D0914000

# FACING
# THE
# ENLIGHTENMENT
# AND
# PIETISM

Contributions to the Study of Religion
*Series Editor: Henry W. Bowden*

# FACING THE ENLIGHTENMENT AND PIETISM

Archibald Alexander and the Founding of Princeton Theological Seminary

## LEFFERTS A. LOETSCHER

A PUBLICATION OF THE PRESBYTERIAN HISTORICAL SOCIETY

CONTRIBUTIONS TO THE STUDY OF RELIGION, NUMBER 8

GREENWOOD PRESS (GP)

WESTPORT, CONNECTICUT • LONDON, ENGLAND

**Library of Congress Cataloging in Publication Data**

Loetscher, Lefferts Augustine, 1904–
    Facing the Enlightenment and pietism.

    (Contributions to the study of religion, ISSN 0196-
7053 ; no. 8. A Publication of the Presbyterian Historical
Society)
    Bibliography: p.
    Includes index.
    1. Alexander, Archibald, 1772–1851.    2. Theologians—
United States—Biography.    3. Presbyterian Church—
Clergy—Biography.    4. Clergy—United States—Biography.
5. Princeton Theological Seminary.    I. Title.    II. Series:
Contributions to the study of religion ; no. 8.
III. Series: Contributions to the study of religion.
Publication of the Presbyterian Historical Society.
BX9225.A5L63    1983        207'.74967 [B]        82-11995
ISBN 0-313-23677-1 (lib. bdg.)

Library of Congress Catalog Card Number: 82-11995
ISBN: 0-313-23677-1
ISSN: 0196-7053

First published in 1983

Greenwood Press
A division of Congressional Information Service, Inc.
88 Post Road West
Westport, Connecticut 06881

Printed in the United States of America

10  9  8  7  6  5  4  3  2  1

# CONTENTS

# FOREWORD

For more than a century "Princeton Theology" stood for staunch conservatism and rational defense of Calvinist tenets. Its stronghold was a seminary, established in 1812, that produced generations of loyal sons who made its theological outlook a force to be reckoned with in Reformed circles, particularly among Presbyterian churches. Except for an 1854 biography, we have known little about the institution's founder. But in this volume we now have a thorough and systematic study of the man who was instrumental in making Princeton categories influential for such a long period of time.

The late Professor Loetscher taught for decades at the seminary which he chose to study, and this last work of his is something of an affectionate farewell. He did not share the old assumptions that characterized its viewpoint in the last century, and so he reviewed the bygone mindset with both detachment and a fondness bred from long historical acquaintance. As a senior American church historian, Loetscher blended the biographical and institutional aspects of this study into the larger context of American culture, depicting salient features that affected religious developments after the Revolutionary War. His broad focus allows for deeper appreciation of republican growth south of New England. Beyond that, he concentrated on significant events in Presbyterianism, the most influential denomination in the middle states, to trace early national trends that did not depend on Puritan precedent. Within that setting, the life of Princeton seminary's founder emerges with sharp personal highlights and appreciable understanding of his cultural grounding.

Archibald Alexander stamped the new seminary and its subsequent outlook with his personality. Loetscher demonstrates here how Scottish Common Sense philosophy affected Alexander's early years and made him wary of speculation—in deism as well as in emotional revivalism. But his own experiences produced a curious blend that made him sensitive to both scholarly inquiry and religious intuition throughout his life. Loetscher was not quick to pigeon-hole Alexander, but rather allowed the young educator to express himself fully, acknowledging manifold ideological inputs and pursuing many directions to intellectual maturation. The resulting portrait is a realistic one that informs us about early experiences as a college president and Philadelphia pastor where he continually warned against extremes in "rational Christianity" (outgrowths of the Enlightenment) and "enthusiasm" (distorted pietism). After an especially valuable chapter describing increased emphasis on professionalism for ministers in nineteenth-century America, we can discern the real impetus behind establishing Princeton as a nursery of vital piety and sound theological learning.

Alexander's conception of ministerial duties gave a distinctive attitude, not new structure, to theological studies. Princeton's curriculum did not differ much from prior educative patterns, and actually constituted a late nineteenth-century graft on the seventeenth-century stock of Reformed scholasticism. Though Alexander was personally moderate and fair minded, he nevertheless fostered in his institution a static view of history that denied progressive change, a commitment to biblical inerrancy, and a refusal to cooperate with either those caught in error or those who compromised denominational priorities. Princetonians claimed to be open to critical study, but they actually underscored timeless truths in their lectures, manifesting a nonhistorical approach that produced undeviating adherence to orthodox conclusions.

In displaying the scope of this framework, Loetscher added another dimension to this book by utilizing unpublished materials. He relied on Alexander's published works, of course, but more importantly, he used manuscript lecture notes and student outlines of curricular presentations that have never been scrutinized before. With these sources Loetscher achieved a systematic overview of Alexander's perspective on epistemology, psychology, piety, apologetics, ethics, Bible study, and pastoral responsibilities. Throughout the exegesis he has demonstrated that Alexander was fascinated with philosophy, but adhered to the Bible and prefabricated truths. Intuition first led to him to trust those truths, but he perpetuated them in a system that reversed the psychological order of events. So the architect of "Princeton Theology" admitted that simple faith was the ultimate guide in religion, but he used an ardent rationalism to challenge speculation in religious thought. One of the lasting contributions of this important volume is to bring out these inner conflicts in Alexander's thought, explaining at the same time how his formal system became a formidable nexus that resisted major theological changes over the next hundred years.

Henry Bowden

# PREFACE

For decades much attention has been devoted to the study of New England Puritanism under the brilliant leadership of the late Perry Miller and other scholars. While intellectual and social interpretations of their character and influence differ, the significance of the Puritans' impact on American life and culture is widely recognized.

More recently, attention has been turning to ecclesiastical and theological relatives of the New England Puritans, the Old School Presbyterians, who, somewhat later in time that their Puritan neighbors, built elaborate theological and ecclesiastical structures which had important impact on an influential minority of Americans of the Middle and Southern states, in the areas both of culture and of social life.[1] The capital of Old School Presbyterianism was at Princeton, New Jersey, in the early days of the college there,[2] and continued for a century after that in Princeton Theological Seminary. Numerous doctrinal dissertations in leading American and some European universities have been written on aspects of Princeton Theological Seminary's history and influence, but no full-length work has been published in recent times on the man who laid the foundations for this long-enduring chief citadel of late American Calvinism—Archibald Alexander.

Alexander's particular formulation of the Christian faith emerged at a point where the Enlightenment and Pietism—two antagonistic but partially parallel movements—were confronting each other. Amid the subjectivism and flux of the times, he sought a foundation for objective and absolute certainty. The system of religious thought which he set forth had great appeal for some intellectuals and particularly for the rising business and planter classes, many of whom had acquired a degree of higher education and whose careers in business or plantation management required social stability for greatest success. Colleges in which these rising classes had received their education—very often denominational colleges—offered the traditional classics and mathematics, and sometimes included interesting examples of the current progress of the natural sciences, but all were taught more descriptively than critically. Thus these graduates were ready to receive eagerly and uncritically the elaborate scholastic theology—or at least its conclusions—which confirmed their world view and promised the necessary degree of stability to the social structures which they headed.

Alexander was followed by a succession of able and dedicated scholars who elaborated, sharpened, and deepened his work while essentially maintaining his presuppositions, objectives, and methods. This involved ever-new debates with leading scholars in America and Europe, which resulted in further amplification rather than in basic revision of the Princeton Seminary positions. When, in the twentieth century, differences of viewpoint and policy emerged within the Seminary faculty itself, the Presbyterian denomination, which had ultimate control of the Seminary, after a four-year visitation, reorganized the Seminary's structure in 1929. Under the courageous leadership of Dr. John A. Mackay, who came to the Seminary's presidency in 1936, the Seminary immediately began to move onto new theological and ecclesiastical ground. In fairness, therefore, both to the present faculty and to its honored predecessors, the author will distinguish between their respective theological positions by referring to the views of the founder and of his direct heirs as "the Old Princeton Theology."

# FACING
# THE
# ENLIGHTENMENT
# AND
# PIETISM

# 1
# ROOTS IN VIRGINIA

Archibald Alexander of Virginia gave to Princeton Theological Seminary distinctive characteristics which it retained for more than a century. As the seminary's first professor and as a man of strong convictions, he was the principal formative influence on the institution. Who was this man, and what were the forces that formed his personality and his views?

Religious experience was the central interest in the life of Archibald Alexander. He was a direct product of the inwardness of Western civilization, which had been increasing ever since the Renaissance and the Protestant Reformation. Both Continental rationalism and British empiricism had opened profound questions concerning the method by which people acquire valid knowledge; and "mental philosophy," a forerunner of modern pyschology, was encouraging introspection to explore the workings of the human mind. For many, man was becoming the measure of all things, and religion itself would soon be viewed by the avant-garde as the unfolding of the human spirit and its integration with the cultural and cosmic environment.

Alexander was born and reared in Virginia in the most stimulating period of its history, when it was producing an amazing number of national statesmen—of whom Washington, Jefferson, Madison, and John Marshall were only a few—and was evincing vitality in many other areas also.[1] Alexander's formative years were located at a point where the Enlightenment and Pietism—two of the most creative forces of the seventeenth and eighteenth centuries—came into sharp conflict. Under this stimulation, the Christian heritage came vigorously alive in his inner experience, and he devoted his life to interpreting that heritage.

Archibald Alexander's grandfather was one of the pioneers who planted in the Valley of Virginia a civilization that contrasted with Virginia's older and more aristocratic Tidewater. The pattern of life in the Tidewater, which extended from the eastern coast to the falls line of the rivers, was set by the large tobacco planters.[2]

Very different from the Tidewater was the civilization which developed west of the Blue Ridge Mountains and east of the Alleghenies in the Valley of Virginia. Starting in 1732, Scotch-Irish and Germans came up the Valley from Pennsylvania along "the Great Philadelphia Wagon Road," a route which for many years continued to be an active Indian trail, the so-called Great Warrior's Path. Massacre by Indians was an ever-present threat until after the French and Indian War. In fact, Archibald Alexander's own grandmother was killed by Indians.

Because of the Pennsylvania origin of most of the early settlers and because of the continuing connection of this road, the Valley for a time remained almost an economic and ecclesiastical—though not a political—colony of Pennsylvania. Even before the American Revolution, however, many forces were drawing the Valley closer to eastern Virginia. New east-west roads through gaps in the Blue Ridge were diverting Valley farmers from Pennsylvania markets. Common government from Williamsburg and common interests in the French and Indian War and in the American Revolution, in both of which the Valley was deeply involved, did much to strengthen ties with eastern Virginia. The Piedmont, lying between the Tidewater and the Valley, was socially and culturally akin to the Valley. For the Presbyterians of both of the Piedmont and the Valley, ties with Pennsylvania were crucially important. Until the revival of 1789, many of the principal leaders of Virginia Presbyterianism had come from Pennsylvania, but the revival raised up a promising new generation of native Virginian religious leaders, of whom Archibald Alexander was one of the most important.

Unlike the typical large tobacco plantations of the Tidewater, the Valley economy was based on small farms with varied crops and livestock. In the earlier days, cattle were often driven on the hoof through the Valley to Philadelphia. Slaves were few, though their number increased. Visitors often complained of the crudeness of life. When Archibald Alexander was a boy, the area was barely a generation beyond frontier, and he later recalled that he was born in a house "built of square logs" and was often awakened by "the hideous howling of hungry wolves."[3] But conditions in the Valley developed rapidly. By the time of the American Revolution, earlier log cabins were being replaced by frame houses furnished with some comforts. Small elementary schools, often taught by local parsons, arose; and Tidewater patterns of political government, with important regional variations, took form, as did a modified social stratification.

The Valley was overwhelmingly committed to the patriot side in the American Revolution, contributing money and foodstuffs to the cause, while its sons fought on near and distant battlefields. Alexander was eleven years old when the Revolution ended, and much later recalled that as a young schoolboy he "frequently saw companies of backwoodsmen, with their rifles, brown hunting-shirts, and deer's-tail cockades, passing on to the theatre of conflict."[4] A decade after the war, as a young preacher, he echoed the fervor that had gripped the Valley in those testing days: "Who wd. have supposed that the thirteen united states, in their defenceless situation . . . wd. have been able to maintain their rights and liberties against a british army of disciplined troops? We were frequently driven to the last extremity."[5] The postwar economic depression and inflation were severely felt, and for a time even imperiled the support of elementary education.[6]

It was to this Valley of Virginia that Archibald Alexander's grandfather, who was also named Archibald Alexander, came as a pioneer settler. He had emigrated from northern Ireland "about the year 1736" to the vicinity of modern Norristown, Pennsylvania. Converted in the Great Awakening, he traveled about with the revivalist John Rowland, and remained an interested church layman for the remainder of his life.[7] A few years later, with other Scotch-Irish, he migrated to the southern part of the Virginia Valley, at Timber Ridge, near modern Lexington, where he found good pasturage for his cattle. This first Archibald Alexander —"Ersbell" as neighbors called him—became a highly respected leader in the new community.[8] He served as captain of a company of rangers which did a tour of duty on the western frontier, along the Kanawha and Ohio Rivers. In 1747 he purchased some 980 acres from the estate of Benjamin Burden, to whom much of modern Augusta and Rockbridge Counties had been granted by the Crown.[9] Ersbell had been well educated in Ireland and had, like a few of the more intellectual settlers, "brought with him a number of good books, to which he added as he had opportunity." He was a good example of the eagerness of these pioneers to keep alive the values of their culture. His grandson reports that he conducted gratuitously a night school in his own house where he taught the "three R's" to young men "who had little or no opportunity of improving themselves."[10] Religious interests were not forgotten, for he and his neighbors built "meetinghouses" at New Providence and at Timber Ridge.

Ersbell had little desire for wealth, but his son William—young Archibald's father—acquired holdings which later came to be among the most valuable lands in the area.[11] William Alexander married the daughter of a wealthy landowner and became merchant as well as farmer, a vocation in which he sometimes traveled at least as far as Baltimore. In later years he built a house in the center of Lexington which in the twentieth century was still marked for tourists because of its later connections. Thus, while not aristocratic in the Tidewater sense, the family had become quite substantial. By the middle of the next century, William's grandson, writing privately to his brother, reported: "Almost all our relations in Rockbridge are well off, and live in some degree of style."[12]

This William Alexander, living on the frontier, had less opportunity for education than his father had had in northern Ireland, but, no doubt stimulated by his father's intellectual interests and library, "acquired a considerable fund of knowledge." He supplied his own indentured servant as schoolteacher, and later donated land for a schoolhouse.

William Alexander, according to his son, was less interested in religion than Ersbell had been. Dancing had long been a necessary accomplishment among the graceful Tidewater aristocracy, but when prosperous Presbyterians of the Valley aspired to it, judgment fell. William Alexander was temporarily suspended from church privileges for encouraging a local dancing school. But soon afterwards he was restored, served as church elder and as treasurer of the Synod of Virginia, and was elected a commissioner to the national body of his denomination, the General Assembly, meeting in Philadelphia in 1791. His wife was, according to the word of her grandson, "a retiring and humble, but affectionately pious woman."[13]

It was into this new but vigorous, moderately prosperous, and sincerely religious family that Archibald Alexander was born near modern Lexington on April 17, 1772. He was the third of ten children.[14] Like other boys in that outdoor life, he was physically active, becoming an excellent swimmer, horseman, and rifle shot, which contrasted strangely with the extremely sedentary habits of his later years. Very slight of build and short of stature (he was only five feet seven inches tall at maturity), as a youth he looked much younger than he was, a fact which tended to heighten a certain inherent modesty.

At the age of five, young Archibald—who later claimed that he was already able to read the New Testament by that time—began his schooling under an indentured servant of his father in a log hut, where he studied from a "horn book" and where pupils of all ages read aloud simultaneously.[15] It is indicative of the irregular pattern of schooling of that time that he was sent to five different schools before the age of ten, with results that failed to impress him. But at the age of ten he came under the teaching of William Graham, whose influence on his entire later intellectual life was decisive.[16]

Inasmuch as Archibald Alexander was one of the pioneers in the whole American theological seminary movement, it is appropriate at this point to examine briefly the educational ideals of his day. The curriculum of the American higher education had its roots in the middle ages, where "scholasticism" had created a synthesis between Christian theology and the logic and science of Aristotle. Knowledge was viewed somewhat statically as a fixed body of truth to be assimilated by the student. The Renaissance stimulated increased interest in Greek and Roman culture which brought widened horizons and vitality; while the Reformations, both Catholic and Protestant, further deepened religious experience and led to social and cultural reorientation. These new movements brought new subject matter into the curriculum, but remarkably soon, the older scholastic presuppositions and methods began to structure and permeate the new materials.

British universities had a formative influence on American higher education. Harvard College, founded in 1636, was directly modeled after Cambridge University, which, through its tutors, was giving solid training in the Greek and Latin classes, logic, and philosophy, but showed less interest in the new natural sciences. During the century, 1540–1640, the religious controversies then current were an absorbing interest at Cambridge University. Scottish universities did not influence New England in its earliest years, but their influence a little later on higher education in Virginia and in the middle colonies was direct and important. The Scottish universities, except Edinburgh, found their models not in Oxford and Cambridge, but in the older universities of Paris and Bologna. Andrew Melville, returning to Scotland in 1574 after study at the Geneva Academy, introduced the logic of Peter Ramus, thus weakening, at least for a time, the hold of Aristotelian scholaticism.[17] In England, when the Act of Uniformity of 1662 excluded non-Anglicans from Oxford and Cambridge universities, these dissenters founded dissenting academies which greatly influenced both higher education and theological education in predominantly non-Anglican America. The new academies were far less bound by medieval tradition than were the older and more prestigious universities, and their curricula from the beginning reflected newer educational interests. They introduced elocution and English prose and poetry, gave greater attention to mathematics and the new sciences, and were able to condense into four years a combination of liberal arts and professional training for the ministry. Obviously their work in Scholastic philosophy and in classical culture was not as thorough as that of the universities, but their example had great appeal to practical-minded Americans.[18]

Americans of course were eager to perpetuate the highly prized culture which they had inherited from Europe. But in the process of transplanting it from its native European soils to the New World, great changes—some unavoidable and some deliberately planned—took place. Almost from its earliest days, American higher education had been torn by an inner struggle for self-identity. What is the purpose of so-called higher education? Is it to strengthen community by undergirding it with a common body of fixed knowledge? If so, what body of knowledge is to be thus chosen? Is higher education to "develop the mind," with the mind divided into "faculties," particular disciplines developing particular "faculties"? Is higher education to develop a cultural "feel" and appreciation and thus to lay the foundation for a particular style of life? Or is education to supply the special body of knowledge and skills required for particular professions? How is the inherited curriculum related to these various ends?

Some leading Americans in the late eighteenth century were coming to the conviction that the inherited curriculum was based on aristocratic and theological presuppositions which were out of harmony with the practical and increasingly democratic spirit of American life and the critical spirit of the Enlightenment. The Enlightenment saw education, not as the appropriation of an arbitrarily selected body of knowledge, but as the development of the mind in critical and constructive processes, which might be directed toward any worthy or useful body of material. Such a concept basically altered the purpose and vastly broadened the potential scope of education, while at the same time—if it betrayed its own highest ideals—it could lead to mere training in ad hoc techniques, unworthy of the name of higher education. From the end of the eighteenth century, the battle was fully joined between those who desired to retain as much as possible of the traditional classical curriculum with its fixed body of knowledge and its professional and genteel ideals, and those who conceived higher education more in terms of mental processes and of expanding areas of knowledge and changing needs. The clergy in general favored the more classical type of curriculum into which so much of theological presuppositions had been built, and which constituted the principal basis of their own professional training. Quite correctly they also sensed that if this traditional curriculum were radically altered in the new directions, the influence of Christianity on American culture would be greatly reduced. Paradoxically, the pagan classics—by this time, of course, properly expurgated and domesticated—had become the educational bulwarks of Christian orthodoxy which must be stoutly defended. If the curriculum revisions so vigorously urged by the Enlightenment were carried through, the resulting "secularized" curriculum would have to be supplemented for ministerial candidates by a superadded theological curriculum—unless enough of the general curriculum could be pushed back into secondary education to make room in the four college years for professional education. The various aspects of this problem were still in flux in late eighteenth-century America.

Virginia Presbyterians in the eighteenth century greatly needed institutions of higher education. They were concerned to preserve their cultural heritage and at the same time to advance the interests of the denomination. The two objectives were closely intertwined, for denominations themselves were important supporting centers of both social structure and culture. The need for an educated ministry was also a major factor in the founding of Presbyterian colleges in Virginia.

Before the revival of 1789, there were very few candidates for the Presbyterian ministry.[19] One factor in this was undoubtedly the great difficulty experienced by the small and scattered congregations in supporting their ministers, a difficulty which became acute during the American Revolution and especially so in the period of currency inflation during and after the Revolution. Thus Hanover Presbytery felt constrained to vindicate one minister who, needing more remunerative employment,

had abandoned his parish without authorization. Heirs of another minister were still struggling after his death to collect his salary arrearage. Frequent tensions between ministers and congregations must also have
made the ministry seem less attractive as a vocation. Most ministers
served more than one congregation at the same time, which divided their
energies and created rivalries for their services. The Presbytery of Lexington, organized out of Hanover Presbytery in 1786 and composed of
the churches west of the Blue Ridge Mountains, created a committee at
its first meeting to visit all its constituent congregations and to inquire
whether their ministers were fulfilling their duties and whether the congregations on their part were meeting salary obligations.[20]

In spite of such logistical difficulties, the church in Virginia pressed
heroically forward and cried out for more ministers. Available ministers
were used strategically; settled pastors were assigned by presbytery to
itinerate for a period among newer settlements, while ministers without
pastorates were often appointed to a different congregation each Sunday.
Often it was simply impossible to export either money or men to the
frontier, as Hanover Presbytery was forced to inform synod during the
war in November 1775. But requests for ministers from newer regions
kept coming in. When in 1779 ''a greater number of the inhabitants of
Kentuckey'' [sic] pleaded for a minister, the best presbytery could do was
to promise to ''send them [ministerial] supplies as soon as possible.''
Four years later, the Rev. David Rice, a valuable future leader, went out
to Kentucky. As late as 1802, Hanover Presbytery in the Piedmont,
occupying a territory estimated at 60,000 square miles, was served by
only eleven ordained ministers and two licensed preachers.[21]

Virginia Presbyterians, in spite of the widely lamented shortage of
ministers, strove heroically to enforce high standards of ministerial education for ordination, an ideal which underlined the need of more adequate facilities for their education. While the records are not complete in
detail for every candidate, it would appear that Hanover Presbytery in
the late 1770s, in addition to oral examinations on various disciplines,
was requiring as written ''pieces of trial,'' a ''homily'' or popular sermon, a lecture or expository sermon, and an ''exegesis'' which seems
more properly to have been a thesis often bearing a Latin title. While
thus striving to maintain high standards of ministerial education amid
the dislocations of the war, presbytery in 1778 did express the hope that
theological education might be drastically reformed to include more
theological study while shortening the total time of preparation, which
would make the ministry at once more accessible and more practical in
orientation. This emphasis on specifically theological instruction foreshadowed the rise of theological seminaries separate from colleges,
though the abridgement of liberal arts desired by the presbytery was,
quite properly, not to be effected.

In the face of the shortage of ministers, it was difficult for presbytery to reject a dubious candidate. One such was definitely rejected, only to be accepted the next year. A candidate from another denomination whose academic qualifications fell below Presbyterian requirements was accepted on the grounds of his proven "usefulness," "because in the present state of religion, & of our Churches, men of liberal education & real piety cannot be obtained in sufficient numbers."[22]

The scarcity of ministers gave opportunity to imposters, and presbytery found it necessary to send a circular letter to its congregations warning them against the "inroads of false preachers or persons introducing themselves as preachers of the Gospel without a regular introduction into that office agreeably to the Rules of Christ." In the face of these ministerial shortages, presbytery, after due deliberation, felt forced "unanimously" to oppose a recommendation of the denomination's highest body that three years of theological study be a prerequisite for ordination.[23]

Virginia had the second oldest college in the American colonies—William and Mary at Williamsburg, chartered in 1693. This institution did not meet the educational needs of Presbyterians, for it was strongly Anglican at a time when denominational lines were sharply drawn, particularly the lines between the established church of Virginia and the dissenters. But until at least the middle of the eighteenth century, William and Mary exerted a powerful influence on the class that dominated Virginia life.

Particularly significant, not only for William and Mary, but for higher education throughout Virginia, were the educational views of Thomas Jefferson. In 1779 Jefferson reported to the Virginia Assembly three bills for improving public education. The third of these bills would create a free public library, while the first two contemplated a system of education on the three levels of primary schools, grammar schools, and university. On the primary level, every county was to be divided into districts, each district to have a school where there would be taught reading, writing, arithmetic, and the history of Greece, Rome, England, and America. All nonslave children, male and female, would be entitled to three years of free schooling, and a very few, selected for their exceptional ability, would have expenses paid until they graduated from the university. Thus all citizens would have sufficient basic education to protect the republic from tyranny, and persons of outstanding native ability, however lacking in financial resources, would be elevated to public leadership in an aristocracy not of wealth but of ability. Grammar schools, constituting the second level of education in Jefferson's bill, were to teach Latin and Greek, English grammar, geography, and advanced arithmetic. The third and highest level of education in Jefferson's bill was to be William and Mary College, drastically transformed into a university, giving courses in moral philosophy, law, medicine, the fine arts, history (including ecclesiastical history), mathematics and science, and ancient and modern language.

This was an amazingly advanced conception for its day. Jefferson's proposed "grammar schools" had obvious resemblances to the *Gymnasien* of nineteenth-century Germany, and gave promise of removing from the university curriculum merely preparatory work—which long after Jefferson's time would continue to clutter it—thus enabling the university to devote itself entirely either to advanced scholarship or to professional education. His program for the university closely resembled the historic four "faculties" of European universities—philosophy, theology, law, and medicine—except that it did not include theology other than ecclesiastical history. But dissenters' objections to thus exalting an Anglican college, and fears of increased taxation, caused the Virginia legislature to reject Jefferson's bills.[24]

Amid the great political and social changes of the later eighteenth century, American education was in flux. Both the Enlightenment and America's intense practicality—the two were not identical—demanded new educational objectives, new curricular subjects, and new methods. Many ideas, once vital, had now become "inert," to borrow Whitehead's term, and there was revolt against them.[25] Some innovations were being adopted from the English dissenting academies and Scottish universities, but change was slow, for higher education did not yet have a broad base in popular support and thus was less responsive to popular desires than it later became.

In what direction would American higher education move? Would it develop, as advocated by Jefferson and as accomplished in nineteenth-century Germany, in the direction of a greatly elevated university curriculum made possible by concentrated and advanced secondary schooling? Or would American education be confused in purpose and so diversified in function that secondary education would not be able to complete a recognized level of preparation which would then have to be completed in college? This alternative would preclude the college from confining itself to truly advanced work and would postpone professional education to later postgraduate years. Jefferson's voice on the subject was clear and strong, but America was not ready to heed.

Presbyterian higher education in Virginia came into being and developed in the larger environment of which William and Mary College and Thomas Jefferson's views on education constituted an important part. But Archibald Alexander's harsh opinion of William and Mary in the late eighteenth century, expressed decades afterwards, was quite representative of the attitude of many Virginia Presbyterians at that time, when he referred to the college as "little more than a school of law & infidelity."[26] Nor were the radical Enlightenment views and practical emphases of Jefferson what Virginia Presbyterians desired in higher education.

Instead they sought to develop their own institutions of higher education, and in doing so were deeply indebted to the older Presbyterianism of Pennsylvania and New Jersey. This Presbyterian aversion to Jefferson's educational ideals had some parallels to Presbyterians' later rejection of Enlightenment influences in Samuel Stanhope Smith's far milder innovations at the College of New Jersey.

An important proportion of the earliest Presbyterian ministers in Virginia had studied at William Tennent's "Log College" in Pennsylvania or at schools conducted by former Log College students. The College of New Jersey (later Princeton University), after its chartering in 1746, became for a time the chief supplier of Presbyterian theological education to Virginia, and a systematic but not overwhelmingly successful effort was made by Virginia Presbyterians to raise money for the New Jersey college.[27]

Meanwhile Presbyterians of the Valley were developing educational institutions of their own. An early settler, Archibald Alexander's great uncle Robert Alexander, who had the Master of Arts degree of Trinity College, Dublin, opened an elementary school in Augusta (now Rockbridge) County in 1749. This work was taken up and carried on until 1774 by the Rev. John Brown, a graduate of the College of New Jersey, who, as he served different pastorates in the Valley, moved the school with him, his last location being at Mount Pleasant, near modern Fairfield. Hanover Presbytery now interested itself in the project, and on October 13, 1774, appointed William Graham, who had graduated from the College of New Jersey the year before, to "manage" the school "under the inspection of" Mr. Brown. At the same meeting, presbytery urged its congregations to contribute toward the support of the work. The next year, presbytery visited the school in a body, and was "well pleased" with the work in Latin and Greek and the "orations" which they heard, and appointed John Montgomery, another recent graduate of the College of New Jersey, as Graham's assistant. In 1776 the presbytery gave Graham more permanent tenure as principal, and voiced their revolutionary patriotism by changing the school's name from Augusta Academy to Liberty Hall. With money appropriated by presbytery, Graham purchased in Philadelphia "philosophical [scientific] apparatus" for the school. Partly under the inducement of gifts of land and money by neighbors, the institution was moved half a dozen miles from Mount Pleasant to Timber Ridge where modest buildings were erected, with presbytery reserving to itself "the Right of Visitation forever."[28]

The brightest promise of this fresh start for the school failed for a time to materialize. Because of wartime inflation, Graham's combined income as teacher and pastor proved inadequate, and he took to farming, about a mile west of modern Lexington. Most of the students moved with him, and in 1782 the school received from the state a charter which Archibald Alexander, a bit optimistically, claimed "made the institution a college in every thing but the name." The charter named twenty trustees, one of whom was Alexander's father, who had donated to the enterprise land across the North River (now the Maury River) from his home. A stone building was later erected for the school, the picturesque ruins of which were still standing in the twentieth century about a mile west of Washington and Lee University.[29]

Archibald Alexander at the age of ten, after six years of elementary education, entered Liberty Hall in 1782, the year of its charter. An education at the College of New Jersey carried some prestige in late eighteenth-century Virginia, as Philip Vickers Fithian noted in his colorful diary. Archibald Alexander, who had been prevented by precarious health from studying there as planned, went out of his way on a number of occasions to imply that he had received at Liberty Hall the practical equivalent of a Princeton education. Thus Alexander much later reminisced:

A number of young men were regularly graduated in the academy, precisely as they were at the College of New Jersey. For Mr. Graham established precisely the same course of instruction in the academy, which the classes pursued at Princeton. The very same class-books & text books were put into the hands of the students. And even Dr. Witherspoon's manuscript lectures on moral philosophy & Criticism were transcribed by the students & regularly recited.

One suspects that the lectures of the famous Dr. Witherspoon did unexpected double duty in many another institution also.[30] But extant notes on Graham's lectures reveal theological influences from Jonathan Edwards utterly foreign to Witherspoon.[31]

The curriculum of Liberty Hall in 1793—just four years after Alexander completed his course—as reproduced from the examination record of a graduate of that year, was basically the long-familiar staple of classics and mathematics: Latin and Greek, arithmetic, algebra, geometry, geography, navigation, surveying, logic, criticism, and rhetoric. This particular student's record strangely omits the natural sciences ("natural philosophy") which Graham emphasized and regarded as strong evidence of God's activity. By 1803 the curriculum had been regularized as a four-year college course. Satisfactory examination in Virgil and Greek New Testament was a requirement for admission, after which the first year was devoted to Latin and the Greek classics, with the decidedly modern-looking option of substituting French (a subject which John Witherspoon had included at Princeton) for Greek. In the second year, mathematics, surveying, and navigation were studied, and the third year was occupied with natural sciences and geography. In his last year the student concentrated on English grammar, logic, "belles lettres," and "the Law of Nature and of Nations," a subject already long emphasized at William and Mary College under Jefferson's influence. In logic, Locke and such exponents of the "Scottish Philosophy" as Thomas Reid, Dugald Stewart, and Hugh Blair (author of a widely used textbook on rhetoric, 1783) were studied.[32] Thus Washington Academy (the former Liberty Hall) exhibited a combination of the old and the new that noticeably paralleled instruction at Princeton.[33] In both curricula, each year successively concentrated on a limited number of subjects, Washington Academy carrying this concentration even farther than was done at Princeton.

Young Alexander won high standing at every public examination and was reported to his father to be a lad of great promise, but he himself felt, on sober later judgment, that he had made very little academic or moral progress during his years at Liberty Hall.[34] The truth would seem to be that this brilliant and genial and rather shy youth had not yet found motivation that would fully arouse his somewhat easy-going nature. Such a new orientation of his life was soon to come to him, when he left home and became deeply involved in the struggle between Enlightenment doubt and pietistic faith which was taking place in many areas of Virginia at that time.

# 2
# WHAT IS "CONVERSION"?

A critical question surrounds the interpretation of Alexander's religious experience. He was—be it said to his credit—extremely modest and reticent about his own inner spiritual life. Though he preached much, both immediately after professing Christian faith and in later years, his sermons and his numerous other later writings contain almost no autobiography or, least of all, direct disclosure of his own inner religious development. The fullest source on his inner life during the period surrounding his conversion is the biography by his son, which was written after the Old-School–New-School Presbyterian division of 1837. One of the important issues underlying the Old-School–New-School controversy was revivalism, many (though not all) New School men supporting the revivalistic innovations of Charles G. Finney and, in general, favoring revivalism somewhat more heartily than did the Old School. It was often charged that Old-School religion was coldly intellectual and totally lacking in the fervor of revivalism. Many Old-School leaders vigorously denied this and asserted emphatically their deep interest in revivals that were properly defined and conducted.[1] Alexander's biographer avows the apologetic purpose of demonstrating that his father was no mere "rigid book divine, who had grown up in cold forms, without acquaintance with great outpourings of the Holy Spirit."[2] So far as Archibald Alexander's own manuscript reminiscences (on which his biographer at this point leans heavily) are datable, they appear to have been drafted not before 1839, and some as late as 1849, that is, all well after the Old-School–New-School rupture of 1837.[3] The critical question must therefore be raised: In the light of the New School accusations, had Alexander's memory unconsciously reconstructed or at least reinterpreted his inner experiences of half a century earlier? We have already observed a number of factual self-contradictions in the narrative. From the nature of the case, a definitive answer is perhaps impossible, but a partial answer may be sought by discovering whether his later views and attitudes as these emerged were compatible with the description he gave of his own youthful religious experience. The answer appears to be a definite affirmative in the light of written sermons and a journal, both from the early period.

We have suggested that the setting for the change in religious life described by Alexander was the sharp tension that existed in his time and locale between the Enlightenment and Pietism. The Enlightenment, with greater confidence in the efficacy of its method, sought to apply human reason critically in challenging old traditions and authority and to apply reason constructively in rebuilding human conceptions and institutions on the foundation of reason. Mathematics was its model and the development of the natural sciences its most spectacular achievement. It emphasized toleration and the humanitarian service of man. In the eighteenth century, when American nationalism was aborning, Enlightenment principles were built into the very structure of American political and economic life. Deism, a child of the Enlightenment which, in its most typical form, sought to reconstruct religion on a purely rational basis, was a shock that galvanized the churches into feverish counteractivity. But in spite of the stimulus which it received from French prestige, deism as a religion soon proved to be intellectually superficial and emotionally unsatisfying. The churches' sharply fought and quickly won outward victory over it left the churches blind to the fact that the most important influence of the Enlightment on religion was not its direct influence through deism, but its indirect influence through American cultural and social institutions which the Enlightenment had so large a part in forming. The churches' preoccupation in the eighteenth and early nineteenth centuries with deism, the floating crest of the iceberg, and their comparative indifference to the much deeper and more important substance of the Enlightenment left much unfinished business for the churches in the late nineteenth and twentieth centuries. The early Unitarians—who were not deists, but whose solution was inherently unacceptable to the evangelicals—were more aware of the importance of the Enlightenment's real challenge than were the evangelicals.

Deistical principles—"infidelity" as they were sometimes called—alarmed the church to vigorous counteraction. These critical views served as the catalyst which precipitated religious conviction in Archibald Alexander. As early as 1735, Governor Gooch of Virginia lamented that "free thinkers multiply very fast." Two years later, Sir John Randolph's will reflected incipient deism, and in 1741 the Rev. Hugh Jones commented that in the Virginia church he found "enthusiasm, deism and libertism" side by side. Archibald Alexander reflected the opinion of many concerning William and Mary College of the 1770s when he later commented, "The fact is indisputable, that for many years, scarcely any young man however piously educated, left that seminary without being infected with the doctrines of Hume and Voltaire."

Nor did the Virginia Valley escape these innovating forces. Recalling the situation at Liberty Hall shortly after the Revolution, Alexander wrote:

Infidelity . . . formerly unheard of began to show itself in this retired part . . . and some of the larger students brought into the academy some of the infidel writings of Voltaire & Hume whose doctrines were greedily embraced by those whose morals had become corrupt. . . . Generally, however, the students cared as little about infidelity as they did about religion.

The account of Liberty Hall parallels Lyman Beecher's famous description of Yale College a few years later, as Alexander proceeded to say: "During the whole period of the writer's continuance in this academy, there never were more than two professors of religion among the students." "About this time," Alexander added, "the condition & prospects of the chh. were as gloomy as they well could be. Vice & dissolution were completely triumphant." Only one (not Alexander himself) "had the least idea of seeking the holy ministry." But Mr. Graham, at least, "stood firm" both in doctrine and discipline. Alexander recounted with particular poignancy the apostasy of his own cousin at Liberty Hall a few years later, who revolted against his strict rearing and then sought, in deistical doubts, a refuge from the sharp scourges of conscience. Though Alexander himself had not read "infidel books," popular conceptions of the peril and power of deism loomed large before him.[4]

Revivalism in Virginia provided a sharp antithesis to the rationality and "coldness" of contemporary deism. The Great Awakening in the South, where it arrived later than it did in the Middle and New England colonies, had been smothered by the preoccupations and violence of the American Revolution. Amidst widespread lamentations over immorality and spiritual decline, there appeared, among Virginia Methodists and Baptists in 1785, another revival which might be called the beginning of the famous Second Awakening. The Methodist phase of this movement was strongest in the southeastern counties of the state, with some of its representatives conducting meetings near the Presbyterian College of Hampden-Sydney in Prince Edward County. The Baptist phase of the revival had its chief strength in the northeastern part of the state, reaching its climax in the years 1787–1789, the place and time where Alexander first encountered it.[5]

As Alexander looked back on this early stage of his life, he recalled little reason to expect that he was about to experience deep religious interest. As a child he had received formal religious instruction and had even experienced an occasional fleeting moment of religious concern. But he described himself at that point as lacking both Christian knowledge and religious feeling. His previous memorization of the Shorter

Catechism and much of the Larger had been "without reflection," and he had been terribly bored by his pastor's sermons. Though his home church and much of Valley Presbyterianism had been founded by "New Side," that is, revivalistic, Presbyterians some two generations or more earlier, this tradition seems almost to have died out in Alexander's boyhood environment. "My only notion of religion," he later recalled, "was that it consisted in becoming better. I had never heard of any conversion among the Presbyterians" (though he immediately added the names of a "few pious people"). He considered his father as belonging "to the more liberal and accommodating" type of Christianity, and he himself was accustomed "to laugh at any who gave signs of extraordinary devotion."[6]

An interesting sidelight on Alexander's inner resources at this time shows him capable of deep feeling and suggests possible parallels between his religious development and the emerging romantic movement. Looking back on his childhood in scenic Rockbridge County, Alexander recalled the great stimulus that his imagination had received from two neighboring mountains. He was quite overwhelmed with emotion when he first saw the famous Natural Bridge at the age of fourteen or fifteen. "The feeling was as though something within sprung up to a great height by a kind of sudden impulse." Such an emotion, he concluded, is very fleeting, and the object which produces it cannot be adequately represented by any work of art.[7]

Alexander's father, without consulting him, had secured his appointment as private tutor in the family of General Posey in the Wilderness in Spotsylvania County, in northwestern Virginia, twelve miles west of Fredericksburg. This was on the edge of the older and more aristocratic Tidewater. "Though somewhat decayed in wealth, the Poseys maintained much of the style which belonged to old Virginia families." During this year, Alexander, thrown on his own resources at the age of sixteen, experienced an intellectual awakening and the beginning of what proved to be for him an even more important religious and personal reorientation.[8]

One could almost say that it was at the hospitable board of General Posey that the Old Princeton Theology was born. The contending deism and Pietism of the day were represented by the cast of characters that gathered from time to time around General Posey's table. A neighbor, Major William Jones, "a good-natured, luxurious, skeptical man," who was somewhat interested in the Cartesian philosophy, "plainly insinuated that religion was a disease of weak and superstitious minds, and that all that was necessary for a cure was an acquaintance with philosophy."[9] At the opposite end of the religious spectrum was Mrs. Tyler, an aged lady who had known better days financially and had "found a refuge" with the Poseys. She had been an Anglican, but since discovering evangelical light had become an ardent and unashamed Baptist.[10]

Her well-intended but insistent aggressiveness forced everyone to fly whatever religious colors he possessed. Between these two extremes, others represented various median positions of the day. Mrs. Posey, "who professed to be a 'seeker,' defended the Baptist opinions, and so did old Mrs. William Jones, who I believe was a truly pious woman." Posey himself, a commander of riflemen in the recent Revolutionary War,[11] was sceptical, refusing to believe in "miraculous" conversion; but he remained open to persuasion, adding that "he would credit it, if Mrs. Posey should ever profess that she had experienced it."[12] Young Alexander, feeling desperately inadequate at this juncture of his life, and even in mature years disinclined to force unsolicited opinions on others, undoubtedly did more listening than talking.

Meanwhile, good Mrs. Tyler served as Alexander's spiritual director. Recounting her own religious experience, she told how she had been "gay and fond of admiration," and when Baptists entered her community, she had attended their meetings expressly to ridicule. But "an aged stranger" addressing the worshipers had stabbed her conscience. After deep inner anguish, she embraced "the plan of salvation" and courageously joined the "despised" Baptists. Alexander, listening in silence, was deeply impressed. Mrs. Tyler also succeeded in taking him to Baptist meetings with her.[13]

As it happened, the Baptist revival, already mentioned, was coming to its height during the period of Alexander's visit, with vigorous expression in the vicinity of the Posey residence. There were in Virginia at that time two types of Baptists, "Regular" and "Separate." A few Regular Baptists had settled in Virginia as early as 1743, and by 1765 had expanded sufficiently in northern Virginia to organize the Ketocten Association. A much stronger impulse to the Baptist movement in Virginia was supplied by a few Separate Baptists who, having withdrawn from Congregational churches in New England as a result of issues growing out of the Great Awakening, moved to North Carolina. By 1767 these Separate Baptists, having come into Virginia from the south, were encountering the Regular Baptists and were soon spreading over most of the northeastern part of the state. The Separate Baptists were notable for their tremendous evengelistic zeal, fervent emotionalism, and peculiar pulpit mannerisms, such as the "holy whine." The contempt and persecution which greeted them seemed only to stimulate their zeal. It is estimated that by 1775 all types of Baptists in Virginia totaled some 10,000, and twice that number fifteen years later. They had become a very serious challenge to denominations earlier in the region, including the Presbyterian. By 1790 some Presbyterians in the Valley were doubting the validity of infant baptism, and the Synod of Virginia had to emphasize the warrant for administering this sacrament to infants. Later still, Hanover Presbytery found it necessary to define again conditions which parents must fulfill to be eligible to present their children for baptism. A highly promising Presbyterian ministerial candidate, Conrad Speece, temporarily abandoned his candidacy because of scruples about baptizing infants, a problem which was soon to trouble Alexander himself.[14]

Mrs. Tyler would have preferred to take her young protégé to visit the more conventional "Regulars," but as they had no meeting in the vicinity, she took him to the local "Separates." The congregation was in the midst of revival. Founded ten years before with twenty-five members, "in '88, they enjoyed the smiles of Heaven, in a precious revival. . . . The church increased to one hundred and thirty."[15] A strange sight here greeted Alexander's eyes. He recalled that the speaker, "a stout, corpulent man . . . took off his coat and neckcloth, threw open his collar, and generally became so earnest that before he was done he was black in the face. In every sermon he gave an account of his own experience." Seeing Alexander present he "inveighed against learning." The meeting exhibited "enthusiastic responses and outcries . . . leaping, contortions, swooning, and convulsions." Poor Mrs. Tyler was humiliated, and insisted on taking him to the more distant meeting of the "Regular" Baptists north of the Rappahanock River. Here at a large outdoor gathering, Alexander was "too much occupied with the strange and promiscuous assembly to pay much attention to the discourse." But he did notice that here too the preacher was critical of learning.

More personal was Alexander's conversation with another Baptist, a mechanic who was building a mill for General Posey. The millwright suddenly asked him whether he believed in the second birth. Alexander, taken aback, answered that he did. The next question inevitably followed as to whether he had experienced it. Alexander answered frankly, "Not that I knew of." The conversation ended with the disturbing words, "Ah, if you had experienced this change you would know something about it!"[16]

Even at this early stage, Alexander, in spite of the negative comments of the evangelistic exhorters, did not conceive of intellectual attainments as antagonistic to deep religious life. All the time that he was engaged in inner struggle, he fulfilled his duties as tutor to the four children of the household and devoted more time than ever before to a broad program of reading. His responsibility for tutoring caused him to feel—perhaps with characteristic overmodesty—that he was "well-grounded in nothing but the grammar." Working nights to keep ahead of his pupils, he acquired a more accurate knowledge of Latin, which with further study later was to be the key that would unlock for him the theological literature of the seventeenth and earlier centuries of Western Christianity. Late in life, Alexander was to claim that "during the half century then past, he had read more Latin than English."[17]

Private libraries of the Tidewater gentry in the eighteenth century commonly included a broad range of subjects, with writings on religion well represented.[18] Alexander appears to have had the run of his host's library in addition to a "trunk of classical and scientific books, sent to me from home at my request," and he "was seldom without a book in his hand, except when he was giving up his mind to solitary meditation," a self-discipline which his former teacher, William Graham, had strongly recommended. The reading which he reports, though scattered, was quite impressive in substance and range. He acquired some broad historical perspective by perusing "with much avidity" the widely popular and informing but uncritical multivolume compilations *Ancient History* and *Roman History* by the French Jansenist Charles Rollin and the more scholarly multivolume *History of England* by the exiled French Huguenot Paul de Rapin, which in the opinion of the English historian, C. H. Firth, "remained until the publication of Hume's, the standard history of England," though suffering from the author's lack of access to important documents. Alexander seems to have had at least an introductory knowledge of philosophy at this time and an acquaintance with the significance of Isaac Newton, though he admitted with commendable honesty that his reading of John Locke's *Essay on Human Understanding* while here was "with little comprehension of the argument," but hastened to emphasize that "Mental Science became afterwards my favourite study."[19]

An agonizing dilemma was beginning to confront Alexander. He was deeply impressed with the earnestness and fervor of the zealous but ignorant revivalists whom he met. But, on the intellectual side, his historical reading had made him aware that there were non-Christian religions whose adherents were equally confident of the truth of their doctrines, and he knew, too, that "many intelligent men in the country" followed deism in rejecting Christian revelation. He had never heard of any published defenses of Christianity on a respectable intellectual level. While he was in this quandary, glancing over the trunkful of books sent him from home, his eye was caught by the title "evidence," and he began reading in earnest Soame Jenyns's *A View of the Internal Evidence of the Christian Religion*, first published a dozen years earlier. "At every step," he later recalled, "conviction flashed across my mind, with much bright and overwhelming evidence, that when I ceased to read, the room had the appearance of being illuminated. I never had such a feeling from the simple discovery of truth."[20]

What particularly captivated Alexander, torn as he was by internal struggle and surrounded by the highly emotional Christianity of the Baptists, was Jenyns's emphasis on the "internal evidences" of Christianity. This type of apologetic appealed to the religious and moral sense of the individual as the ultimate norm of truth and acceptability. While

Jenyns was certainly no revivalist, subjective method which he employed made it possible for the evangelical reader to use his own own inner
spiritual experience as the foundation for an intellectual defense of
Christianity. This suggestion that a synthesis was possible between
Christian experience and rational intelligence delivered Alexander from
the agonizing dilemma of choosing between them. Faith could be saved
without forfeiting intelligence.

Jenyns's method was a radical departure from the "objective" method
of "external" evidence used by early antideistical writers to prove Christianity's supernatural character from the biblical miracles and fulfilled
prophecies. By contrast, there was a strong romantic note in Jenyns's
emphasis on Christianity's value for man. Jenyns explicitly made his
apologetic independent of whether or not the biblical books contain
errors or were written by authors other than those whose names they
bear. One can only conjecture what the "Old Princeton Theology" of the
nineteenth century would have been if Archibald Alexander and his
theological heirs had accepted this broad view of Scripture from the
author whom Alexander regarded so highly. On the other hand, Jenyns
did not wholly escape the weakening of the objective and historical
foundation of Christianity to which this type of apologetic is liable.
Alexander made no comment on, and perhaps did not notice at the time,
the smug, static view of society found in this and in other writing, for
which Jenyns's famous contemporary, Dr. Samuel Johnson, roundly
denounced him.[21]

Alexander's spiritual mentor, Mrs. Tyler, had weak eyes and often
asked him to read to her from the writings of John Flavel, an English
Presbyterian Puritan who was ejected from his church living by the Uniformity Act of 1662, but continued to minister furtively to his former
parishioners of Dartmouth in Devonshire. In typical Puritan "plain
style," his sermons dealt with inner experience, moral conduct, and
abstract doctrine. His logical thought, without much concrete illustration, moved clearly and rapidly. Flavel's writings had been popular
among Virginia Presbyterians from their first settlements, even where
few other books were owned. One Sunday evening, Alexander was
reading to the whole Posey household, by request, a sermon of Flavel on
Revelation 3:20: "Behold I stand at the door and knock." During the
course of the reading, he was so overcome by emotion that he retired
hastily to his room, where he says, "I was overwhelmed with a flood of
joy. It was transport such as I had never known before, and seldom
since. . . . I was filled with a sense of the goodness and mercy of
God. . . . It soon occurred to me that possibly I had experienced the
change called the new birth." He later declared, "To John Flavel I
certainly owe more than to any uninspired author."[22]

Meanwhile Alexander kept reading. He supplemented his growing knowledge of Christian doctrine with "Jenks on Justification by Faith."[23] The only commentary he could find in the house was that by Burkitt.[24] Mrs. Tyler pressed into his hands one of the numerous attacks on infant baptism by the English Baptist commentator and controversialist John Gill. "This perplexed me not a little," says Alexander, "for I had a strong predilection for the way in which I had been educated, especially as I found that Flavel was a Presbyterian." His extensive reading while at General Posey's and immediately thereafter centered in the writings of the seventeenth-century Puritans and their direct heirs of the next century. While his favorite was Flavel, he also read John Owen, Richard Baxter, Philip Doddridge, George Whitefield, and Joseph Alleine.[25] Conversations that he had with William Graham a little later, on such subjects as justification by faith and regeneration, showed that solid theological reading and thinking was beginning to undergird his more subjective introspections.[26]

But it is not surprising to discover that at this period in his life, Alexander had fluctuating inner experiences of anxiety, conviction, elation, despondency, and confidence which closely paralleled the type of experience made familiar by innumerable Puritan diaries. The emphasis of the Baptist millwright on the new birth as something that could be consciously experienced jolted him, for it was utterly foreign to his earlier environment.[27] It is interesting that the first spiritual elation which he reported was in response not to a fervid exhorter, but to the solid writings of Soame Jenyns. It was in this period that he began private prayer, wandering alone into the outdoors, like Jonathan Edwards. At a spot on the nearby Wilderness Creek, "with his knife, he made a booth of arbour," and "to this sequestered spot he used to retire for prayer, taking some volume with him."[28]

When Alexander was overcome with emotion while reading Flavel to the Posey household, it occurred to him that possibly he had experienced the change called the new birth. With this exaltation, there began for him a period of agonizing introspection and fluctuation. He supposed that if he were now regenerated, he would henceforth live without sin. Therefore, when he next transgressed (he was honest enough to admit to himself the fact of transgression), he fell into despair.[29]

By the end of the year at General Posey's menage, Alexander had finally achieved an improved working knowledge of Latin, had acquired a hasty overview of history and philosophy, and had made a very modest but earnest beginning in biblical study and theology. What was to be most significant for future years, he had become deeply concerned about the meaning for him of the Christian gospel. These were no small extracurricular accomplishments for one year or less in the life of a lad only recently turned seventeen.[30]

Soon after returning home to the Valley, Alexander found himself involved in another area of the revival. John Blair Smith, president of Hampden-Sydney College, and a College of New Jersey classmate of William Graham, invited Graham to preach for him in Prince Edward County, east of the Blue Ridge. Graham took along Alexander and another young man. Smith was an heir of the Great Awakening, his father, Robert Smith, and two of his uncles, Samuel and John Blair, having been prominent in that movement. Methodist and Baptist preaching in the vicinity had contributed to making people revival-conscious. When three Hampden-Sydney students became "serious," President Smith openly encouraged them and became the leader of the revival among Presbyterians over a wide area. Graham, whose previous preaching had always been intellectual and conscientious, but cold and not very effective, was stimulated by the prevailing atmosphere to preach a powerful sermon, and presently carried the revival back with him to the Valley.[31]

During the revival at Hampden-Sydney, Alexander, "having never spoken freely to any one of my own religious exercises," was amazed by a youthful exhorter. "How a person so young should have the courage and ability to speak in public and before such an audience, I could not conceive."[32] While at Hampden-Sydney, Alexander privately sought the counsel of John Blair Smith, who had made a very favorable impression on him. He told his counselor of his religious experiences, admitting that he had subsequently sinned. To this Smith replied, "in his decided, peremptory way, that then they were certainly not of the nature of true religion, which always destroys the power and dominion of sin; and he proceeded to account for the joy I had experienced, on other principles."

Poor Alexander, finding his former anxieties now verified, was shattered once again. Now he determined to achieve the deepest agonies of conviction of sin. "I rolled on the ground in anguish of spirit, bewailing my insensibility," but apparently to no immediate avail.[33] During his journey home from Hampden-Sydney to Lexington, he was engaged in private meditation and prayer "at the edge of a wood, . . . when I was suddenly visited with such a melting of heart as I never had before or since." His tears flowed profusely "under a lively sense of the Divine goodness" and his own ingratitude. Like Jonathan Edwards acknowledging that there had been some neuroticism in the Great Awakening, Alexander in retrospect inclined to downgrade this particular experience as "a sudden change in the animal system, and a relief arising from a vent found for tears."[34] While he was again meditating alone in the woods a few days later, his spirits sank to a new low. He now concluded that he would "certainly be lost forever," even while acknowledging "the justice of God in my condemnation." With the matter seemingly finally settled, he "felt no need of prayer or further waiting on God."

But he was about to experience more permanent deliverance. That same day, he told a local minister that he had just come to the conclusion that he would "certainly be lost," because he "had not yet in any degree experienced those convictions without which I could not expect to be saved." The minister offered the timely reply "that no certain degree of conviction was prescribed"; that the only value of conviction was to show the need of Christ; " 'and this,' he added, 'you have.' " Looking back over the years, Alexander recalled, "This mere possibility of salvation, after having given up all hope, was like . . . life from the dead." Back home in Rockbridge County, "I resolved . . . to devote myself entirely to prayer, fasting, and the Scriptures until I should arrive at greater hope." He later felt that in association with fellow-seekers, "telling over our private exercises was carried to an undue length." Once again, alone in the woods, he tried by the earnestness of his own prayer to capture heaven by storm. But the effort ended only in exhaustion and despair. Like Martin Luther, he found that "the more I strove the harder my heart became." About to quit, he cried to God, when, "in a moment, I had such a view of a crucified Saviour, as is without a parallel in my experience." He now expected to enjoy continually elevated feelings, "but before a week had elapsed, darkness began to gather over me again." It seems that a more stable state of mind came to him only as he abandoned such agonizing introspection and gave himself to a faith that was more objective and did not seek continual psychological confirmation. Looking back from the age of seventy-seven, over his early anxiety and seeking, Alexander wrote, "I am of opinion, that my regeneration took place while I resided at General Posey's."[35]

A number of implications emerge from this account of Alexander's youthful religious experience as he himself later remembered and interpreted or reinterpreted it. Most conspicuous is the dualistic assumption that all people are divided into two categories, the "saved" and the "lost." Another assumption, less emphatic in Alexander's narrative, is that many, though not necessary all, of the "saved" can have assurance that they belong to this felicitous group. But there is no demand that conversion be "dated," and some uncertainty remains as to whether Alexander's own conversion was exactly "datable." Another clear implication of these recollections is that it is extremely difficult for a person to distinguish by introspection between genuine Christian experience and mere excitation of the nervous system. The sequence clearly moved in the direction of basing confidence on objective, external realities (in this case on God and divine grace) rather than on the degree or quality of subjective awareness and appropriation. In this area, too, the problem of knowledge—epistemology—so important in post-Renaissance culture, is found to occupy a central position. It was only after major attention was shifted from subjective psychological phenomena to God himself, whom he believed he had experienced directly, that Alexander reached stability and assurance. This direct concentration on the subject of knowledge itself, rather than on the mental image of the object, was quite in accord with the so-called Scottish Philosophy. Alexander's turning at this point in his life from subjective frustrations to an "objective" base of faith became a central characteristic of his faith and of the entire Old Princeton Theology. Alexander's thought, as more fully developed a little later, based this "objective" knowledge of God on the Bible, an assurance made still more objective and absolute by some of Alexander's later followers in the concept of biblical "inerrancy."

# 3
# EDUCATIONAL
# BACKGROUND

Alexander, looking ahead to further education, was urged by his relative General Andrew Moore[1] to consider going to the College of New Jersey. But when Graham advised him first to take additional work at Liberty Hall, he consented, much to the chagrin of Moore and their common relatives. Meanwhile, Alexander fell sick of a serious fever which for weeks kept him helpless. After a slow convalescence, he chose, with characteristic misgivings concerning his own qualifications, to study for the ministry under the direction of Mr. Graham, to whom Alexander's cousin John Lyle similarly applied. A little later the band of ministerial candidates had grown to more than half a dozen.[2] Inasmuch as Graham was an active pastor in addition to being the head of Liberty Hall, Alexander's program of theological study was a kind of blend of the two early methods of ministerial education—the method of "apprenticing" with a pastor, and the method of taking a year or so of graduate study in divinity under a professor or president of a college.

Alexander never ceased to extol Graham as a teacher and to emphasize in particular the permanent influence that Graham had on his intellectual life. It seems desirable therefore to take a closer view of this somewhat unusual man.[3] William Graham and his opposite number at Hampden- Sydney College, President John Blair Smith, were about the last of the line of Pennsylvanians on whom Virginia Presbyterians depended for the basic leadership of their work. The young Virginians and their successors whom Graham and Smith educated in their respective colleges permanently took over the leadership of the Presbyterianism of their region. By then the younger Presbyterianism of this oldest colony had come to full maturity and was soon setting the pace for some aspects of the life of their denomination as a whole.

William Graham was born in 1746 of Scotch-Irish parentage in Paxton Township on the Pennsylvania frontier, some five miles from the site of modern Harrisburg. Youthful vitality found expression in a love of dancing, a recreation which he later somewhat humorlessly condemned on the ground that it preoccupied the mind and displaced all solid thinking. Converted at about the age of twenty-one, he tardily began preparation for the ministry, a little later entering the College of New Jersey where he graduated in 1773, a classmate of the Rev. John Blair Smith and of the famous "Light Horse Harry" Lee.[4]

The Presbytery of Hanover in 1775, desiring to support education in the Virginia Valley, invited Graham to take charge of their academy, which a little later became Liberty Hall. The year after arriving in Virginia, Graham entered into an unhappy marriage which had a souring influence on his personality and adversely affected his career. Soon after assuming leadership of the Virginia school, Graham made a money-raising journey on horseback as far as Boston. It was a broadening experience which enabled him to see various types of society and which provided the opportunity of firsthand acquaintance with the emerging "New Divinity"—as yet unknown in the Valley—of such theologians as Joseph Bellamy and Samuel Hopkins, disciples of Jonathan Edwards. In later years he often referred to a conversation he had had with Bellamy. This experience might well explain the fact that he had a more favorable opinion of the theology of Jonathan Edwards than did his Princeton teacher, John Witherspoon. But he was not impressed by the widely practiced reading of sermons. In sum, he found New England quite insular but very stimulating, a reaction which may well have been an incentive to Alexander to undertake a similar New England odyssey some years later.[5]

As a preacher Graham was diligent in scholarship and preparation, but his delivery was cold and flawed by distracting mannerisms. His ministry was notably ineffective until the revival of 1789, when his preaching became vital and dynamic and his services were in wide demand. That he was held in respect by his peers even before the new dynamism in his preaching is evidenced by his election as the first moderator of the new Synod of Virginia in 1788. In what Alexander called "the greatest error of his life," Graham planned to found a utopian community, purchased 6,000 acres of land along the Ohio River in 1796, and resigned as rector of the academy. Hoped-for settlers did not arrive, and he died a financially ruined man in 1799.[6]

One of the most important activities of Graham's life was his instruction of candidates for the ministry. For a number of years before the revival of 1789, no candidates appeared, but following the revival, more than half-dozen, of whom Alexander was one, presented themselves. Also following the revival, the Synod of Virginia in 1791 proposed two centers of theological education, one of them to be in Rockbridge County, with Alexander's father, William Alexander, as its treasurer. The next year the trustees of Liberty Hall offered the use of their property for carrying out synod's plan, an offer which the synod accepted. But denominational interest in the project soon cooled, and a few years later, for various reasons, Graham resigned.[7]

Meanwhile, however, after the revival, Graham zealously instructed Archibald Alexander and the other students for the ministry. He devoted one day a week to hearing students' papers and to discussing theological subjects with them, in addition to which Alexander himself had almost daily consultations with him. The students also engaged in stimulating theological conversations among themselves. Like Alexander later, Graham continually urged his students to think independently, but nearly all at the end of the course thought as he did, and he was not pleased if their conclusions differed from his own. Graham gave particular attention to the developing psychological studies of his day, a subject which shed new light on the long-standing interest of Puritanism and revivalism in inner Christian experience. This psychological illumination of Christian experience was to be a lifelong interest of Alexander. In his work under Graham, Alexander studied "a compendium of Turretin in Latin" and such writers as the English Puritan John Owen and Jonathan Edwards. Graham also set great store by Bishop Joseph Butler's *Sermons* and his *Analogy*, a work of which Alexander later made much use.[8]

Alexander's education did not include introduction to German philosophy or theology, but he was indoctrinated in the principles of Scottish common-sense realism, which became the philosophy which underlay his own theological thinking and writing. He eagerly devoured Hugh Blair's widely influential *Lectures on Rhetoric and Belles Lettres*, recently published (1783), which was based on the Scottish philosophy. Graham himself had acquired the writings of such leading exponents of "common sense" as Thomas Reid and James Beattie.[9]

Because of the importance of Scottish common-sense realism in supplying the philosophical presuppositions and base of Alexander's theology, it is desirable to summarize the thought of Thomas Reid, its early and leading exponent, and after that the thought of Witherspoon and of Graham as transmitters of this philosophy to Alexander. This Scottish common-sense philosophy emerged in the latter eighteenth century, a "golden age" of Scottish culture which produced outstanding works in philosophy, history, belles lettres, natural science, social science, and economic development, numbering such brilliant names as David Hume, Francis Hutcheson, and Adam Smith.

Thomas Reid, like Immanuel Kant a little later, was awakened from "dogmatic slumber" by the brilliant critique of David Hume, who declared that our only certain knowledge is of the stream of our own mental "impressions" and asserted that these impressions give no proof of the existence of an external world, or of the continuing identity of one's own self, or even the existence of a "self" at all. The only reality that is certain for us, said Hume, is the stream of our own subjective impressions or ideas.

Reid traced the root of Hume's scepticism back through Berkeley, Locke, Descartes, and even Aristotle to the conception that our senses do not give us awareness of the external world itself, but only of images or ideas of that world. If we have only images or ideas, Reid conceded to Hume, it does become impossible to affirm that these mental images are related to an external world, or that they represent any reality beyond themselves. In fact, Reid conceded further, if we have only detached and atomized ideas, it becomes impossible to affirm the continuing identity of the human self or even the existence of such a self.

Hume's conclusion is an impossible one, Reid argued. It flies in the face of the universal "common sense" of mankind, and, if taken literally, would make rational thought and even life itself impossible. Therefore, said Reid, Hume's sceptical conclusions must be rejected, and, in order to validate that rejection, his premises also must be repudiated. That is, our sensations are not of mere mental impressions or images, but of external reality itself. There are, said Reid, no intermediary, detached "images"; we sense the material world directly.

In developing this position, Reid was in effect rejecting also the possibility of the simultaneous existence of two levels of reality—a level of common sense, everyday living where things are what they seem to be; and, contrasted with this, another level of more ultimate reality, which was being explored by mathematics, science, and philosophy, a rationally reconstructed reality very different from the world of "common sense." In denying the reality of any such universe of rational reconstruction and later of scientific reconstruction, and in insisting that nothing could be accepted as reality which could not be squared with "common sense" and practical living, Reid was turning his back on what was to be, under the leadership of Kant and of Kant's numerous philosophical heirs, a major development of the nineteenth century. Reid was, in effect, locking himself into a seemingly safe and sure, but very static and limited, universe.

Reid, having rejected Hume's conclusions and therefore also Hume's premises on the basis of common sense, found it necessary to secure a foundation for his own constructive building. Such a foundation he discovered in "first principles," or axioms—"self-evident truths," like those underlying mathematics, which do not need to be proved, indeed cannot be proved because there is no more ultimate knowledge by which they can be verified. All valid knowledge is based on these first principles, said Reid, and if they were to be rejected, to that extent knowledge would be impossible. These first principles are not "innate" in the sense that they are fully formulated in the mind of an infant. Rather, every normal human mind has the potentiality of recognizing as true these first principles as soon as they are clearly presented. At this point Reid is in trouble because, on investigation, he has to admit that "first principles" are not as clear-cut and absolute as his needs require. Able men in different cultures and in different eras have differed as to what are first principles. Reid rather lamely offers arguments by which the truth of a disputed first principle can be established.[10]

This is one of the weakest joints in Reid's armor. If, after all, first principles need demonstration and vindication, what has become of their self-evident ultimacy? First principles are discerned by common sense, he tells us, but he wavers between treating common sense as an unerring source of absolute truth and treating it as yielding less assured conclusions. Thus, on the more confident side, common sense is "the voice of God"; "clear and steady apprehension" leads invariably to "sound judgment"; and "matters of universal agreement can be accepted as first principles." But when he removes common sense from the area of implied intuition and relates it to concrete rational processes, its conclusions appear more fallible. Though common sense is an "inward light . . . given by heaven," it is given "to different persons in different degrees."[11]

Reid's "common sense" was thus a somewhat fluctuating concept. To the extent that it was something innate, intuitive, and absolute, it could be confirmed by universal consensus, and was a radically leveling principle which transformed everyone potentially into a competent philosopher. But to the extent that common sense was related to rational processes and to a particular historical context, it lost much of its absolute character and leveling tendencies. In later hands, this philosophy often resorted to counting noses in the effort to establish a first principle by "universal consensus." Reid, in the earliest and ablest of his published writings, *An Inquiry Into the Human Mind on the Principles of Common Sense* (1765), made sparing use of the concept "common sense." But it was a magic wand that seemed to accomplish so much so easily that in later works he—and even more his later popularizers—waved it more frequently and more carelessly.

The area in which the Scottish philosophy stimulated William Graham and his pupil Archibald Alexander most vigorously was in psychology, by encouraging the introspective analysis of the operation of their own minds. Graham had particular zeal in this direction, and Alexander who, as we have seen, was already deeply involved in agonizing spiritual self-analysis, quickly caught the contagion and entered upon a lifelong interest in so-called mental philosophy. The problem of how we acquire knowledge and the validity of our supposed knowledge, which had dominated philophy from the time of Descartes, inevitably brought in its wake new study of the operations of the mind itself. René Descartes, Thomas Hobbes, John Locke, George Berkeley, David Hume, and David

Hartley all made major additions to the emerging study of psychology. The originality and value of Thomas Reid's contributions to the new discipline have been debated, but one could hardly study his writings seriously without sharing the growing interest in psychological questions.

Reid accepted the subject-object dualism of Descartes, but saw the mind concerned not only with perceiving objects outside itself, but able also, by introspection, to view itself as having such perceptions. Reid sought by strictly "empirical" methods of introspection to discover laws of the mind analogous to the laws of mechanics discovered by physical science. While Reid's easy appeals to "common sense" and lack of sharply defined methodology were inadequate to accomplish the task he proposed, his distinction between the mind's viewing its ideas and the mind seeing itself viewing these ideas was perhaps his most important philosophical contribution.[12] This suggestion proved particularly stimulating to a vigorous mind prone to introspection, such as William Graham's, and to a religious spirit deeply involved in self-searching, such as Archibald Alexander's.

In the field of ethics, Reid displayed the same wavering between absolutism and relativism that was present in his philosophy as a whole. In ethics, as in epistemology, Reid at times wrote as though a person would have sure knowledge of first principles. All men have these principles "written in their hearts"; conscience perceives them intuitively. God himself implanted this "moral sense" in man as "a light within." "Conscience commands and forbids . . . without the labour of reasoning." "Every man of common understanding, who wishes to know his duty, may know it." But over against these intimations that conscience—which apparently was common sense expressing itself in the area of ethics—was an absolute norm, Reid gave clear indications that conscience was, after all, quite relative and fallible. Conscience "grows and develops" and depends very much on "being duly cultivated and exercised." In fact, it "is not so strong and vigorous by nature, as to secure us from very gross mistakes with regard to our duty. Our natural power of discerning between right and wrong, needs the aid of instruction." Thus a man may act very wrongly from a perfectly sincere but uninstructed conscience.[13]

Reid divided the powers of the mind into two—the understanding and the will or affections. Only when the will is operative can there be moral action; the will is man's "active" power. But moral liberty is not mere ability to do whatever one desires. True moral liberty is free choice based on moral judgment. Thus man's understanding or reason, in spite of all that was said about intuitive common sense, is given a decisive role in ethics, because it is "self-evident" that man's reason should control his will and passions.[14]

Reid was struggling for an absolute ethic. Maybe it was a residue of

Calvinism that caused him to reject the optimistic view held by Lord Shaftesbury and Francis Hutcheson that man is naturally benevolent, that self-interest coincides with the general welfare, and that one's own "taste" (perhaps not so different from Reid's "conscience" as Reid supposed) is the basic guide in the closely related areas of aesthetics and ethics. Reid somewhat weakened his position by accepting the suggested linkage between aesthetics and ethics, which forced him to assert absolute norms in both areas—a particularly difficult position to establish for aesthetics. Reid was equally emphatic in combatting the subjective relativism of Hume's ethic, insisting that ethical action should be guided not by feelings, but by judgment "expressed by a proposition." Whether Reid's vacillation between intuition and reason can support an absolute norm would seem to be a fair question.[15]

Reid shared the emphasis of Shaftesbury and Hutcheson on freedom from self-interest—"disinterestedness"—as necessary to the highest kind of benevolence. He agreed with them, too, in saying that benevolent affections are implanted in man by the Creator, and that the man who, forgetting his own happiness, gives full expression to benevolence will be the one who attains happiness. This is true because God, who is wise and benevolent, rules all things. It is important to note that, for Reid, in sharp contrast with the Utilitarians, the ethical value of an action depended not on the result accomplished, but on the motive or "intention" of the doer.[16]

Archibald Alexander's introduction to the thought of Thomas Reid and of other Scottish "common-sense" philosophers came indirectly through his instructor William Graham, who had been taught the Scottish philosophy by President John Witherspoon at the College of New Jersey.

John Witherspoon was not a research scholar or a highly original thinker. But he was a man of large outlook, strong practical sense, and vigorous leadership. When he graduated from the University of Edinburgh and entered upon his ministry in the Church of Scotland, a great era of Scottish culture was reaching full development. On coming to the presidency of the College of New Jersey in 1768 he brought with him the Scottish common-sense realism. His lectures on moral philosophy, published posthumously from syllabi distributed to his students, summarized some of his philosophical positions. His realism opposed both the idealism and the materialism of the day. It was a sharp dualism between God and man, body and soul, subject and object.[17] He strongly emphasized reason, suggestive of the Scottish Enlightenment in which he had been educated at Edinburgh, but with a scholastic rather than a radical critical turn. Thus he offered rational proofs for the existence of God and in a traditional way analyzed the divine attributes. He defended moral philosophy against the strictures of Jonathan Edwards, saying that "if the Scripture is true, the discoveries of reason cannot be contrary to it," and suggested that reason can supplement revelation: "There may be an illustration and confirmation of the inspired writings from reason and observation, which will greatly add to their beauty and force."[18]

In the true spirit of common-sense realism, appeal to first principles quickly solved epistemological problems: "That our senses are to be trusted in the information they give us, seems to me a first principle, because they are the foundation of all our after reasonings." Those who followed Berkeley and Hume in denying "the reality of the material system" were peremptorily dismissed:

Persons who would maintain such principles, do not deserve to be reasoned with, because they do not pretend to communicate knowledge, but to take all knowledge from us. . . . The immaterial system is a wild and ridiculous attempt to unsettle the principles of common sense by metaphysical reasoning, which can hardly produce any thing but contempt in the generality of persons who hear it.

Witherspoon cited with approval "some late writers" and " authors of Scotland" who have invoked "first principles or dictates of common sense" in refutation of Hume's denial of causal power and of personal identity. Reflecting the importance attached to consensus, Witherspoon argued for belief in the existence of God from "the consent of all nations, and the universal prevalence of that belief."[19]

In ethics, Witherspoon exhibited the same fluctuation between intuition and reason as did Thomas Reid. Witherspoon sought an absolute ethic, based on its ability to produce happiness, but on first principles discovered by conscience. He considered this drawing of principles of duty "from the nature of man" as analogous to the inductive methods of natural science, with intuitive conscience playing a large part in the derivation of these "first principles" of conduct. He reasserted tradition against Shaftesbury and Hutcheson when he took the position that aesthetics and ethics do not have parallel norms; nor does benevolence constitute the whole of virtue; nor does the "general good" supersede "the particular principles of duty which he [God] hath impressed upon the conscience." Though Witherspoon said much about intuitive conscience, his real ethical norm was a somewhat undefined combination of conscience and reason. "We ought to take the rule of duty from conscience enlightened by reason, experience, and every way by which we can be supposed to learn the will of our Maker." He also compromised by combining intention and results as the tests of the ethical value of an action. Unlike Reid, Witherspoon distinguished three "faculties—"the understanding, the will, and the affections."[20] In his theological views, some of Witherspoon's positions foreshadowed in a skeletal way the later "Old Princeton Theology" of Archibald Alexander and Charles Hodge.[21]

William Graham, the Princeton graduate who had a formative influence on Archibald Alexander, was imbued with the common-sense realism taught by Witherspoon. Graham's commitment to this Scottish philosophy can be seen in an extant copy of a student's notes on his lectures, written just a few years after Alexander had completed his studies at Liberty Hall.[22]

Graham, even more than Reid or Witherspoon, appealed unashamedly, over the heads of experts, to plain common sense: "We are not to consult the opinions of metaphysicians. We shall appeal to the common sense of mankind. . . . When you come with your logical definitions and metaphysical reasonings the subject is so involved in darkness that scarcely the refined, much less the plain man can understand you." All reasoning, he said, must assume as its foundation "first principles," which "cannot be demonstrated, yet they are seen by immediate perception."[23]

Descartes's attempt to prove his own existence was unnecessary, according to Graham, because one's own existence is a first principle other than which nothing can be more certain. Following Reid, Graham rejected the view held by Locke and others before him that we sense only images in the brain and not the external world directly; and rejected also Locke's subjectivizing of secondary qualities. Contrary to Berkeley, Graham declared that the trustworthiness of the senses and the existence of the material world are first principles; and, as against Hume, he found continuing self-identity and causality also to be first principles.[24] In discussing certain first principles, Graham found them attested by the consensus "or at least the majority" (!) of mankind, and saw man so "constituted" by his Creator that he cannot avoid believing in these axioms. The chief purpose of education, he said, is to "open the first principles of Science" so that the student can build his later thought and activity on these.[25]

Graham's "psychology" consisted partly in defining terms to describe what he found by introspection. Witherspoon still spoke of three "faculties" of the mind,[26] but Graham went beyond his teacher at this point and followed Locke in rejecting such "faculties." In a quite modern spirit, Graham found emotions permeating the knowing process, which could have had extremely important implications for theology and for a relation in theology between reason and spiritual experience. "Every perception," Graham said, "is attended with emotion." He devoted a great deal of attention to the emotions and at times showed an almost modern interest in the problem of motivation. Emotions are "pliant" and take their character from the object. He noted basic resemblances between bodily appetites and certain nonphysical desires such as lust for wealth or power, with the difference that bodily appetites can be temporarily satiated, but not these nonphysical lusts. He seemed to assume the widely held idea of a "Great Chain of Being" when he asserted that there are objects in nature suited to the gratification of each human desire. Though never having studied medicine, he appeared to be aware of psychosomatic connections when he pointed out that the body influences the mind, and the mind the body.[27]

In spite of his realization of the presence of emotion in the knowing process and the influence of the body on the mind, and in spite of the large role that his "Scottish realism" assigned to common sense, Graham still regarded "reason" with the veneration characteristic of his era. In his anonymous *An Essay on Government*, he wrote as though it were possible for "the honest inquirer after truth" to pursue truth with "an honest unprejudiced heart," even though admitting in the same pamphlet that "custom has greater influence with many than reason."[28] His definition of reason was consistent with his rejection of mental "faculties" and is suggestive of associationist psychology: "Reason is that series of energies by which I discover things not before known or that which brings a train of ideas to view through the medium of known and acknowledged truths or finds out the connection and dependence of known truths."[29]

Graham's treatment of the will was also consistent with his rejection of the faculty psychology: "The will is the soul choosing and determining. It is not a distinct being." We do not choose without a motive, and the strongest motive always prevails. The will has no "self-determining power," for this would mean that an act of will is determined by one previous to it and that by a still earlier act of the will *ad infinitum*. Here he reflected Jonathan Edwards. Suggestions of associationist psychology appeared again in his statement, "The power of thinking then means no more than that the soul is capable of turning itself to and fixing its attention on any subject." He frankly declared he did not know what a "free will" is, because he had "no conceptions of its opposite bound will." He rejected the definition of "moral liberty" as "the power of acting as we please," because it ignored the distinction between mental [moral?] and physical [natural?] motions, and also overlooked the fact that in society liberty must be consistent with law.[30] Scattered through Witherspoon's *Moral Philosophy* were a number of attacks, some explicit and others implicit, against various views of Jonathan Edwards. By contrast, Graham's treatment of the will has some interesting parallels with Edwards's thought on the subject.

Graham's great interest in the inner workings of human personality enabled him in sermons to describe specific aspects of Christian experience with a clarity and analytic power that startled his hearers, "for it seemed to them as if he could read the very inmost sentiments of their minds; which he described more perfectly than they could do themselves."[31] The same was often said later of Alexander himself. In both Graham and Alexander there was frequent coinciding of the growing interest in mental philosophy and the widespread revivalism of the day. Graham's recognition of psychosomatic connections led him to adopt toward the emotional excesses of revivalism an attitude of religious neutrality similar to that of Jonathan Edwards. When the mind suddenly becomes aware of such grand truths as "the awful majesty of God," "free pardon," and "a title to everlasting happiness," "the mind may be affected so as to produce commotions in the body." Such a phenomenon neither proves nor disproves a divine working. "The wise man therefore had rather let it alone."[32]

In the area of ethics, Graham, in spite of his theological orthodoxy, seemed ready to accept tacitly the definitions of the task as formulated by those who were attempting to reconstitute ethics on a purely naturalistic and empirical basis. Graham, following the Scottish common-sense realists, conceived of "empiricism in this field as the discovery of first principles by introspection followed by the inductive drawing of inferences from these principles." Thus he said that a right knowledge of moral science is obtainable only "by reflecting upon the operations of our own mind—a want of this attention is the reason why moral science has been involved in so much obscurity."[33]

Graham diverged sharply from Witherspoon in agreeing with Shaftesbury and Hutcheson that "taste [that is, in the arts] and the moral sense are nearly allied." He saw an inductive element in taste, for "a general knowledge of nature and the relation of things is necessary to form an accurate taste." Presumably he would see conscience also as involving induction from experience. Something of Hutcheson's conception of harmony appears in Graham's statement, "Any instrument or machine that is neatly made and fitted to answer the end for which it was intended is beautiful." This kind of "harmony," transformed from aesthetics to ethics, leads to utilitarianism. There is more of the mellow spirit of Hutcheson's "moderatism" than of the extreme spirit of some of Jonathan Edwards's followers in Graham's statement that "benevolence" should not only transcend one's own interests, but should also include concern for such interests. Disinterested benevolence alone is impossible, for man cannot "act without motives, or altogether independent of his own happiness."[34] Alexander, as against Samuel Hopkins, followed Graham in legitimizing a carefully limited degree of personal happiness as a proper ethical goal.

Witherspoon, as we have seen, taught that the ethical value of an action was to be measured by both the intention of the doer and the consequence of the deed. The latter emphasis, of course, faces in the direction of utilitarianism. Graham, by contrast, was emphatic in measuring ethical value by intention alone.[35]

In theology, according to Alexander, Graham was "strictly orthodox, according to the standards of his own church, which he greatly vener-

ated; but in his method of explaining some of the knotty points in theology, he departed considerably from the common track."[36] Some might
regret that bitter eighteenth- and nineteenth-century controversies over
the conundrum of the relation of God's foreknowledge and man's freedom did not follow Graham's easy common-sense dismissal of the whole
question: "Preordination can have no influence on human conduct if it
be not known."[37] Graham, reflecting contemporary optimistic views of
man as well as his own emphasis on man's reason, embraced a "light
scheme." This taught that regeneration came when, by the influence of
the Holy Spirit, divine truth was perceived in its true nature by man's
mind. Alexander sharply rejected this opinion of his teacher and insisted
on the more supernaturalistic view that regeneration involves a "physical" change (that is, a change in man's nature, or "phusis," not a change
in man's physical body) wrought in man's being by the direct action of
God.[38]

In discussing the atonement, Graham held to the governmental theory,
which was gaining ground among New England Congregationalists. This
view taught that the death of Christ was grounded not in the inherent necessities of God's justice, but in God's need to maintain order in a universe of rational creatures by proving that wrongdoing inevitably
receives a penalty.[39] Here, as in some other cases, Graham showed
greater kinship with New England thought than was characteristic of
Alexander or of later Old School Presbyterians. Graham defined guilt as
"an obligation to suffer punishment," a definition which was later
greatly emphasized by the Old Princeton Theology, but which had
very legalistic and external implications concerning moral obligation.
Graham noted that morality presupposed rationality ("a capacity to deliberate") and a social context ("morality is the acting of a being under a
law").[40]

It is further evidence of the widespread influence of the Baptists in Virginia that Graham himself—like his students Alexander, Conrad Speece,
and others—for a time was persuaded to doubt the warrant for baptizing
infants. Graham had overcome his doubts on this question "some years"
before 1799,[41] which warrants a conjecture that his yielding to Baptist
suasives might have occurred during the revival a decade earlier when
Baptist outreach was particularly effective. It was characteristic of
Graham's honesty that in a pamphlet written to defend infant baptism,
he stated very forcefully the arguments against it; and it was characteristic of his independence that he found no previous writings in its defense
fully satisfactory. But when he developed his own argument for the baptism of infants, it was, after all, strikingly lacking in novelty. In quite
traditional fashion, he justified the practice on the basis of God's
covenant with Abraham (and even with Adam) and on the analogy of the
rite of circumcision. Alexander felt it necessary to apologize for the

mediocrity of the pamphlet, but it did show Graham's characteristic honesty and independence.[42]

Graham's views on political theory appeared in a pamphlet which he published in 1786 when he intended to become a citizen of the projected state of "Franklin." At that time his ideas were quite radically democratic, but after he was defeated as a candidate for the Federal Convention from Virginia (he was opposed to ratification), his active political interest ceased, as did that of many other clergymen in these decades, and his political views also became much more conservative, a change of which Archibald Alexander seemed to have approved.[43]

In his pamphlet, Graham saw all citizens equal and originally possessing a monopoly of legislative, executive, judicial, and military power. Man's fall into sin made government necessary, and men entered into social "compact" defining the powers of government and securing liberty, property, and religious freedom to all.[44] Graham defined a "republic" as "a government, by equal and just laws, made by common consent," and, like James Madison, he seemed aware of the danger of faction and of tyranny of the majority—"the dominion of one community over another community or of one set of men over other men." He desired to maintain the separateness of legislative, executive, and judicial powers, and, at a later date—again like Madison—desired a system of checks: "a proper balance of power sufficient . . . to prevent oppression." He favored a universal franchise with electoral districts of equal population in order that every citizen might have the same voting weight, an ideal more fully approximated in the twentieth century by decision of the Supreme Court. But by 1796 Graham already seemed quite disillusioned concerning the possibility of personal liberty: "No government can be framed . . . in which the people can enjoy a tolerable share of liberty."[45] Alexander's views reflected little or no influence from Graham's earlier economic and political liberalism.

In view of Graham's radically democratic view in his early years, one would expect him to have been vigorously opposed to slavery. According to Alexander, "when he first arrived in Virginia . . . he held slavery in great abhorrence." But as with many another living amidst slavery, his views on this subject changed—probably in conjunction with his shift from radically democratic to more aristocratic political ideas. "He became a slave-holder, and continued such until the day of his death." Notes on his lectures of 1796 quote him as conveniently harmonizing Christ's Golden Rule with social stratification. This Rule does not command emancipation, he said, but only the giving to each person what each has a right to expect in his particular relationship. Neither common sense nor revelation teaches that slaveholding is wrong, he added. "That Christianity was not designed to change men's civil relations is evident from the 7th chapter of I Corinthians." The slaves are unfit for liberty, and if freed might unite against us. It is striking that the lecture immediately preceding these statements still voiced such radically democratic ideas as short terms of political office with frequent rotation. Writing in 1799, Graham noted, with apparent complacence, that "it may . . . be impracticable for a believing master to give his servants a christian education." The matter must therefore be "left to the judgment of every christian master." Such a tragic change in outlook bears mute witness to the subtle and powerful forces of the time.[46]

Graham's readiness to take an independent stand on social questions was seen during the "Whiskey Rebellion" of 1794 when the Synod of Virginia urged obedience to the hated excise tax on whiskey. Whiskey, being more economically transportable than whole grain, was a staple of the back country and of the Valley, and such leading figures as Jefferson were critical of the tax. Graham opposed the synod's action, boldly declaring that "the whiskey boys" were suffering an injustice. Militiamen sent out to suppress the insurrection threatened violence against Graham, and he withdrew from the scene.[47]

The exact duration of Alexander's study of theology under Graham is not specifically stated. It could not have started before the spring of 1790, the date when the youth began to recover from a serious illness; and it did not extend beyond October 1, 1791, the date when presbytery licensed him to preach, following which he immediately entered upon extensive pulpit labors.[48] But in this period and in earlier years of pre-theological study, Graham was the major influence on Alexander's intellectual development, according to Alexander's own often-repeated testimony.

# 4
# APPLIED THEOLOGY

As a result of the Great Awakening earlier in the eighteenth century, the Presbyterian Church expected all its candidates for the ministry to have an acquaintance with what was called "experimental religion"; that is, they must have an experience of Christian faith of which they were conscious and which they could describe intelligibly. Alexander, who had deeply probed his inner life, still had misgivings. But Graham and other friends prevailed upon him to place himself "under the care of presbytery," the first step in seeking ordination.

Lexington Presbytery had come into separate existence in the autumn of 1786, but had received no candidate for the ministry until the spring of 1790, when Alexander's cousin John Lyle, a convert of the recent revival, presented himself. In that and the next year, Lyle, Alexander, and a number of other candidates who had been stimulated by the revival, came forward. In spite of the longstanding shortage of ministers, presbytery was quite exacting in its three-stage requirements of receiving a candidate under its care, subsequently licensing him, and still later ordaining him.

Alexander came before Lexington Presbytery at its meeting on October 27, 1790, not long after he had begun the study of theology under Mr. Graham. Presbytery having received "a favourable Account of his moral & religious Character and literary Accomplishments" introduced him to a Conference in which having given a "naritive [sic] of his religious Exercises, and of his Evidences of Faith in Christ and Repentence [sic] towards God together with his Call and Motives to the Gospel Ministry and a specimen of his skill in Cases of Conscience," he was received by presbytery "under their Care as a Candidate for the Gospel Ministry."[1]

At this same October meeting, presbytery assigned to Alexander written papers—"Parts of Trial"—which were the customary prerequisites for licensure. He was to write an "Exegesis" (a strange misnomer) in Latin on the subject, "Are we justified by faith alone [?]," an exercise which he found quite difficult in view of his still imperfect facility with the language. He was also assigned a homily on "What is the Difference betwixt a dead & living Faith [?]," a topic presumably selected because of its relevance to the recent revival. At the meeting of presbytery the next April, Alexander read his exegesis and homily and was examined in "the Latin & Greek languages" and in such liberal arts of the day as "Geography, Natural Philosophy, Astronomy, Criticism, and Moral Philosophy." The presbytery sustained the examinations and ordered him to be ready at the next meeting to "lecture" on Hebrews 6:1–6 and to preach "a popular sermon" on Jeremiah 1:7: "But the Lord said unto me, Say not, I am a child: for thou shalt go to all that I shall send thee, and whatsoever I command thee thou shalt speak." Alexander, who was physically small and very boyish in appearance, "disliked exceedingly" this text, but accepted it obediently.[2]

The same meeting of presbytery in April, 1791, which continued Alexander's examinations, elected his father, William Alexander, as an offical delegate ("commissioner") to the denomination's national General Assembly to meet the next month in Philadelphia. When his father declined the election, presbytery conferred the commission on Archibald, who was already a "ruling elder," though only a lad of nineteen. This election gave him the opportunity of visiting the capital of the nation, which was the leading metropolis of North America, and of seeing many of the denomination's leading figures.

Alexander rode all the way to Philadelphia on horseback, accompanied by Mr. Graham, who was also a commissioner, and was joined a little later by their friend, John Blair Smith, president of Hampden-Sydney College. Almost like Luther first viewing Rome, he recalled, "I felt a great awe on my spirits at the thought of entering the great city," and added, "My impression was that all eyes would be directed towards me." But he was relieved to find that "they took no notice of us." The opening sermon at the Assembly was delivered by the Rev. Dr. Robert Smith, father of Samuel Stanhope Smith and of John Blair Smith. Dr. Smith "wore a very large white wig, coming down far over his shoulders, and being short in stature presented an appearance somewhat grotesque. Most of the clergy wore wigs; all from the cities and great towns wore powder, as did many gentlemen whom we met in the streets."

The Rev. Dr. Ashbel Green of the Second Presbyterian Church, Philadelphia, was not a commissioner, "but came every day and sometimes engaged in discussion. . . . His appearance was dignified and lofty. . . . I was filled with admiration to hear so fine a man talk seriously about religion; for I had imbibed the prejudice widely prevalent among the Methodists, that men or women who dressed fashionably and wore powder and the like ornaments, must be destitute of religion." (Alexander himself, while not slovenly, never gave much concern to dress.) Like numerous contemporaries, Alexander was tremendously impressed by the person of Samuel Stanhope Smith of the College of New Jersey, as "the most elegant [person] I ever saw. . . . The thought never occurred to me that he was a clergyman." By contrast, "Dr. Witherspoon was as plain an old man as ever I saw, and as free from any assumption of dignity." But Alexander hastened to add, "All he said, and everything about him bore the marks of importance and authority."

The official enrollment of the Assembly was only forty-five, and Alexander noted how very few there were from the South. Distance and difficulty of travel were a serious hindrance to such intersectional church gatherings. Alexander attested the fact that the so-called Second Awakening was earlier in Virginia than in the Middle states when he later recalled "that he found [at the Philadelphia meeting] less of that warm and impulsive religion which the revivals of Virginia had made dear to him, than he expected. But he often recurred with pleasure to the animated piety . . . of Mrs. [Andrew] Hodge, a venerable Christian lady of Philadelphia" whose home he had frequently visited during his sojourn. She was the grandmother of Charles Hodge, Alexander's later student, junior colleague, and successor.[3]

In the September (1791) following the Assembly meeting, Alexander completed his examinations for licensure. He preached the opening sermon of presbytery on the hated text, "Say not, I am a child," without in any way referring to his age or youthful appearance. After he had also read his lecture and been examined in divinity, had "adopted" the Westminster Confession of Faith, and had answered the constitutional questions put to candidates, presbytery on October 1, 1791, "licensed him to preach the everlasting Gospel of Christ, as a Probationer for the holy Ministry within the Bounds of this Presby." Like some of the worthies of the ancient church shrinking from ecclesiastical preferment, Alexander remained reluctant to be licensed up to the last moment, and was prevailed upon only by Mr. Graham's repeated urgings. Alexander poignantly remembered: "During the service I was almost overwhelmed with an awful feeling of responsibility and unfitness for the sacred office." He withdrew outdoors, as had become his recent custom in crises, "in very solemn reflection and earnest prayer. My feelings were awful, and far from comfortable." Alexander intended to return home for further study after being licensed, but the highly succesful launching of his preaching career now prevented that.[4]

Alexander's first sermon, written as a theological exercise in October 1790, was read before the class and criticized by Mr. Graham.[5] It has been preserved, and, as the earliest available formulation of his thinking, it has considerable interest. Preaching on Acts 16:31: "Believe on the Lord Jesus Christ and thou shalt be saved," he divided the sermon into three parts. The first part analyzed the nature of faith in Christ, the second dealt with the connection between faith and salvation, while the third described the nature of salvation itself. The second and third parts, while developed with notable clarity, were quite conventional in doctrinal content and in their apropos citing of Scripture. The first part, however, occupying about half of the sermon, reflected fresh thinking and vital experience. The influence of Graham's Scottish common-sense realism was evident when Alexander denounced "the unprofitable janglings amongst subtle metaphysicians," and "the obscure and perplexing labyrinths of their metaphysical reasoning." Alexander implicitly—perhaps even unconsciously at this early stage of his career—assimilated Scottish intuitionism to the Calvinistic doctrine of illumination by the Holy Spirit when he added, "Yet the meanest and most unlearned of the children of God can be made to understand the true nature of saving faith, because he has the experiences of it in his own soul; he has the witness in himself." "Saving faith is no mere speculative faith." Here was an implied parallel to Thomas Reid's insistence that only what squared with everyday experience could be accepted as intelligible truth. But Alexander did not here or later—as some of the more radical scions of pietism actually did—reduce theological content to doctrines that can thus be subjectively "experienced." It is notable how central the "experience" of "saving faith" appears here without the rational explanations and defenses which in later years became so important in his formulations.

It will be recalled that some two years before this, young Alexander, to his great delight, had discovered from Soame Jenyns's book the "internal evidences" of Christianity. In this first sermon he regarded the subjective experience of faith as an internal evidence of Christianity—an evidence which, he warned, might become "clouded," as he had sadly found in the recent violent fluctuations of his own religious introspections.

One catches an echo of the widespread eighteenth-century connection of virtue and happiness in the dubious implications of Alexander's declaration, "In the very nature of things an unholy being cannot be happy . . . for God has wisely joined moral & natural good and moral & natural evil together." The mature Alexander would not be satisfied with so easy a theodicy.[6]

Alexander's second sermon, written the month before his nineteenth birthday, is also extant. Presumably it too was prepared as an exercise in his theological education. The sermon dealt with two basic questions: the relation between ability and moral obligation, which was being widely discussed in New England and elsewhere at that time and for decades thereafter; and the related problem of the nature of God's action in human regeneration.

After the manner of Jonathan Edwards, Alexander distinguished between "moral inability" and "natural inability." Natural inability is inability caused by circumstances outside of oneself, and is not blame-worthy; but moral inability is inability caused by one's own nature and is culpable. Alexander did the very thing that Charles G. Finney was later to castigate severely—he announced with great emphasis that man totally lacked ability to turn to God. "O careless sinners . . . you are unable to come unto Christ. . . . You cannot because you will not . . . as you labour under such an inability, you therefore are inexcusable. . . . I do believe the very strongest of you can no more determine your hearts to love God at this time, than you can command the sun to stop in his course." In accordance with Scottish common-sense empiricism, he urged his hearers by introspection "to attend to the exercises of your own minds" to confirm the fact of moral inability. Finney later argued that such a view left man hopeless and immobile. Alexander, on the con-trary, argued that the illusion that one had the ability to turn to God whenever he might choose to do so created "a false sense of security." Like Finney, Alexander created a sense of crisis, but from opposite pre-mises. Paradoxically, Alexander, by telling men that they could not turn their wills to God and that all depended on the initiative of God's grace, caused them to cry out for that grace. If this result followed, he would have said that it was because God had been in the process, and had initi-ated their concern.

Alexander's discussion of the nature of God's action in human regener-ation appears to be a veiled and incomplete argument against the "Light Scheme" of his instructor, William Graham, which taught that regenera-tion occurs when God's truth comes to be understood by the human mind. This seemed to Alexander to assume too much competence in human beings and also to err in giving the crucial role to the reason rather than to the will. Human beings labor under no "natural inability" to turn to God, Alexander argued. Therefore they do not need "a change of any natural faculty of the soul," but "the turning of those natural fac-ulties" toward God. "A new moral disposition . . . is given . . . by the teachings or illuminations of the Holy Spirit." He seemed almost to com-bine his own avowed position with the position which he was refuting when he said, "A view of the moral character of God in the face of Jesus Christ has a transforming efficacy upon the soul and may very likely be the means which the Holy Spirit uses in this great work of conversion." Alexander further astutely suggested, against the Light Scheme, that if the coming of this "light" was the cause of regeneration, then the previous lack of the light was for human beings a "natural inability" (being a cause outside of themselves), and they must therefore all along have been blameless—an intended *reductio ad absurdum* of the opposite view.

Alexander reflected something of Edwards and behind him of Shaftes-bury and Hutcheson when he spoke of the corrupted moral "taste" of the unregenerate. In regeneration "the Spirit of God changes the corrupted disposition of the heart and gives the soul a divine relish for heavenly things." In Alexander's conception of the Christian life there was always a large place for "affections," "heart," and the will. Christianity was never to be restricted to the mind alone.[7]

Even as a youth, Alexander did not dodge hard questions. This can be seen in the homily which he read before Lexington Presbytery in April 1791 on "The Difference between a Living and Dead Faith," which has been preserved. Reminiscing half a century later, he commented that "the view taken of the subject is not materially different from that which I should now take."[8]

Young Alexander, in the true spirit of the Protestant Reformation, insisted that mere assent to Orthodox doctrine does not constitute saving faith, nor does confidence in "exercises" experienced in revivalism. He almost echoed the Lockean language of sensory experience employed by Jonathan Edwards when he said that persons of dead faith, "having no spiritual discernment cannot see his [Christ's] beauty for it is a spiritual excellence which . . . cannot be perceived but by the influences of the Holy Spirit enlightening the mind." He contrasted merely speculative knowledge with knowledge by the "heart"; "A dead faith is nothing more than an empty notion or speculative opinion," whereas a living faith "is firmly seated in the heart, and influences the will and affections in such a manner as to become a ruling principle of action." Merely speculative faith cannot believe in eternal things "as they are in themselves."[9]

A living and a dead faith also differ in their effects, he continued. "A living faith is always accompanied by love"—love to God, love to Christians, and love to all men, or "benevolence." In this emphasis on benevolence, again like Edwards, he coincided with a central theme of Enlightenment thought. Without adopting Edwards's penetrating distinction between specifically Christian benevolence and general benevolence, Alexander—boldly despoiling the Egyptians and claiming a central Enlightenment theme as a Christian monopoly—claimed that only the true believer could desire the happiness of all people. In discussing universal benevolence, this lad of nineteen—two decades before the founding of the American Board of Commissioners for Foreign Missions and half a century before the founding of the Presbyterian Board of Foreign Missions—defined the essence of Christian faith in terms that necessitated foreign missions: true believers "earnestly desire the whole world to come to the knowledge of him [God], and it is their habitual determination to do what in them lies to bring mankind to a saving acquaintance with him."[10]

In his "trial sermon" which opened the meeting of Lexington Presbytery in September 1791, Alexander discussed the nature of the gospel ministry. This has special interest in view of the fact that most of Alexander's adult life was to be devoted to educating students for the ministry. From what has already been evident of his great emphasis on inner spiritual experience, on illumination by the Holy Spirit, on consciously "tasting" God's grace, and on the sharp contrast between a "living" and a "dead" faith, one might suppose that his conception of the ministry would be quite charismatic, including a supernatural, mystical "call." On the contrary, Alexander took a quite rational and institutional view of the ministry. Pietism and tradition are not fully synthesized here. "Extraordinary impressions or impulses from God are not now to be expected in order to evidence a call to the Ministry, and . . . those who make them the foundation of their call, are in great danger of being deluded." Instead, Scripture describes for us "the character of a Minister." It is the Spirit of God who calls to the ministry, but he operates "not by immediate revelation" or "by an unaccountable impulse," but "by enlightening the person's mind, to see that he is possessed of those marks, by which a call is distinguished in the word of God." Alexander enumerated five such "marks" or qualifications for the ministry: (1) An "experimental acquaintance with religion"; (2) certain "natural abilities," "improved" by study; (3) "sincere desires to serve God in the ministry"; (4) a door to ministerial service "opened by the providence of God"; and (5) "the approbation of those whom God has appointed, to judge of these prerequisite qualifications." All this quite accorded with Calvinistic orthodoxy in the way it combined subjective and objective elements of a true call and in the recognition it gave to ecclesiastical authority.[11]

For a few years in this period of his life, Alexander kept a journal whose tone was similar to that of numerous Puritan diaries fluctuating from dejection over personal shortcomings to elation over evidences of divine grace. On his twentieth birthday, for example, he wrote: "Twenty years of my life are past, and gone, never to be recalled, but what have I done for God, alas! . . . When I reflect upon my life what is there but an [one] continued stain and blot."[12] The fact that most of the journal was in cipher shows that spiritual exhibitionism was not his purpose. As the years passed, he seems to have become less introspective and less concerned about subjective fluctuations, and more calmly confident in the divine object of faith.

Alexander began his public preaching immediately after October 1, 1791, the day when presbytery formally "licensed" him.[13] He had planned to return home for further study, but ministers in the northern end of the Valley pressed him to help them. His first sermon after licensure was preached near Winchester on the spur of the moment when he was unexpectedly called upon. General Daniel Morgan, the hero of the battle of Cowpens, was among his hearers.[14] Much of his preaching was in and around Charles Town in Berkeley County, now Jefferson County, West Virginia. In his first preaching there, his sermon outline was blown off into the congregation, a fact on which he later commented: "From that time for twenty years, I never took a note of any kind into the pulpit; except that I read my trial sermon at ordination." He could not memorize sermons effectively, but early developed great fluency and power in preaching without notes, a method which was characteristic of Southern ministers in contrast to the widespread custom in contemporary New England of reading sermons. On the way home he preached in Staunton at an Episcopal church which "was crowded, and all the gentry of the town were out, including Judge Archibald Stuart,[15] who had known me from a child." Stuart expressed surprise at the knowledge of mental philosophy which the young preacher had revealed in his analysis of the inner life, an interest which he had acquired from Mr. Graham.[16]

Soon after returning home, Alexander was again dissuaded from remaining to study, and in April 1792 accepted appointment by the Synod of Virginia to be a missionary in the lower Piedmont,[17] even though he felt he "knew nothing" about the people of the region. His orders were to proceed with another licentiate as far east as Petersburg and then to return west alone by a more southern route along the North Carolina border. During the course of this itineration, he met and was entertained by the venerable Devereux Jarratt, an Episcopal clergyman who had been a notable leader in the previous Great Awakening and had fostered early Methodism. Throughout his recollection of this missionary journey, Alexander made special mention of his contacts with converts of Whitefield or of Samuel Davies. He seemed eager to get firsthand accounts and authentic representation of the spirit of that movement. But his lifelong interest in the "religious affections" was never divorced from scholarly inquiry. It was while on this missionary tour that he first saw a Hebrew Bible, and he acquired a copy for himself as soon afterwards as possible. He found preaching a stimulant, and returned home greatly improved in health. Soon afterwards, he accepted a call to be copastor with Drury Lacy of six churches in the Piedmont, where he had recently been itinerating.[18]

Alexander kept a record of his preaching for fifteen months after being licensed, which covered his itinerations in the Valley and in the Piedmont. Of 183 sermons identified by county where he preached, 68 were delivered in the Valley and 115 in the Piedmont. The county in which he preached more often than any other was Berkeley at the north end of the Valley. Only seven of the sermons were in his native Rockbridge County. He preached in six of the counties along the North Carolina border a total of fifty-three times. He did not preach in the northern half of the Piedmont, and Dinwiddie County was the nearest he got to the Tidewater. Fifty of the sermons were preached in private houses; others in courthouses and churches.

The way he used Scripture was striking. Of the 123 sermons for which texts are given, only 8, or barely 6 percent, are from the Old Testament, a sharp contrast with early New England Puritan theocratic fondness for the Old Testament. From the gospels, sixty-six texts, or more than 53 percent, were chosen, with Luke a heavy favorite. The epistles provided forty-one texts, but Acts and Revelation only three and five, respectively. The extremely high incidence of New Testament selections no doubt reflects the young man's fervent evangelicalism, but suggests also that he had not yet thought deeply about Christianity's historical roots, institutional character, and cosmic relationship. From May through July, 1792, he recorded attendance in round numbers, ranging from 8 to 800, the average being just under 200, an extremely encouraging response considering the fact that many of these audiences were gathered for the occasion where there was no congregation of his denomination. He later recalled that for his ministry in the Valley as a licentiate he received "not one cent, and indeed expected nothing." "I never thought of compensation for what I did, not considering my labours as of any real value."[19] This recollection is corroborated by the contemporary record he kept of his preaching. It lists no compensation before the spring of 1792, after which, while synod missionary, he received honoraria at eighteen meetings, totaling less than sixteen pounds in British currency. In the last few months he added somewhat stereotyped comments on the reaction of his hearers, such as "serious," "solemn," "attentive," "affected," or—much less frequently—"unattentive," "careless," and in one case even "lawless."[20]

This preaching experience in the Valley and in the Piedmont contributed greatly to Alexander's development. He had to adapt his thought and language to all sorts of people, some of whom had had little contact with church, others of whom had had but slight general education, and many of whom could understand only the plainest speaking. This forced him to develop clarity and directness. In spite of his modesty and self-disparagement, he was thrust into leadership. He had to secure places for meetings, enlist promoters, and assert his own convictions as he confronted ever varied audiences of his seniors.

At that time in Virginia, Alexander tells us, it was expected that a minister or ministerial candidate staying overnight would conduct family prayers. But when he and a preacher friend were spending the night at a tavern and offered to lead the heterogeneous guests in "family" prayers, all scurried away to bed. The experience contributed to his conclusion "that it was not a duty to insist on having family worship in taverns, unless the people were serious & free from company."[21] Many pastoral services during this period were more rewarding, as when, by request, he visited an aged and illiterate couple who in their concern had spent most of the preceding night trying to spell out portions of the New Testament. They were overcome with emotion as he talked with them. "Here was a family," he later commented, "of whom the heads had grown gray without having ever attended public worship; and who until now knew no more of a Saviour than the heathen. But they were now like persons come into a new world."[22]

Looking back on this period, Alexander recalled two characteristics of his preaching: great rapidity of utterance—"I ran on until I was perfectly out of breath"—and a habit of "looking steadily down upon the floor" to avoid losing his train of thought. In later years his eyes acquired complete freedom and many a hearer's attention was fixed by their piercing gaze. His voice, "though not sonorous, was uncommonly distinct and clear" so that he could be heard in the biggest churches or even at large outdoor meetings. But, he adds, "I was so conscious of my own defects, that often after preaching I was ashamed to come down from the pulpit."[23]

Alexander's biographer gives a more favorable, and undoubtedly truer, picture of the young preacher. His youthful appearance—he seemed even less than his twenty years of age—his "incomparably clear" and "flute-like" voice, his spontaneity and earnestness combined to make a powerful impact on audiences. His popular sermons, if we may judge from a few datable manuscripts and from contemporary comment, had an intellectual foundation and a gift of imagination notable for so young a man. After the blowing away of his manuscript, he inclined to extemporaneous utterance, for which he had a great gift. Although he was much in demand as a preacher throughout his life, many thought that his most popular and effective pulpit work was accomplished in these earliest years.[24]

Life on the road, stopping at homes which possessed few if any books, left him, during this period of itinerancy, little opportunity for study except from the pocket Bible which he carried with him. Many of his sermons were composed while in the saddle, an exercise which developed his natural powers of logical, consecutive thinking. But his keen intellectual interest remained alive in spite of such deprivations. It was while on these journeys that he first saw, to his great delight, an aged minister's copy of the Septuagint, with its translation of the Old Testament into Greek. "I seized it with great avidity, and read as much as I could during the time I spent there." In the same house, he read an English translation of Chrysostom on the priesthood and Riccaltoun's exposition of Galatians.

Many of Alexander's sermons survive in manuscript, though very few of them are datable. But one sermon is marked (in another hand) "Aged 20, 1792," which connects it with the period of his itinerancy in the Piedmont. The psychology of the sermon seemed to waver between the traditional view that man's mind should control his personality and the

Edwardsean view that the "affections" are blended with "intellect" in that control. Preaching from the text, Romans 8:6, "To be carnally minded is death: but to be spiritually minded is life and peace," he found the "fall" not injuring man's "faculties," but diverting the mind from viewing "the glorious perfections of God" to viewing merely "objects of sense," thus putting "fleshly propensities" in control. This threw "all the powers of the man" into "disorder and confusion" and produced "the most horrid consequences" that God is neglected and hated, while "the carnal appetites" govern life. This disaster is remedied when the Spirit of God both enlightens the mind and changes the heart. The mind now becomes "spiritual" and regulates the "inferior propensities," and to this extent "the soul is restored to its primitive beauty and harmony," with every propensity regulated by "conscience," conscience apparently being regarded as a function of reason.[25] The definition of virtue in terms of "beauty and harmony" again suggests a Shaftesbury-Hutcheson-Edwards lineage, but the role assigned to reason faces in a more traditional direction. There also seems to be the intimation that evil inheres in the body, and virtue in the mind.

Alexander proposed that his hearers test whether they were "spiritually minded" or "carnally minded" by watching the direction of their spontaneous thoughts. But with more emphasis he proposed that they examine the direction of their affections as apparently the more basic criterion. "The carnal mind altho it may some times think of God never can love him nor delight in him." He then proceeded to emphasize that it is the "affections" which determine action: "The actions of the life will correspond always with the affections of the heart, for they proceed from them, are the external expressions of them."[26] This view, if carried through consistently, would challenge the traditional supremacy of reason, which was implied elsewhere in this sermon. The young preacher was developing a theology of the affections. It is also noteworthy that he had already assimilated the psychological view—presumably from his teacher, Graham—that "our minds are continually engaged in thinking about something."[27]

On April 27, 1793, a "call" for Alexander's services as pastor was presented to him from four "collegiate," or associated, churches with six preaching points, in the lower Piedmont. But as he was still a missionary of synod, action was postponed until the October meeting of presbytery. The year before this, three of these churches had unsuccessfully tried to secure the pastoral services of William Graham. We have previously seen the great hesitation with which Alexander had sought licensure, a reluctance stemming from excessive modesty, a very high view of the ministerial office, and a certain temperamental hesitation to make crucial decisions. Although he had by then had more than five months to consider this call, he asked the October meeting of presbytery to give him "until to morrow morning to return answer to Presby." and then, the next day, he "informed Presb he had not clearness to give a decisive answer to sd. Calls; but wished to retain them under Consideration." Accordingly, at his request, his home Presbytery of Lexington dismissed him to Hanover Presbytery, the body having jurisdiction over the calling churches. By November he had not made up his mind, but Hanover Presbytery gave him permission to preach in the calling churches, and on June 7, 1794, ordained him. Finally, in October 1794, a year and a half after being invited, Alexander accepted calls from two of the four churches—Briery and Cub Creek. Part of his reason for hesitation had been the inefficiency of two ministers serving four widely scattered congregations on horseback, rather than dividing the task between them. Even as it was, less than a year later he secured a ministerial colleague to aid in serving the two churches.[28] In April 1797, Alexander resigned as pastor of the Cub Creek Church, and in November 1798 he resigned as pastor of the Briery Church. In February 1801 he was called back to the Briery pastorate, and in November of that year he was invited to be pastor of the Cumberland Church. Briery offered him £ 70 a year and Cumberland $200, each for "one half of your ministerial labours." Not until April 1802 did he accept these calls, and then remained pastor of both churches until he left Virginia in 1806.[29]

Such pioneer Presbyterian clergy in Virginia as William Robinson and Samuel Davies had preached in this area in the 1740s, and between 1755 and 1760 both Cub Creek Church in Charlotte County and Briery Church in Prince Edward County secured an installed pastor. John Blair Smith, president of Hampden-Sydney College, had served these two churches, and they had been chief centers of the revival of 1787–1789. Alexander's son, a generation later, ministered for several years in this area, living with the same family as his father had done. The son was quite taken with the life of Southside Virginia. "There is no portion of the State or country," the son wrote, "where the bright side of the planter's life is more agreeably exhibited. . . . The proprietors enjoy the comforts and luxuries of life in a high degree, and almost every family has some man of liberal education within its bosom. Hospitality and genial warmth may be said to be universal."[30]

Even the virtue of hospitality could be overdone, the senior Alexander discovered when early one day he dutifully undertook a pastoral visit to his most remote parishioner. In spite of his repeated protests, "chickens were chased in all directions; fires were kindled, closets were searched, and I soon found that we should scarcely be able to get away." The planter, summoned from the fields by his wife, must shave and change his clothes before being seen by the minister. At last, late in the day, "an enormous dinner" was spread, followed by a thunderstorm which delayed departure almost until sunset. "Thus," concluded Alexander woefully, "a whole day was wasted in visiting one family, and that without the least benefit." Disappointed, he devised a plan of small preaching services in private homes in different areas, but he found that this imposed an undue burden, for the hosts invariably served dinner to all present.[31]

This gracious living came at a high price, for much of it depended upon the labor of slaves who were more numerous in the Piedmont than in the Valley. Late eighteenth-century humanitarianism and evangelicalism did not lack strong critics of slavery. Thomas Jefferson and many another prominent Virginian advocated emancipation, and various Baptists and Methodists opposed slavery. The more prosperous Presbyterians were less inclined to challenge it. But Alexander's close friend John H. Rice was deeply concerned. In 1827, in a letter to Alexander, he was pessimistic about any effective influence from the church against slavery.[32]

Many of the churches themselves were directly involved in the institution of slavery. This was true of the Briery Church which Alexander served. In 1766 the church received some three hundred pounds sterling which it invested in the purchase of slaves to be hired out for the support of the minister. The services of those owned by the church in 1774 could hardly have been very profitable, for all but four of the nine were under seventeen. While there is no explicit official mention of the church's slaves during the years of Alexander's pastorate, 1794–1806, the very sketchy records show that the church still owned slaves in 1819; so it is to be supposed that part of the church's revenue was derived from this source during Alexander's pastorate.[33]

It was customary to make a very sharp distinction between evangelization and emancipation. Samuel Davies did notable gospel work among the slaves, instructing and baptizing large numbers of them and also teaching them to read. The Cub Creek Church under the ministry of Drury Lacy, a contemporary of Alexander, claimed some 200 black communicants. Alexander himself was much interested in gospel work among blacks and was designated by presbytery to receive books for circulation among them.[34]

The whole question of whether conversion to Christianity and the Christian baptism of a slave legally terminated his servitude was a matter of concern in the colonial period, but a firmly negative answer was worked out. A somewhat different aspect of the matter, namely whether Christian masters should sponsor for baptism infant children of their slaves, came before Hanover Presbytery in 1780, and again in 1793. Finally in 1795—the year after Alexander joined this presbytery—it was decided that "no general rule respecting this could now be fixed upon, but that Christian Masters must act in this case according to the light of their own Minds, & the Circumstances in which God had placed them. The question was upon this dismissed."[35]

As pastor, Alexander moderated the session, the governing body of the Briery Church, while his copastor, Matthew Lyle, served as clerk. A chief function of sessions in those days was to exercise discipline when the conduct of members seemed to require it. One man accused of "slander" was acquitted because only one testified against him and that without being cross-examined. Another person was admitted to church membership after professing "repentance" for allowing dancing in her home on the "Sabbath." Another member after confessing to drunkenness was suspended from church privileges "until he give satisfactory evidence of repentance." Alexander seems to have discharged with judicial fairness and moderation the disciplinary ideals of the day.[36]

Meanwhile Alexander utilized every available opportunity for study, often, because of the heterogeneous nature of available books, reading in such diverse subjects as the history of the Arabs and Edward Stilling-fleet's *Irenicum*, an Anglican attempt shortly after the Restoration to reconcile Presbyterians and the Church of England. He also made some limited purchase of books, including the publications to date of the Scottish common-sense philosophers, Thomas Reid and Dugald Stewart. He also studied public speaking firsthand by hearing the venerable Patrick Henry and the rising young John Randolph of Roanoke. His comments analyzed with sophisticated detachment the techniques that gave the famous spellbinders mastery over audiences.[37]

A few of Alexander's extant sermons are datable for the years of his Virginia pastorate. For a man still in the early twenties, they show considerable understanding of such basic human experiences as disappointment, suffering, sickness, death, as well as joy, pride, and self-deception. His sermons frequently proposed, with noticeable resemblances to Puritan discussions, self-tests as to whether one was really a Christian. Many of them also battled against the still expanding influence of deism.[38]

In a sermon on Corinthians 16:22, "If any man love not the Lord Jesus Christ let him be Anathema Maranatha," Alexander again emphasized the psychological primacy of the affections: "Affections govern and move the will." Later in life he would emphasize the primacy of the intellect. The ethical quality of an affection is measured by the character of the object that attracts it. This ethical criterion of ends, reflecting perhaps the early influence on him of Edward's emphasis on benevolence, differed diametrically from Alexander's later ethical criterion of motives. Christ, said Alexander, "is in himself the most lovely and excellent of all beings." Love for Alexander therefore was a supreme virtue. Eighteenth-century eudaemonism was quietly accepted, for he frankly avowed that "the desire of happiness is innate in every living creature." He did not condemn this seeking of happiness, but only the search for it in the wrong objects, and thus turned the discussion to an emphasis on the joyousness of true Christian faith: "God is the only satisfying portion of an immortal soul."[39]

Following his deep-seated assumption that the affections determine human action, Alexander agreed that those who oppose Christianity (he undoubtedly had deists in mind) reject it not for intellectual reasons but "because it is inconsistent with the course of conduct which they are inclined to pursue." They are excluded from faith by "some beloved lust or darling pursuit." One thinks of the similar ethical argument used by President Timothy Dwight against deism. A striking lack of empathy appears in both cases. Later in life, Alexander reversed this position, arguing that the deists' conscience showed that all people are endowed with a moral sense and arguing against deism on intellectual rather than on moral grounds. Alexander added the warning that some people reject Christianity from a desire to appear independent and different. Turning attention to dangers at the opposite extreme, Alexander reiterated a favorite theme of his that seemingly spiritual inner experiences are no guarantee of the genuineness of one's Christianity. While not inherently evil, such experiences may be merely an elevation of "animal spirits." Thus he built and ever maintained a platform from which to criticize revivalistic excesses. Even outward virtues and regularity in religious exercises afford no sure proof that one is really a Christian. By contrast, somewhat vaguely, he offered three tests of one's Christian standing: (1) being "United to Christ . . . by the operations of the spirit"; (2) wearing "the image of Christ. This is Holiness. . . . It consists principally in love to God and to Man"; (3) by following "the example of Christ. To imitate him."[40] These are essentially the two central tests familiar to Calvinism of the "witness of the Holy Spirit" and a holy life.

Young Alexander was not blind to epoch-making events that were unfolding in Europe. French influence in America had been strong ever since the French Alliance of Revolutionary War days, and the increasing radicalism of French thought was a powerful stimulus to deism in America. When the French Revolution began in 1789, many Americans, remembering their own Revolution, strongly sympathized with it. But with the execution of Louis XVI and with the Reign of Terror that followed it in 1793–1794, many Americans had serious misgivings.

In the critical year 1794 Alexander took the occasion of a day of thanksgiving to express his views on America's national life and her relation to contemporary events in Europe. He preached from Psalm 2:11, "Rejoice with trembling." Alexander thanked God that the United States had the gospel in contrast with such "heathen" areas as Africa, Asia, and even parts of Europe, like Lapland and northern Russia. Here was a wide geographical outlook and potential missionary interest, though noticeably lacking in empathy. Even in much of Europe, "the thick gloomy clouds of popish darkness overshadow the minds of the people." Even in 1794, he was still open-minded toward the French Revolution and dared to hope that by it there was "a door opened for the spread of the Gospel in its purity which we expect will soon take place when that country comes again to a state of peace and tranquility."[41] Clearly, his support of the French Revolution was less wholehearted at this juncture than that of some American preachers such as his seminary colleague Samuel Miller.

The American Revolutionary patriotism of Alexander's boyhood in the Valley echoed in his summary of the hardships suffered "in a long & bloody war," and the victory finally achieved for liberty. He praised "the wisdom & the firmness of that great man," Washington, raised up by the providence of God who works through secondary causes.[42] Alexander's teacher, William Graham, had opposed ratification of the Federal Constitution, and Alexander's praise for that document was somewhat guarded.[43] In commenting on the Constitution, Alexander injected a cryptic comment that seemed critical of slavery—an institution which many leading Virginians of the day were criticizing—but he did not develop his ambitious allusion. "I do not know," he said, "a Nation under heaven . . . where the rights of men are so well secured—To this there is only one exception, which distorts the political features of our Country, with which it is not my business to meddle and which I shall forbear to mention."[44] This halting criticism was representative of what many in Virginia were thinking at the turn of the nineteenth century.

Quite characteristic of the emerging American nationalism of the period was his emphatic detachment from Europe. America "by a kind Providence" was enjoying "a state of peace & tranquility" while much of Europe was "involved in the horrors and devastations of war."[45] Although Graham had expressed some sympathy with the malcontents in the Whiskey Rebellion, Alexander felt thankful that "the insurrection is suppressed," and urged against "unreasonable quarrelling with the laws," noting that "we must expect as members of so large a community to make sacrifices, of our particular interests in many cases for the good of the whole."[46]

In sharply contrasting America's spiritual and military condition with that of much of the rest of the world, it was not the conscious intention of the preacher to foster national smugness. He warned that nations, unlike individuals, do not face judgment in a future life, but here and now, and are punished by God for their national sins, of which America has many.[47]

Deism, whose influence Alexander had seen as a boy at Liberty Hall soon after the American Revolution, had been steadily gaining strength in Virginia and in other parts of the United States in the intervening years. Before 1794, deism found its chief following among the more sophisticated upper classes, who had made little attempt to popularize it. But in 1794, Thomas Paine, already famous as a brilliant patriotic pamphleteer of the American Revolution, published his *Age of Reason*, Part One. Written in France, where Paine had supported the early stages of the French Revolution, it was for Americans a bold and sensational, if not original or profound, attack on the Christian Bible in an effort to overthrow the foundations of clerical power. Paine's book circulated widely in Alexander's vicinity, and those who were in sympathy with it occasionally attended his church services. A sermon which he preached against Paine's book is extant, but he modestly stated that Bishop Richard Watson's famous *Apology for the Bible* was a better rejoinder to Paine than anything he himself could produce.[48]

Ignoring Paine's argument, borrowed from Hume, that no kind of testimony could verify a miraculous deviation from the uniformity of nature's laws, Alexander's sermon argued that the apostles who witnessed to Christianity were not deceivers and furthermore that they were not self-deceived by their senses. In establishing the latter argument, Alexander drew on Scottish common-sense philosophy to assert that "it is universally agreed that the testimony of our senses is the most certain evidence which we can have." Over against Paine, Alexander throughout magnified the miraculous character of Christianity and the conception of miracle as deviation from nature's otherwise uniform processes.[49]

Paine found the concept of revelation to some men by Scripture an aristocratic idea contrasted with the democratic idea of revelation to all men through nature and reason. This argument did not trouble Alexander, who confidently defended a Calvinistic predestined inequality.[50] Paine also argued that a true "revelation" of God would have to be contemporary and direct to an individual, and would cease to be "revelation" if received indirectly from a written record. Alexander did not answer this by emphasizing the witness of the Holy Spirit in personalizing and individualizing revelation. Instead, Alexander identified the written record with divine revelation, implying among other things that the "revelation" is a body of objective information.[51] This scholastic external conception of revelation was later to create many problems for the Old Princeton Theology. When Paine raised the acute historical problem of how absolute revelation could be embodied in such a changing historical medium as written ideas, Alexander in answer apparently contradicted himself and almost seemed to stand on later "neo-orthodox" ground when he upbraided Paine for demanding that God "must communicate to his word one of his incommunicable perfections [i.e., immutability] & thereby deify it." But Alexander did not stop to deal with the complex problem which this answer implied. Was he suggesting that Scripture partakes of the relativity of all the rest of history? This was not the path which he and the Old Princeton Theology were to follow. By a clever turn, following the example of Bishop Butler's *Analogy*, Alexander then asked by what right Paine claimed to find in nature an absolute and immutable revelation. Alexander also reminded

Paine that the epistemological problem for natural religion parallels that for Biblical revelation—some men see no evidence of God in nature.[52] This frontal attack on deism's mediating position could, of course, in the hands of Alexander as in the hands of Butler, drive an opponent not to orthodoxy but to atheism. Quite congenial to both the nineteenth and the twentieth centuries—perhaps reflecting the spirit of Edwards or antici-patory of the romantic movement—was Alexander's defense of mystery in religion against Paine's shallow rejection of all reality that could not be rationally comprehended.[53] More typically the Old Princeton Theol-ogy when fully developed would seek to defeat rationalism on rational grounds rather than thus to argue the limitations of reason.

A sermon by Alexander on holiness, in 1795, made partial use of seventeenth- and eighteenth-century efforts to rebuild ethics on a natu-ralistic basis. By nature, said Alexander, man has "a moral sense or con-science," without which he would be "incapable of forming any notion of holiness or morality." In the spirit of Scottish realism, Alexander then asserted that although this "moral sense" has been "greatly perverted," it has enabled men to agree in "some first principles of morality, which are discovered by intuitive evidence." He accepted enough of the eudae-monism of his time to assert that choice of virtue will be accompanied by "exquisite delight" and pursuit of evil by "unspeakable pain." It is this moral "faculty" which distinguishes man from the brutes and makes it possible for him to be conformed to the character of God and to delight in him.[54] Having exalted so highly man's intuitive moral sense, Alexan-der then, at a stroke, destroyed much of what he had just built when he declared that by man's fall into sin, "the image of God is entirely defaced."[55] If man was so completely ruined by the fall, how could he retain natural religion or a true moral sense?

In this sermon, at the age of twenty-three, Alexander was already teaching the rudiments of "imputation," a doctrine which he later asserted vigorously against New England and New School Presbyterian theologians, and which Charles Hodge was to elaborate at greater length. The doctrine was considered by some to be the counterpart of the Protes-tant emphasis on justification by grace through faith alone. Before he has performed any good works, the believer is given legal standing before God as already righteous and holy—in the holiness of Christ "imputed" to the believer's account, before the believer has actually performed any righteous deeds whatever. The doctrine thus offers a rational description of justification before "sanctification" has produced in the believer any good dispositions of his own, but it can lead to an "antinomian" and quite unethical conception of what Christian holiness really is.  Does holiness include a holy nature, or merely the status of being accepted by God? Supporters of the doctrine of course would not acknowledge such an antithesis. The doctrine was to loom large in the theological tradition which Alexander founded, but at this early date he only touched on it, and did so in a way which carefully connected imputation with holy living. "The design of the Gospel . . . is not merely to produce right disposition in the soul," he said, "but to produce an alteration in the state of man as he stands related to the law & government of God. . . . By faith the merits of the Saviour are applied to us so that the condemnation of the law is removed, and the spirit is given to produce holiness in the soul."[56]

Philosophy and psychology during the era of the "Enlightenment" were having much to say about inner "illumination" of one sort or another. Alexander himself—perhaps under the stimulus of William Graham's "Light Scheme"—was giving much thought during these years to the connection between the renewal of the convert's inner being and his spiritual illumination. Graham, in spite of possible naturalistic implications, gave primacy, as we have seen, to the mind's perception of spiritual truth as the power that renewed the Christian's inner being. Alexander, however, gave the primacy to God's act of renewing man's spirit as alone enabling man to perceive spiritual truth. Regeneration is "an entire change produced in our nature by which our sentiments, affections, purposes and conduct are altered. . . . It extends to all the faculties." This true "illumination of the mind" is "the beginning of holiness" and "immediately produces love to God." Thus this illumination does not operate in man until after he has been regenerated.[57]

While Alexander was busy trying to interpret the Christian gospel to his age in the light of contemporary psychological and ethical thought, he became, at the age of twenty-five, president of a struggling young college. The experience acquired here would later be of inestimable value in leading an infant seminary with almost no American seminary precedents to guide him.

# 5
# THE LEADER MATURES

It has been said that the Presbyterian Church was "one of the strongest influences on formal education" in Virginia in the period following 1790.[1] This influence was exerted through academies and periodicals, and especially through the two colleges, Washington College (originally Liberty Hall) and Hampden-Sydney College.

Hampden-Sydney College in the Virginia Piedmont opened in 1776, attaining a student enrollment of more than a hundred in its first year. But the college suffered from the distractions of the Revolutionary War and from the fact that its first two presidents—Samuel Stanhope Smith and his brother, John Blair Smith, both College of New Jersey alumni—were followed by an interregnum of eight years during which the college lacked a president.

Archibald Alexander arrived in 1797 as the college's third president one month after his twenty-fifth birthday. He had come with some reluctance, for the college, as he later recalled, was at that time "as low as it could be to have an existence"; but "the trustees were determined to resuscitate it if possible."[2]

Alexander immediately took hold of the financial problem, proposing, at his first meeting with the trustees, that students pay their tuition and room rent upon entering the college. Shortly after his arrival the trustees had raised the charge for students' board by 25 percent, which less than eight years later was raised by another 20 percent. But in spite of everything, within less than two years the college was owing Alexander nearly half a year's salary, and periodic arrearages continued to appear. Even in the face of these shortages, Alexander admitted a penniless student without tuition and was sustained in this by the trustees.[3]

The curriculum of Hampden-Sydney, as planned by the first president, Samuel Stanhope Smith, who had served as a tutor at his alma mater, copied in broad outline the Princeton curriculum, but with greater attention to the study of English. There was of course the customary Greek and Latin, with work also in mathematics, natural sciences ("Natural

Philosophy"), history, geography, and "the science of Morals" (the familiar "moral philosophy"). Under the college's second president, John Blair Smith, the students were divided into three classes—sophomore, junior, and senior. The staples of Latin, Greek, and mathematics (the latter being quite extensive) continued to be taught. If the listing of "Philosophy" means "natural philosophy," natural sciences were included. History and English, as originally projected, were retained, and now there was mention of a "French master," reflecting Witherspoon's introduction at Princeton of courses in spoken French. For a time it was even permitted to substitute French for Greek, but this was rescinded as detrimental to the students' "improvement in science." As early as 1775, in planning for the college, Hanover Presbytery had voted £300 for the purchase of scientific "apparatus." Following this precedent a quarter of a century later, the college trustees, under President Alexander, appropriated £100 to procure "a Philosophical and Mathematical Apparatus" which was housed in a room with the library. Students paid for the use of library books, and this revenue was plowed back into the purchase of additional volumes. Thus the curricular tradition into which Alexander came as president reflected strong modernizing tendencies.[4]

When Alexander arrived, he found that as a result of the demoralization that had followed President John Blair Smith's resignation, even the division of students into annual classes had been abandoned, and he restored class structures. Under Alexander we find the trustees appointing a committee "to attend the Examination of the Students who are candidates for a degree." Such attendance by trustees at the oral examinations of degree candidates was widely current among colleges at the time and among theological seminaries in the early nineteenth century. Information is lacking concerning details of the curriculum under President Alexander, but six years after his leaving, the subjects taught were very similar to what he had found on arriving—the classical languages, much mathematics (with the addition of navigation and surveying), natural sciences, history and geography, English, moral philosophy, with the omission of French and the addition of law (in this resembling William and Mary College), logic, and "the Philosophy of the human mind," the last mentioned perhaps added during Alexander's administration, in view of his own great interest in mental philosophy. There is thus every reason to suppose that Alexander retained with little change the basic curriculum of classics and more modern practical subjects which his two predecessors had developed as a result of Witherspoon's influence.[5]

Alexander had now entered what he later considered his best years. His young manhood, until he left Hampden-Sydney, was characterized by frequent change and movement, which stimulated his development and saved him from narrowness and pedantry. The complexities that burden twentieth-century industrial and academic administration had not yet emerged, so that although he was heading a small college, serving a pastorate, and frequently preaching elsewhere, he found time for some of the most intensive study of his life. We are told that he expanded both the range and the depth of his learning. He found that the exactness of his knowledge was permanently sharpened by the practice of "drilling" his students, an exercise highly regarded in that day, which would clarify knowledge even if not stimulating critical mental processes. His mind was stimulated, too, by frequent metaphysical discussions with his colleagues at the college.[6]

Although detailed information is lacking concerning Alexander's complete program of reading during these years, clues are available. In an undated letter to Charles Hodge, apparently written in the middle 1830s, he revealed something of the openness of his mind and the range of his questions in this earlier period. Temporarily, amid the rapidly expanding Virginia Methodism, he apparently toyed with the idea of attributing to man's will much greater freedom and initiative than was customary among Calvinists. Discussing Hodge's recently completed commentary on Romans, Alexander, then living in Princeton, wrote:

Forty years ago, I was led to study the first part [of Romans], i.e. from hearing an Arminian preacher expound it very ingeniously, on Arminian principles. For some time, I hesitated whether his exposition was not correct; but after studying it *intensely*, as I travelled on my mission, I came ultimately to the same views of its meaning, as those wh. you have given in your commentary.[7]

A close friend, Drury Lacy, indicates that in 1801 Alexander held millennial views similar to the "postmillennial" beliefs of Samuel Hopkins,[8] which were widespread among early nineteenth-century evangelicals, and which proved to be a great incentive to missionary outreach and moral reform. Alexander, however, seldom referred to millennial beliefs.

To Baptist views Alexander gave even more consideration than to those of the Methodists. Starting about the year he came to the college presidency, 1797, Alexander had such serious doubts as to the rightfulness of infant baptism that he declined to adminster it for some two years. His cousin and colleague in the ministry, Matthew Lyle, took the same position, as did also Conrad Speece, who served for a time as tutor in the college, and who, unlike the other two, actually became a Baptist for a short period.

It is another evidence of the great influence of the Baptists in Virginia that they made such an impression on these young Presbyterian leaders. In the case of Alexander, this was not altogether surprising. It will be recalled that it was an elderly Baptist lady in the home of General Posey who had first led him to serious religious interest, and had thrust into his hands a writing by the English Baptist John Gill.[9] Alexander had also been favorably impressed with the zeal of the Baptists in the revival, and his current concern for the purity of the church lent appeal to the Baptist doctrine of a "believers' church." Unlike his friend Speece, Alexander, as already noted, was more deliberative than impulsive, and entered upon an extensive biblical and historical study of Christian baptism.

The English Baptist Abraham Booth argued that baptism is a "positive institution," and that for such institutions Christians must have explicit biblical precepts. Booth therefore dismissed every defense of infant baptism which was based merely on inference from scripture or on ecclesiastical tradition. Alexander was so shaken by the argument that he told his friend Drury Lacy that "if his [Booth's] premises were true, he had established his point."[10] Alexander and his cousin found help in a dissertation by George Campbell, a Scottish "moderate" and principal of Marischal College, Aberdeen, which asserted that although in the Old Testament Septuagint and in New Testament Greek the words "hagios" and "hosios" are both commonly translated as "holy," they have quite different meanings, the former signifying "consecrated" or "devoted" in an external and formal sense applicable even to physical objects, while the latter signifies holiness as a disposition of the heart in an ethical or religious sense. Using a Greek concordance to the New Testament, the two inquirers found that the former, more external term, was used to address churches collectively, and hence they concluded that Scripture does not assume that every church member is necessarily a converted person. This elimination of the "believers' church" dogma of the Baptists at least left room for inclusion of infants in the church. Applying this distinction of terms to I Corinthians 7:14, where it is said that one believing parent causes the children of the union to be "holy" ("hagia"), they concluded that children of Christians properly belong to the consecrated community, the church.[11]

Even this did not fully answer in their minds Abraham Booth's assertion that a "positive institution" such as Christian baptism depended on explicit biblical precepts. But as they examined more closely some of the "positive institutions" of the Bible, they discovered that many details are left to inference. Scripture, they found, gives no precepts as to who is to administer the Lord's Supper, nor when, nor how often. Likewise in the case of baptism, they found that such matters as who is to administer it and the time and mode are left to inference or discretion. This discovery opened the way for the use of postbiblical ecclesiastical resources. An English Baptist, Robert Robinson, was suggestive of the more modern *Sitz im Leben* emphasis when he stressed the importance of discovering the circumstances of those to whom the biblical authors wrote, in order to understand how they might be expected to construe the writings addressed to them.[12]

Seeking to discover presuppositions concerning baptism which were held at the time of the apostles, Alexander and his cosearcher turned to later Christian writers. Tertullian, in the second century, they observed, opposed infant baptism, but never charged that the practice was an innovation. Origen and Cyprian in the third century, and Augustine in the fourth and fifth centuries, and many other Church Fathers not only attested the universal acceptance of infant baptism in their own day, but more importantly revealed no evidence that there had ever been a controversy to replace an hypothetical earlier practice confined to adult believers. In the light of this testimony of later centuries, the young scholars felt justified in inferring that the biblical authors and their original readers considered children of believers as included in the consecrated community and baptized them. Concerning the mode of baptism, Alexander and his friend felt that this was a matter of indifference, for even if it could be shown that immersion was the method employed in New Testament times, Scripture nowhere enjoins this method.[13] Alexander was now reaffirming Presbyterianism's concept of the church which was a more organic view than that taught by the Baptists. But, interestingly, he never applied to society or to the social issues of his day parallel organic concepts. The impact of revivalism and other individualistic forces had weakened American Presbyterianism's inherited organic concepts although Presbyterianism did retain (perhaps with some sociological inconsistency) the practice of infant baptism.

This detailed contemporary testimony of Lacy's letter is supplemented by Alexander's own recollection from "nearly half a century" later.[14] His recollection emphasized even more than did Lacy's account the argument from church history, and added arguments from the Jewish rite of circumcision and from Jewish baptism of proselytes, particularly as based on the seventeenth-century Anglican, Henry Hammond, and on John Lightfoot, a member of the Westminster Assembly and distinguished Hebraist of that day and on the eighteenth-century writing of William Wall, a high church Anglican.[15] Alexander found traces of infant baptism in the New Testament, and was also much moved by the ecumenical consideration that it was unthinkable that the Baptists were the only true Christian Church on Earth. And, besides, what historical evidence was there that Baptists had maintained through the centuries their "valid baptism"? This question about baptism was for these few years a very pressing personal problem for Alexander, and served as an important stimulus to his critical thinking and to his biblical and historical studies. Although he thus finally returned to his inherited view regarding baptism, he had shown notable open-mindedness and readiness to give the most serious consideration to a quite different view. It is evident also that he was developing in scholarly methods of research. Interestingly, it was in this year, 1799, when Alexander was concluding his struggle over the question of baptism, that his former mentor William Graham published a pamphlet on the issue, which, as previously noted, Alexander later regretfully pronounced quite mediocre.[16] Its arguments were certainly more conventional than those now being employed by Alexander himself. He was evidently outgrowing the teacher from whom he had received so much stimulation.

As the eighteenth century came to a close, deism was reaching the peak of its influence in Virginia, and was very strong in the vicinity of Hampden-Sydney College. It was during these years that William E. Channing, later Unitarian leader, coming from a New England home characterized by moderate Calvinism to be a tutor in the Randolph family in Virginia, found his religious faith temporarily shaken by the religious radicalism of the environment. In fact deism was so widely associated with Virginia in the popular mind that when Alexander was visiting in New England in 1801, "it was every where a matter of curiosity to hear an orthodox man from Virginia, which was supposed to be given up to Deism." A judge told Alexander that he had thought "almost all the educated Virginians to be Deists." Washington and Hampden-Sydney Colleges were important centers of antideistical influence in the state.

Alexander, addressing himself to the situation in Virginia, frequently devoted portions of his preaching to elaborate antideistical arguments, while the sermons of his faculty colleague, John H. Rice, in this period, were "principally argumentative, and especially directed to the demonstration of the truth of the Christian religion, and its vindication from the objections of infidels." The common foe was forcing ministers to consolidate their strength. Alexander reported to a Connecticut periodical that ministers met together in nearby Bedford County, Virginia, in December, 1801,

to consult upon the best measures for uniting their efforts in defense of Christianity against the torrent of vice and infidelity which threaten to overflow the land. Their meeting was remarkably harmonious,—prejudice and party-spirit seemed to have no place amongst them, but with one accord they consented to a scheme of friendly intercourse, and general union.

One immediate result of this cooperative effort was a local religious revival.[17]

The early nineteenth century, however, witnessed the rapid decline of deism in Virginia. By 1810, Rice was calling Alexander's attention to the reduced proportion of those who considered church attendance "beneath" them. In 1816 a Virginia friend informed Alexander that religious conditions in the Piedmont counties of Orange and Albemarle were "very encouraging." After visiting Charlottesville—seat of Jefferson's university—he reported that "the charm of infidelity seems to be broken in this region. Many have renounced their sentiments, & some are serious inquirers after truth." Regarding the religious climate of Virginia as a whole, he reported:

I am everywhere told, that a very favourable change, has within a few years been experienced. There is an increasing attention to religious instruction, & an earnest desire to have it statedly . . . . There is an impression daily gaining, no body knows how, that religion is necessary to the temporal, as well as the spiritual interests of men.[18]

But the "peril" of deism had been deeply impressed on Alexander during the formative period of his intellectual development, and it had permanent influence on his thinking and on the early history of the seminary whose initial character he was to have so large a part in forming.

One indirect evidence of the permanent influence on Alexander of deism's challenge was his lifelong esteem for the writings of such eighteenth-century British opponents of deism as Samuel Clarke and Joseph Butler. Just before the close of the century, Alexander began to acquire some experience as a theological educator, directing the ministerial studies of his friend, John Holt Rice. The program of reading he drew up for his pupil was an arduous one and was described as "very liberal" for that era. In view of the pressing contemporary challenge of deism, it is not surprising to find, among assigned books, Samuel Clarke's *A Demonstration of the Being and Attributes of God*.[19] Clarke was an Anglican of liberal views who, like his contemporary, Bishop Joseph Butler, sought to refute the deists by rational argument. After the death of John Locke, some—a little extravagantly—considered Clarke to be England's leading philosopher. If he was not profoundly original, he did have broad interests, being knowledgeable in classical and biblical studies, Newtonian physics, philosophy, and theology. *The Scripture Doctrine of the Trinity*, which he published in 1712, brought down upon him the ire of the orthodox, for in it he declared that the Scriptures do not teach the doctrine of the Trinity. This of course gave great encouragement to the radicals of the day, but he presently denied charges that he was either a Unitarian or an Arian. Perhaps his greatest writings were his Boyle Lectures of 1704 and 1705, the former published as *A Demonstration of the Being and Attributes of God*, directed partly against Thomas Hobbes and Benedict Spinoza. To meet materialists and atheists on their own ground, he made no use of Scripture. Starting with the basically mathematical concepts of infinity and eternity, he sought, by a mathematical method of pure reason, to establish God's existence and attributes.[20]

Clarke asserted that something has existed from all eternity. Otherwise present reality must at some point in time have emerged out of nothing without even a cause. Therefore either there must from eternity have been one unchangeable and independent Being, or else there must have been an infinite succession of changeable and dependent beings without any original cause at all.[21] In pronouncing the latter alternative unthinkable, Clarke revealed the sharp distinction which he everywhere implied between being and becoming. His universe was basically static, consisting of motionless existences or "orders" which were related to each other in numerous ways, but which never changed one into another. Though he did not use the phrase, we see here in Clarke a favorite eighteenth-century concept, "the great chain of being." These motionless existences change only when moved by an outside force. This assumption was in sharp contrast with the dynamism of the nineteenth and twentieth centuries, where process and change are inherent in reality itself. Clarke leaned heavily on his static conception of the universe to refute the materialists as when, for example, he said that matter could not produce intelligence, because intelligence is "a distinct quality."[22] Elsewhere he developed this argument in a form that ran counter to later physics: "If the Atheist will say that the Motion in General of all Matter is necessary; it follows that it must be a Contradiction in Terms, to suppose any Matter to be at Rest," a conclusion which he confidently pronounced "absurd."[23]

Clarke ostensibly rejected the Anselm-Descartes ontological argument for God's existence, yet borrowed from it to say that it is impossible to think of a universe apart from the concepts of infinity and eternity. But these "attributes or modes" can exist only if they inhere in a Being.[24] A modern reader cannot avoid wondering whether this argument proves the existence of an infinite and Eternal Being, or merely the necessity for thought of such normative ideas as infinite space and infinite time.

Clarke's static presuppositions came indirectly to view again when he argued for the unity of the self-existent Being. The necessary existence which he had predicated of this Being does not admit of variation or plurality, and the variety which we see in the universe could not have been self-produced, but must have been caused by this one ultimate Being.[25]

What Scholastics have called God's "incommunicable" attributes—infinity, eternity, omnipotence, and the like—lent themsleves far better to Clarke's a priori or mathematical treatment than did God's "communicable" (personal or moral) attributes such as intelligence and benevolence. Here Clarke was forced to resort to the a posteriori "cosmological" argument that the intricacy and beneficent nature of the universe showed that the Creator was intelligent and benevolent. In so doing, he went on to imply that this is the best of all possible universes.[26]

Like other representative thinkers of the eighteenth century, Clarke sought to establish ethics on the foundation of reason, again by a mathematical method. Goodness consists in the "fitness of all things"—that is, in discerning and maintaining the proper relation between the existing "orders" or entities of which the universe is composed. "Intelligent beings," unless they are "depraved," can disern these proper "Relations of Things" and can direct their actions accordingly unless their wills are corrupted by self interest.[27]

Clarke's world-view was not only mathematical, but specifically Newtonian. For Clarke, as for Isaac Newton, space and time had an objective and absolute existence. Space is an infinite reality, and observed phenonema are located "in" it. The "orders" are located in space and time, and experience consists of experiencing relations between these fixed orders. The philosopher Leibniz challenged Clarke, asserting a more modern view that space and time are merely concepts by means of which we understand the relations between realities.[28] Such a critique would of course prepare the way for the dissolution of Clarke's static universe with its predictable relations between unchanging "orders." Very much of Clarke's "objective"—and static and mathematical—outlook remained in Alexander's mature apologetics, as will be evident later.

The reaction of Alexander's pupil and colleague John H. Rice to Clarke's book is illuminating. Rice, who was an omnivorous reader, seems to have had an aversion to metaphysics. He attended the frequent metaphysical discussions in the little academic community with understanding, but did not participate in them. The ambivalence of Clarke's argument is understood by the fact that the reading of his book caused young Rice temporarily to lose his religious faith, which was soon restored, not by argument or discussion, but by prayer.[29] One recalls the quip of the deist Anthony Collins that no one doubted God's existence until Clarke undertook to demonstrate it.

A modern reader, looking across the great divide of nineteenth-century romanticism to view the battle waged by Clarke and his fellow apologists against deism, is startled by the degree to which the opponents of deism shared deism's method and confidence in reason. Archibald Alexander's theological repertoire now included not only the immediacy of spiritual experience derived from revivalism, but also seventeenth-century Scholastic Calvinism, the Scottish philosophy, and rationalistic apologetics. Could spiritual intuition and rational intellectualism be synthesized into a viable theological unity? Or to state the issue in different words, how would the Enlightenment and Pietism be related to each other? This problem would be the key to the life work of Alexander and of his immediate theological heirs.

Alexander had originally hesitated to accept the presidency of Hampden-Sydney College, and the work had certainly not been without its discouragements. By the spring of 1801, therefore, he felt ready "to accept any situation of greater usefulness which might be presented." Besides, his health was unsettled, and he desired to visit New England, as his teacher William Graham had done years before to great personal advantage. Accordingly, he resigned the presidency in April 1801, and was elected by Hanover Presbytery a commissioner to the General Assembly which was to meet in Philadelphia in May 1801. The college trustees, after an unsuccessful attempt to secure a successor, left the presidency vacant in the hope that Alexander could later be reelected.[30]

Though Alexander was only twenty-nine years of age, his visits to the General Assembly in Philadelphia and shortly afterwards to New England were something of a professional triumph, in sharp contrast to his bashful entrance into the American metropolis ten years before. He journeyed to Philadelphia on horseback, was robbed en route, and was seized with a brief illness that forced him to seek help among strangers. But once arrived in the city, he soon got his bearings in that larger world. Here he entered into association with, among others, Jonathan Edwards the Younger, president of Union College in Schenectady; Ashbel Green of Philadelphia, already a power to be reckoned with; and John McMillan, distinguished missionary to western Pennsylvania. Now, too, he met for the first time Samuel Miller, the copastor of the United Presbyterian Congregation of New York City.[31]

With the resurgence of spiritual vitality that was emerging in this period, the church undertook annual narratives of "the state of religion," which eventually became routinized procedures in Presbyterian judicatories at every level during the nineteenth century. Alexander must have been quite vocal in the two sessions of the Assembly which discussed the current "state of religion," for he was appointed to the committee, along with McMillan and one other, to draft the Assembly's views on the subject. The committee's report reflected the fact that the tide was already turning against deism, noting that "in most places, infidelity does not assume that bold and threatening aspect which it did for some years past, but seems to be in some measure abashed." "From many of their churches, the Assembly have heard the most pleasing accounts of the state of vital piety. Revivals, of a more or less general nature have taken place in many parts, and multitudes have been added to the church," this being particularly true "in the northern and eastern Presbyteries." Qualified but definite endorsement was given to the famous Kentucky revival, still in its early stages:

Many circumstances attending this work are unusual; and though it is probable that some irregularities may have taken place, yet from the information which the Assembly have received, they cannot but exceedingly rejoice in the abundant evidence given them that God has visited that people, and poured out his Spirit remarkably upon them. . . . In the middle and southern Presbyteries, appearances are now so encouraging.

The situation in the crucial frontier regions seemed particularly promising: "our missionaries" there have had some success, "and churches are rapidly forming, which will soon need settled pastors." "The prospect of the conversion of the Indians is now more flattering than it has ever been before." Along with his committee colleagues, Alexander was now seeing the work of the church in national perspective.[32]

This Assembly laid another task on Alexander. The Assembly resolved that "Mr. John Chavis, a black man of prudence and piety . . . be employed as a missionary among people of his own colour, until the meeting of next General Assembly." Because such duties "are attended with many circumstances of delicacy and difficulty" it was decided that "some prudential instructions be issued to him by the Assembly." The ambivalent relation of black evangelization to the social status quo was reflected in the Assembly's feeling that if Chavis would follow such instructions, "the knowledge of religion among that people may be made more and more to strengthen the order of society." Following the example of Samuel Davies, Alexander for some years had been interested in bringing the gospel to blacks, and he was appointed, along with three others, to a committee "to draught instructions to said Chavis, and prescribe his route." The instructions were drafted, duly approved, and delivered to Mr. Chavis along with his missionary commission.[33]

Missionary outreach into the rapidly expanding west was the dominant interest of this Assembly, and Alexander was appointed, along with Ashbel Green, John McMillan, and six others, to a strategically important committee to decide whether existing missionary funds were adequate and to recommend how such work should be conducted.[34] Alexander himself at this time was without professional connections, and the Assembly a week later appointed him "a missionary for six months, in Virginia and in the state of Georgia, at such time and in such manner as the state of his health will admit." He was at the same time appointed "to solicit donations for the use of the General Assembly."[35]

This same General Assembly received from the Congregationalist General Association of Connecticut a proposal to consider "establishing a uniform system of church government" for Presbyterians and Congregationalists on the frontier. The Assembly, under the leadership of a committee chaired by Jonathan Edwards, Jr., responded with specific proposals for such cooperation and instructed Archibald Alexander and two other elected representatives to convey this action to the Congregational General Association soon to meet in Litchfield, Connecticut.[36] Thus was born the famous "Plan of Union" which was to be one of the dominant factors in the history of both American Presbyterianism and Congregationalism for more than a third of a century. Alexander's planned visit to New England had suddenly acquired an official character: he was now going as an elected representative of the General

Assembly to the General Association of Connecticut, and as the cobearer of an epochal communication.

After recovering from another attack of fever—which, to his own surprise, proved to be the last he ever suffered—with a companion, Alexander set out on horseback for New England. En route he saw Princeton for the first time and there visited President Samuel Stanhope Smith, who had known Alexander's father and grandfather in Virginia and whose imposing presence had so impressed him at the General Assembly ten years before. Stopping at New York, he became better acquainted with Samuel Miller. He arrived at Litchfield in time for the opening of the meeting of the General Association to which he was accredited. The General Association had originated the proposal of cooperation between Presbyterians and Congregationalists, and now readily adopted "without discussion" the more detailed implementation which the Presbyterian General Assembly had drafted in response.[37]

The most important aspect for Alexander himself of his New England tour was the direct contact it gave him with theological and ecclesiastical conditions in New England at a crucial turning point in the religious history of that region. American Calvinism was in process of disruption, and New England was the eye of the hurricane. Even in the seventeenth century, New England Puritanism had given ominous evidences of internal instability. How could its ideal of a "regenerate" church be permanently maintained along with infant baptism and political establishment? What was the relation of inner spiritual experience and "the witness of the Holy Spirit" to outward conduct and to ecclesiastical structure? And how was God's almighty, gracious sovereignty to be harmonized with human decision and responsibility in an age that was increasingly emphasizing human ability and initiative? Well before the end of the seventeenth century, such problems were plaguing New England Puritanism, and fond adherents were lamenting a "religious decline for these and other reasons."

The outburst of spiritual fervor in the Great Awakening of the 1730s and early 1740s amid the increasing force of the Enlightenment precipitated polarization between head and heart and between objective and subjective emphases in religion. The cleavage revealed by the Awakening had its European antecedents in the critical rationalism and the Pietism, respectively, of the Enlightenment era. From the time of the Great Awakening—to go no farther back—the emerging "Arminian" or "liberal" party in New England was giving serious theological response to some of the leading presuppositions of the Enlightenment. Their principal opponents also, under the leadership of Jonathan Edwards, Sr., showed awareness of Enlightenment ideas and, with notable freshness and originality, sought to refute these or to incorporate some of them into Calvinistic orthodoxy.

In this respect the New England which Alexander was visiting differed greatly from his native Virginia. True, deism was widespread in Virginia and had made noticeable headway in William and Mary College. Virginia Presbyterians, as we have seen, were acutely aware of deism and were vigorously combatting the Goliath. They hastily seized such anti-deistical weapons as Samuel Clarke and other English apologists had forged. But their external and uncritical use of these rationalistic defenses altered the content and method of their own theology far more than they themselves realized. Unlike the heirs of New England Puritanism, Alexander and the Presbyterians of Virginia had not yet undertaken a critical and constructive evaluation of recent cultural trends to analyze in detail what aspects of these were unassimilable and what aspects might well improve or revise their own theological heritage. Such an evaluation, stimulated by sharp theological discussion and controversy, was well under way in New England, and this investigation was in process of establishing New England's theological leadership of America for another century. It was into this highly stimulating and somewhat perplexing theological ferment that Alexander came in 1801.

Actually three major parties had emerged in New England by the time of Alexander's visit—Arminians, Edwardseans, and Moderate or Old Calvinists—although ecclesiastical division did not result from these differences until a few years later.

The Arminians, or liberals, are not to be confused with the evangelical Arminianism of John Wesley, whose theological stance was nearer to that of Edwards than some at one time supposed. The New England Arminians, whose position developed gradually during the eighteenth century, were the most direct representatives within the New England churches of the critical rationalism of the Enlightenment. They found their most advanced following among the more prosperous and sophisticated groups in eastern Massachusetts, particularly in and around mercantile Boston. Under the influence of such Enlightenment emphases as God's benevolence and man's moral ability and the necessity of freedom for moral accountability, Arminians attacked doctrines like original sin (in which even the guilt of Adam's sin was "imputed" to his descendants), eternal punishment, election, and man's inability to respond by himself to God's offer of grace. As more complacent views of man's spiritual condition emerged, some felt less need for atonement by a divine Redeemer. Thus before the turn of the century, some—but not all—Arminians were questioning the superrational doctrines of the Trinity and orthodox Christology and were asserting the Arian view that Christ was less than God, but more than man. A few were going beyond this to the full Unitarian position that Christ was only a man, though Unitarianism in New England is not dated as a separate movement until the election of the Unitarian, Henry Ware, to the Harvard faculty in 1805.[38]

While Unitarianism was highly influential in stimulating theological reconstruction and cultural expansion in New England over a period of many years, it remained numerically a minority movement. The main stream of theological and spiritual influence in New England and considerably beyond that area was represented by Jonathan Edwards and his successors, known as Edwardseans or "consistent Calvinists." Responding to the Arminian emphasis on man's ability, Edwards asserted that man has full "natural ability" to do whatever he is inclined to do unless physically prevented, but that he lacks "moral ability" to change his own inclinations, which are determined by his nature. And his nature, because of original sin, is corrupt until God's grace regenerates him. Virtue consists in benevolence to Being in general in proportion as it possesses true being.

In dealing with the problem of God's permission of sin, Joseph Bellamy and Samuel Hopkins, early disciples of Edwards, sought to reconcile Calvinistic emphasis on God's sovereignty with Enlightenment concern for man's happiness by seeking to prove that by permitting sin God was increasing the total happiness of his creatures. Hopkins went beyond Edwards to teach "mediate" imputation of Adam's sin: a child is not born "guilty," but is born with a corrupt will which causes him inevitably to choose sin, whereby he himself then incurs guilt. Thus Edwardseanism was moving toward acceptance of the Enlightenment dictum that "ability limits obligation." With his strong interest in the will, Hopkins taught that only man's affections and will are "depraved," leaving the intellect of the natural man morally unimpaired. Thus all "sin" tends to be reduced to particular "sins," an advanced form of nominalism. In regeneration, God gives man a new will, and man then expresses this renewal in conscious conversion, which is considered separate from regeneration. This central emphasis on the will was of course an incentive to Christian activism, and seemed to some hypercritics to imply that unregenerate man has the "ability" to obey God and lacks only the "inclination" to do so. Coupled with this emphasis on man's will, Hopkins sought to save his Calvinism by a hyper-Calvinistic teaching—further heightened by his follower, Nathanael Emmons— that God is actually the one who moves the wills of all men to do everything that they do, though not actually himself guilty of their sinful deeds. Opponents were quick to charge that this doctrine made God himself the author of sin, a charge which the Hopkinsians vigorously denied. Hopkins also denied the efficacy of the means of grace when used by the unregenerate. In another area, Hopkins went beyond Edwards's emphasis on benevolence by asserting that true benevolence is "disinterested" to the point of a willingness to be damned for the glory of God, and by teaching that all sin is rooted in selfishness. Under the influence of humanitarian considerations, Hopkins, like most Edwardseans other than Edwards himself, moved toward the "governmental" view of the atonement, which taught that the necessity for an atonement was not rooted in the justice of God's own nature, but in the needs of God's government, which required him to demonstrate to his subjects that sin must be penalized. Hopkins's distinctive views, supplemented by Nathanael Emmons and other followers and distorted by opponents, came to be known as "Hopkinsianism," and were an important source of contention among both Congregationalists and Presbyterians.

A third theological party among the heirs of New England Puritanism at the time of Alexander's visit, in addition to the Arminians and the Edwardseans, was the Old Calvinists, or more descriptively, the Moderate Calvinists. They were probably the largest of the three groups. As their name implies, they had not repudiated the Calvinistic heritage, but many had become somewhat indifferent to theological precision, unconsciously making accommodations to the spirit of the times and casually allowing altered meanings to slip into old terms.

Alexander's New England tour soon brought him into direct contact with leading Hopkinsians, and he noted varying opinions among them. Dr. Nathan Strong of Hartford, a mild Hopkinsian, was reacting against more extreme views, and even praised Alexander's doctrines when the young visitor preached for him.[39] At Newport, Rhode Island, Alexander spent a day with Samuel Hopkins, who was now almost eighty years old. He commented that "Dr. Hopkins had nothing assuming or dogmatical in his manner, but showed a childlike simplicity and entire submission to the will of God." But his pastoral labors were "by no means successful," and when Alexander preached the Sunday afternoon sermon for him, there was "a mere handful" of hearers.[40] More stimulating was Alexander's visit at Franklin, Massachusetts, with the arch-Hopkinsian, Nathanael Emmons, who was still in his fifties. Preaching a sermon on Christian love in the presence of Emmons, Alexander chose common ground and repudiated, as did all good Hopkinsians, the idea that true Christian love can be selfish. On the ride home, Emmons embarrassed Alexander with his praise of the discourse and declared that "there was nothing in the sermon which he did not approve." Alexander often afterwards referred to Emmons with great respect, and in a lecture years later said: "It has generally been acknowledged, that Hopkins, [Stephen] West & Emmons were eminently pious men, & I believe it, having had some acquaintance with two of them."[41]

In interpreting Hopkinsianism at this time, Alexander distinguished sharply between the theology of Edwards himself, whose "follower" at this time he himself still claimed to be, and "the ultraism of Hopkins, Emmons, and others," which he definitely repudiated. In making this sharp disjunction, he defined "Hopkinsianism" by the three doctrines popularly—and quite dubiously—considered its distinguishing characteristics: God is the author of sin, willingness to be damned is a sign of grace, and the means of grace are of no true spiritual value to the unre-generate.[42]

When Alexander reached the vicinity of Boston, he encountered far greater extremes of theological diversification. Surprised that "there was as yet no public line of [theological] demarcation among the clergy," he proceeded in his later recollections to identify by name men professing Unitarian, Arian, Edwardsean, Universalist, humanitarian, "rigid Trinitarian," and Arminian views. He found Harvard College "not yet fully under Unitarian influence," but rapidly moving in that direction, since "all were for making little of doctrinal differences." Already, "all the young men of talents in Harvard were Unitarians." He whimsically noted that all eight of the Congregational ministers in Newburyport dif-fered from each other in their theological positions.[43]

Ashbel Green, the distinguished Philadelphia clergyman with whom Alexander had recently associated at the General Assembly, had reacted even more negatively against this broad inclusivism when he had visited New England ten years before. After attending a meeting of the General Association in Boston, Green commented:

They are so diverse in their sentiments that they cannot agree on any point in theology. Some are Calvinists, some Universalists, some Arminians, some Arians, and one at least is a Socinian [Unitarian]. How absurd it is for men of such jarring opinions to attempt to unite. . . . To such a meeting as this, for the purposes of amusement, relaxation or sociality few would probably object. But for the purposes of church government, to me, at least, it appears ludicrous.[44]

A few native New Englanders protested these theological divergencies, most notable of whom was Jedidiah Morse, minister at Charlestown, Massachusetts. Amid the chaotic situation, Morse, who was himself an Old Calvinist, sought to create a clear cleavage by combining Old Cal-vinists and Hopkinsians against Unitarians. A few years after Alexander's visit, Morse founded a periodical, the *Panoplist*, and had a prominent part in founding Andover Seminary, both projects bringing together Old Calvinists and Hopkinsians against Unitarians. Ashbel Green, during his visit, had found Morse highly congenial, and main-tained lifelong connections with him.[45]

Alexander also met Morse, who entertained him at Charlestown, invited him to preach, and introduced him to some of New England's leading dignitaries at the Harvard Commencement.[46] Undoubtedly the two felt some theological kinship, but Alexander records no partisan identification with Morse at this time. Perhaps this was partly because of Alexander's adherence to much of Jonathan Edwards's theological posi-tion, but it also reflects a basic difference in personality between Ashbel Green's outspoken and strongly partisan temperment and Alexander's greater inclination toward mildness and conciliation.

During the tour Alexander, on invitation, preached frequently, expressing particular delight at seeing in Hartford recent converts of the Second Awakening which had begun previously.[47] His preaching at this period of his life must have been unusually moving, for we are told of six separate cases of persons who, many years later, said that the course of their lives had been permanently changed by sermons they heard from him at this time.[48] The surprise often expressed that a Virginian was orthodox may have been partly a by-product of the bitter denunciations, especially in New England, of the Virginian presidential candidate Jefferson as an "infidel" the year before.

Alexander noticed many differences in church customs. Hearers were much more given to praising sermons than in Virginia. There was much interest in church music, but, he felt, not always to good advantage. "Choirs were found everywhere, and this singing was very much confined to them. This struck me unfavourably." For the first time in his life, he preached in a gown, and got tangled in it climbing the steep stairs to the high pulpit. Dr. Emmons in a conversation with him defended the clerical wearing of bands and cocked hats in public as a "badge of their profession."[49]

Alexander returned home by way of New York, Princeton, Philadelphia, and Baltimore, preaching in all of these places. As an indirect result of his tour, he received calls to a professorship at Dartmouth College in the summer of 1802 and to a pastorate in Baltimore, neither of which he accepted.[50] A lasting significance of the journey was the personal contact it gave him, at a formative period in his life, with men and theological movements which were to affect the remainder of his career.[51] Ashbel Green had been so alienated by New England's theological diversity that it caused him totally to abandon the sympathy for the region that he had inherited from his more liberal New Side Presbyterian father. Alexander also reacted negatively against what he considered to be the disorderly pluralism of the region, but with his more moderate temperament he reacted more gradually than did Green. His close association with Green in Philadelphia a few years later undoubtedly further increased this negative reaction. Although Alexander never entirely lost clear traces of the influence of Edwards's thought, this New England experience caused him to build into the Old Princeton Theology a determined exclusivism that would allow no ecclesiastical unity with any kind of "heretical" views. This strong doctrinal exclusivism remained a notable characteristic of the Old Princeton Theology from the time of Archibald Alexander to the days of J. Gresham Machen, and was the issue that touched off the division of the Seminary in the 1920s. If Alexander's need of the objective and absolute authority of the Bible resulting from the agonizing fluctuations of inner spiritual experience in his conversion experience became a chief cornerstone of the Old Princeton Theology, this contact with a disruptive pluralism in New England on its part produced an aversion to pluralism and church mergers as another basic characteristic of the Old Princeton Theology.

On an undated occasion during this period of his life, Alexander, mounted on horseback and accompanied by an armed servant, made ''a long journey of exploration'' into what later became the state of Ohio. He used to tell his children anecdotes of ''meeting a bear at night'' and of coming suddenly on a camp of hunters who had made a rich killing. He told them, too, that at Chillicothe, the best room in the best house still had the stump of a tree protruding from its earthen floor.[52] Thus, before finally leaving Virginia, Alexander had had some direct acquaintance with every major section of the country, including the frontier.

Before Alexander accepted the invitation of the trustees to resume in May 1802 the presidency of Hampden-Sydney College,[53] he entered into marriage. On his way north to the General Assembly, he had visited the Rev. Dr. James Waddell in Louisa County, Virginia. Waddell had become blind, and was read to by his wife and by his daughter Janetta. Alexander had met the daughter before, but was now so impressed with her beauty and filial devotion that he asked and received her promise of marriage. They were married on April 5, 1802, less than a year after his return from New England. Like many earlier leaders of Virginia Presbyterianism, the bride's father, Dr. Waddell, had been born in northern Ireland and educated at a ''log college'' in Pennsylvania. He served pastorates in the ''Northern Neck'' of Virginia, in the Valley, and in Louisa County. A tall slender figure of courtly manners, he was noted for his pulpit eloquence, which William Wirt praised extravagantly in a somewhat sentimental but popular essay. It revealed something of his own irenic spirit when Alexander, in commenting on Waddell, extolled the fact that, though thoroughly orthodox himself, Waddell ''was disposed to treat with great respect those who differed from him.'' Waddell had married a first cousin of President Wiliam Henry Harrison. She was the daughter of a prosperous Scotch-Irish elder in Waddell's first pastoral charge. Alexander's marriage proved to be a most happy one, his wife being a woman of grace, intelligence, and devotion, whose memory has been fondly eulogized by her son.[54]

# 6
# A SHORTAGE OF MINISTERS

As the eighteenth century drew to a close, there was increasing interest among many Virginians in the religious revival. George A. Baxter, rector of Washington Academy, visited the famous Kentucky revival in its fourth year and sent a prevailingly favorable description to Alexander at Hampden-Sydney College. Alexander forwarded Baxter's article, together with his own endorsement, to the *Connecticut Evangelical Magazine*. But in a letter to his sister, Alexander, like Jonathan Edwards, refused to approve the widely challenged nervous disorders, declaring that "those extraordinary bodily appearances furnish no evidence of a saving operation of the Holy Spirit." By 1804, one minister was reporting improved church attendance and even "more Tears" at one of his own conventional services than in the more widely touted revivals in Kentucky and Tennessee. But here, as nearly everywhere, revivalism tended to be cyclical, and Hanover Presbytery, suffering from loss by westward migration and other causes, lamented: "We observe the gradual decline of religion among us. Our congregations are annually decreasing in number. Some are taken from us by death, others remove to distant places." By 1810 John H. Rice was complaining to his friend Alexander: "I think the state of religion in this country worse by some degrees than when you left it" (in 1806).[1]

These were years of growing population and of extensive movement to the frontier. Virginia had had the largest claims to western lands before the various states ceded their claims to the United States during and after the Revolutionary War, and Virginians retained great interest in the West. Virginia Presbyterians, whose chief strength at this time was in the Piedmont and the Valley, were in the forefront of this thrust westward, moving not only westward into Kentucky, but also northwest and southwest. By 1799 the Synod of Virginia contained presbyteries in parts of what was or later became Ohio, Kentucky, Tennessee, and western Pennsylvania, although not all of these areas had been settled predominantly by Virginians. By 1803 the new synods of Pittsburgh and Kentucky took over the more westerly presbyteries.

Statistics reflect the drain which this westward movement placed on the ministerial manpower of the Synod of Virginia. Though the national denominational statistics are flawed by the failure of some presbyteries to submit figures, the ratios for a decade are illustrative. For the ten-year period, 1795–1804, the average annual number of "ministers settled" in the synod was 35.8; ministers "without charge" (without settled pastorates) 4.4; "licentiates" 5.1; and "vacant churches" 41.1 Thus, during this period, there was an average of 4.33 times as many vacant churches as there were available personnel (that is, as there were "ministers without charge" and "licentiates" combined). This was almost exactly twice the denomination's national ratio of 2.19 times as many vacant churches as available personnel for these same years, and even that was causing anxiety in the denomination. It is interesting to notice, too, how much more efficiently the Virginia Synod was using its manpower than was the church at large. In the synod there was an average for the period of 8.14 times as many "ministers settled" as there were "ministers without charge," whereas in the church at large, the ratio was only 5.06 times as many. This is no doubt partly explainable by the likelihood that the newer regions had fewer retired ministers on their rolls and perhaps more missionaries coming in from outside. But in spite of the accentuated need of ministers in the Synod of Virginia the ratio of ministeral candidates (represented in these statistics by "licentiates," although this category included only the most advanced level of candidacy) to ordained ministers (that is, "ministers settled" plus "ministers without charge") was a little below that of the denomination as a whole. Thus in Virginia there was for the ten-year period an annual average of one licentiate per 7.88 ordained ministers, whereas in the church as a whole there was one licentiate per 7.31 ordained ministers. With these special needs, Virginia showed an interest in measures for ministerial procurement and education somewhat greater than did the denomination as a whole.[2]

As early as 1771, Hanover Presbytery, the oldest presbytery in Virginia, was taking steps to found what became Washington and Lee University in the Valley, and three year later made plans for founding what became Hampden-Sydney College in the Piedmont. Ministerial education was an important part of the purpose of both of these institutions.[3] By 1794, more than a decade before a national overture by Ashbel Green on the same subject, Hanover Presbytery took action to subsidize the education of individual ministerial candidates, and directed one of its ministers, the young Archibald Alexander, to prepare subscription blanks for the purpose. Three years later, presbytery found that "something considerable had been done" with this project and, at the request of presbytery, Archibald Alexander proposed a plan, which was adopted, for a permanent endowment to support two ministerial candidates.[4]

Hanover Presbytery should probably be credited with the first action by any judicatory of the church (as distinct from a private letter written by Dr. Samuel Miller of New York a year before) explicitly looking toward the founding of a theological school. In responding to an overture sent by the General Assembly to its presbyteries, Hanover Presbytery on April 4, 1806, took an action going far beyond what the Assembly had proposed: "The Presbytery were of opinion that this important object [education for the ministry] might be best obtained, by the establishment of a presbyterial institution embracing a theological Library and school within their Bounds." Presbytery appointed President Alexander chairman of a committee "to solicit donations, and do all other things which may to them appear expedient for obtaining and establishing a Theological Library & school at Hampden-Sydney College."[5] In September the trustees of the college met this proposal by preparing to confer with presbytery regarding the matter.[6]

This decision of presbytery to create a theological seminary was no empty resolution, but expressed specific ideas as to what theological education should be. The ideal was Bible-oriented in a scholarly way. Theological education must preeminently include instruction in the original languages of Scripture, because translations can never capture the full and identical meaning of the original and because the living languages into which translations are cast continually change in meaning. Not only here, but in its emphasis on the need of studying the history and culture of biblical times in order to understand the biblical message, this report to presbytery showed notable historical awareness. Apologetics was necessary to convince hearers of the truth of the Bible and of the gospel. Ancient church history was valuable for throwing light on the nature of Christianity. Science, which was currently expanding rapidly, should also be studied. A large view of the minister's social and cultural role is reflected in the declaration of Alexander's committee that well-educated clergy now had the opportunity to give permanent character to the United States, which was still in its formative youth. Here is reflected the ideal of "a Christian America" and even of what has later been called the "cultural establishment of Christianity." Scanning these broad needs of clerical preparation, the report, with a modesty suggestive of Alexander's pen, lamented that "there are so few amongst us who are not entirely destitute of this kind of learning."[7]

At this same time, the Reverend George A. Baxter, rector of Washington Academy in the Valley, felt it necessary to defend the ideal of a highly educated and salaried professional ministry against competing charismatic views. While not promoting a theological seminary, he demanded a theological curriculum very similar to that outlined by Alexander's committee, which was decidedly superior to what was currently available.[8] Soon afterwards, in an address to its constituent congregations, Hanover Presbytery echoed the self-searching regret expressed by Alexander's committee that "in the bounds of this presbytery, there are very few ministers possessing the knowledge, the zeal, and the piety united which ought to belong to the ministerial character," and urged support for the projected theological seminary.[9]

Thus Virginia Presbyterians, with Alexander playing a leading role, were in the forefront in their own denomination, and not far behind the most advanced trends anywhere in the nation, in seeking a more adequate and acceptable structuring of theological education. This ideal would soon be expressed in a new type of American institution—theological seminaries and college divinity schools. Here in Virginia, before the General Assembly had taken action looking toward the creation of a national seminary, local efforts were being launched which eventuated in 1812 at Hampden-Sydney College in a theological school which later became "Union Theological Seminary in Virginia," at Richmond. Had Alexander not left Virginia when he did, this Virginia seminary would probably have opened before 1812. Thus when Alexander did leave Virginia in 1806, he carried with him a lively interest in theological education and valuable experience in its promotion.

In yet another area, Alexander while still in Virginia, was a prominent participant in one of the newer experimental forms of religious expression. In October 1803 the Synod of Virginia appointed him and six others as a committee to publish, if it was found to be feasible, "a periodical for the dissemination of religious knowledge."[10] The result was the *Virginia Religious Magazine*, published in Lexington in three volumes from October 1804 through 1807. Only one religious periodical had previously appeared in the South, a Baptist publication in Georgia.[11] Evangelical and missionary interests were already producing in these years such religious journals as the *New-York Missionary Magazine* (1800), the *Connecticut Evangelical Magazine* (1800), and the *Massachusetts Missionary Magazine* (1803).[12]

General periodical literature had been developing in America since before the middle of the eighteenth century. In abbreviated and popular form, this democratic medium presented to the reader a wide spectrum of interests, much of the material being freely excerpted from British books and periodicals, often without acknowledgement. As the nineteenth century dawned, the growing nationalism was seeking to assert a distinctively American literary character, though still borrowing from abroad. The specifically religious press developed along similar lines, with a pot-pourri of original or excerpted articles on missions, biblical exposition, brief doctrinal articles, sermons, news of revivals, congregational life, deathbed utterances, and the like.

The Preface to the first issue of the *Virginia Religious Magazine*, after noting that distance from the New England states made it impractical to depend on their religious periodicals, uttered a clear sectional declaration of cultural independence: "The sources of information are as open to us as to them, and the means of conveying it equally within our reach." The quarterly announced that its "leading design" was to "convey information" concerning the great work of missions being done in such widely extended areas as among the Hottentots, the "Hindoos," the Pacific islanders, the American Indians, the white frontiersmen, "and in many other places." In spite of "the rage of infidelity" these missionary exertions—probably the greatest "since the days of the apostles"—give hope of the near fulfillment of biblical prophecies concerning the coming of Christ's kingdom. This prospect "calls aloud for the exertions of every one" for "many vices are yet to be banished from society." But in spite of some hortatory rousements, the Preface seemed fairly complacent about the existing moral level of the churches and of American society.

The Preface proposed, by means of "extensive correspondence," to receive news of Christian activity from every part of the world and especially concerning missions. To help parents, there would be lively and interesting materials for children. For busy adults, brief articles would quickly give the gist of important subjects. The reader was promised that many of these short essays would be "the productions of his own country, and perhaps some of them of his own neighborhood."[13] Here, as in more successful later religious periodicals, promotion, in true democratic fashion, was reaching for mass appeal, with clear echoes of the rising American literary nationalism. It is no wonder that before many years, theologians were complaining that popular religious journals were seducing laymen—and even ministers—away from more solid intellectual fare.

As the first year of publication neared completion, the report to synod revealed that the journal was facing the discouragements common to such projects. "The work has been deserted by almost all the members" of synod, and "original matter has not been furnished in sufficient quantity to ensure success." But with more than 400 subscribers and a profit of some seventy odd dollars, the project at least was solvent. Vocal support was easy and it was "unanimously voted" to continue publication.[14]

In introducing their second volume, the editors significantly called attention to the difficulties in inland Virginia—"so remote from the seaport towns"—of establishing connections with national and worldwide sources of religious news. The editors implied a conception of the church which transcended denominational and even national lines when, in pleading for contributions of news, they noted—very evidently in the light of recent American developments in political journalism—that even in the civil sphere, democratic government cannot be adequately maintained "without some vehicle of political information."[15] But in spite of such emphasis on the importance of their paper, the editors, near the end of their second year, were forced to admit to synod that the number of subscribers had fallen to "about 344," "much below what was expected." With flagging enthusiasm, the synod voted to continue publication for "the ensuing year," which then proved to be the publication's last.[16]

Throughout the life of this journal, nearly all the articles were either anonymous or written under pseudonyms; but one entitled "An Enquiry into the Nature of Conscience" and signed by the initial "A" bears some evidence of Alexander's hand. The article conceived conscience's "judgment" as a rational evaluation of a contemplated action by comparison with an accepted moral norm. Just as for Jonathan Edwards a "motive" was the "cause" of an inclination of the will, so here conscience's judgment is the "cause" of conscience's approval or disapproval of an action. The norm by which judgment is guided should be the Scriptures, but appeal, the article charged, is too often made to some false or inadequate norm. Acting in ways approved by conscience brings pleasure, while acting in ways disapproved by conscience brings pain. Thus pleasure or pain is the result of moral action, but not the norm for it. Because of man's fall, the writer rejects every merely intuitive moral standard. Alexander's authorship of this article is somewhat problematical. One misses entirely the emphasis on "benevolence" which might still have been expected from Alexander's Edwardsean sympathies at this stage of his life. It should be noted also that the norm of ethical action is viewed in an external and legalistic way that provides no principles facilitating application to changing social situations.[17]

Alexander's close friend Conrad Speece asserted that conscience operates by comparing actions with "a standard of duty," but went beyond "A"'s article in stating that many duties are "immediately and intuitively evident." In another article, almost in Edwardsean fashion, Speece defined piety partly as "love to God" which includes "joy in his infinite excellency." In an extended series that had clear overtones of the Enlightenment, Speece developed much more fully the thesis that piety promotes happiness.[18]

One of the most important and informing items in this journal was a serial piece cast in fictional setting and entitled, "A Conversation at Mr. Jervas's." Through Alexander had moved to Philadelphia the year before its publication, he and his friends Rice and Speece all participated in this literary dialogue. "Paulinus" has been identified as Alexander, and "Philander" as Alexander's friend Speece.[19]

In one of the earliest portions of the "Jervas" series, an idyllic word picture was painted, where on a Sunday evening "Mr. Jervas" was surrounded by his loving family and thirty happy slaves. His daughter summarized the morning sermon, and slave children recited catechism which had been taught to them by their parents. Mr. Jervas reported that at first the slaves had been reluctant to attend, but now they loved it.

Whereupon an interlocutor asked, Were you not afraid "that giving them such instructions would inspire them with high notions of liberty, and make them both troublesome and dangerous?" On the contrary, replied Mr. Jervas naively, "the readiest way to incline them to act as they ought is to train them up according to the precepts of the gospel . . . . The best and most enlightened christians are best servants [slaves]." If all the slaves were Christianized, "plots and insurrections and all the horrid ideas, which now haunt the minds of so many people, would no more be apprehended." He told of a dear old lady "who frequently observed, that the preachers, who instructed her servants in the doctrines and duties of religion, were of much more advantage to her than all the overseers she ever employed."

The conversation achieved its highest level of unreality in the proposal that only "men of piety" be appointed as overseers, and that they be required on Sundays to read religious books to the slaves. Such phantasy was perhaps partly explainable by the fact that in the Valley and Piedmont, where this journal circulated, the greater abuses of large slave plantations were less known. But in spite of this effusion of piety, the speaker's conscience seemed troubled, for he added: "I am saying nothing now, as to the lawfulness of the holding of slaves by the people of this country in present circumstances."[20]

This particular Jervas cameo was apparently an effort, however crude, to supply motivation for Hanover Presbytery's much more sober and realistic injunction that masters give religious instruction to their slaves on pain of receiving God's judgment on themselves.[21] Previously the journal had published a notably explicit and courageous denunciation of the sexual exploitation of female slaves. "Incontinence prevails to an alarming extent in our country" and is "a crime of the greatest magnitude," which "leads to the misery of our servants, . . . is a source of misery to the offspring of such vicious connections," is a particular indignity to the humiliated male slaves, and "leads to the corruption of the whites." In fact, it is "no uncommon thing in this country for men, who rank high in society, to see and even to hold their children in slavery!—to bequeath them as they do their horses! and sometimes to sell them . . . for the support of their luxury!!" It evidences the deep roots of the slavery evil that this writer also, in the midst of his damning diatribe, felt constrained to say, "I do not at present plead for their emancipation, because I do not see any opportunity either of promoting their happiness or the happiness of society by such a measure."[22]

As the conversations at the fictitious Mr. Jervas's proceeded to later stages, they clearly reflected the fact that Virginia Presbyterianism in Alexander's day was finding itself hard pressed by more uninhibited, more charismatic, less formal religious groups which had less theological structure, and a more flexible and less educated ministry which was much closer to the social and cultural level of plain people. In a word, Presbyterians in Virginia were being overwhelmed and numerically outdistanced by the Baptists and Methodists, and apparently felt threatened also by the backwash from the current religious extravagances of their own ecclesiastical children on the Kentucky and other frontiers. Such vigorous young Presbyterian leaders as Alexander, Rice, and Speece, in the "Jervas" conversations, reacted to these "sectarian" tendencies by an emphasis on "churchliness" which went considerably beyond views usually voiced by Presbyterians of their time. Indirect references which they made to unnamed rival religious movements amid the heat of competition sometimes did their opponents less than justice.

Thus Alexander, in these conversations, suggested greater use of the Christian calendar, while Speece pled for more adequate church buildings. "There is not a church in this part of the state," Speece complained, "as good as a Dutchman's barn."

They are generally poor, miserable leaky hulls, which let in wind and water. . . . Churches ought to be elegant buildings, and constructed . . . to inspire worshippers with awe and solemnity. . . . And though instrumental musick in churches is exploded, among us, yet were I to consult my own taste, I would have a good organ at every place of worship.

Somewhat anticipating Protestanism's later use of pedagogy, Alexander offered a surprising reply: "I agree with you; but would go still farther," and use "paintings in churches." "The objects of sense have such an influence upon us . . . that it would be a happy thing accomplished if we could inlist the senses in the cause of religion." Still more startling in those "revival" days—even though, as usual, penned under his pseudonym "Paulinus"—was Alexander's broad-minded declaration:

Among Roman Catholicks, there is almost universally to be found more zeal, at least more appearance of devotion, and piety, and more attachment to religion, than among Protestants. I think that this can be accounted for, only from the circumstance that among those people, the senses, as I said, are employed in the service of religion.

He went on to say that "superstition derives not from liturgy but from lack of religious instruction," and charged that there were "thousands" in America "who know nothing of popery" or church art, but among whom there are "formal professors and superstitious observances."[23] A serious warning concerning the future of Protestant orthodoxy was implied when another interlocutor said that in a preaching tour of the state, he had found even professing Christians "totally ignorant of the meaning of the terms most commonly in use in Christian discourses, such as Regeneration, Sanctification, Adoption, and the like." Related to this theological ignorance was the widespread sectarianism which he had encountered, with its bigotry and proselyting, quite devoid of the zealous piety often found in such movements.[24]

In the continuing dialogue, Speece picked up this pessimistic note to lament the woefully inadequate financial support of the clergy as compared with the "honours and emoluments" offered to other learned professions. "I therefore greatly fear," Speece continued, "that the clerical office will in process of time be deserted by men of learning and genius, and filled with unlearned clerks, who will only burlesque their profession, and bring religion into contempt." It was not flattering to his Baptist former coreligionists when he asked, concerning Virginia, "Except a few Episcopalians, and about thirty Presbyterians, how many men of learning are in the ministry?"[25] At this point Alexander suggested that an additional explanation for current religious problems was to be found in Virginia's continuous stream of emigration to the newer settlements. By the time young people have received religious instruction, he said, they will be "wandering in the wilds of Louisiana [purchased less than four years before], or seeking a habitation on some distant frontier." Because of his static ideals of indoctrination in a "given" religious and cultural heritage, Alexander interpreted this population mobility as a bar to all progress rather than as a stimulus to it. "This shifting and moving of the people, in fact, stops the progress of every kind of improvement whether of religion, literature, agriculture, or manufactures."[26]

Another theme of the dialogue was the question so pressing for early Puritans and for the Reformed faith in general, "Am I really a Christian or not?" Here, in spite of much revivalism in the environment, the conviction was strongly expressed that the answer is not to be sought in "a particular experience," because as persons differ "in the character, disposition, and structure of mind . . . it is not to be imagined, that any man's experience is just like another's." When such an error is taught, honest inquirers will be disheartened and less sincere persons will artificially imitate the required model. Thus multitudes are diverted from gospel truth and "from the cultivation of pious, holy affections, and from the works of faith, of charity, and patience, to the business of working up the passions." "Preaching of this kind has been too common . . . so that now, the majority of christians do not go to church to be instructed in the duties which they owe to God and their fellow-creatures . . . but they go with the intention of having their feelings excited." Here was really an attack on the religious subjectivism not only of superficial "revivals," but—probably unconsciously—on the increasing turn of Western culture since the Renaissance to the human subject rather than to the divine object as the starting point of religion. In his later theology Alexander stressed "objective" aspects of Christianity in a way that flew in the face of much of his contemporary culture, and even threatened to undercut the intellectual foundation of his own vital Christian experience. "Religious affections, as far as they are genuine," continued Alexander ("Paulinus"), "will produce good works." While "an experience of grace" is not ignored, emphasis here falls on the side of good works as the basic test of one's being a Christian, creating a real danger of legalism. It is significant that Alexander, who was a consistent advocate of a sane and intellectually guided revivalism, here and elsewhere associated himself with sharp castigation of revivalistic excesses. The discussants found a chief source of this harmful emotionalism in "the physical state of our country," and proposed as the principal remedy more adequate education of ministers.[27]

Many of the topics treated "at Mr. Jervas's" revolved around the need for improved ministerial education, and to this central theme the friends now devoted concentrated attention. After noting with gratification the encouraging financial response to a current effort at establishing a theological school (presumably the effort begun by Hanover Presbytery the year before), they emphasized that theological education should be thorough rather than hurried. The candidate's preseminary work should provide "a broad foundation that his mind might be enlarged and liberal"—solid work in Greek, Latin, and mathematics and acquaintance with "the general principles" of the natural sciences. On the seminary level, he should study Hebrew and Greek, biblical history, the laws and customs of the ancient Jews and of their contemporary nations, objections to and evidences for Christianity, church history (including its background in secular history), and the history of doctrine, with particular attention to patristics. Only after acquiring this preparatory foundation should the student enter the climactic stage of his program, the study of "the doctrines of the scriptures . . . from the scriptures themselves." It was interesting that a mind set was to be so consciously created for the student before he could turn for himself to the "source" of religious authority, "the Scriptures themselves." For "relaxation" and "the refinement of his taste" the minister-to-be should read the best of the Latin and Greek classics and of modern poetry and prose. This ambitious course of study, which would require "at least four or five years," very closely resembled the theological curriculum which Alexander's committee had proposed to Hanover Presbytery the year before[28] and much of what later became the curriculum of Princeton Seminary.

There followed vehement denunciations of ignorant fanaticism, and warning that "unless the friends of learning and true piety exert themselves to the utmost of their powers, in a few years our country will become a mere hot-bed of enthusiasm," with the imminent danger of seeing "acted over again the scenes of desparate madness and frenzy which disgraced the madmen of Munster" (the German locale in 1533–1535 of Anabaptist religious innovation and social violence). Perhaps part of this anxiety was produced by reports about former Virginians who were caught up in the current unrestrained religious emotionalism of the Kentucky and Tennessee frontiers. Here, as frequently elsewhere, Alexander and his colleagues ominously linked religious sectarianism with social disorder. In the face of the supposed imminent peril of religious wildness, one of the conversationalists at "Mr. Jervas's" proposed to have "all men, of all creeds, to unite in one general effort to support the church of Christ" by adequately undergirding theological education.[29] The American Education Society, a nondenominational enterprise here nebulously foreshadowed, was later repudiated by Alexander and his Old School Presbyterian confreres in an era when denominational definitions were tightening.

It is clear that in the face of the envisioned perils of ignorant fanaticism and of social dissolution, some in Alexander's circle in Virginia were reacting vigorously against "sectarian" tendencies; were viewing "churchly" traditions much more sympathetically; and in particular were reemphasizing the necessity of very solid education for ministers. This deep concern for theological education Alexander carried with him when he left Virginia, a concern closely related, as we have just seen, to the desire for social stability in the face of mobility and "fanaticism."

Meanwhile, at Hampden-Sydney College, Alexander had been facing mounting problems of discipline, a widespread phenomenon in American colleges ever since the Revolutionary War, a problem which had undoubtedly heightened his evaluation of social stability. During his first presidency, there had been concern about student irregularities, but disciplinary problems grew much worse after his resumption of the presidency in the spring of 1802. Students were challenging authority by destroying fruit trees, firing off pistols, "unlawful gaming," and the like. Shortly after Alexander left, his successor, together with the presidents of the other two Virginia colleges, felt constrained to petition the Virginia legislature for authority to summon witnesses and to administer oaths in proceeding against student disorders. Alexander had had as much as he cared to endure, and on November 7, 1806, he presented his resignation to the college trustees, which was accepted six days later. His departure, he later acknowledged, had been somewhat hasty and impatient (which was quite uncharacteristic of him), but he added: "What I did rashly, Providence ordered for good."[30]

Alexander's eight years as college president were years of marked personal growth. He studied diligently; he gained experience as a teacher; he was active in ecclesiastical affairs at every level; he became personally acquainted with church leaders in the South, in the middle states, and in New England; he had direct contact with varying types of denominational life and religious expression; he gained experience in academic administration; and he left Virginia with a deep conviction of the need of more adequate methods of theological education. In spite of this, according to his son, he "never felt himself completely at home at the head of a college."[31]

Alexander had been invited in the spring of 1806 to preach in the vacant pulpit of the Third Presbyterian Church in Philadelphia. He had declined the invitation at the time, but when it was renewed in September, he preached there two Sundays and received a call to the pastorate. To accept this post, he resigned the college presidency and left the South to make his home in America's largest city.[32]

# 7
# A PHILADELPHIA ORIENTATION

The Philadelphia to which Archibald Alexander came in 1806 was not only the largest city on the continent, but also the nation's economic and cultural capital and, from 1790 to 1800, the political capital as well. Even before the Revolution, Philadelphia's trade with Europe and the West Indies, together with coastwise shipping, had made it an important commercial center. The winning of national independence stimulated a real estate boom, while the early stages of the French Revolution created new opportunities for Philadelphia shipping, and some local manufacturing developed also. In spite of the damage to American commerce by France and Great Britain as the Napoleonic Wars progressed, and in spite of Jefferson's damaging embargo on American exports in 1807, Philadelphia's growth was continuous and rapid. According to the United States census, the population of Philadelphia City increased from less than 29,000 in 1790 to more than 53,000 by 1810, while the population of Philadelphia County outside of the city more than doubled in the same period to exceed 57,000.

In view of the great inequality of wealth and influence, social distinctions were much emphasized in Philadelphia, though less so than in colonial times, when the heritage of European stratification was more operative. Before the Revolution, the typical dress of a mechanic, even on the street, was a leather apron, buckskin breeches, check shirt, and flannel jacket. But after the Revolution, tradesmen were assuming the attire of gentlemen, much to the chagrin of the latter. Meanwhile the gentry themselves were abandoning their earlier more pretentious dress.[1] In a society of great economic opportunity and rapid upward mobility, the concept of fixed social "station" was inevitably eroded.

Church life in Philadelphia was highly diversified, with some mutual toleration among the denominations, a good will which Dr. Benjamin Rush—the famous patriot, physician, and sermon taster—inclined to ascribe more to indifference than to love.[2] The three most important religious bodies in Philadelphia at the time were the Quakers, the Presbyterians, and the Episcopalians. Even before the Revolution, the Quakers had declined greatly in numbers and influence, becoming dissatisfied as they prospered with the plain dress and simple worship of their society, many becoming Presbyterians and more becoming Episcopalians. The Episcopalians included a disproportionately large number of the wealthy and influential, many of whom had been Loyalists in the late war. The Presbyterians, some of whom also had been Loyalists,[3] were perhaps the most numerous religious body, distributed in the city among four congregations and including many leading citizens. Philadelphia, during Alexander's years there, was virtually the capital city of American Presbyterianism. It was there that its first presbytery had been organized in 1706, and it was there that its national General Assembly met in twenty-one of the twenty-four years from the first Assembly through the year that Alexander left the city, including every year while he was there.

Dr. Alexander's pastorate of the Third Presbyterian Church for somewhat less than six years was successful outwardly as well as in more basic values. In spite of an undertone of dissension, which had existed also during the ministry of his predecessor,[4] the membership increased more than 50 percent. The greater concern of parents in those days for securing baptism for their children was reflected in his having baptized 306 persons, including no doubt some adults.[5] At Communion services, following the Scottish pattern, worshipers gathered around long tables upon presentation of tokens evidencing good standing. Concerning a Communion in May 1812, the minutes of session reported, "The number of communicants who sat down [was] not less than 300 (many members of the Assembly partook). Gloria Deo!"[6] The General Assembly was currently meeting in the nearby First Church, and no doubt some of its members came to have another look at Alexander whom this Assembly was considering for the first professorship in the projected theological seminary at Princeton. He was elected to the position nine days later.[7]

Alexander's church was located at Fourth and Pine Streets, four blocks south of the city's main street (High Street—later named Market) and two blocks north of South Street, which at that time was the city's southern boundary. In America in the early nineteenth century, quite unlike in the twentieth, many of the most prosperous citizens chose to live in the inner cities, with the less fortunate living in the suburbs. Alexander's church was adjacent to residences both of the wealthy and of the least privileged. One of the city's most desirable residential areas extended two blocks east from his church and three blocks north. St. Peter's Episcopal Church, with a fashionable congregation, lay in this area, one block away. In sharp contrast, two blocks still farther east was the Delaware River with its shipping and traffic. Also the region below South Street and extending west from Sixth Street was occupied by an increasing number of underprivileged whites. And one block south and three blocks west was the earliest center of black population in the city.

Soon after settling, Alexander described his parishioners as "with few exceptions of the middling class,"[8] including "a great number of persons from the neighborhood of the Navy-yard, with a goodly proportion of shipmasters and pilots."

The predominating ingredient in the congregation was the old-fashioned Scotch and Irish Presbyterianism . . . with a disposition on the part of some to look with distrust on hortatory preaching, and any measures toward revival as savouring of newlight and methodism. . . .The situation was one fitted to make a young Virginian minister feel the transition from a religious climate of great fervour and freedom.[9]

Apparently few of the more influential people residing immediately to the east attended Third Church. It was at that time Dr. Ashbel Green's Second Church that proved most attractive to more privileged Presbyterians in Philadelphia.

Alexander analyzed his new parishioners not only sociologically, but also religiously, and sought to meet them where he found them. "The truth is," he wrote to his sister in Virginia a few months after arriving, "there is much less religious knowledge among the people here than in the country. . . . These require very plain preaching, and when they become serious need to be taught the very first principles of the doctrine of Christ."[10] But already his plain dealing was accomplishing its purpose. He told of a "deistically inclined" out-of-town visitor who was "induced by his relative . . . to attend our meetings. Since he went home, he has written that he has determined to turn his attention to religion and to change his manner of life." Also, Alexander added,

We have several instances of awakening and hopeful conversion since I arrived here. . . . Among the poor I have found some choice spirits, . . . one man in particular, who is too infirm to come out, and who is supported by the congregation, edifies me every time I call to see him. . . . I find myself greatly benefited by my visits to the sick and afflicted; and it leads me to preach in a strain which otherwise I should not have thought suitable to a great city.[11]

If Alexander, as an editor of the *Virginia Religious Magazine*, had felt isolated from national and world events, in Philadelphia he need feel so no longer. Two decades before his coming, Philadelphia had been torn between French sympathizers and British sympathizers as people tensely watched the unfolding of the French Revolution. Presently thousands of French émigrés, including Louis Philippe and the redoubtable Talleyrand, were swarming into Philadelphia. As late as 1808, Jacob J. Janeway, copastor with Ashbel Green of Philadelphia's Second Presbyterian Church, and like many other leading Presbyterians an ardent Federalist, testified that "Philadelphia was the headquarters of the excitement" and feelings there still "ran high."[12]

The second half of the eighteenth century, especially the 1790s, had constituted a kind of "golden age" of Philadelphia's culture.[13] Two blocks north of Alexander's church was the residence of Dr. Casper Wistar, physician and scientist, who during the winter months held weekly cultural soirees attended by the intellectually elite of Philadelphia and dignitaries from abroad, until his death in 1818. Philadelphia has been called the "port of entry" for the Enlightenment into America.[14] For a time the Enlightenment brought in its wake a vigorous deism which radiated out from Philadelphia. As early as the 1760s, many even among the less educated were embracing it. "The Universal Society," a deistical group, was organized in Philadelphia in 1790, and in 1800 a short-lived deistical newspaper, *The Temple of Reason*, was published in Philadelphia and New York.

One product of Enlightenment influence was the building in 1794 of a Universalist Church on Lombard Street directly behind the church which Alexander later served. The same year, Joseph Priestley, an English nonconformist minister, supporter of the American and French Revolutions, famous in chemistry as the discoverer of oxygen, and a zealous Unitarian, came to Philadelphia. Two years later he preached in the Universalist Church "to a numerous, respectable, and very attentive audience" which included Vice President John Adams and members of Congress. Later in the same year, Priestley organized "The Society of Unitarian Christians of Philadelphia."[15] Neither Universalism nor Unitarianism is to be identified with deism, but both of them, like deism, found the Enlightenment a congenial climate.

In entering into closer association with Dr. Ashbel Green, Alexander was allying himself with one of America's determined antideists. Green was ten years older than Alexander and the unmistakable leader of the Presbyterian group in the city. His proud bearing, powdered wig, and formal attire cut a striking figure on Philadelphia streets long after others were adopting a simpler style. As a young man he had been chaplain of Congress and a frequent guest of President Washington. Green was cast in a large mold—strong in purpose, energetic, and dominating, with an unperturbed self-assurance that exasperated opponents. He was ardently devout, sometimes loquaciously so, but his piety often savored more of conscientious labor than of spontaneous delight. He was an able preacher, an opponent of slavery, a national leader in missions, and tireless in the numerous new enterprises that Christianity was developing in this era.

As a youth in the Revolutionary army, Green had found his Christian faith shaken by the deism of the army officers. In the characteristic fashion of that day, his doubts took the form of questioning the divine authority and inspiration of the Bible. The reading of Samuel Clarke's *Demonstration of the Being and Attributes of God* and of John Leland's *A View of the Principal Deistical Writers*[16] convinced him that the antideists had the better of the argument, but this still left him unsatisfied. So to the Bible itself he turned with the prayer "that God, in whose existence and attributes I believe, would help me to form a just opinion of the truth or fallacy of that book. Proceeding in this way, I had not gone through the four evangelists, till all my skepticism left me; and to this hour it has never returned."[17] This experience of one who had had a strict Christian rearing is notable for its stimulation by the threat of deism, and for its culmination in the typical Reformed conjunction of the written Word and the illumination of the Holy Spirit, which in his case had been preceded by, but had proved more decisive than, rational apologetic argument. Green claimed that he had drafted President John Adams's proclamation of March 1799, which denounced dissemination in the United States of "principles, subversive of the foundations of all religious, moral, and social obligations" and asked that citizens "implore His [God's] pardoning mercy, through the Great Mediator and Redeemer."[18]

It is not surprising that Alexander found much in common with Green and that he later received from Green strong support in laying for Princeton Seminary a foundation that sought to combine rational apologetics with spiritual experience based on the Bible and on the illumination of the Holy Spirit. But Alexander, though genuinely modest in spirit, was too independent a person to become any man's satellite. The same would be true of Princeton Seminary. Although its ties with Philadelphia were sometimes particularly close, theologically and otherwise, it never became a satellite of that city, but always retained the national character which its founders planned for it.

Less than a year after being called to Third Church, Alexander was elected moderator of the 1807 General Assembly, his denomination's highest honor. It thus became his duty to preach the opening sermon at the Assembly of 1808, and he made it a wide-ranging survey of the church's theological foundations and ecclesiastical life. "Truth," he said, "is the subject of knowledge. It is the object of faith, and furnishes the proper motives to all pious and benevolent affections." But truth is vast and, he added modestly, "the number of truths, which can be known by man, is comparatively small, and of attainable truths there are few which are absolutely necessary."[19] Alexander then invoked his Scottish realism to assert that, though "there are no innate ideas, . . . there are some . . . self-evident principles, to which every rational mind assents, as soon as they are proposed. I believe moreover," he added, "that there are such truths in morals, in which all men do as certainly agree as in any mathematical axioms."[20] Alexander here as elsewhere often treated the knowledge of God and interpersonal relations after the model of Newtonian mathematics, a pattern which the Old Princeton Theology would follow with increasing consistency. "These [self-evident truths]," Alexander continued, "are the stock on which all others [all other truths] must be engrafted" by a process of deduction. According to Alexander, natural theology was a necessary foundation for revelation. "If there were no such thing as the light of nature, . . . a revelation might be addressed, with as much reason, to a brute as to a man." But this light of nature is not sufficient, for "the truths, most important to the peace and salvation of men, are revealed only in the sacred scriptures," for "Christ himself is the truth. . . . To 'preach Jesus Christ and him crucified,' includes the whole range of doctrines taught by the apostle Paul."[21]

Almost like Philip Schaff nearly forty years later,[22] Alexander warned the church against the opposite extremes of "rational christianity" and "enthusiasm," outgrowths, respectively, of the Enlightenment and of a distorted Pietism. At the moment, he considered the threat of rationalism less serious from deism than from Unitarianism. Perhaps he was thinking of the impact on Philadelphia of Joseph Priestley, who had died only four years previously, and of the Universalist Church situated practically in his congregation's backyard. But against all forms of "rational Christianity" he found comfort in the thought that "no religion will engage the attention of people generally, unless it be calculated to interest their feelings." Actually, however, Alexander fought a lifelong war on both fronts—against deism and against enthusiasm. "Enthusiasm," he charged, "is likely to spread more extensive mischief among the unlearned, than any species of free-thinking. . . . The wild ebullitions of enthusiasm when they subside, leave their subjects under the fatal influence of some absurd opinions which become the creed of a new sect," of which early nineteenth-century America provided many examples.[23]

The experience of national independence, population mobility, innovative economic activities, increasingly heterogeneous population, and other forces were creating denominational tensions and diversification. This stimulated greater awareness of the practical and spiritual need for Christian cooperation and serious thought about the nature of the Christian church and its unity. It is not surprising, therefore, to find Alexander, in this sermon to his denomination's national gathering, urging Christian unity. "That the church of Christ . . . ought to form an undivided body is . . . generally admitted," he said, "yet it is a matter of dispute wherein this unity consists." He denied that Christian unity is unity of organization of people of diverse views. Rather, he declared, "truth and an agreement in the acknowledgement of truth, are the only solid foundation of christian unity and peace." But "what truths shall we require others to acknowledge, before we will unite with them?" Alexander asked. "I answer," he replied, "only such as are necessary to be known and received, in order to constitute a person, a sincere disciple of Jesus Christ." This was an amazingly broad definition of the theological bounds of the church (presumably he was speaking of the denominational church and not of Calvinists' intangible worldwide "visible church") for one who, less than thirty years later, endorsed (though he did not lead) the exclusion of New School Presbyterians from his denomination. Alexander, almost like Alexander Campbell, noted the accumulating process inherent in creed building, and speculated that when an error disappeared, the portion of the creed condemning that error might be eliminated, were it not that such deletion might seem to endorse the error. Undoubtedly referring to current bitter divisions among Presbyterians in the Kentucky frontier revival, Alexander warned his hearers: "Our body [the Presbyterian Church in the United States] is now large and widely extended. Some diversity of opinion and practice may be expected; but the progress of schism (which has already made its appearance) would be a most disastrous event."[24]

Alexander's sermon to the Assembly touched upon an issue which was still being discussed in the late twentieth century among denominations which practice infant baptism—the relation of baptized children to the life of the church. The practice of infant baptism in its heyday goes back to a society which conceived of itself in organic terms and has had fluctuating fortunes since the rise of individualism in the Renaissance, and especially in America. Invoking the theology of the Presbyterian creed, Alexander reminded his hearers that baptized children are "members" of the church and that this obligates the church to "a careful attention to the religious education of children." But Alexander was fully aware that with the rise of revivalism, a more individualistic conception of church membership was becoming widespread "which savours of greater strictness and purity, which considers none as properly members of the visible church, but such as exhibit evidences of vital piety." Alexander rejected this theory of the church outright, because "all attempts of man to draw a visible line between the regenerate and the unregenerate are ineffectual," although he did say that the church should exclude the heretical and the immoral and should examine applicants as to their religious knowledge and their lives. "All those," he said should be "admitted into the visible church . . . who acknowledge Christ to be the anointed prophet of God and Saviour of the world, and who profess a desire to be instructed in his religion."[25] This statement by Alexander concerning conditions for "admission" to church membership reveals the unresolved ambivalence in denominations practicing infant baptism between the concept of church membership by birth and the newer revivalistic concept of membership by individual choice and qualification. This contrast parallels the contrast between older static societies where one's "station" was fixed by birth and modern dynamic societies based on individual initiative.

Historically, by far the most important part of Alexander's moderatorial sermon was his proposal that the church should found regional theological seminaries devoted to the preparation of ministers. But that proposal will be discussed later in another context.

A sermon dated 1808, and therefore within Alexander's Philadelphia years, analyzed the struggles of inner religious life. In language that was more heightened than customary for him, he depicted the convicted sinner "filled with pain and anguish" after the pattern of "a lingering and agonizing death by crucifixion," and suffering "days & nights of bitterness & woe." In the midst of this, it is God who "works a repentance," and the "love of sin is henceforth extinguished."[26] "But the commencement of this change, is not so clear and obvious . . . as many pretend. . . . It is the deceitfulness of the heart . . . which perplex[es] the investigation."[27] Here was the quest for "assurance" which had so occupied seventeenth-century Puritanism. Alexander, it will be recalled, thought he could, though with some difficulty, date his own conversion, but he did not consider dating essential.

In those who have run to a great length in open sin, . . . the beginning of the work of grace, is much more easily traced. . . . But this is not the case, with those who have had impressions & desires from early life. They cannot . . . so distinctly recollect their conviction & conversion. . . . Such experience, altho the precise date of conversion cannot be ascertained, is as satisfactory as the former.[28]

For the surest evidence of true conversion, Alexander, like post-Calvinists including Jonathan Edwards, looked principally to good works. Acceptance by God was received through faith, not through works, but this acceptance was evidenced by works. For self-testing Alexander suggested that one who is really "dead to sin" will find sin "loathsome," will choose its "renunciation," will "never be satisfied" by it, will desire its "reign . . . in our world . . . to . . . end," and will "feel a peculiar attachment to others, in whom they suppose the same change has taken place." It is interesting that all of these tests are on the level of attitudes rather than of actions. "This attachment," Alexander added,

is very different from mere party-spirit which unites members of the same sect; for it does not embrace all who may belong to our own Community, but only such as appear to us to be engaged in "mortifying the deeds of the body"— and it goes out of the sect to which we may belong, & embraces with cordial esteem those of other denominations, who appear to be Christians.[29]

This last-mentioned tendency to realign professing Christians was a common characteristic of Pietism—to substitute the individual's recognition of "true" Christians for a particular denomination's theological and historical criteria of church membership. Alexander did not actually carry this tendency all the way to ecclesiastical realignment, but such an implication, even though unintentional, was clearly here.

Only a very few sermons of Alexander can with certainty be assigned to his Philadelphia years, and these contain more theology than his modest claim to simple preaching would lead one to expect. An undated sermon identified as "Preached at the Third Presbyterian Church, Philadelphia," reflected current discussions coming out of New England concerning the nature of free will. "We acknowledge that the will of man is free," said Alexander,

because to be forced to choose is a contradiction in terms; but still there is a moral certainty that the volitions of the will, will be coincident with the disposition of the heart. There is no restraint upon an unregenerate sinner to hinder him from turning [,] yet as long as he is left to himself there is a moral certainty that he will not reform. . . . But many . . . seem to be of opinion that God does just as much towards producing repentance in those who continue in their sins as in those who turn unto God. . . . This conception of grace . . . allows to man a share of the credit of his own salvation.[30]

This conclusion was for Alexander unthinkable.

With his high view of human reason, Alexander made the "will" "the chief seat of this depravity." Thus Alexander could regard human reason as to a degree unimpaired by man's "Fall," and could make the will the real culprit. "However strong the motives may be which are proposed [by the reason]," he continued, "a right choice will not be made until the heart is renewed." Alexander, at least to a degree, saved reason from the ravages of the "Fall," but at the price of acknowledging that this reason was not adequate to the task of redemption. For that, redeemed affection (of the "heart") was necessary.[31] In the Enlightenment era of reason and science, Alexander was saying in effect that reason was fully adequate to advance science and to discover moral truths, and even to reason objectively about theology; but only a spiritual force could renew human life in the image of God. Here was a dualism—a division of labor, though not a contradiction—between reason and faith, between the Enlightenment and Pietism. Each had its proper role, and each was operative within its proper bounds.

Alexander insisted that this divine renewal of a person's inner nature or "heart" did not contravene the freedom of that person's will, but that "all the acts and exercises of this new nature are in perfect coincidence with laws by which free agents are governed."[32] Closely related to his assertion that divine grace did not impair human freedom was his observation that the emotional reactions of individuals to divine grace differed widely.[33]

Presbyterianism in a young and rapidly expanding nation was continually torn between the ideal of a highly educated ministry and the hard fact of ministerial shortages. The problem was less acute in Philadelphia than in the Virginia Piedmont and Valley, which were in closer touch with the frontiers, but was by no means absent. Thus more than twenty years before Alexander came, Philadelphia Presbytery urged that lay elders of vacant churches provide for "the decent & devout performance of all proper religious offices . . . such as prayer, singing of Psalms, reading a portion of the holy Scriptures, with . . . such printed Discourses as appear to be most conformable to the sense & spirit of the Gospel."[34] One wonders how well this last-mentioned expedient would compete with the fiery Methodist and Baptist lay preachers. At other times, Presbyterian pastors, including those of leading churches, were commissioned by presbytery to leave their own pulpits for a Sunday or two to supply vacancies.[35] In spite of this shortage of ministers, Philadelphia Presbytery continued to demand the required "trials" of ministerial candidates similar to those applied to Archibald Alexander in Virginia.[36]

But there were occasional exceptions to the strictness with which Presbyterians guarded occupancy of the pulpit, one of the most notable exceptions being that of Joseph Eastburn, a deeply religious mechanic who was a member of Ashbel Green's Second Church. People in spiritual or psychological need often resorted to his shop and found help, and soon he was exhorting in public with notable acceptability. This confronted the governing presbytery with a problem. How could they utilize Eastburn's zeal and talents and at the same time preserve the distinctness and special qualifications of the clerical office? They resolved the problem by declaring: "The Presbytery of Philadelphia, viewing this as an irregularity, and considering that it might prove an inconvenient precedent, determined to give him a license to preach, under certain restrictions; not, however, as a candidate for ordination, to which he did not aspire." The solution appeared to be an ideal one for all concerned: Eastburn could render all the service he aspired to, and the strict requirements for entrance into the professional ministry would in no way be infringed upon. Eastburn continued preaching at the prison, the hospital, the city almshouse, and especially to sailors thrown out of work by Jefferson's embargo. He even "supplied the pulpits of all the Presbyterian churches with much acceptableness when the pastors were unwell or absent."[37]

Apparently it was the example of Eastburn's notable lay service that inspired Alexander to organize the "Evangelical Society," for he twice recounted the story of Eastburn and the organization of the Evangelical Society in immediate sequence. Alexander came to his Philadelphia parish just before the national voluntary societies were being formed, but at a time when local nondenominational groups for the purpose of missions of social concern were coming into existence, and he played a prominent role in this earlier movement in Philadelphia.

In less than a year after arriving at Third Church, Alexander was impressed that while commendable work was being done in "sending the Gospel to the heathen, and to the ignorant on our frontiers," little was being done to reach the religiously "destitute" right in Philadelphia. He was concerned that so little use was being made of Presbyterian lay people for active religious service. Clearly, this insufficient Presbyterian lay activity in the face of the expanding society and the shortage of fully trained ministers was related to the sharp functional cleavage in the Presbyterianism of that day between the laity and the professional clergy whose special training and functions had to be defended against the vigorous attacks of the contemporary sects. At the same time, Presbyterians were making inadequate use of their own lay elders, an office which the Reformed and Presbyterians had developed early in the Reformation era. Alexander was quick to note the anomaly that many lay people were zealous and aware of the situation, but viewed the spiritual need "without putting forth a hand, for they knew not what to do, and were afraid to go out of their proper sphere." Laymen were already beginning to dominate the more sectarian religious movements in America, but the era of expanding lay activity and influence in the more conventional Presbyterian and Congregational denominations was dawning.

As Alexander saw it, the problem for Presbyterianism which emphasized the authority and special functions of a theologically trained professional ministry was how "a plan might be devised by which pious laymen might be advantageously occupied in giving religious instruction to the ignorant, without touching on the peculiar duties of the Pastoral office." The question of available ministerial time for this kind of outreach was compounded by the fact that, for ministers, "preparation for the pulpit was then . . . deemed more indispensable than it has been by many since." This seemed to imply, as Alexander looked back, that the later activism of ministers had detracted from their theological study and pulpit preparation.

Alexander approached his objective of trying to increase lay activity by drafting "a constitution for an 'Evangelical Society,' not to raise funds, nor to employ others to work, but an association of which every member was to be a working man." After securing the informal endorsement of the Presbyterian ministers of the city, he invited about twenty laymen from the Presbyterian churches, who "seemed greatly pleased, and all expressed a willingness to do something." They divided into committees of two and went out on Sunday evenings "into the lanes and by-ways, and into suburbs" and "gathered children and adults into little societies for instruction and prayer." A note of condescension was not entirely lacking, as we read that "even men of high standing in society were found collecting the young and ignorant in the remote and obscure parts of the city." Some of the workers were so eager that they met "with their little flocks" on weekday evenings also. They even conducted street meetings in which, on occasion, they felt threatened by physical violence. Most of these groups "became the germs of flourishing Sabbath Schools," while some stimulated the erection of school houses and even the founding of churches. The Society's work also inspired the conducting of popular Sunday evening church services.[38]

Perhaps the most notable service of this Evangelical Society was the help it gave in organizing the nation's first Presbyterian church for blacks. From his early days in Virginia and continuing throughout his life, Alexander had a special concern for bringing the gospel to blacks.

The earliest center of black population in Philadelphia was on Lombard Street from Sixth to Seventh Streets, three or four squares from Alexander's church. By 1810 blacks constituted about one-tenth of the population of Philadelphia. Slaves were used as domestic servants or even hired out by their owners as mechanics, a practice which stirred some ire among white workers. By 1780 a Pennsylvania law provided that children born to slaves were to be emancipated at the age of twenty-eight.

Meanwhile blacks were feeling the need of organizing their own community under their own leaders, and in 1794 the first black church in America was organized in Philadelphia, the First African Church of St. Thomas, an Episcopal Church at the corner of Fifth and Adelphia Streets. Two years later, at Sixth and Lombard Streets, Bethel African Methodist Episcopal Church was erected, and this new denomination expanded notably.[39] Dr. Benjamin Rush aided in founding the African Methodist Church, seeing in the work both social and missionary possibilities. "I conceive," he said, "it will collect many hundred Blacks together on Sundays, who now spend that day in idleness. . . . And who knows but it may be the means of sending the gospel to Africa, as the American Revolution sent liberty to Europe?"[40]

Meanwhile, Presbyterians were not idle. When Dr. Alexander heard that John Gloucester, a black slave in Tennessee, was being considered for Presbyterian licensure, he persuaded the master to release him for ministerial service in Philadelphia. Presently Gloucester was preaching on streets and in private homes, gathering a church. In the summer of 1809, Dr. Alexander and a committee of the Evangelical Society, finding that some sixty blacks had signed a paper expressing a desire to have a Presbyterian church, agreed to aid them in raising money for a permanent building.[41]

The Evangelical Society's appeal to the public for funds, along with spiritual goals, stressed social benefits. The black community, the appeal said,

is daily rapidly increasing . . . and many come here with habits very little compatible with the peace and good order of civil society. Your officers of police . . . your prisons and workhouses can all attest, how much need there is of a reformation among the blacks of this place. This degraded state of manners cannot justly be attributed to any national inferiority, but must be ascribed to the circumstances of their having so lately emerged from a state of abject slavery calculated to paralyze every noble faculty of the mind, and extinguish every moral sentiment; but every day furnishes us with increasing evidence, that the African race is not inferior to the inhabitants of the other quarters of the world, either in the natural endowments of the understanding or the heart.[42]

This last was a clearcut denial of inherent racial inferiority, a charge which a few decades later, as the slavery controversy became more heated, was to be increasingly used as a defense of slavery. In the light of the menacing picture just painted, the appeal addressed the self-protection of potential donors. "Will not every friend of virtue and good order among the whites, lend his aid in promoting this work? Are we not bound by every consideration, of justice, of charity, of humanity, and of self-interest, to give our best assistance towards civilizing and reforming this numerous and increasing class of inhabitants?"[43]

The appeal then honestly confessed the white man's guilt and—in a spirit of true Calvinism, without at all excusing this guilt—saw the possibility of God's overruling providence.

Shall we suffer them to perish through lack of knowledge . . . when we have been accessory, as a people, in bringing them into their present wretched situation. The injury which has been done to this race of people by tearing them away from their friends and native country, and subjecting them and their posterity to a heavy yoke of bondage, cannot now be fully repaired; but that which was originally a crime of the most crying injustice and oppression may, under the direction of a gracious Providence, prove eventually to be a blessing of the first magnitude, by bringing them in reach of the Gospel of Christ.[44]

If Alexander had a part in drafting or endorsing this appeal (and he must have had, in view of his dominant position in the Evangelical Society) it reflects the ambivalence with which he and many another slaveholder past or present viewed the institution of slavery.

Before the end of 1809, the First African Presbyterian Church of Philadelphia had secured a charter; by the following October it had purchased lots on Seventh Street near South Street; and on May 31, 1811, the new church building was dedicated.[45]

Dr. Alexander was also prominent in the creation of the Philadelphia Bible Society, the first such organization in the United States. Dr.

Benjamin Rush reported that on December 12, 1808, he himself had opened a nondenominational meeting of "25 citizens at Mr. Ralston's for the purpose of establishing a Bible Society."

A Constitution . . . was subscribed . . . with great zeal and cordiality. [Episcopal] Bishop [William] White presided at this meeting. Two previous meetings were held at Mr. Ralston's to prepare the business for the above meeting, at which were present Mr. Ralston, the Revd. Messrs. Archd. Alexander and Jacob Janeway and Benjn. Rush.

Alexander was also elected one of the original "managers," a position which he held until he left the city.[46]

It was characteristic of the emerging voluntary society movement that laymen—especially merchants with contacts in England, where they caught inspiration from similar earlier movements—played a leading role. Robert Ralston was typical of these. A merchant with connections in London, he was treasurer of the Evangelical Society's funds for the First African Church and also treasurer of the Bible Society. In days when Philadelphia had been the national capital and Second Presbyterian Church had reserved pews for the president and the vice president of the United States, Ralston had occupied a front pew adjacent to the front pew of Mary Hodge, grandmother of Charles Hodge and widow of Andrew Hodge, another leading merchant.[47]

The new Bible Society divided into teams to solicit gifts, and used these to purchase English and German Bibles and New Testaments for free distribution in the city and its environs. Copies were also given to Benjamin Wickes, a devout sea captain, for distribution among his sailors and in Canton, China. When at home, Wickes was a leading member of Alexander's Third Church. Bibles were sent to the West Indies and to Alexander's friend John H. Rice, "to be distributed among the slaves who can read, in Virginia." Copies for distribution were also given to "the missionaries of the German Lutheran Church," to the Episcopalians, and to the Moravians. The *Third Report* of the society in 1811 noted with satisfaction that there were now fifteen Bible societies in the United States, but "our society was first established."[48]

In its *First Report*, the Philadelphia society acknowledged that it "owed its existence, in a great measure, to the noble example afforded by the British and Foreign Bible Society," and heard that "a handsome donation" had been promised by the British society "to the first society of a similar kind established in the United States." Mr. Ralston was therefore requested "to give information through his correspondent in London" of the formation of the Philadelphia Society and to send a copy of its constitution. The British responded with a generous donation of £200, twice what the Americans had hoped for. The gift was accompanied with the unsolicited but farsighted advice that the Philadelphia society "be enlarged, so as to comprehend the whole Union in one Society."[49] The Philadelphians failed to follow this good advice, and even when a number of younger local societies united to form the American Bible Society, they maintained their own separate existence. Before that time, Alexander had moved from the city, and Ralston, with his large interests and vision, became one of the leaders of the national society.

Meanwhile, this *First Report* of 1809, amid the turmoil of the Napoleonic Wars, reflected an expanding view of the potential impact on the world, not only of the American nation, but even of the city of Philadelphia. "In the convulsed state of the European continent," said this daring report, "perhaps there is no spot on earth, from which the light of divine truth might be sent forth more successfully, to various and distant parts of the benighted world, than from this city." The managers of the society even declared it to be their hope that "before the present generation shall have passed away the holy scriptures shall be read by all the principle [sic] nations under heaven."[50] Young America was a nation in a hurry. But Alexander himself was not inclined to indulge in extravagances of this kind, and seldom even referred to the much-discussed hope of a millennial kingdom.

It will be recalled that Alexander in Virginia was a founder of one of the nation's earliest religious quarterly periodicals. In Philadelphia he planned a church newspaper, but left the city before the plan could be carried out. But a young printer whom he had interested in the project followed through, and for a number of years published *The Christian Remembrancer.*[51] Alexander also had in view organizing a tract society, especially for distributing Christian literature among sailors who docked not far from his church, and who were much on his mind. No society was founded, but a few tracts were printed including prayers composed by Dr. Alexander himself.[52]

In those days churches were extensively supported by renting pews, a system which conspicuously seated worshipers according to their wealth, or at least according to their generosity or financial pretensions. While it provided a convenient source of needed revenue, it had the inevitable effect of making the poor feel ill at ease or positively unwelcome. Alexander in Philadelphia was quite early in his sensitivity to this problem, related to his concern for the poor and for city missions. He left a manuscript from this Philadelphia period which contemplated erection of "a free church, a church, the pews or seats of which should never be appropriated to particular persons, but left open for all who might choose at any time to occupy them." He assumed that the pulpit of such a church could be supplied on Sunday evenings by the city's pastors and on some Sunday mornings by visiting ministers "who may happen to spend the Sabbath in the city." He even drafted a constitution for this contemplated "Society for Promoting Religious Knowledge Among the

Poor," a title which itself reflected the more openly acknowledged stratification of society in that era. The dream was much more interdenominational than Alexander became a quarter of a century later, for this "constitution" provided that "any three" of the Executive Committee elected by the members of the Society "shall be authorized to invite any preacher of any Christian [presumably "evangelical"] denomination to preach in the aforesaid church."[53] This was an early date to be entertaining the ideal of a "free" church, but there is no evidence that it produced concrete action at this time.

The increased humanitarian spirit of the eighteenth century, together with expanding wealth, had produced a growing number of charitable institutions in Philadelphia, so that by 1828 Mathew Carey was able to list some thirty of these.[54] The early nineteenth century, as already noted, saw a rapidly expanding interest in Christian outreach and social concern on the part of laymen. But early in this century, Christian women in Philadelphia were also engaging in active enterprises, although it would be a century and a quarter before they would be made eligible for ordination as Presbyterian lay elders.

In 1804 the women of the Third Presbyterian Church of Philadelphia during the pastorate of Alexander's predecessor, Philip Milledoler, had in conjunction with the women of Ashbel Green's Second Church, organized a society to educate poor girls in Philadelphia. The work had originated in a religious revival in Milledoler's time, and was incorporated during Alexander's pastorate. The organizing plan provided for securing "a suitable House or Room" and the selection as "Preceptress" of "a capable woman of an unexceptionable moral and Religious character chosen at a joint meeting" of the participating women of the two churches. By the women of each church a committee or six "shall be appointed quarterly . . . to assist the Preceptress in the performance of her duties, and . . . in instilling in the tender minds of the Pupils sentiments of piety."[55]

In 1808 Philadelphia women organized the nondenominational "Female Hospitable Society," noticeably paralleling in structure and method the voluntary societies of the era which were controlled by men, and only slightly later in time than they. One objective of this Hospitable Society was "to procure old clothes, cloth remnants, etc., and make them over for the use of friendless orphans, also to become acquainted with such, and give them sympathy and help." In 1811 Dr. Janeway, addressing this Society which was holding its meeting in Alexander's church, commented that in the three years of its existence, it had "afforded relief to many hundreds of poor and sick females, and imparted religious instruction to many, ignorant of the path of duty and the way to eternal life."[56] Dr. Alexander had the stimulating experience of living in Philadelphia when that city, in the spirit of the times, was beginning to develop new forms of religious activity and social service and of being involved in the leadership of these enterprises.

Alexander was also concerned with more traditional social goals. American Calvinists followed the Puritans' legalistic views of Sunday observance rather than John Calvin's broader and more evangelical New Testament conception. The nineteenth century's economic diversification and growing variety of life-styles was causing increasing departures from sabbatarian ideals, especially in towns and cities. In 1807 the Synod of Philadelphia, which included Philadelphia Presbytery, for the first time since its reorganization in 1788, seriously contemplated legislative lobbying. This was something relatively new for American Presbyterians, but they and other denominations would resort to it increasingly. The Synod expressed "deep concern" over "the general disregard and profanation of the Sabbath. . . . They [the Synod] consider that institution as essential to the prosperity of the Christian religion, if not to its very existence" and unless "the profanation of that holy day" be checked, "consequences the most injurious, both to religion & to civil society are to be apprehended." The Synod appointed Alexander and five others as a committee to secure the support of the Presbyterian Synod of Pittsburgh and of other denominations in the state as well as of the Synod's own constituent presbyteries and their congregations in this endeavor to secure desired action from the Pennsylvania Legislature.[57]

Clearly, this sabbatarian issue was one of the opening guns on a much wider front than that of strict Sunday observance. It was a symbolic outpost of the domination of American life and culture by the Puritan tradition. Were the heirs of this tradition to maintain or regain their domination, or was their guiding influence to be swept away by a pluralism and a secularism whose ultimate destination no one could foresee? To those who held this sabbatarian ideal, nothing less than cultural and social stability seemed at issue. And in a sense, they were correct in their realization that their sabbatarian tradition was interwoven with a much larger social and cultural pattern.[58]

One member of the Philadelphia Synod's Sabbath Committee reported the next year "that the Committee . . . found so many circumstances & considerations to discourage, if not to forbid, the contemplated application to the Legislature of Pennsylvania, that they had not attempted it." The committee report did not elaborate on the difficulties it had encountered, but the Synod was not to be deterred, and reappointed two members of the committee (not including Alexander) to pursue the original goal. Though the renewed committee continued to report for several years, the record shows no concrete accomplishments.[59] But the issue would long be pursued by the heirs of Puritanism. The fact that Dr. Alexander was not included in the renewed committee perhaps reflects the fact that, though he was a man of strong convictions, throughout his life he was disinclined to force those convictions on others. But Ashbel Green was a man of more aggressive temperament than Alexander, which is reflected in his church session's "unanimously" memorializing Congress in 1810 against Sunday mail delivery, which was considered by many at the time to be a burning issue.[60]

A traditional bugaboo of strict Puritanism was the theater. When a theater was built in 1758 on the far side of South Street, just outside of Philadelphia city limits, the Presbyterian Synod unsuccesfully urged Pennsylvania's governor and legislature to suppress it. Two years later this same company built a larger theater within two blocks of the future site of Alexander's church, still on the safe far side of South Street, later to be honored by the occasional attendance of President Washington. The theater was still being used during Alexander's pastorate.[61]

National attention was turned to theatrical performances when on December 26, 1811, in a theater in Richmond, Virginia, scenery caught fire from an open lamp and some seventy-five people perished in the resulting conflagration and panic. The emotional shock that followed inspired many sermons. Alexander, preaching by request, expressed the universal sorrow in language that was for him unusually grandiloquent. But, like many others at the time, he could not resist the opportunity of inserting a brief warning against the supposed evil of theater attendance. "I feel it to be incumbent upon me," he said, "to give my public testimony against [theatrical exhibitions] as being, notwithstanding the partial good which may result from them, unfriendly to piety— unfriendly to morality . . . and unfriendly to true delicacy and genuine refinement."[62] In less than a month after the fire, the Presbyterian ministers of Philadelphia had together drafted a resolution against theater attendance, secured the adoption of this by their governing sessions, to be read from their pulpits, and had agreed to preach against theater attendance.[63]

Alexander's time in Philadelphia was not all spent in preaching, pastoral visitation, and social concern. In the city he had access to better libraries, book sellers, and stimulating personal contacts. He had a penchant for language study and read extensively in the Latin theology of the sixteenth and seventeenth centuries, "including Romanist and Lutheran, as well as Reformed," whose volumes became an increasing part of his library. He continued his diligent study of the Greek New Testament and began a more advanced study of Hebrew under the guidance of "a learned Jew," developing the regular habit of reading at least a chapter a day in the Hebrew Old Testament. He also acquired and diligently studied volumes on the history and practice of textual criticism and biblical interpretation.[64] He was now able to purchase scholarly theological volumes for his Virginia friends John H. Rice and Conrad Speece.[65] He found in James Patriot Wilson, pastor of the First Church, a dedicated and stimulating scholar, unlike Alexander, something of a recluse.[66]

By the time Alexander left Philadelphia in 1812, his theological stance had changed noticeably. We have seen that in his early preaching in Virginia, the ideas of Jonathan Edwards were conspicuous, but his reaction against the pluralism which he witnessed in his New England visit in 1801, followed by his intensive studies in Philadelphia of seventeenth-century Reformed scholasticism—and perhaps also the influence of his senior colleagues Green and Wilson, especially the former—had definitely shifted his theological center to that scholasticism. Alexander himself, says his biographer, "has left on record the statement, that on his return from New England, and during his residence in Philadelphia, his views, which had been somewhat modified by eastern [New England] suggestions, began to fix themselves more definitely in the direction of the common Westminster theology."[67] By the time Alexander left Philadelphia, the basic pattern of the Old Princeton Theology was fixed, but, as we shall see, it would be erroneous to assume that all vestiges of Edwardsean influence on his thinking had disappeared. It was significant also that during this Philadelphia period, he was "silently acquiring reputation as a theologian of original and clear views, and strict adherence to Reformed tenets."[68]

The year before he left Philadelphia, Alexander told his sister that "religion in this place is at present in a languid rather than a thriving state,"[69] and later he commented that the church contained some "who are not of the right spirit,"[70] as his predecessor had sensed, and as was to become evident in the attempt to call Alexander's successor.[71] But in announcing to the congregation his intention of leaving, Alexander could say, "Since I have been your pastor, no event has occurred to disturb that peace and harmony which should ever exist between minister and people."[72] And he could later recollect: that he "had on the Sabbath large assemblies of attentive people; and the preaching did not seem altogether without saving effect. The congregation appeared one and all to be pleased with my services, and many strangers as well as members of other churches came to hear me."[73] But even so, he regarded "his sojourn in Philadelphia as the least agreeable portion of his life." His son explained this fact as due at least partly to his preference for the open country life of Virginia and Princeton over the more crowded life and ways of the city.

Alexander's preparation for building an American seminary had been greatly enriched by the fact that he now had had personal contact with every major area of American life—South, Middle states, New England, city, country, and frontier. He had read widely, confronted many viewpoints, and even changed somewhat the orientation of his own thinking. At the age of forty he was ready to begin his greatest life work. But before evaluating that, we must trace the steps by which the new seminary came into existence.

# 8
# A PRIVATE LETTER

The first proposal for what later became Princeton Theological Seminary came from the Rev. Dr. Samuel Miller, pastor of the First Presbyterian Church in New York City. It came in the form of a letter to Dr. Ashbel Green of Philadelphia on March 12, 1805, very near the beginning of the rapidly growing movement in the United States to found theological seminaries that would be separate from colleges and divinity schools that would be distinct departments of colleges. In his letter, Miller made the clear proposal: "It appears to me, that we ought, forthwith, either to establish a new theological school, in some central part of our bounds; or direct more of our attention to extend the plan and increase the energy of the Princeton establishment" (that is, the College of New Jersey, founded in 1746).[1] Dr. Miller's letter suggested three reasons for founding a seminary, which were also three central issues in the emerging seminary movement.

The first reason which Dr. Miller's letter proposed for founding a Presbyterian seminary was denominational competition. In every society there are conflicting forces simultaneously making for disunity and for unity. This has been true of the Christian church through the centuries, but in early nineteenth-century America, forces making for denominational diversification and rivalry were particularly strong. Need was felt for national and group self-identity in the somewhat amorphous new American republic. Both the Enlightenment and Pietism, much as they differed from each other, fostered individualism with its variety of beliefs and life-styles, a tendency further encouraged by the new separation of church and state. And the breathless race to capture the frontier stimulated denominational competition, an effort that paralleled the bitter sectional political rivalry in organizing the new territories.

Miller's denominational zeal had recently been aroused by claims of his Episcopal neighbor on Wall Street, the Rev. John Henry Hobart of Trinity Church, that only a church with bishops in apostolic succession could have a "valid" ministry or sacraments. Miller considered it important that the alternative Presbyterian view of such matters be early instilled into candidates for the ministry.[2] It should, however, be added that reaction to Episcopalian high church claims was not an expressed motive of other founders of Princeton Seminary. A more important denominational stimulus to the founding of Princeton Seminary was the prior organization of seminaries by the Reformed Dutch at New Brunswick, by the Associate Reformed at New York, and by the Congregationalists at Andover. A few years after his letter to Green, Miller was coauthor of an address by the General Assembly to its churches. This address referred to these earlier seminaries, and then warned: "Unless we imitate their laudable example, the consequences will probably be, that in a few years, while they rise and flourish, we shall decline, and fall into a state of discouraging weakness and inferiority."

Miller was closely in touch with Jedidiah Morse, a chief founder of Andover Seminary, gave him hearty encouragement, and was even considered for a professorship there. But Miller, like Ashbel Green, felt that Andover could never adequately serve distinctively Presbyterian interests, and he welcomed the prospect of four great seminaries (the three just mentioned plus a Presbyterian one), each serving its own denomination and each national in scope and influence.[3] Like Ashbel Green and Archibald Alexander after their respective visits to New England, Samuel Miller was strongly committed to a Presbyterian denominationalism which refused to compromise its distinctiveness, and this became a conspicuous characteristic of Princeton Seminary for more than a century.

A second reason which Miller, in his letter of 1805 to Green, offered for proposing a theological seminary was the shortage of ministers, which had already been noted among Presbyterians in Virginia, in Philadelphia, and in the nation as a whole. This shortage involved the serious question, could the church's ministerial leadership be rapidly increased in needed quantity without lowering its intellectual quality? This was the form in which at least three of the leading American denominations (Congregationalists, Presbyterians, and Episcopalians) defined the question. But there was another dimension to the problem of increase of ministers which these and other churches did not at the time fully face, and which they began adequately to define only in the late twentieth century: namely, the problem for religious communication and transmission which was created by cultural diversity. Would highly academic seminaries, organized to produce the traditional type of cultured parish minister, be able adequately to meet the religious needs of uprooted settlers and of others of varying cultures and life-styles?

At the very moment that Miller was writing his letter of 1805 to Green, the Presbyterian Church—if it had been in a mood to interpret such signs of the times—was receiving dire warnings that some innovations in the nature and function of the ministry, as well as a broadening in the concept of the church itself, might be needed. The year before Miller's letter, a General Assembly Committee on the State of Religion, chaired by Miller himself, had commented in a baffled way on the amazing religious revival taking place in Kentucky and Tennessee. The committee, noting the "extraordinary nature" of the revival with its "great bodily agitations," forbore "to express any opinion as to the origin and nature of some of those circumstances which have attended the . . . revivals," but nonetheless found "increasing evidence that it is indeed the work of God."[4] Could the nature of the church be defined in such a way as to make room for both of these two conflicting comments? The very year of this report, Barton W. Stone led out of the Presbyterian Church in Kentucky a "New Light" group, which, uniting later with the movement founded by Thomas and Alexander Campbell, became the important groups of Disciples and Churches of Christ.

Meanwhile, Presbyterian expansion in the revival area led to the organization of the Cumberland Presbytery, in the year that Miller's committee presented its perplexed report. This presbytery immediately became a storm center, with the result that in 1813 a separate Cumberland Presbyterian denomination was organized. In this Kentucky-Tennessee revival, Presbyterians lost not only Stone's "New Lights" and the separating Cumberland Presbyterians, but also many who joined the rapidly growing Shaker movement. In these divisions there were involved important differences of attitude toward such issues as revivalism, Calvinistic theology, ministerial education, the nature of the ministry itself, and even the nature of the church; but underlying all of these disputed matters were basic sociological differences and differences of life-style which greatly increased the difficulty of effective communication, both verbal and nonverbal.[5] Amid the rapid expansion of the times, the Presbyterian Church would soon replace the numbers lost from these divisions. But would the Presbyterian and other denominations, as they founded early seminaries, be able to develop a ministry that could communicate the Gospel on a variety of cultural levels and through the medium of varied types of spiritual experience? The Kentucky-Tennessee estrangements did not augur well for an affirmative answer. This problem at the opening of the nineteenth century constituted a kind of turning point in the history of American Protestantism both numerically and sociologically.

Pietism, in the form of revivalism, has deeply affected the course of American religious history. The Great Awakening of the eighteenth century in effect proposed that self-consciousness of inner religious experience be the test of a true Christian. In a way this basic principle—as Schleiermacher later showed—was in accord with trends in Western culture since the Renaissance that would make the individual, and particularly the individual's consciousness, the source and norm of truth and reality. The Great Awakening had focused on conversion in a manner that went beyond Puritanism,[6] but in spite of Jonathan Edwards's highly creative work, the Great Awakening in general did not radically challenge inherited theological structures.

The second Awakening—particularly in the Kentucky-Tennessee revivals—carried the tendencies of the Great Awakening much further, openly challenging scholastic Calvinism's conceptions of God's sovereignty on which much of that theology had been built. The Enlightenment had already made this challenge from a different basis and with different results. Some among revivalists, in the pattern of the Campbells' "primitivism," challenged all existing creeds and theological structures in favor of the more elastic concept of "the Bible only" as a religious authority. Many converts now joined those who rejected infant baptism, which was historically associated with organic concepts of society, in favor of "believers' baptism" and localism in church government as against authoritative national church structures. These tendencies to reduce structure and central authority reflected some of the deepest trends that had been developing ever since the Renaissance, and also had special appeal to frontiersmen who were the farthest removed of all Americans from the European heritage of feudalism and medieval Catholicism, and therefore the most open to the newer forces of Enlightenment and Pietism. Increasingly, modern culture was starting with inner consciousness and moving out to external reality, rather than starting from the outer cosmos and moving in. Of course, the Kentucky-Tennessee revival was far from thoroughgoing subjectivism, but it did shift some of the emphasis from the theological, ecclesiastical, and liturgical structures of religion to its inner experience. This, of course, is very far from saying that those who historically emphasized religious structure were devoid of religious inwardness. But at the very least, a different emphasis was emerging.

All of this posed a profound challenge to the previously dominant Calvinistic bodies, some of which were already feeling their way toward a median position that would be somewhere between old conceptions of sovereignty and structure on the one hand and greater freedom and individual experience on the other. Presbyterians charged their critics on the Kentucky-Tennessee frontier with inadequate education of the ministry, and there was some truth in the allegation, resulting from necessity amid the shortage of ministers. But more importantly, there was implicit in the frontiersmen's ecclesiastical revolt also a basic criticism of the assumptions underlying traditional theological education. The deeper issue was not the quantity of theological education, but the nature and purpose of that education and its relation to the cultural environment—particularly to an increasing inner-directedness of culture. The

Presbyterian Church, facing this frontier situation, soon came down firmly on the side of traditional structures of theology and church government with a high degree of outer-directedness. The founders of Princeton Seminary were in the forefront of this position.

The result of this Presbyterian policy was what might have been predicted. The denomination lost the numerical predominance which it had shared with Congregationalists, Baptists, and Episcopalians at the end of the American Revolution. But it did become the leading American denomination during the years preceding the Civil War in founding colleges and, jointly with the Congregationalists, for a time led the way in nondenominational cooperation in the various voluntary societies.

In addition to denominational rivalry and the need for a much larger number of ministers thoroughly grounded in the heritage to take care of the expanding and moving population, Miller's letter of 1805 to Green offered a third reason which was widely influential in the American movement to found seminaries: dissatisfaction with the contribution which the colleges were currently making to ministerial education. For Miller this took the form of dissatisfaction with the role of the college on which Presbyterians of that day chiefly depended, the College of New Jersey in Princeton. Thus his letter suggested that the only alternative to organizing an independent seminary was to "direct more of our attention to extend the plan and increase the energy of the Princeton establishment."

Many of the colonial colleges had been founded to make possible the maintenance of a broadly educated ministry, well grounded in classical culture. As time passed, however, these colleges became concerned to meet more adequately the needs of the increasing proportion of students who were not preparing for the ministry. John Witherspoon, as president of the College of New Jersey, by his broad vision and influential contacts, particularly in the middle and southern colonies, gave the college a greatly enlarged role in educating students who became statesmen and nonclerical professionals. As already noted, his curriculum reflected the changing orientation. From the outset, the College of New Jersey had been much influenced by the English "dissenting academies" and their divergence from the curricular rigidity of Oxford and Cambridge universities. This vigorous heritage made further change somewhat easier. Witherspoon retained the Greek and Latin classics, but also made new place for public speaking, offered French as an option, and advanced the teaching of the natural sciences, reflected in his securing of David Rittenhouse's famous "orrery," an ingenious machine which reproduced the motion of the heavenly bodies.[7]

After his death in 1794, Witherspoon was succeeded in the presidency by his eloquent and able son-in-law, Samuel Stanhope Smith, who had been virtually acting president while Witherspoon had been taking a prominent part in the political activities of the Revolutionary War, and again during Witherspoon's declining years. In a plea to the New Jersey Legislature for funds in 1796, President Smith envisaged the college as the nation's leading cultural center south of New York, playing a national role, with enlarged faculty and broadened curriculum.

Smith's most important influence on the curriculum was to reduce the role of the Greek and Latin classics and to expand still further the teaching of the natural sciences. This change drew criticism. The pagan classics had long been considered an essential part of ministerial education. The classics reflected wide understanding of human experience and gave a linguistic and logical training that aided theological conceptualization and pulpit utterance. With the addition of Hebrew, they developed facility in language which was essential to the study of the Scriptures in the original Hebrew and Greek. There were those in the early nineteenth century, on the other hand, who saw no comparable value for the future minister in the study of science. Many were not yet fully aware that science was ushering in an entirely new world view of which theologians and preachers must take account: others, though sensing that basic changes were in the air, preferred to continue with business as usual.

President Smith recognized value in the classics, but discerningly pointed out in a letter to Dr. Benjamin Rush that social change had reduced their worth by making the study of them in America "hasty and superficial."[8] He secured a Scotsman, John Maclean, as professor of chemistry, and told a correspondent, "I am resolved, if possible, to have in future one of the best [collections of scientific] apparatuses on the continent."[9] He was not able to confine to freshman year, as he had hoped to do, the dull drilling in the grammar of ancient languages as then conducted, but he did persuade the trustees to admit students to a special program emphasizing natural science, for which a certificate was awarded instead of the regular diploma.[10] He secured the purchase of extensive scientific equipment, including such items as "Prism, Astronomical Quadrant, Equatorial Instrument, Magnetical Apparatus."[11]

Not only did President Smith's reduced emphasis on classics, with increased attention to science, seem to some to make his curriculum less effective for educating ministers; but along with this was a growing suspicion that his own orthodoxy was not above question. Following the example of Witherspoon, Smith adhered to Scottish philosophical realism, which though its emphasis on "common sense" lent itself readily to a defensive orthodoxy, also contained important strains of Enlightenment rationalism. More of the spirit of the Enlightenment than of strict orthodoxy appeared in the tolerance of diverging views expressed in some of his letters to individuals.

Smith had a strong personal interest in scientific matters. He told a friend that "the character, and manners and state of society" of the

American Indian was "an object that merits the attention of literary societies."[12] He himself wrote a very knowledgeable study of the cause of variety in the human species that had implications concerning the relation of reason to revelation, which was a central issue in much of the theological discussion of the late seventeenth, eighteenth, and early nineteenth centuries. The strictly orthodox, facing the omnipresent emphasis on reason, sought to show that revelation in Scripture was not contrary to reason—was even confirmed by reason—and contained important truth not discoverable by reason. At the opposite extreme, the more radical deists charged that revelation added nothing to reason, was even contrary to reason, and must be rejected. Many positions lay between these extremes. Smith's treatise on variety in the human species, while holding the biblical view that all men are descended from a single pair, made no use of biblical or theological material, but based its argument entirely on natural causes. Of course Smith was no deist, but in the typical spirit of science and the Enlightenment, he was assuming that reason has independent authority. A modern edition of the treatise has clearly pointed up the question which this raised: "If the findings of science and the dictates of Revelation failed to coincide, what then?"[13] Here lay potential peril for the orthodox.

Smith's tendency to give a degree of autonomy to reason, independent of revelation, provoked sharp criticism when he applied the principle to a concrete social institution, marriage. In 1804 a clergyman of Virginia wrote in alarm to Dr. Ashbel Green, who was a trustee of the College of New Jersey, citing a rumor that President Smith was telling his classes that polygamy was not contrary to the law of nature. Green, deeply concerned, ordered one of the tutors to investigate and report back to him exactly what Smith was saying. In his lectures as later published, Smith wrote: "I confess I cannot perceive, from the opinions, and example of the wisest men of antiquity, that the law of nature has provided any definite rule upon the subject [of polygamy]."[14] Thus he seemed to some to imply that there was no moral evil in polygamy for those who were without the light of Christian revelation.

A fire that severely damaged Nassau Hall on March 6, 1802, had the indirect effect of undermining Smith's administration. He and the trustees responded heroically to the emergency, drafting appeals and organizing solicitors throughout the country. Enough was collected to recondition Nassau Hall and erect new buildings. Student enrollment increased, and in 1806 the largest senior class in the history of the college to date was graduated.[15]

But the fire had a sinister by-product. Smith, with deism and the French Revolution fresh in mind, considered the burning to be a deliberate act of students imbued with "irreligious" and "jacobinic" principles.[16] The trustees, too, considered the fire a deliberate act,[17] and tightened college discipline inexorably. Students were required to testify against fellow students, and suspects were punished en masse. President Smith, always the serene gentleman, failed to fight for his own and the faculty's prerogatives against trustee encroachment, and the trustees virtually took over the detailed administration of the college. The situation exploded with a major student riot in 1807. To be sure, this was not a purely local phenomenon. Amid the rapid changes through which the nation was passing, American higher education in general was suffering growing pains with student upheavals a common phenomenon. But the situation reflected very adversely on Smith's administration.

Meanwhile President Smith sought to mend his ecclesiastical fences by increasing the college's emphasis on ministerial preparation. As early as 1758, solicitations in Great Britain by Gilbert Tennent and Samuel Davies had secured an endowment of annual scholarships for ministerial students at the college,[18] which had been increased by later gifts. In September 1803 the college took a decisive step by instituting a "Professorship of Theology."[19] This could develop into what at Harvard and Yale a little later became full-fledged divinity schools. After the Princeton trustees had called Dr. Ashbel Green to the new chair, without President Smith's previous knowledge, Smith urged Green to accept the call, with what inner feelings one can only conjecture.[20] When Dr. Green declined the call, the trustees immediately invited the Rev. Henry Kollock, pastor at Elizabethtown, New Jersey, who accepted the appointment.[21]

Presently the divinity students were granted greatly reduced boarding rates and the use of a separate building known at the time as Divinity Hall.[22] The curriculum taught by Kollock was certainly wide ranging for a one-man operation, touching the major fields of theological study—reading of the Old and New Testaments in the original languages, biblical criticism, "Christian and Jewish antiquities," church history, theology, and "the duties of the pastoral office," taught variously by means of lectures, recitations, and student papers. In addition to these offerings by Professor Kollock, President Smith lectured on metaphysics, natural theology, logic, and Christian evidences. Both teachers attended the weekly two-hour meetings of the Theological Society, a widely used structure in early nineteenth-century theological education, where there was greater opportunity for student initiative than in formal class meetings.[23]

President Smith was so pleased with the setup that he addressed a letter to the Presbyterian General Assembly of 1806, reminding the Assembly that a purpose of the founding of the College of New Jersey had been to educate for the ministry, and that "the Trustees of the institution have ever been attentive to this great object." Summarizing the tuition-free curriculum, he noted that the program was open to graduates of all colleges.[24]

Here, granted a supporting environment, was a very promising beginning that might have developed into a university divinity school. The
Assembly did Smith the courtesy of recommending his program "to the
attention of all their Presbyteries and the youth concerned," but it was
too late. About the year 1803 or 1804, the ecclesiastical tide had
definitely turned against Smith. Smith and Green had been good personal friends. In fact, it was Smith who, long before, had persuaded
Green to choose the ministry rather than the law as a vocation,[25] and
after Green became a trustee at the college, their numerous close contacts for a time were very friendly. But by 1804 Green was confiding to
his nephew that he and Smith were not "on as good terms as we once
were," and Green was spying on him as one who was weakening the
foundations of monogamy.[26]

At about the same time, Samuel Miller also turned against Smith's
regime. Perhaps it was the rumor of Smith's lecture on polygamy that
had tipped the scales, for as late as 1803 Miller had described the college
very favorably and had urged Kollock to accept the call to Princeton.[27]
But by 1805, as seen in his letter to Green, Miller was pressing for a new
institution to educate ministers. In fact, by 1805, Miller was so concerned about the need for more ministers and the supposed inadequacy
of the college under Smith as a source of ministerial supply that he
hurried to write two additional letters on the subject before the General
Assembly was to convene in mid-May, 1805—a second letter to Dr.
Green and one to a mutual friend urging him to emphasize the matter to
Green. In these additional letters, Miller referred again to the desirability of counteracting the Episcopal polemic and to the need for more
ministers, but did not again propose the founding of a theological seminary.[28] Miller, in his original letter of March 12, 1805, to Green had specifically urged that "you will devote your leisure time between this and
the meeting of the Assembly to the consideration of the subject [of founding a theological seminary, or of remedying alleged shortcomings of the
college], and the preparation of some plan to be acted upon by them [by
the Assembly]."[29]

Miller's letter urging that Green propose to the General Assembly of
1805 either a new theological institution or the drastic alteration of ministerial preparation at the college must have given Green pause. After all,
he was a leading trustee of the college. He had been acting president of
the institution in parts of 1802 and 1803 during Smith's absence on an
extended money-raising tour, and had been formally commended by the
board for his services.[30] He was clearly a possible candidate for succession to the purple. If now he, as a trustee, were to use the Assembly to
put pressure on his fellow trustees for drastic revision of the college's
role in ministerial preparation, or if he were to propose a new theological
seminary which would overshadow President Smith's recently introduced theological professorship, such action would certainly be an irre-

versible crossing of the Rubicon. Clearly Green was not ready for such a breach, and instead presented to the Assembly of 1805 an overture which was both constructive and noncontroversial.

The central concern of Green's overture, as of Miller's letters, was the shortage of ministers. But the resemblance ended there. Without even mentioning the founding of a theological seminary, Green's overture after emphasizing the need of perhaps twice the existing number of ministers—provided that they were properly qualified—proposed two remedies for the shortage. One remedy was more adequate financial support of those already ordained, suggested in the face of the renewed attacks on a learned and salaried ministerial profession which increasing democratic tendencies in American life were bringing in their value. The overture's second remedy was to urge greater initiative by presbyteries in seeking out promising ministerial candidates; in directing them to appropriate institutions or to suitable individual instructors; and in subsidizing their education where necessary. No new curriculum or educational structures were proposed. Rather, in the spirit of the times, the emphasis fell on more efficient action—clearer definition of responsibility and more vigorous promotion.

The Assembly postponed action on Green's overture until the next year, asking that meanwhile "the Presbyterians instruct their commissioners [to the next Assembly] respecting the measures which they may think advisable."[31] When the General Assembly of 1806 examined the responses of the presbyteries to the overture on the supply and education of ministers which had been sent down to them the preceding year, it was discovered that there was "a general coincidence of [favorable] sentiment on the subject." The Assembly thereupon appointed Dr. Samuel Miller chairman of a committee to make recommendations that would "carry the design into complete effect."

Miller's committee expressed alarm that the number of vacant churches was increasing proportionally faster than the number of candidates, but, perhaps recognizing the diversity and cultural pluralism of American life, refrained from laying down injunctions binding on all presbyteries. Instead, the committee contented itself with recommending to its presbyteries "to use their utmost endeavours to increase, by all suitable means in their power, the number of promising candidates"; to choose their places of study and inspect their progress; and to report annually to the Assembly what they had done in this matter. Probably because the committee's task was limited to making recommendations concerning the overture referred to it, Miller did not introduce into the report anything of his earlier private proposal of a theological seminary; but the report did declare the increase of a learned ministry to be a denominational priority and emphasized that every local presbytery shared responsibility for such increase.[32]

The same Assembly rejected a proposal to authorize the appointment of catechists, "as it would be dangerous to the church to employ illiterate men as exhorters, or catechetical instructors."[33] Even in the face of its currently unfolding catastrophe in Kentucky, the church was resolutely insisting on a single cultural level of ministry. Potential worshipers who could not tune in on this wave length were left to turn elsewhere.

Meanwhile, in private correspondence, Dr. Samuel Miller continued to press for a theological seminary. Less than two weeks before the General Assembly of 1808, he wrote again to Dr. Green. This letter reflected Green's increasing alienation from President Smith and the fact that by this time Green himself was thinking seriously about the founding of a seminary independent of the college, although he had not yet publicly advocated it. Miller understood that Green, though a trustee of the College of New Jersey, was now so dissatisfied with the institution as to doubt whether the contemplated seminary should be located in Princeton at all. "Perhaps you did not mean to suggest the latter doubt," wrote Miller, who had himself become a trustee of the college the year before.[34] Miller then went considerably beyond anything he echoed from Green to give extended reasons why the proposed seminary should be neither connected with the college nor located in Princeton. He was particularly concerned that the seminary be under a board of control separate from that of the college.

In order to guard against degeneracy, both in principle and practice, to which such institutions [theological schools] are liable, and which most of those in Europe have actually exhibited, I think every Trustee ought to subscribe our Confession of Faith, before taking his seat . . . and perhaps to do this every fifth or sixth year thereafter. But this obviously could not be done by all trustees of Princeton College.

Perhaps nothing could be done for ten years to remedy the alleged shortcomings of the college, so "why wait an hour for a favorable change in that institution?" Miller urged. "Precious time is wasting. . . . Might not a committee be appointed, this spring [presumably at the approaching Assembly], to digest and report a plan to the Assembly of 1809?"[35]

Miller's next letter, four days later, reflected the fact that Green still had misgivings about the seminary project because of the existence of "prejudices . . . against divinity schools." But Miller was persistent. "I was aware" of these, he replied, "but I did hope that we might venture to encounter and resist these prejudices, in the open field, with confident hopes of victory." "If we cannot have a single great school, then I am clearly of opinion that one in each Synod holds the next place on the scale of expediency." Miller hoped, in some unaccountable way which he did not explain, if there must be many seminaries, that these might later all become one, and thus avoid running "the risk of having our church divided into seven or eight parties, or separate interests." He clearly saw that multiple seminaries might become centers of separate viewpoints and divisive loyalties, but was quite unrealistic in assuming, in so vast a country as the United States with such great diversity, that religious pluralism, even within the same denomination, could be avoided. This pluralism was a fact which Princeton Seminary for more than a century would seek to overcome; or, failing that, to resist.

Apparently Green was toying with the idea of a seminary which would teach both the liberal arts and theology, reflecting the fact that the question as to the new form in which theological education in the United States would be institutionalized was still very much in flux. At this stage it is not clear whether Green desired that the proposed seminary itself teach a full four-year, liberal arts program and follow this with a separate and distinct professional curriculum for ministerial preparation; or whether he contemplated some telescoping and integration of the two within the seminary. At any rate, Miller came out clearly for the pattern which was already emerging in the American professions—a traditional and complete liberal arts course after which would be added, in piggyback fashion, a subsequent professional curriculum, very loosely related to it, if at all. "Shall we systematically abandon the idea of requiring our young men to produce a diploma from some college?" Miller asked. "Shall we erect a new college?" Miller's objection to thus including both higher education and theological education in a single institution was on the grounds of expediency rather than of principle; it would unnecessarily offend the College of New Jersey and it would be too costly. The decisive factor in his mind seems to have been that it would be more feasible simply to add by means of a separate institution to the existing liberal arts program of the existing colleges whatever additional theological education might be necessary for a minister, with no suggestion for integrating or even interrelating the two. Green was thinking of proposing an overture at the approaching Assembly of 1808 which apparently would be for a seminary that would include both liberal arts and professional ministerial training in the seminary itself. Miller urged that this idea be postponed until there could be further deliberation; but if Green insisted on going ahead with such a combined institution, Miller would support him.[36]

# 9
# THE COLLEGE AND
# THE SEMINARY

The next advance toward the founding of a seminary was made by Dr. Archibald Alexander while pastor of the Third Presbyterian Church in Philadelphia. In preaching the opening sermon at the General Assembly of 1808 as retiring moderator, Alexander made the first recorded proposal to the General Assembly that the church should found theological seminaries. Like Dr. Miller's letter to Dr. Green, he emphasized the shortage of ministers and, also like Miller, echoed current ecclesiastical criticism of college curricula, doubting

whether the system of education pursued in our colleges and universities [presumably he had in mind the College of New Jersey under President Smith] is the best calculated to prepare a young man for the work of the ministry. The great extension of the physical sciences, and the taste and fashion of the age, have given such a shape and direction to the academical course, that, I confess, it appears to me to be little adapted to introduce a youth to the study of the sacred scriptures.

The statement clearly reflected presuppositions of his own concerning curriculum. While recognizing that the Assembly had already made some constructive proposals for theological education (as in its suggestions of seeking out candidates and raising money growing out of Dr. Green's overture of 1805), he considered these "inadequate to the object." Unlike Miller who favored one central seminary for the church, Alexander proposed regional theological seminaries of the type he had worked for in Virginia. This reflected more of states' rights tradition than Miller's national ideal. "In my opinion," he told the Assembly,

we shall not have a regular and sufficient supply of well qualified ministers of the gospel, until every presbytery, or at least every synod, shall have under its direction a seminary established for the single purpose of educating youth for the ministry, in which the course of education from its commencement shall be directed to this object.[1]

Here, in the church's highest judicatory, was a concrete proposal of an institution that presumably would not include the liberal arts curriculum of a college, but would concentrate entirely on the specialized objective of professional education for the ministry, an academic type which was just emerging on the American scene.

Dr. Ashbel Green had declined to participate in the founding and promotion of Andover Seminary, feeling, on both theological and sectional grounds, that the project was not suited to Presbyterian needs. But Green was not encouraged by Alexander's proposal at the Assembly to press openly for a Presbyterian seminary. Green's break with President Smith had by this time become public. Two years before this, Dr. Benjamin Rush—who had a plethora of ideas on education—in a letter apparently to Green, was advocating theological seminaries separate from colleges. This would be more economical for the students, Rush argued; it would separate them from "the follies and vices" of secular students; it would concentrate on theological subjects; and it would foster godliness.[2] It would seem that Rush was not contemplating a theological education on top of a complete liberal arts course, but as a specialized substitute for the broader liberal arts college curriculum. Green's presbytery of Philadelphia, following his own new public commitment to the seminary idea, instructed its commissioners to the coming General Assembly of 1809 "to use their best endeavors to induce the Assembly to turn their attention to the institution of a theological school, for the education of candidates for the Ministry in our Church, to be established at some central or convenient place within their bounds."[3] If this Philadelphia action reflected Green's views, he seems to have been won over to Miller's desire for a single seminary, and, for the moment at least, to the limitation of its curriculum to theological subject matter.

The Assembly readily responded to the Philadelphia proposal, and appointed President Timothy Dwight of Yale (who was present as a Congregational delegate) chairman of a committee to make recommendations on the matter. The membership of this committee attested the broadening base of the movement for a seminary, in that it included neither Miller, Green, nor Alexander. The Assembly adopted the committee's recommendation to send to the presbyteries for their reply the next year the following three alternative proposals regarding a seminary or seminaries.

1. "One great school in some convenient place, near the centre of the bounds of our Church," as one alternative, had the advantage "that it would be furnished with larger funds, and therefore, with a more extensive library, and a greater number of professors."

The system of education pursued in it would, therefore, be more extensive and more perfect; the youths educated in it would also be more united in the same views; and contract an early and lasting friendship for each other; circumstances which could not fail of promoting harmony and prosperity in the Church. The disadvantages attending this mode would be principally those derived from the distance of its position from the extremities of the Presbyterian bounds.

2. The second proposal was "to establish two schools, in such places as may best accommodate the northern and southern divisions of the Church." The advantages and disadvantages of this proposal, said the committee, "will readily suggest themselves from a comparison of this with the other two."

3. The final proposal was "to establish such a school within the bounds of each of the Synods." The advantages here would be convenience of access, accommodation to regional needs, and the prospect of better response from local loyalties. The disadvantages would be less concentration of funds, resulting in smaller library and faculty and a more limited curriculum and less breadth of acquaintance among the prospective ministers of the church.

If either of the first two alternatives were chosen, the resulting seminary or seminaries should be under the General Assembly; if the last alternative were chosen, the seminaries should be under the control of the respective synods and should be supported by them.[4] The questionnaire was obviously loaded in favor of seminary education, since it assumed that an affirmative answer would be given to one of the alternatives.

Dr. Miller, apprehensive lest a majority of the presbyteries would vote for two or more seminaries, and uncertain where Dr. Green stood on the matter, urged on Green some positive reasons for a single national seminary. Miller's strongest argument was that one seminary would cement the national unity of the church in the face of differences in "Psalmody, Church government, Sealing Ordinances, &c." It is interesting that he did not here mention doctrinal unity as a desideratum. Miller was quite aware of varying sectional and cultural tendencies in the country, but suggested that "the different habits & feelings at present existing in different parts of our country can be consulted by selecting Professors from such different portions of the church as will render them, strictly speaking, representatives of the whole."[5] That is, national unity in the church would be better served, he felt, by bringing differences together where they might achieve mutual understanding and adjustment, rather than leaving them to diverge further separately.

Miller's desire that the contemplated seminary would span and strengthen the national unity of his denomination closely paralleled the feelings of nationalism and patriotism and that were sweeping the country at the time. Two decades earlier, the Constitutional Convention had achieved a closer unity of the states. The superpatriotic "War Hawks" were soon to lead the self-confident young nation into the War of 1812, to be followed by a political "era of good feeling." A national literature based on distinctively American experiences and scenes was about to arise. In the religious sphere, early local voluntary societies were on the point of merging nationally. Jedidiah Morse's *Panoplist,* on the eve of the founding of Andover Seminary, lamenting prevailing divisions among the heirs of New England Puritanism, had emphasized the unifying influence that might be expected from a single institution for theological education. "Difference of education, we find, has produced difference of opinions. Sameness of education, then, we may reasonably hope," an anonymous writer had fondly suggested in Morse's periodical, "will be productive of similarity in opinions."[6] But ecclesiastical Humpty-Dumpties—as both Congregationalists and Presbyterians were to discover—were not to be put together quite so easily or held together.

Miller's and Morse's sectional myopia that sought to foster national unity under the aegis of the Northeast quite overlooked Southern and Western sectionalisms. Alexander's Virginia-born proposal of regional seminaries was more realistic, even if in some respects less efficient. In spite of Miller's temporary victory, it was inevitably the regional pattern of seminaries which ultimately emerged, the geography and sectional feelings of the nation being what they were. Undoubtedly both Miller and Morse also had in view imposing strict orthodoxy on their respective denominations if each could have a single truly "orthodox" seminary.

Samuel Miller was never metaphysically minded, but he had a historian's—even a politician's—keen eye for strategic forces. New England was preempted by Congregationalism, and besides, Miller, Green, and Alexander looked askance at the theological reconstruction in process there. The Middle states would of course be the projected seminary's home base. But the College of New Jersey had strength in the South, and the contemplated seminary might well hope to render major service there, especially as competition from New England would be minimal in that region. The West, including western New York, then being settled by New England Yankees, seemed, in spite of recent setbacks on the Kentucky and Tennessee frontier, to be promising mission territory for a truly national seminary. Ashbel Green, the recipient of Miller's exhortations, was, from his experience in leading the Assembly's Committee of Missions, fully alert to geographical realities.

There was still another aspect to the national character urged for the projected seminary which Miller did not mention and which perhaps was not yet fully realized. If the seminary were made dependent on the General Assembly and thus on the whole church, it would have a deeply vested interest in maintaining and preserving the unity of the denomination. But over against this vested interest in unity, there might arise in the seminary a divisive compulsion to impose on the whole denomination its own conceptions of theological truth. This might tempt the seminary and its supporters to manipulate ecclesiastical forces so that the Assembly, which controlled the seminary, would always be dominated by theological views congenial to the seminary. Or, alternatively, forces hostile to the seminary and to its convictions might gain control of the Assembly. These were some of the potential perils, in contrast with the great possibilities of unity and strength inherent in a seminary of national character for which Dr. Miller was ardently pressing.

During this year, 1809–1810, it was the responsibility of the presbyteries to indicate to the General Assembly of 1810 whether they preferred one national seminary, or two, or more. Dr. Samuel Miller—hardly an impartial judge in the matter—was chairman of the seven-member committee of the 1810 General Assembly which analyzed the votes of the presbyteries. It was found that of the church's thirty-six presbyteries nine did not vote. Six voted against founding any seminary at the time. One presbytery favored two seminaries. The remaining twenty presbyteries divided evenly, ten voting for one seminary and ten for regional seminaries under the respective synods. Miller's committee handled this critical situation with aplomb. First it noted that a majority of all the presbyteries of the church (twenty-one out of the thirty-six) "have expressed a decided opinion in favour of the establishment of a Theological School or Schools." There had been some concern in the church lest, if there were only one official seminary, all presbyteries would be required to send all their candidates to it, and also lest the seminary's faculty might wrest from presbyteries the right to license candidates to preach,[7] fears which proved quite groundless. The committee took advantage of this misunderstanding to draw the somewhat dubious conclusion that "as several of the objections made to the first plan [for a single seminary] are founded entirely on misconception . . . it seems fairly to follow that there is a greater amount of Presbyterial suffrage in favour of a single school, than of any other plan."

On recommendation of Miller's committee, the Assembly voted that it would "immediately attempt to establish a seminary," while leaving its geographical location to future decision. There were to be "at least three Professors, who shall be elected by, and hold their offices during the pleasure of, the General Assembly" who would "give a regular course of instruction in Divinity, Oriental and Biblical Literature, and in Ecclesiastical History and Church Government, and on such other subjects as may be deemed necessary." It was intended to provide for the students tuition-free instruction. Apparently there were some in the church who feared that this formalizing of ministerial education might be injurious to spiritual life—an implied antithesis between mind and heart, and between structure and spontaneity—for the action declared that "the General Assembly . . . do hereby solemnly pledge themselves . . . that in forming and carrying into execution the plan of the proposed seminary, it will be their endeavour to make it, under the blessing of God, a nursery of vital piety, as well as of sound theological learning."

Agents were appointed in all major areas of the church to solicit funds, but presbyteries and synods were left free to support the projected institution or not at their own discretion, and to send or not to send their ministerial candidates to it. The Assembly assured the church that the seminary's professors "shall not in any case be considered as having a right to license candidates to preach the gospel," this prerogative remaining with the presbyteries.[8] Thus Presbyterians sought to assimilate the projected seminary—as they eventually did missionary, publishing, reforming, and other new organizations of the early nineteenth century and later—to their inherited governmental pattern of four ascending judicatories. Such functions were not anticipated when these judicatories were created in the sixteenth century, and the effort to integrate these and other local, regional, and national functions into the earlier judicatorial structure created problems which are still being discussed in the late twentieth century.

Finally, this Assembly of 1810 commissioned Dr. Miller and his friend from Newark, the Rev. James Richards, to draft an address to the churches soliciting their support for the project. The address, probably written by Miller, noted that "near four hundred vacant congregations" required more ministers. Furthermore, the rising general level of education and culture in American society "will render it impossible for the religious teacher to maintain weight of character and permanent influence, if his knowledge be scanty, and his literature circumscribed." Perhaps there was also a hidden intimation here that the education of the average minister, under pressure of the shortage of personnel, had declined not only relatively, but absolutely. The address called pointed attention to the fact which Miller had previously emphasized to Green that three other denominations—the Dutch Reformed, the Associate Reformed, and the Congregationalists—had already founded seminaries, and were threatening to leave Presbyterians behind in denominational competition. The concentrated efforts of a very few had secured the formal adoption by the church of the seminary proposal. How successful would they be in broadening the base of support and making the undertaking viable?

Part of the action of this Assembly was to create a committee of seven chaired by Dr. Green and including Miller, Alexander, Richards, and a New York colleague of Miller, Dr. John B. Romeyn, "to digest and prepare a plan of a Theological Seminary, embracing in detail the fundamental principles of the institution, together with regulations for guiding the conduct of the instructors and the students, and prescribing the best mode of visiting, of controlling, and supporting the whole system." The committee was instructed to report to the next Assembly.[9] Five of the seven members were trustees of the College of New Jersey, and a sixth was soon afterwards elected to that board.

Dr. Green himself drafted a "plan" for the seminary, which was presented to the Assembly of 1811 for its action.[10] The plan was admirably composed, setting forth in clear language the evangelical presuppositions of the time, and providing brief but adequate guidelines for the seminary's structure. Like all viable constitutions—with due respect to Green's claim of originality—it grew out of the concrete situation, skillfully summarizing motive and structural suggestions, many of which had been voiced during the preceding years of discussion.

Dr. Green's draft of the plan contained a highly controversial article entitled "Of the Theological Academy." It should be noted that Andover Seminary, founded two years before, was institutionally connected with a previously existing academy, Phillips Andover. But the curriculum in Green's skeletal proposal of an "academy," with its definitely collegiate content, does not indicate direct influence from Phillips Andover. The theological academy of Green's Plan was to be "established, at the place of the Theological Seminary, and in connexion with it," and to be under the same board of directors as the seminary. It was to have two professors, one of "languages" and the other of "mathematics and natural philosophy," both to be chosen by the General Assembly. These professors need not be ministers, but they must make the same confessional subscription as the seminary professors. Professors of the seminary would contribute to the curriculum of the academy by teaching courses in Hebrew, logic, metaphysics, moral philosophy, rhetoric, and belles lettres. At least two-thirds of the students admitted to the academy must be preparing for theological study. That this intended "academy" was not merely preparatory to college but also included a college course is evident both from its curriculum and from the explicit statement: "The studies and exercises of the Academy shall be calculated to prepare youth for the Theological Seminary, from the beginning to the end of their Academical course."[11] This proposal reminds one of Roman Catholics' beginning of the training of priests in their early years in order to assure full indoctrination and church loyalty. Before the end of September 1810, the completed draft of the plan was being circulated for study and was being discussed long before the Assembly convened.[12]

A month before the Assembly of 1811 met, Miller, with great interest, commented to Green on an idea connected with the name of their fellow trustee of the College of New Jersey, Governor Bloomfield. Bloomfield's proposal seems to have contemplated founding a theological seminary which would be at once autonomous and yet organically connected with the College of New Jersey. Dr. Romeyn, a New York pastor and a trustee of the college, was enthusiastic for the idea, but the practical-minded Miller had little hope of its acceptance by the trustees, since it would involve renunciation by the trustees of their proper responsibilities.[13]

At the time the Assembly of 1811 convened, three interrelated basic questions concerning the projected seminary still remained unanswered.

1. What connection, if any, would the seminary have with the College of New Jersey? Would it be under the college trustees, or under the General Assembly, or could a via media be devised which would relate it in some way to both? One possibility, if given strong church support, would have been a fully developed theological department or divinity school at the college completely controlled by the trustees. At that time, and especially a little earlier, this would undoubtedly have been welcomed by President Smith and the college trustees. But for reasons already noted, some of the more outspoken church leaders would not support such a plan. There was, of course, the opposite possibility of a separate seminary under the complete control of the General Assembly. But a few in the church and even among the college trustees were toying with the idea of some kind of incorporation into the college which would, however, not place the seminary under the sole control of the college trustees.

2. In what place would the seminary be located? If a site other than Princeton were chosen, the preceding question would automatically receive a negative answer. If Princeton were chosen, whatever options were inherent in the situation would still remain open.

3. What would be the scope of the new seminary's curriculum? Would it define itself as a professional school of the type that was already emerging in the United States among physicians and clergymen; concentrate entirely on postgraduate work in the theological disciplines; and require of its students as a prerequisite to entrance, graduation from a liberal arts college? Or would the new seminary attempt a curriculum which included liberal arts on the college level along with ministerial professional studies? One can only conjecture whether, if the latter type of program had developed in America after the pattern of many European universities, it might have contributed to closer integration of the curricula of undergraduate and professional studies (with perhaps some reduction in the aggregate length of time) than was actually achieved in the American pattern. Miller, in his wiser moments, had clearly foreseen the financial impossibility of so ambitious a project for his own day,[14] but allowed himself to be beguiled by the dream.

When Green's committee included the proposal of an academy-college along with a theological seminary in the plan that it recommended to the Assembly of 1811, it was confronting the College of New Jersey with a direct competitive challenge at a moment when the college was in a much weakened condition. The college's seemingly promising professorship of theology had lapsed in 1806 when Professor Kollock had resigned because of paucity of students in the program.[15] Although President Smith himself resumed responsibility for theological instruction, and although financial aid was maintained for divinity students their number remained small. In fact, student enrollment in the entire college, after reaching a peak in 1806, had declined by 1812 to less than a hundred.[16] The college funds were low, and President Smith was making a special effort to secure increased church patronage. Under these circumstances, the creation of a denominationally maintained seminary would almost certainly supersede President Smith's flagging theological department. But much more seriously, if a college, such as proposed in the seminary plan, were to be established along with the seminary, under the direct control and support of the church, it would be a dangerous competitor of the College of New Jersey for both funds and students.

In the autumn, shortly following the 1810 meeting of the General Assembly, the college trustees appointed a committee, chaired by President Smith, "to meet a Committee of the General Assembly of the Presbyterian Church of the United States of America and to confer with them on the subject of establishing a Theological Seminary for the Presbyterian Church and to report what they shall do on this subject to this Board."[17] This trustees' committee, in its communication to the General Assembly of 1811, emphasized the college's own services to the church, stating that the college had been founded "principally with a view to promoting the general interests of religion," and that it annually graduated candidates for the ministry. The trustees' committee also emphasized the recent founding of the college's theological professorship, currently occupied by President Smith, and noted that a solicitation of funds for this program had already begun, when the trustees learned of the General Assembly's interest in founding a theological seminary of its own. The trustees, fearing that such simultaneous competition for funds would "look like a schism among the friends of the growing institution" (the "institution" being the college's theological program) and would injure both projects, temporarily suspended these promotional efforts and, through this committee, presented the following six proposals to the General Assembly.

1. That the Assembly establish their contemplated institution at Princeton "under the advantages of the charter of the college of New Jersey," a charter which the committee described as "most extensive in its powers & privileges" and "probably more complete than could be at present obtained for any institution of a similar nature."

2. That the theological seminary students have the use of the college buildings "& all advantages appertaining to the students of the college."

3. That the theological funds of the college "be thrown into a common fund with those which the Assembly may obtain for the same purpose."

4. That the Assembly appoint a committee "to meet a committee of the Trustees of the College with like powers to form a detailed constitution for said seminary, containing the fundamental principles of the said union, never to be changed or altered without the mutual consent of both parties."

5. Previous to ratification of such an agreement, both parties shall be free to solicit funds for their separate enterprises.

6. "That the principal direction of the college in its instruction, government, & discipline, be gradually turned to promote the objects of the Theological institution in proportion as the funds can be so augmented as to compleat it, on the most enlarged scale."

The proposals were signed by the committee's chairman, President Smith.

It is clear that the college trustees were apprehensive of losing the support—both moral and financial—of the General Assembly and of the denomination which it represented. Their sixth proposal even offered (in the case church contributions should warrant) to make the education of candidates for the ministry for the college's chief academic objective, as had been the case before the advent of Presidents Witherspoon and Smith. The trustees proposed that the new seminary be founded in the college's charter and share the college's buildings and theological resources. While nothing was here said specifically as to who would control the project, the proposal of the college trustees logically pointed to absorption of the enterprise by the college, presumably in the form of a divinity school Any form of dual control by college trustees and General Assembly, such as had been suggested by Governor Bloomfield, was not at all feasible in view of the college's independence of all ecclesiastical control ever since its founding.

The General Assembly, meeting in May 1811, received this communication from the college trustees before acting on the plan for a seminary. In response, the Assembly appointed a committee, with Dr. Archibald Alexander as chairman, to meet a committee of the college trustees

to frame the plan of a constitution for the Theological Seminary, containing the fundamental principles of a union with the Trustees of that College, and the Seminary [the theological department of the college] already established by them, which shall never be changed or altered without the mutual consent of both parties, provided that it should be deemed proper to locate the Assembly's Seminary at the same place with that of the College.

This action of the Assembly seemed to relate location in Princeton to some kind of organic connection between the college and the projected seminary, which was not spelled out in the communication from the trustees' committee, but was implied in it.

At the same time, the Assembly, desiring to keep open the option of locations for the seminary other than at Princeton, empowered its committee also "to receive any propositions which may be made to them for locating the said seminary in any other situation if it be found expedient." The Assembly then proceeded to narrow the question of location by determining that "the rivers Raritan and Potomac be the limits within which the seminary shall be located." This eliminated New York, as well as Virginia and points farther south, none of which had been seriously considered as sites, and virtually restricted the selection to Princeton or eastern Pennsylvania, both of which were being discussed.

The Assembly then took additional action on the proposed plan. It added a paragraph at the end of the plan's introduction to announce that one of the reasons for organizing the seminary was "to found a nursery for missionaries to the heathen." Perhaps this insertion was inspired by the fact that foreign missions by American Calvinists had begun the year before with the organization by Congregationalists of the American Board of Commissioners for Foreign Missions. Thus Princeton Seminary was committed at the outset to the support of overseas mission. After making a few slight additional amendments, the Assembly adopted the plan, except that it postponed until the next year action on the articles dealing with the library and with the theological academy, the latter no doubt being postponed to await the outcome of the conference between the Assembly's committee and the college trustees' committee.[19]

Shortly after the adjournment of the General Assembly, President Smith, Dr. Miller, and four others called a special meeting of the college trustees for June 25, 1811, to consider the report of the trustees' committee, of which President Smith was chairman. Apparently the board rejected the report of this committee. Actually the committee's proposals had already been superseded by the Assembly's new action in placing the proposed seminary under the General Assembly. The most important question still pending was, would the Assembly create also a new college? The college trustees proceeded immediately to appoint a new committee, chaired this time by Dr. Green and not including President Smith, "to meet tomorrow morning with a Committee of the General Assembly." The board then adjourned till the next afternoon, awaiting the report of its new committee. At the time appointed, the committee "reported that they had entered into an agreement with the Committee of the General Assembly—after consideration the said agreement was unanimously approved."[20]

The agreement thus adopted between the representatives of the College and of the General Assembly implied that if a supplementary institution were attached to the proposed seminary, it would be only "an elementary school, for the instruction of youth in such learning as usually precedes their entrance into college." The language of this section did not prevent the Seminary from having a secondary level academy affiliated with it; but it promised the aid and good offices of the College of New Jersey to an affiliated program only on the express condition that it be "elementary" and previous to "entrance into college." In the context of the discussion within the church that had preceded, and especially in view of the section of the seminary plan on the academy-college that was still awaiting adoption by the Assembly, this article of the agreement must be construed as a renunciation by the church of any intention of founding a new college in connection with the seminary. In the light of financial realities any idea of the church's creating simultaneously a seminary and a college in the same location had been something of a pipe dream, but it had seemed a real peril to the college, and that danger was now permanently removed.

The college agreed, on its part, that "while the Theological Seminary shall remain at Princeton, no professorship of theology shall be established in the College." The "professorship of theology" as it had previously functioned was a branch of the college curriculum intended to prepare students for the professional ministry. The obvious intent of this provision was to renounce on the part of the college its function of preparing candidates for the ministry, rather than to specify what academic courses would or would not be taught. Thus it was mutually agreed that the seminary would not be a college, and that the college would not include the function of professional ministerial training. By this agreement, basic areas of possible competition between the two institutions were eliminated. There was thus, in the situation that prevailed at that time, a definite *quid pro quo* for each party to the agreement.

The college trustees evinced a strong desire to have the seminary located in Princeton. For some years church influence on the college's board of trustees had been increasing. About the year 1807—the year when Dr. Miller was elected to the board—a number of others were elected who also voiced the criticisms of President Smith's administration current in the church. Such board members, for example, as Green, Miller, Romeyn, Richards, and Hillyer, to name no others, were in close correspondence with each other and sought to bring Smith and the college into line with educational views then dominant in the church. The effort to bring the seminary to Princeton was closely related to this objective. Generous promises were made if the seminary would locate in Princeton. The exclusive control of the seminary by the General Assembly was acknowledged, and there were granted free use of the college library, "every practicable accommodation" in the college buildings, free custodial service of the seminary's funds, and the right of the Assembly "to erect at their own expense, on the grounds belonging to the College, such buildings for the accommodation of pupils and professors as they may judge proper," so long as this did not interfere with the functioning of the college.

To become operative, this agreement depended upon approval by the General Assembly of 1812, but before that Assembly convened, a dispute arose in New York which threatened to influence the location of the seminary and even its character. Miller himself was near the center of the storm, which foreshadowed later "Old School"–"New School" differences. "Hopkinsianism," the moderate alteration of Calvinism previously discussed, became a sharp issue among New York Presbyterians shortly after three leading Presbyterian churches in that city, on the initiative of Dr. Samuel Miller, dissolved their longstanding "collegiate" connection in 1809, with some friction inevitably resulting. Miller and his colleague Dr. Philip Milledoler became pastors, respectively, of two of the churches, while the third, the Brick Church, was left without a minister. After at least four unsuccessful efforts to secure a minister, the Brick Church called to its pastorate Gardiner Spring, a young Congregational licentiate, a Yale graduate, and a former student at Andover Seminary.[21] He was accused of holding "Hopkinsian" views, and it was principally the powerful support of Dr. Miller which persuaded New York Presbytery in 1810 to receive him in spite of these accusations and to install him in the Brick Church pastorate.[22] It was perhaps a feeling of being partly responsible for the predicament of the Brick Church resulting from the dissolving of its collegiate connection that inspired Miller to defend this alleged "Hopkinsian." Also, Miller was in friendly relations with the champion of New England orthodoxy, Jedidiah Morse, who had recently set an example of cooperating with Hopkinsians in founding Andover Seminary. Besides, Miller showed a strange lifelong tendency to fluctuate between the extremes of generous conciliation and impatient controversy. He was, on many occasions, quite broad in outlook and policy.[23]

The General Assembly of 1812, meeting in Philadelphia, was scheduled to decide on the location of the proposed seminary and to act on the agreement with the trustees of the College of New Jersey. News of the theological imbroglio in New York was circulating in the Assembly cloakrooms. Suspicion of the orthodoxy of Dr. Miller and of two ministers of northern New Jersey—Dr. James Richards and Dr. Asa Hillyer—was being whispered, and there were suggestions that the seminary be located in Chambersburg, Pennsylvania, far from the sources of "heresy." On Saturday morning, May 23, the question of the seminary's location was discussed on the floor of the Assembly, but postponed to the next week. That afternoon there gathered at the home of Dr. Ashbel Green an informal but crucially important meeting of more than a dozen, at least ten of whom soon afterwards were elected directors of the seminary. This informal gathering fully cleared Miller, Richards, and Hillyer of any suspicion of "heresy," and at the same time ensured for the seminary a base broad enough to include as directors Miller, Richards, and Hillyer, who openly favored tolerating Hopkinsianism. Milledoler, the arch foe of Hopkinsianism, was so chagrined by this policy of toleration that he withdrew from the denomination the next year.[24]

The way was now clear for the Assembly to decide on the location of the seminary, a question which was closely related to the proposed agreement with the college trustees. An alienated former colleague of Miller in New York who resided near Chambersburg strongly urged Chambersburg as the site, arguing that if the seminary were located in Princeton it would in time dominate the General Assembly to a dangerous degree.[25] But after prolonged discussion, the Assembly somewhat tentatively "Resolved, That Princeton be the site of the Theological Seminary, leaving the subject open as to its permanency," and later the same day adopted the agreement with the college trustees.[26] Meanwhile the college trustees appointed Dr. Green chairman of a committee to persuade the Assembly to make permanent the seminary's location in Princeton, which the Assembly did the next year.[27]

In accordance with the spirit of the agreement with the College of New Jersey trustees, the Assembly of 1812 declined to adopt the section of the plan providing for an academy-college, a proposal which had created such concern in the college, action on which had been postponed from the previous year. Thus the form of the proposed theological seminary had taken definite shape. It had now been decided that an academy-college would not be organically connected with the college nor under the control of the college trustees; and that it would be directly under the denominational General Assembly. Various possibilities had been canvassed, and the result was very evidently the interplay of strongly held convictions and particular circumstances.

At no time previous to the agreement with the college was there a rejection on principle of a divinity school connected with and controlled by the college, provided the theological position of the college could be held to denominational orthodoxy. But of course that was impossible and, from the point of view of the college, highly undesirable. Nor was the idea of founding a new college and seminary in conjunction, both under denominational control, rejected in principle. But the agreement with the College of New Jersey trustees, now ratified by the General Assembly, ruled it out. It should be added, however, that so ambitious a plan was really financially impossible from the outset. What emerged on the American scene, then, not only at Andover and at Princeton, but repeatedly, were theological seminaries independent of colleges and universities, requiring for admission graduation from a liberal arts college and concentrating on studies preparatory to the professional ministry. As compared with college- or university-related divinity schools, there was a danger—not necessarily fulfilled—of isolation from the critical forces of contemporary culture; and there was, on the other hand, the decided advantage of more direct connection with the living church and the worshiping parish. This was the danger and the opportunity which the new seminary confronted for the long future.

The General Assembly of 1812, after amending the plan of the seminary to increase the number of directors to thirty, elected this number. At their first meeting the next month, the directors selected Dr. Ashbel Green as their president, a position which he held until his death in 1848.[28]

The board of directors underwent many changes of personnel, particularly during the four or five years immediately following, but its composition as originally chosen by the Assembly is interesting from several perspectives.[29] In accordance with the provisions of the plan, twenty-one of the thirty members were ministers. Unlike the emerging voluntary societies, where lay influence was very great, the clergy were dominant here, thus facilitating strong theological emphasis. It was a distinguished group, eleven of the thirty (eight ministers and three laymen) being listed in the *Dictionary of American Biography*. Three of the group, including Eliphalet Nott, the famous president of Union College, were or later became college presidents, while two were later professors at other Presbyterian seminaries. Nine of the board were also trustees of the College of New Jersey, reflecting the close interrelation of the two institutions at the time. Two had been officers in the American Revolution. One was the philanthropist after whom Rutgers College was named. Eleven, including five of the laymen, were notably active in the very important voluntary society movement, one, the Rev. Robert Finley, soon afterwards founding the American Colonization Society. Of the seven most recent moderators of the General Assembly, all but one were directors.

In view of Miller's far-sighted emphasis on the national character of the seminary, the geographical distribution of the directors is also of interest. New York was overwhelmingly predominant, eight of the board being from New York City, compared to four from Philadelphia, which was still the largest city. Miller's influence, in spite of a number of recent tensions, undoubtedly was a factor in this New York strength, since seven of the eight were from churches that had been part of the collegiate union or offshoots from it. If to New York City are added three from upstate New York and six from northern New Jersey, the total would be seventeen from New York City's sphere of influence. The four from Philadelphia plus two from eastern Pennsylvania and two from Princeton village, making a total of eight, might be considered as lying geographically within a Philadelphia sphere. This great numerical preponderance of New York is interesting, especially in the light of later somewhat different geographical alignment of forces within the church. One member from Pittsburgh was the most western representative. There were three from the South—one each from Maryland, Virginia, and South Carolina. As this year 1812 antedated the great canal and railroad building era, the geographical concentration of representation in the East did not foredoom the national stature that was contemplated for the institution. Theologically, the board included some who would have no truck with "Hopkinsianism," but also some, like Miller, who were willing to tolerate it.

As for the College of New Jersey, the prevailing theological attitude among its trustees by this time was similar to that which controlled the General Assembly and the infant seminary. Miller told a correspondent in 1811 that the college was "now in a fair way of being restored to its former evangelical character."[30] On August 13, 1812, the college trustees elected a vice-president, and the same evening President Smith, feeling that he had been deliberately superseded, resigned. The next day he presented a characteristically dignified written resignation on the grounds of the ill health which had long afflicted him. The trustees accepted his resignation, granted him an annuity, and, at his request, purchased his library. The same day they "unanimously" elected Dr. Green as his successor. Some had desired Dr. Miller for the post, but the evening before, Miller had pressed every trustee to vote for Green.[31] Smith accepted the blow with the unruffled serenity that had characterized his entire life-style, but a sharp comment to his son-in-law several years later concerning his successor's failure as a disciplinarian revealed how deeply he had been wounded.[32] President Smith later came to be recognized as potentially one of the ablest American educators of his generation.

The village of Princeton, where the General Assembly decided to locate its seminary, was founded on land once owned by William Penn and later purchased by Richard Stockton, grandfather of the Richard Stockton who signed the Declaration of Independence. Located a short distance northeast of the line dividing East Jersey from West Jersey, it was first settled by Quakers in the closing years of the seventeenth century. The moving of the College of New Jersey from Newark to Princeton in 1756 brought into the little village promise of a distinguished future. The Revolutionary War projected the community into the national limelight. General Washington's brilliant maneuvers against Lord Cornwallis at Trenton and Princeton bolstered the colonials' drooping spirits, but enemy soldiers pillaged the homes of the village's two signers of the Declaration of Independence, President John Witherspoon and Richard Stockton, and burned down the house of Jonathan Dickinson Sergeant, another prominent patriot, whose daughter later married

Samuel Miller.[33] The college's Nassau Hall was honored in being a temporary seat of the Continental Congress amid its forced peregrinations. Attracted principally by proximity to the college, the seminary in 1812 cast its lot in this already historic village, situated midway between the young nation's two largest cities, Philadelphia and New York. There was some current debate in the country about the relative merits of urban or rural settings for colleges and professional schools, and, as transportation developed, partisans of the seminary were wont to claim some of the advantages of both types of location.

Who would be chosen as the seminary's first professor? Early in 1810, Miller, consistently with his strong desire that the proposed seminary should be national in character, urged that of the three professorships ultimately contemplated "at least one . . . ought to be selected from the South or West, in order to conciliate those portions of our church." The professors, he added a little later, should be selected "from such different portions of the church as will render them, strictly speaking, representative of the whole."[34] Miller's strongly national outlook appeared again when, writing as a trustee of the college in 1812, he urged that a Western or Southern man be choosen for the vice-presidency of that institution.[35] Similarly, Philip Lindsly, referring to the College of New Jersey a decade later, "had hoped to see a citizen of Virginia as the head of our college."[36] Southern connections were very important to both the college and the seminary. Though extant records do not mention it as a motive, the continuing intention of Virginians to organize a seminary of their own undoubtedly increased the desirability of securing a southerner for the seminary faculty.

The Assembly's election of the first professor in 1812 was a solemn occasion, preceded by "a season for special prayer." On recommendation of the new board of directors, the Assembly fixed the salary at $1800 and a house, a generous stipend for the infant seminary, equal to the salary received by pastors of some of the largest churches, and comparing favorably with the salary of $2,000 paid by the College of New Jersey to its new president, Dr. Green.[37] The Assembly's choice fell on Archibald Alexander to be "Professor of Didactic and Polemic Divinity."[38] He was clearly in the good graces of the college, having received their honorary doctorate of divinity two years before.[39]

Whether or not Miller had maneuvered for Alexander's election, Alexander admirably supplied the Southern connection which Miller had urged. But Alexander's qualifications were far more than merely geographical or strategic. Educated before America had theological seminaries or divinity schools, and long before American doctoral programs had been instituted, and entering upon his professional duties shortly before the American trek to German universities began, Alexander was one of the more learned and scholarly American clergymen of his generation. Given existing presuppositions, the seminary could hardly have chosen a man better qualified to lay its foundations and to cast what was to be its mold for more than a century.

The original plan of the seminary called for "not less than three professors." The third professorship was slightly delayed, but the General Assembly of 1813 proceeded to the election of a second professor. On the nomination of the seminary's board of directors, the Rev. Samuel Miller, D.D., pastor of the First Presbyterian Church of New York, was chosen, at the same salary as Dr. Alexander.[40] Miller had already attained much distinction. Born in 1769, he was three years older than Alexander. Moderator of the General Assembly the year before Alexander, he was active and influential in denominational affairs. He is best known among twentieth-century scholars for having published, nine years previously, his two volumes, *A Brief Retrospect of the Eighteenth Century,* a distinguished pioneering work in the history of American culture.

Clearly, the American seminary movement, of which Princeton Seminary was an early and distinguished representative, was seeking increased professional competence in the ministry. It is therefore important to examine the new emphasis on professionalism that was developing in America at this time and the implications of this emphasis for curricula that would most effectively prepare competent professionals.

# 10
# MINISTERS AS PROFESSIONALS

What kind of minister would Princeton Seminary seek to produce, and what functions would he be educated to perform? A specific concept of the ministry and a theological curriculum are, or at least should be, closely interrelated. How did Presbyterians in 1812 conceive of the ministerial profession?

Nineteenth-century Presbyterians inherited—with some changes, to be sure—the lofty conception of the ministry set forth by their sixteenth- and seventeenth-century Reformed forebears. John Calvin emphasized that God was the sole ruler of his church and exercised this rule by his Word. But because he is not visibly present, "he uses the ministry of men to declare openly his will," and this human ministry is "the chief sinew by which believers are held together in one body." "Through the ministers . . . he [Christ] dispenses and distributes his gifts to the church." Thus, though the ministers' authority is not given to them personally, but solely "to the Word whose ministry is entrusted to them," nevertheless, "God often commended the dignity of the ministry to all possible marks of approval in order that it might be held among us in highest honor and esteem, even as the most excellent of all things."[1] Thus the office of Reformed "minister of the word of God" contained in it seeds of both humility and pride.

The duties and powers of the office were manifold. The minister was to proclaim the word of God by preaching, by administering the sacraments, by pastoral visitation and counseling, and by catechetical teaching. He also exercised the church's awesome "power of the keys" by preaching God's judgment and forgiveness and—in conjunction with lay elders—by administering discipline.[2] The minister also performed marriages, though not always in the earliest period of the Reformation, and inherited some of the powers of the medieval bishop such as participating in ordaining new ministers, and, along with ruling elders, in governing the church both locally and beyond the limits of his own congregation. One might not enter this divinely appointed office without a "call," and the minister was established in it by the act of ordination, which later (though not always in the earliest days) involved the "laying on of hands." Ministry was to the whole church; so ordination was not repeated if the minister moved to another congregation.[3] The academic gown which the Reformed minister wore reflected the academic attainments which his office presupposed and the cultural influence which it was assumed that he would exert. The new clergy of the Reformation era—commonly married and having families—constituted "a new social and vocational class," with its roots in the burgher or middle class,[4] which in nonfeudal America became the highest social class.

In eighteenth-century America this high view of the ministry was still held by Presbyterians, although by that time there were audible overtones of defensiveness. Thus, Samuel Finley, later president of the College of New Jersey, declared in 1752: "A minister of the Gospel is a grand and illustrious Character. . . . In this Function God employed the most excellent Men on Earth." In fact, he later said, "Gospel Ministers succeed in the Room of the Old Testament Prophets," but they should administer their sacred office with humility, as did the late Samuel Blair in whom "condescensions and authority were duly tempered."[5]

It was emphasized, especially by those who were heirs of the Great Awakening, that a minister must be spiritual, and that he should "preach the Gospel with pathetic Earnestness and affectionate solemnity. . . . To lull our Hearers asleep with languid Harangues upon Matters of Everlasting Consequence and infinite Importance . . . this is the most shocking incongruity in Nature."[6] The minister should be not only an earnest preacher but a "skillful Casuist," meaning in this context effective in pastoral counseling. Samuel Stanhope Smith, speaking amid the changes and political animosities that came in the wake of the American and French Revolutions, saw the clergyman also as a supporter of social order, praising the minister who was "an enemy to faction and sedition—abhoring those intrigues, cabals, and slanders that tend to disturb the peace of the state."[7]

To fill this high office, a minister must have solid learning. "T'is our business," said the eloquent Great Awakening preacher Samuel Davies, "at once to familiarize the sublimest Truths to the meanest Capacities. . . . A little smattering of human literature, a superficial Acquaintance with Divinity and experimental Religion, a stock of useless Pedantries, a volubility of Tongue, a Dexterity to amuse the populace with empty Harangues; these are not sufficient."[8] Finley emphasized that the minister "should be able to apprehend things clearly, Methodize his Conceptions regularly, and Reason solidly." He should study "the learned languages, Rhetoric, and Philosophy." He should above all be familiar with divinity, Scripture, and "cases of conscience," meaning variously ethics or pastoral counseling.[9]

With due respect to the Christian earnestness and extensive influence of these good men, a later, more informal and democratic age finds their image of the ministry excessively self-conscious and somewhat pompous. Great emphasis was laid on the proper proportion in which dignity, authority, and "condescension" were to be combined in the minister's bearing and even in his facial expression. Eighteenth-century genteel moderation with its careful balancing of qualities was given a distinctively clerical application. The minister "should neither put on a morose Reservedness, nor soppish Levity; but an affable Gravity, and an inviting Distance."[10] Of the Rev. Aaron Burr it was said that he possessed, in the pulpit, "an Air of mild Gravity, and genuine Benignity."[11] Gilbert Tennent was described as "grave" and "reserved," but as also "affable" and "condescending."[12] Early in the nineteenth century, the bearing of the Rev. Dr. MacWhorter of Newark was portrayed as "affectionate, paternal, and dignified; calculated to inspire respect and dependence and to repel the approach of presumptuous familiarity."[13] This carefully studied posture was obviously intended to preserve high official status for the minister, while still indicating his accessibility for service to the rank and file.

If this part of the picture appears excessively complacent, there were evidences from the same speakers that the eighteenth-century Presbyterian clergyman was also quite consciously on the defensive. Thus Davies warned his fellow ministers that "we should preach the Gospel of Peace with 'a peaceable Spirit' " and should not be "peevish and touchy under Calumny."[14] Finley felt it necessary to defend the ministerial office against social disparagement: "Go to, then, all ye who . . . think it only becomes the meanest of the People, who have no better shift to procure a living."[15] Samuel Stanhope Smith, conveniently forgetting Witherspoon's achievements and even his own, offered the discouraged generalization that "to embrace the office of the ministry is, in our country, to abandon the road of civil honors and emoluments. It is . . . to confine genius and talents to an humble sphere from which they can never hope to emerge."[16]

At the time Princeton Seminary was founded in 1812 and in the years immediately following that event, the concept of the ministry among American Christians in general was a subject of sharp debate, and ministerial functions were undergoing important change. The influence of the "left wing" of the Reformation, which tended to be critical of a professional ministry, had long been strong in America. The Great Awakening had openly criticized "unconverted" and unspiritual ministers, and frontier gatherings were achieving startling popularity and success under the leadership of very informal ministers or of no ministers at all. National "separation of church and state," together with the ending, somewhat later, of the last establishments in individual states, meant that no clergy would receive prestige from a state church or have its professional standards enforced by civil government. Now, more than before, the clergy must secure popular support from an increasingly democratic society. Alexander Campbell's denunciation of the ministerial profession was a sign of the times, well suited to the Jacksonian Era's glorification of the "common man."

The upsurge of evangelicalism that followed the Second Awakening, along with rising democratic tendencies and the developing efficiency and confidence of American mercantile and other economic interests, witnessed a great expansion not only of religious activity in general, but of the influence of laymen in particular. This development of the layman's role competed with the clergy for control of religious affairs; tended to reduce emphasis on theology and other aspects of the Christian heritage and with it all the specialized knowledge that was the ministerial profession's special possession. The rise of lay influence also gave great impetus to Christian unity and in general contributed toward an increasing tendency to identify religious and secular goals.

In no area of the religious life of the time was lay influence more conspicuous than in the rising voluntary society movement. Thus the American Bible Society Constitution of 1816 limited its board of managers to thirty-six laymen, though every minister "who is a member of the Society" was given "the same powers as a Manager himself." The American Tract Society was still more laical, specifying that eleven members of its sixteen-member executive committee must be laymen. Only laymen were eligible to be officers or managers of the American Sunday School Union, though clergymen were invited to attend its meetings.[17]

Within the denominations also, increasing lay activity was needed if the vast work of outreach was to be accomplished, and this contributed to further expansion of lay influence. The shift in power within church structures of course was not without its tensions. Some clergy feared that laymen were trespassing on ministerial prerogatives,[18] and it was characteristic of the democratic spirit of times that some laymen were concerned lest the emphasis on ministerial education represented by the founding of Princeton Seminary would increase the ambition and political power of ministers.[19]

Not only left-wing groups opposed a professional ministry, but even the Presbyterian General Assembly of 1811 found it necessary to refute critics of a salaried ministry within its own communion; and Archibald Alexander, in a farewell sermon to his Philadelphia congregation the next year, felt constrained to defend the propriety and necessity of an economically supported ministry against strong sectarian tendencies in Philadelphia.[20] A New Englander layman carefully calculated the rather meager salary on which he thought a minister would be spiritually and culturally most productive.[21] A prominent Presbyterian layman in New

York City even questioned his denomination's longstanding emphasis on a highly educated ministry. "Ministers," he charged, "are too often a class by themselves—a learned, recluse body, as far removed from the associations, capacities, and sympathies of the people generally . . . as are the Babel tongues of their libraries."[22] Certainly the ministry in this era was not lacking in friends ready to help it cultivate humility.

Other factors, too, were threatening the status of the ministry. Pastorates were becoming shorter; a growing preference for young ministers sometimes exalted vigor and energy at the price of learning and experience; sharp denominational competition kept numerous pastorates at a subsistence level; and the extensive subsidizing of "poor but pious youths" to meet the expanding need of ministers was bringing a larger proportion of men of humble background to the "sacred desk."[23] Dr. Alexander's longstanding friend John H. Rice found the ministerial office in his day "greatly underrated by men of the world; who . . . respect and admire objects in proportion as they are splended [sic] and pompous."[24] This was, to be sure, good for the minister's soul, but it did reflect a marked decline in his professional and social prestige.

In contrast to those (whether church members or others) who belittled or opposed a professional ministry, the American seminary movement greatly magnified the ministerial office, and had as its principal objective increasing the minister's competence as a professional. President Timothy Dwight of Yale, preaching at the opening of Andover Seminary in 1808, declared pastors and teachers to be a gift from God and his chief instrument in saving men. It was not right, therefore, that the pulpit should remain ignorant in a day when adequate preparation was being demanded for lawyers and physicians. For Dwight, and for the seminary movement in general, the emphasis on ministerial education embodied the ideal of a cultured professional who possessed social standing and whose person and office had weight in the community. Thus Dwight said: "If Ministers are respectable; Religion will by mankind in general be respected. . . . If they are dignified; it will be believed to be noble. If they are pious; it will be acknowledged to be real. But if, on the contrary, Ministers are contemptible; Religion will be despised." Social conservatism was built into this conception of ministry. President Dwight went on, in the same address, to envisage the minister, in contrast with the destructiveness of the French Revolution and Napoleonic wars when "ancient establishments . . . are . . . crumbling," as soon to lead the church on in "that illustrious [millennial] day, destined to . . . cover the earth with light and glory."[25]

An overwrought recognition of the problems facing this historic authoritative type of minister, amid the dynamic and democratic forces of the new nation, was voiced by one of the traditional ministry's most prominent exponents, Dr. John M. Mason, Associate Reformed pastor and theological teacher in New York City. Writing in 1810 to a fellow minister in Kentucky—where under other types of ministry churches at that very moment were growing phenomenally—Dr. Mason lamented:

I discern nothing for it but to call in our outposts. . . . I tremble at the anticipation that all, or nearly all, the Western country will be brutalized and paganized. . . . Your talents will be lost, your spirits dissipated, and your heart broken, in a fruitless effort to stem an irresistable torrent. . . . In your Western regions, and in too many others, they are lamentably hostile to a decent provision for the ministry.[26]

This was an over-hasty surrender in a moment of discouragement that seemed to admit the charges of ineffectiveness and worldly motivation that some were leveling against seminary training for the ministry.

More truly representative of the traditional, authoritative ideal of the ministry was a statement by another seminary founder, the Rev. John H. Rice of Virginia, who declared in 1817: "The sphere of the minister's duty is co-extensive with all the relations which man sustains. . . . It reaches to the magistrate . . . to the judge . . . to the legislator . . . to the neighbor . . . to the master." This authority, he suggested in a statement which almost seemed to reflect Revolutionary War views of fundamental law and social contract, derives from the Bible and is also limited by the Bible, limitations which may be enforced by the people against a minister who misuses these scriptural powers.[27]

American Presbyterians in the early nineteenth century retained their historic ideal of the minister as neither priest nor charismatic exhorter, but as divinely appointed proclaimer of the Word of God. To perform this function most effectively he should be a well-educated gentleman of commanding personality, a concept which, as a heritage of the religious awakening, included renewed emphasis on piety. To this ideal there was now added increasing diversification of function. Ministers now were not only, as traditionally, pastors or school or college teachers and administrators. Many of them were becoming or about to become, alternatively, also home missionaries, foreign missionaries, professional revivalists, editors, church and voluntary society executives and promoters, or theological teachers. The ministerial profession was becoming at once more diversified and thus potentially also more specialized.

If the ministerial professional was in transition in America between the middle of the eighteenth and the middle of the nineteenth century, so too were such other learned professions as medicine and law. All were finding it difficult in a changing society to draw precisely a dividing line between real "professionals" and the many who were less qualified. In the face of the great need of such services, how much and what kind of training must be considered minimal?

Ultimately the concept of "professional" depends on a social need which can be adequately met only by the use of a body of specialized knowledge and techniques which are beyond the competence of those not specially prepared. Professionalism further assumes the formal definition by a recognized body (commonly the professionals themselves) of what constitutes competence in the profession, and some system of licensing which will limit practice to those thus deemed competent, or at least give them a public accreditation which is withheld from all others. When first becoming regularized, this involved a kind of vicious circle, for it still left open the question as to who were the "competent" professionals who would authoritatively define the standards and examine the applicants. In the case of the ministry, widely variant requirements for ordination were found in the different denominations, amid the separation of church and state.

This process of definition and restriction of the professions not only renders the important service of protecting the public from those judged incompetent, but it also greatly serves the self-interests of the profession by conspicuous separation of the accepted professionals from all others. Because of the social demand for such services and the skills required for proper performance, the accredited professional is given special economic rewards and an elevated social status. This principle, which of course operated in the ministry also, cannot be invoked as proof of bad motives; but in the early years of the seminary movement it was pointed to by some secularists and by radically democratic religious groups as a ground for criticizing the type of minister which the seminary movement sought to produce.

This function of defining norms for the respective professions and of licensing or accrediting candidates has obvious social and ethical overtones. Will the "in-group" make standards unnecessarily exacting and be unduly restrictive in accrediting candidates, thus giving unwarranted "status" to the profession at the price of an adequate supply of practitioners? Or, contrariwise, will they be unduly lax in standards and admission, thus commending to the public incompetent practitioners? Under such laxity, by a kind of Gresham's law, the inferior practitioners tend to undercut and drive out the better qualified.[28] A tightening of standards, on the other hand, reduces the number of inadequately prepared and leaves the way open for a larger number of the fully qualified.[29] In the ministerial profession, this issue was an important point of difference among the denominations, and, in crucial years of population movement and expansion, combined with a shortage of ministers, gave competitive advantage to some denominations over against others.

Democracy had a somewhat ambivalent influence on the professions in America. In the long run, by superseding the rule of the hereditary feudal aristocracy, democracy left the way open for leadership in government and society by professional experts. But more immediately, the egalitarianism of Jacksonian democracy, by its reluctance to admit that any specialists were superior to the "common man," very visibly lowered professional standards, for example, in the medical profession,[30] in the legal profession,[31] and in the ministry. The frontier had a similar temporary effect.[32] As scholarship, technology, and social complexity increased, however, the professional necessarily became more highly trained, more specialized, and increasingly indispensable, with further heightening of status. The greater diffusion of education, for example, was one of the stimuli that made the seminary movement seem necessary.

Specialized training lies at the center of the concept of professionalism. In colonial days, most of professional education was by the "apprentice" method. Hopefully (though not always) the candidate would first complete a liberal arts course in a college, and then attach himself to a professional, in order from him to "learn by doing." This custom was widespread among doctors, lawyers, and ministers.[33] Some of the most privileged, after completing their college course, engaged in professional study abroad: physicians at Leyden, Paris, London, or Edinburgh; lawyers at the Inns of Court in London; ministers (depending on their denominational affiliation) at Oxford or Cambridge or at Scottish or Continental universities. Ministers were better provided for than were other professionals by the colonial colleges whose earliest curricula were directly adapted to ministerial preparation. But as the colleges began to shift the primary purpose of their curricula from ministerial preparation to more general objectives, some of these institutions introduced a few rather informal courses in divinity for those who had completed the liberal arts program.

The first actual professional school in America was in medicine—the medical department of the College of Philadelphia, founded in 1765. Three years later, a medical school was opened at King's College in New York (now Columbia University) and in 1783 one at Harvard College, with a number of other colleges later following suit. The new schools did not ignore practical experience, at first supplementing rather than replacing the apprentice system, and many of them offering in addition practical experience in hospital work. The demand for practitioners was so great that presently proprietary medical schools were organized for profit, which seriously lowered the quality of preparation.[34] Ministerial education was fortunate in not having a counterpart of such proprietary schools. Medical education gradually began to improve again in the last decade of the nineteenth century, and was raised to an entirely new level by the epoch-making analysis and proposals of Abraham Flexner in 1910.

The first chair of jurisprudence in American was established at William and Mary College under the influence of Thomas Jefferson in 1779, and the college became an important early center for educating lawyers. The first actual law school was begun by Judge Tapping Reeve at Litchfield, Connecticut, in 1784. It was sometimes difficult to distinguish early professional schools from the "apprentice" system, especially when, as at Litchfield, Reeve was for a time the only teacher and continued his active practice of law. In spite of the founding of this and later law schools—most of them unlike Reeve's school as departments of colleges or universities—apprenticeship continued far into the nineteenth century as the method by which most candidates prepared for the legal profession. Instruction in the law schools was by lecture or recitation from textbooks until Christopher C. Langdell in 1871 introduced the "case method" of teaching law, whereby from an analytic study of past cases, the student learned to think legally.[35] As in the case of medicine and law, many ministerial candidates, for a considerable time after the founding of seminaries, continued to prepare by the old "apprentice" method of study under a pastor, or by study at a seminary for a fractional part of the total curriculum.

A perennial problem for professional schools has been the extent to which they should concentrate on practical and concrete techniques, or on broad principles and theory, with large cultural overtones. The speed with which change causes memorized techniques to become outdated, and the social impact which the professions have, far beyond their specialities, warn against a too narrow concentration on technical and procedural matters at the expense of underlying principles and broad objectives.

Talcott Parsons suggested that the function of the lawyer and the physician is to mediate between the particular needs of the client or patient and the resources and demands of society; between dynamic change and social stability. The lawyer seeks to meet the special needs of his client within the requirements of objective law; the role of the psychotherapist is somewhat parallel. The physician brings to the sick the resources for healing which society has developed.[36] Similarly the minister, by the proclamation of the historic Christian gospel of redemption, seeks to reconcile erring human beings with God and to reconcile them and social structures with moral obligations. All of this, to be done most effectively, requires expertise both of knowledge and of technique.

Religious motivation was prominent in the founding of American colleges. Many felt that education must be informed by Christian faith and precepts to create an adequate base for a worthy civilization. The Great Awakening stimulated the organization of important colleges, and the Second Awakening accentuated pietistic emphases in curricula and campus life. Education of ministers, desire to win converts, and denominational rivalry were also among the religious motives for founding colleges.[37] The role of the clergy in college founding, teaching, and administration long was prominent.

This strong religious emphasis in American higher education, inherited from the Middle Ages and from the Reformation and heightened by revivalism, was challenged by the Enlightenment. The Enlightenment's critical spirit implied hostility to metaphysical absolutes and thus collided with traditional formulations of Christianity. Natural science, which at first was developed more outside of the colleges than in them, was bringing in its wake not only technological usefulness, but an altered world view. The Enlightenment's belief in the perfectibility of individuals and of society pointed toward confident social and educational experimentation. The spirit of religious toleration following the American Revolution discouraged denominational emphases, and the rapid thrust toward more radical democracy in the early nineteenth century demanded reconsideration of both the objectives and the methods of higher education. French influence was reflected in Thomas Jefferson's quite secular ideals for the new University of Virginia; and Dr. Benjamin Rush's version of a much discussed postgraduate national university for federal office holders heralded the revolt against traditionalism in education and in favor of immediate practicality.[38]

This ferment of new ideas and expectations was having a powerful impact on the curriculum of American higher education by the opening of the nineteenth century. There were as yet no real "universities" in the young nation, and conceivably the existing colleges might, if secondary schools could have raised their standards to the level of the Continental *Gymnasien*, have been able to give professional training in a lengthened, but continuous and integrated, university course. Instead of this, the American colleges chose gradually to generalize their curricula, reducing classics and other traditional material, and introducing science, which of course had become essential, and various other disciplines, but on a subprofessional, subspecialized level. When professional or graduate education was appended to the college course, problems arose concerning the proper relation between the curriculum of the college and of the professional school and also raised questions whether the great amount of time devoted to the total educational process was being most efficiently used.

Specifically theological education, as it developed in the Middle Ages, Renaissance, and Reformation had its principal home in the universities. This pattern was at first followed by the American colleges. Thus the education of ministerial candidates was a central motive in the founding of Harvard and Yale. More than half of Harvard's graduates in the seventeenth century became ministers, and as late as 1723 two-thirds of its library dealt with theology. In addition to Greek, Hebrew, Aramaic, and Syriac, all Harvard students studied two areas of theology—"catecheti-

cal'' and "biblical." A third area, theology proper, was reserved for ministerial candidates after graduation. Catechetical work consisted in
memorizing and reciting back William Ames's *Marrow of Sacred Divinity,*
later replaced by John Wollebius's *The Abridgement of Christian Divinity.*
In biblical theology the student was required to translate Bible portions
from the Hebrew or Greek into Latin and "to resolve them Logically,''
an exercise which took place twice a day. By the time the graduated student took up the study of theology proper, he had acquired linguistic
tools and some training in method. He was now largely on his own, but
preferably remained at the college to use the library, to attend the president's divinity courses, and to confer with him from time to time. There
was also some practice preaching as well as actual supplying of pulpits.
Some of this postgraduate study consisted merely in reviewing work previously done, and much of the total program—in the early colonial
period at least—was better calculated to confirm orthodoxy than to stimulate independent thinking. The practice of disputations, inherited from
the Middle Ages, was valuable for developing clear and pointed speaking.[39]

The Great Awakening stimulated the "apprentice" method of ministerial preparation. Many more, after graduating from college, now
studied under pastors instead of returning to college for further study in
theology. The Edwardsean pastor-theologians Joseph Bellamy and
Nathanael Emmons were among the most popular of these teachers. Significantly, their instruction in biblical and historical areas was minimal,
but they enabled students to acquire a reasoned system of theology and a
supervised experience in preaching and pastoral work. Vigorous criticism of theological essays and sermons and the extensive use of dialogue
within the group were among the more stimulating features of this type
of instruction.[40] But in spite of some practical values, the "apprentice"
method suffered from the teacher's parish distractions, his inability to
supply in his own person the needed variety of specialties, and the
manse's relatively meager library facilities. The apprentice method was
particularly inadequate at a time when the nation was feeling its way
toward cultural self-expression and wider extension of education and
political suffrage. Other professions were seeking better methods of preparation and stricter standards of professional licensure, and the desire
to improve ministerial education was part of this general trend. Could
the new seminaries and divinity schools develop curricula which would
do justice both to the heritage of the churches and to the contemporary
needs of the new American society?[41]

# 11
# WHAT SHOULD A MINISTER STUDY?

The Enlightenment, with its flair for critical analysis and orderly reconstruction of universal knowledge, gave great stimulus to "theological encyclopedia." This study sought to analyze the nature and appropriate methodology of the various theological disciplines and of their relation to each other, thus offering a road map of the terrain. Theological encyclopedia also viewed these disciplines in relation to the church and to contemporary culture. The German theologian, K. R. Hagenbach, writing in the second quarter of the nineteenth century, gave development and wide currency to a previously proposed fourfold division of theological studies into exegetical (or biblical), historical, systematic, and practical. This arrangement was long used by Princeton Seminary. In spite of advantages of convenience and apparent simplicity, the rubrics in this scheme are not coordinate, the first three—exegetical, historical, and systematic—being based primarily on the subject matter of the disciplines, and the fourth—practical—originally being based primarily on the intended use of the material taught. In addition, such a classification predominantly by subject matter became less meaningful when critical historical method was applied to both exegetics and systematics, and when scholars became increasingly aware of the extent to which philosophical and theological presuppositions influenced biblical conclusions. This necessarily resulted in the crossing of divisional lines and the closer interrelation and interdependence of disciplines. Later the introduction of new disciplines into the theological curriculum necessitated either the arbitrary "squeezing" of these new disciplines to fit existing departmental categories, or the stretching of departmental definitions so far as virtually to rob them of meaning in order to include the new studies. Friedrich Schleiermacher had already begun to revolutionize theological encyclopedia in 1811 by proposing an analysis that gave greater emphasis both to historical and to practical studies than did the earlier tradition which was later set forth by Hagenbach. Theology, Schleiermacher said, is the scientific formulation of the church's religious consciousness, and it finds its culmination in concrete expression through practical theology. In his threefold division of theological studies into philosophical, historical, and practical, Schleiermacher classified both biblical studies and dogmatics as "historical," thus confronting traditional bulwarks of theological stability with historical relativism.[1] Another dynamic classification of disciplines was the twofold one of "historical" and "normative," which was based on the use to which the discipline was put and the method used in it. Studies classified as "historical" would analyze factual evidence and classify and interpret it, whereas "normative" studies would use a more philosophical method. By this pattern, norms are defined by philosophical criticism rather than by either "revelation" or inherited thought structures.[2]

An early pace-setter in the American seminary movement was Andover Theological Seminary, founded in 1808. The ideal was here clearly embodied that theological education was to be a three-year course and that prerequisite to it would be the satisfactory completion of both secondary and college education. Upon fulfulling the seminary's curricular requirements, any student so requesting would be granted a "certificate," but no academic degree. The Andover Constitution in 1807 set forth five fields of study for the projected seminary: "Natural Theology, Sacred Literature, Ecclesiastical History, Christian Theology, and Pulpit Eloquence."[3] If natural theology were bracketed with Christian theology, as was presently done, there was here the familiar fourfold theological encyclopedia of exegetical or biblical, historical, systematic, and practical theology.

Part of the task of theological encyclopedia was to define the proper limits, interrelation, and sequence of the respective disciplines, and this was a question on which for a time the Andover professors differed among themselves. There was some complaint in early Andover—often voiced in later generations in other theological schools—that teachers of the various disciplines were overlapping each other in classroom work. After extended deliberation, the Andover professors agreed that all seminary instruction had a common object and also that the respective disciplines often dealt with the same subjects, but that each should focus primary attention on its most proper subject matter and methodology. Obviously the discussion was skirting but not quite reaching the twentieth-century realization that the various theological disciplines can cross-fertilize each other by mutual criticism of presuppositions and methodologies. It was agreed that biblical studies should precede systematic theology and that both should precede a concentration on practical theology. But what was the role of church history? Some of the Andover faculty, apparently reflecting the new historical insight, thought that church history was "an important means of understanding the doctrines of revelation." But others objected that "if we should undertake to expound the Scriptures . . . by the various clashing opinions and unauthorized practices which have prevailed among Christians since the Apostolic age, we should be greatly perplexed, our faith might be unsettled." Therefore church history was safely relegated to the final year, after the student had been fully indoctrinated by the study of the Bible and theology. The sequence that resulted at Andover, which was maintained for many years, thus was: first year, sacred literature; second year, Christian theology and natural theology; third year, sacred rhetoric (previously called "pulpit eloquence") and ecclesiastical history.[4] This distribution of the theological disciplines into separate years of study, while offering the opportunity of greater concentration of focus for such students as might be competent to concentrate, would certainly hinder cross-fertilization of disciplines in general, reducing, for example, the likelihood of an historical approach to Scripture, or of an examination of the theological presuppositions used in biblical interpretation, or of the relation of these studies to actual preaching.

Princeton Seminary was organized close on the heels of Andover, with very similar presuppositions and objectives. It is not surprising, therefore, that there were noticeable resemblances of structure and emphasis in the curricula of the two institutions.

The original "plan" of Princeton Seminary, as adopted by the General Assembly of 1811, set forth a kind of capsuled theological encyclopedia. Recognizing that adjustment and change would be inevitable, the plan wisely concentrated on desirable attainments rather than on specific courses. In order to receive the seminary's "certificate of approbation" (as with Andover, granted instead of a degree), the student, in oral examinations conducted by the professors in the presence of the board of directors, must show that he has "laid the foundation for becoming" (1) "a sound biblical critic"; (2) "a defender of the Christian faith"; (3) "an able and sound divine and casuist"; (4) "a useful preacher and a faithful pastor"; and (5) "qualified to exercise discipline, and to take part in the government of the Church." Each of the above objectives in the light of the description given of it can readily be identified, respectively, with particular theological disciplines as follows: (1) with biblical studies; (2) with apologetics; (3) with church history (which the plan mentioned as a resource for this particular objective) and theology, including both systematic theology and ethics; and (4) and (5) with practical theology. If apologetics and ethics be subsumed under systematics, there is here found essentially the fourfold classification into exegetical (or biblical), historical, systematic, and practical theology, as later elaborated by Hagenbach.

Biblical studies are broadly conceived in the Princeton plan. The student must become "well skilled in the original languages of the Holy Scriptures." Also he "must be able to explain the principal difficulties which arise in the perusal of the Scriptures" (an exercise part of which at least might well have been subsumed under apologetics). Historical context is not to be ignored, for the student "must be versed in Jewish and Christian antiquities" and "must have an acquaintance with ancient geography and with oriental customs." Strangely, nothing is explicitly said about exegetical study.

Apologetics is treated in the limited context of the already fading deistical controversy whose "principal arguments and writings" the student "must have read and digested." This somewhat belated emphasis may be partly explained by the fact that the three most prominent members of the committee that drafted the plan had had direct and somewhat agonizing personal contact with deism in three of its American strongholds—Chairman Green in Philadelphia, Miller in New York City, and Alexander in Virginia and Philadelphia. Natural theology, listed later under theology, would also be serviceable to apologetics. It is obvious that the plan sought to utilize philosophy to defend the faith against outside attack rather than to define the faith in generic terms or to analyze the philosophical presuppositions of theological work.

Theology proper is summarized merely in terms of its proposed subdivisions: "Natural, Didactic [systematic], Polemic, and Casuistic [ethics]," but these—especially if extended to include apologetics, already listed—offer wide coverage. Symbolics appears in the unpromising dress of sectarian competition using a proof-text method, for the student must acquire the ability "to support the doctrines of the Confession of Faith and Catechisms by a ready, pertinent, and abundant quotation of Scripture texts."

Church history as a discipline is summarized in three brief but very comprehensive lines, which include not only "the history of the Christian Church," but also "a considerable acquaintance with General History and Chronology." As in the summary of biblical studies, historical context is admirably stressed. One can almost see Samuel Miller's hand in the committee's drafting of this particular emphasis, for Miller was always very strong in stressing context in history, though he never reached the stage of fully supplementing this with the newer view of history as process.

In the plan's treatment of practical theology, works of religious devotion are not overlooked, for the student "must have read a considerable number of the best practical writers on the subject of religion," though no class instruction in this area is indicated. Great emphasis is laid on the analysis, composition, and delivery of sermons, half a dozen of which must be written out in full and submitted for criticism. Attention is also given to "pastoral care." Church government is to be studied in a very broad historical setting, this also benefitting from Dr. Samuel Miller's unfailing contextual method of approaching the study of human groups and societal structures. But this broad approach appears here to have also a sectarian angle. The student "must have studied attentively the form of Church Government authorized by [sic—not "required by"— they were not quite "divine right" Presbyterians] Scriptures, and the administration of it as it has taken place in Protestant Churches." The teaching of church government presently became and long remained one of the major responsibilities of the professor of ecclesiastical history. If, contrary to the apparent intent of the plan, church government is classi- fied under practical theology, then practical theology occupies a full 40 percent of the space here used to outline the curriculum. There was of course no implication that this fortuitous ratio should become norma- tive, and the actual time and thought devoted in the curriculum to the practical area of preparation were very much less than 40 percent. But the clear purpose of the seminary founders was to provide preparation for the pastorate. All the members of the General Assembly's committee which drafted the plan were pastors, and the first professor who did most to cast the seminary's mold came directly from the pastorate, as did also the second professor.[5]

The plan called for a minimum of three professorships, and the titles of their proposed fields give additional indication of what were intended to be the main structural lines of the curriculum. The three were "Didactic and Polemic Divinity," "Oriental and Biblical Literature," and "Ecclesiastical History and Church Government."[6] Here again are three of the four divisions later elaborated by Hagenbach—exegetical or biblical, historical, and systematic. The practical field was far from for- gotten, for instruction in preaching and pastoral care was to be offered by those teaching in other fields. This was not a bad idea, contributing to the close interrelation of Practical Theology with the other disciplines, quite possible when, as here, two of the three other disciplines were taught by successful former pastors.

The projected plan could readily be interpreted as making the oral examination before the board of directors the climax of the entire curric- ulum. Such an examination before a committee of the board of trustees was the current practice of the College of New Jersey and of many other institutions. In the case of the seminary, this procedure—with drastic modifications, to be sure—could conceivably have developed into the type of comprehensive examination conducted by universities on the European continent, which constitutes the climax toward which all pre- vious academic work points, and which establishes both the breadth and penetration of the student's preparation. But no such development took place on the American scene in this period. Instead, the oral exami- nations became an increasingly superficial formality, tedious to the decreasing number of members of the governing board who bothered to attend them. Emphasis rather was placed quite atomistically on the ex- aminations in individual courses, which could then be safely dismissed by the student and left unrelated to his other equally atomistic studies. The seminary's plan, unlike the young science of theological encyclopedia, neither stated nor implied what if any were the relations between the several disciplines of theological study, and almost left the impression that each subject was quite autonomous and self-sufficient.

Comments pertinent to the constructing of a theological curriculum were offered at the inauguration of Dr. Alexander in August 1812. Dr. Miller, in this sermon on that occasion, suggested, although in a regrettably fleeting way, a quite modern inductive approach to the problems of curriculum which was not common in his day, when he sought to relate curriculum directly to the actual work of the ministry by asking "what . . . a minister . . . must be qualified to perform." But his answer to the question was disappointing, for he mentioned only two functions of a minister, the duty "to explain the scriptures" and "to perform his part in the judicatories of the church." This implied that the curriculum should concentrate on preparing preachers and leaders of church polity (with of course the broad cultural and theological base which the seminary's founders envisaged for these tasks). But there was no intimation of what might be implied for curriculum building in the great diversification and specialization of ministerial functions which was just beginning to take place.

As the seminary began its work, Alexander, who had been elected to his professorship barely two months before, faced the Herculean task of creating a three-year curriculum with no specialized experience for the undertaking and with few American precedents on which to draw. He was at the same time confronted with a serious dearth of suitable books in English to be used for texts, as he reported to the directors: "The knowledge sought was often contained in massy folios, and mostly in foreign languages; and such books as would have been convenient in size, & suitable for our purposes, in many instances, were out of our reach; or so few copies could be obtained that the whole class could not pursue the study at once." In an era antedating photographic duplication, Alexander laboriously did "the best in his power to supply this deficiency, by collecting scraps making translations & abridgments from every work which he could find suitable to his purpose."[7]

After three years, as the original students completed their course, Alexander was able to report to the board of directors that the seminary curriculum had been fully organized as follows:

- *Third Class* (lowest): winter term (six months): Hebrew language, scriptural chronology, biblical history, Jewish antiquities. Summer term (three months): Scriptures in English, biblical history, original languages of Scripture, and portions of *The Four Gospels, Translated from the Greek, with Preliminary Dissertations and Notes, Critical and Explanatory* by the Scotsman George Campbell (2 vols., 1789).

- *Second Class:* winter term: scriptural chronology, sacred geography, biblical and ecclesiastical history, didactic theology. Summer term: didactic theology, ecclesiastical history.

- *First Class:* winter term: didactic and polemic theology, ecclesiastical history and church government. Summer term: pastoral care, composition and delivery of sermons.[8]

*TABLE 1    CURRICULA OF EARLY AMERICAN THEOLOGICAL SCHOOLS*

| Year | Andover (1807) | Princeton (1815) |
|------|----------------|------------------|
| Junior Year | Sacred Literature | *Winter Term* (6 months<br><br>Hebrew Language<br>Scriptural Chronology<br>Biblical History<br>Jewish Antiquities<br><br>*Summer Term* (3 months)<br><br>Scriptures in English<br>Biblical History<br>Original Languages of Scripture |
| Middler Year | Christian Theology and Natural Theology | *Winter Term* (6 months)<br>Scriptural Chronology<br>Sacred Geography<br>Biblical History<br>Ecclesiastical History<br>Didactic Theology<br><br>*Summer Term* (3 months)<br>Didactic Theology<br>Ecclesiastical History |
| Senior Year | Sacred Rhetoric and Ecclesiastical History | *Winter Term* (6 months)<br><br>Didactic Theology<br>Polemic Theology<br>Ecclesiastical History<br>Church Government<br><br>*Summer Term* (3 months)<br>Pastoral Care<br>Composition and Delivery of Sermons |

Through a number of nonacademic exercises and meetings in the various years, the seminary also made extensive provision for worship and the development of religious experience. Table 1 shows the curricula of four early American theological schools, Andover, Princeton, Harvard, and Yale.

TABLE 1 *(continued)*

| Harvard (1828) | Yale (1835) |
|---|---|
| *Total Curriculum* = 50 term-meetings (A term-meeting was one class meeting every week for term) | Mental and Moral Philosophy |
| | Exegetical Theology |
| Biblical Studies (22 term-meetings) | |
| German (8 term-meetings) | |
| Ecclesiastical History and Christian Institutions (5 term-meetings) | Systematic Theology |
| | Exegetical Theology |
| Theology (7 term-meetings) | |
| Practical Theology (8 term-meetings) | |
| | Preaching |
| | Pastoral Theology |

As compared with Andover, Princeton Seminary introduced church history into the second year along with didactic theology instead of postponing it to the third year, thus suggesting at least a theoretical possibility that the study of theology might be influenced by historical considerations, though there is no evidence that this possibility attained any degree of fulfillment. Both seminaries devoted the classwork of the entire first year to biblical studies, but Princeton gave to this material fractional time in the second year also. Princeton apparently gave less class time than did Andover to practical theology, devoting to it only the short summer term of the final year, whereas at Andover practical theology shared an entire year with one other subject. While a twentieth-century reader notices the high degree of concentration on one or a few studies at a time, this concentration is noticeably less at Princeton than at Andover, the Princeton curriculum more frequently scheduling different disciplines simultaneously. This would increase the physical possibility of interdisciplinary criticism and stimulation, though for reasons already discussed, this was not yet an important factor in American seminary life. The scheduling of preaching and pastoral care by themselves in the very last term at Princeton offered the hope that in these exercises the student would utilize the resources acquired from his now completed biblical, historical, and theological courses. But it also meant that his earlier study of those fields had been deprived of the practical relevance and motivation that simultaneous work in the practical disciplines might have supplied.

A comparison with the early curricula of Harvard Divinity School and of Yale Divinity School is also illuminating. Harvard Divinity School, which became a separate department of the college in 1819[9] (though some have claimed a date a few years earlier), built its curriculum on a quite different pattern from that of Andover or Princeton. Unitarian Harvard was in revolt against dogmatisms, and drastically reduced instruction in both systematic theology and ecclesiastical history. The early assumption seems to have been that a properly scholarly and critical study of the Bible, uncorrupted by erroneous dogmatisms and historical aberrations, would confirm the Unitarian position. The new divinity school thus gave overwhelming emphasis to biblical studies, and presently led the nation in introducing the new critical methods in that field.[10] On the other hand, the notable interest of Harvard men in moral philosophy[11] could scarcely be related to the divinity school's meager single-unit course in ethics. In reducing theology and exalting biblical studies, Harvard seems to have assumed that each student could form his own independent theological conclusions from the direct study of Scripture.[12] This approach, like that of contemporaneous Andover and Princeton, differed widely from the twentieth-century hermeneutical assumption that one inevitably approaches biblical interpretation with theological presuppositions, which should be critically examined early in the process.

Five fields of instruction were planned at Harvard, though financial stringency prevented their immediate realization: "natural religion and the evidences of revealed religion; Hebrew; Biblical criticism; ecclesiastical history and pastoral theology."[13] If Hebrew be subsumed under biblical studies, here to be sure was the familiar fourfold arrangement, but proportionate distribution of class time differed greatly from that at Andover and Princeton Seminary.

Detailed recommendations made in 1828, though not fully carried out, represented the Harvard school's curricular ideal in this early period. Each of the three years was divided into three terms. The curriculum totaled what might be called fifty term-meetings, if one term-meeting be defined as one class, meeting every week for a term. (Each class meeting was of more than one hour's duration.) The preponderant emphasis on biblical studies is seen in the fact that of the total of fifty term-meetings, twenty-two were devoted to biblical studies (thirty, if the eight term-meetings for the biblically motivated study of German be included); "Ecclesiastical History" and "Christian Institutions" together received only five term-meetings; while theology received seven (of which only three were given to "Christian Doctrine" and one to ethics); and practical theology was given eight.[14] Thus there was even less attention given here to church history than at Andover and Princeton, with only one-tenth of the total term-meetings devoted to it, clearly reflecting the early Unitarian revolt against tradition.

It is interesting to observe that the number of class meetings decreased each year, perhaps suggesting that as students matured they gave more time to private reading. There was less tendency here than at Andover and Princeton to concentrate on one or two disciplines per year, for, in spite of the great emphasis at every stage on biblical studies, at least three different disciplines were always presented in the same year. Such concomitant study gave added opportunity for mutual criticism and stimulation on the part of the respective disciplines, had the presuppositions and methods of the era been conducive to it.

Yale Divinity School, emerging as a distinct administrative unit of the college in 1822, was directly in the evangelical tradition of the late President Timothy Dwight. The curriculum core as recorded in 1833, when properly amplified, is representative of the opening decades as a whole. The junior class concentrated on mental and moral philosophy under Dr. Nathaniel W. Taylor and on exegetical theology; the middle class on Dr. Taylor's systematic theology and on further exegetical studies; while seniors focused their attention on practical theology, including both preaching and pastoral theology. Like most of the theological curricula of the day this was supplemented by somewhat more informal but basically academic student organizations such as a "Rhetorical Society" in which students participated and over which a professor presided.[15] As with the early Edwardsean pastor-theologians, theology dominated the curriculum and Dr. Taylor was for decades the school's outstanding figure. He had come from a successful pastorate in New Haven and he sought to present a modified Calvinism in a form that would be readily preachable in a context of religious awakening. Also like the early Edwardseans, Yale Divinity School gave considerable attention to practical theology, devoting to it the chief emphasis of senior year, formal class instruction in these subjects being limited to this one year. A similar approach to practical theology is apparent at Andover, Princeton, and Yale. All three confined to senior year class instruction in practical theology, Princeton and Yale devoting all of the closing period of instruction to it.

The most notable weakness in the early Yale curriculum was in church history, a weakness evident also in the early Harvard program. Of the four early curricula here surveyed, that at Princeton Seminary seems to have devoted most attention to church history, alloting to it half the time of two long winter terms and of a short summer term. This was perhaps due to the influence of Dr. Miller, who had great interest in history, extensive knowledge for his day of the major developments in church history, and a strong sense of the interplay of environing forces. But, like his colleagues at Princeton Seminary, and like nearly all church historians in America before the impact of German idealistic historiography, he failed to view history as a continually transforming process. Unlike the other three institutions, this static concept of history, which resisted the newer concept of process, became one of the central characteristics of the Old Princeton Theology and, along with biblical inerrancy and unwillingness to compromise denominational distinctives, contributed to an increasing ideal of resistance to change. It would appear that of the four early theological institutions here viewed, Andover and Princeton treated the four areas of biblical, historical, systematic, and practical theology in the most evenly rounded way, though there is little evidence that they explored critically the mutual interrelation of these several disciplines.

How were these broad principles of theological education fleshed out concretely in the case of Princeton Seminary? Fortunately, extant lectures of Dr. Alexander illustrate the way he related his chosen heritage of ideas to the thought and action of his day. Regrettably, Dr. Miller's lectures have not been preserved as fully. To Dr. Alexander's teachings, which became the enduring foundation of the Old Princeton Theology, we now turn.

# 12
# PSYCHOLOGY AND RELIGIOUS EXPERIENCE

For the opening class of Princeton Seminary in 1812, Dr. Alexander was ready with a lecture on the "Nature and Evidence of Truth."[1] Here in seed were the explorations in epistemology, psychology, apologetics, and ethics which he considered essential foundations for the study of theology proper. Quite in keeping with the Seminary's plan, "natural theology," with its strong confidence in reason, was thought to be the appropriate preparation for "revealed theology." The Seminary's *Catalogue* of 1831 listed these subjects for first-year students under the title of "Studies Preliminary to Theology," leading up to "Didactic [systematic or doctrinal] Theology" in the second year. In 1832 the *Catalogue* listed these preliminary studies more specifically as "Mental and Moral Science" and "The Evidence of Natural and Revealed Religion." Four years after Alexander's death, these courses disappeared from the *Catalogue*, much to the disappointment of his son,[2] but some similar material was included in the lectures and writings of his successors, often under different headings.

It could be said that this collection of Alexander's "Studies Preliminary to Theology" represent an eighteenth-century graft on the seventeenth-century stock of Reformed scholasticism, all set forth in the epistemology of the Scottish philosophy. The eighteenth-century introductory material is based on a world-view formed by Newtonian science, whereas the earlier seventeenth-century Reformed scholasticism which constitutes the body of theology thus introduced was formed in an atmosphere of pre-Newtonian rationalism out of which the Newtonian world-view emerged. The two are not completely assimilated to each other in Alexander's thinking. The eighteenth-century elements reflect far greater awareness of the larger world being opened up by natural science and by the widened geographic contacts of the immediately preceding centuries, as well as by the desire to reconcile these newer experiences and ideas with Christianity, an ambition that sometimes carries with it in Alexander unintended intimations of naturalism. Interfused with these eighteenth-century elements are Alexander's defense of strict seventeenth-century orthodoxy. If seventeenth-century and eighteenth-century rationalism remain at times separately identifiable in Alexander's thinking, still more visibly separate from both is the ever-recurring strong emphasis on a semirevivalistic type of piety which is not fully assimilated to either, least of all to the eighteenth-century type of rationalism, which is conspicuous throughout Alexander's thinking.

Dr. Alexander read widely, and skillfully adapted material gleaned from sources whose main thrust was in some cases quite alien to his own thinking. As he was not essentially a systematic thinker, we shall, therefore, in presenting his thoughts introductory to Didactic and Polemic Theology, select materials from various writings of his and arrange them under the successive headings of Epistemology, Psychology, Piety, Apologetics, and Ethics, reserving the last two of these topics for the next chapter. Alexander did not offer a formal course on piety, but it colored all his thinking and teaching and found concentrated expression in his informal Sunday afternoon "conferences" which deeply influenced many students.

Alexander, the father of the Old Princeton Theology, was its most philosophically minded early representative. Less disciplined and systematic than his successor, Charles Hodge, and far less architectonic, although broad in outlook and interests, he did not, like Hodge, aspire to relate theology to the whole range of human knowledge. While explicitly stressing the central authority of the Bible for theology, Alexander's extensive manuscript lectures show more interest in philosophy and in the writings of theologians than in the interpretation of biblical books or passages. One must go to Alexander's manuscripts fully to appreciate this overwhelming preponderance of metaphysics in his thinking.

Clearly his metaphysics predetermined his negative attitude toward the new biblical criticism, echoes of which were coming from Germany. And his metaphysics also predetermined to a large degree the interpretation he gave to the biblical text itself. His sympathetic son and biographer averred almost as much when he said that "it used to be a common remark, that students who had been imbued with Dr. Alexander's metaphysics were sure to swallow his entire system."[3] Thus it is appropriate to begin the analysis of Alexander's thought with his metaphysics rather than with the biblical studies which came first in the Seminary's curriculum and which for a few years were part of his academic responsibility.

Dr. Alexander was very much aware of the historic impact of philosophy on theology, as when he told his students, "No cause produces so many changes in Theology as the different Philosophical systems which prevail at different periods of the world."[4] "Avoid metaphysical subtleties," he warned, but immediately qualified the statement with the explanation, "By metaphysical subtleties I w[oul]d be understood to mean such discussions as are removed beyond the limit within wh[ich] we have distinct & certain perceptions."[5] Alexander, like many Old School Presbyterian scholars of his day, eagerly read and heartily endorsed the direct empirical observations of natural science, but was very wary of hypothetical or speculative inductions that went beyond these direct observations. Thus he, and especially his heirs, felt seriously threatened by the more revolutionary conclusions that science was able to draw from its observed data.[6]

"God," said Alexander, "has set a bound to the human intellect as he has to the sea, beyond which it cannot pass." If one presses beyond this, one risks "debilitating his intellect, and producing a habit of skepticism."[7] There is implied here a closed body of knowable facts rather than the more modern dynamic concept of knowledge growing unpredictably by hypothesis and testing out of previous knowledge. His rejection of "speculation" and his strict confinement of the sources of knowledge to "experience," while welcoming additions to the factual superstructure of knowledge, would tend to prevent critical analysis or reconstruction of the foundations of existing systems of thought including his own. And yet, in spite of his avowed concern to limit reason, Alexander actually granted a very large role to rational inferences in the elaboration and defense of his own theology.

Alexander was deeply interested in the problem of knowledge (episte-mology), which was the starting point of modern philosophy. How, according to Alexander, do we attain that knowledge of "distinct & certain precepts"—obviously akin to Descartes's "clear and distinct ideas"—which for Alexander lead to "sound and legitimate reasonings"? He had respect for Descartes, and gave an important place to that philosopher's dualism between mind ("thinking substance") and matter ("extended substance"), emphasizing also a dualism between the observing subject and the observed object. These two dualisms seemed to Alexander to make it possible to study reality with both detachment and accuracy.

More basically, however, Alexander departed from Descartes's rationalism in favor of British empiricism, including his adoption of John Locke's emphasis on the derivation of knowledge from simple ideas received from the senses.[8] On this principle Alexander based his conclusion that the knowledge of God is not innate, nor is it derived from intuition. Rather, he said, the knowledge of God is derived from "empirical" experience—by that he meant observation of God's works as seen in nature and in scriptural revelation.[9] But he rejected Locke's teaching that secondary qualities (such as sound, color, and odor), are only in the mind of the observer, a concept which, as further extended to primary qualities by George Berkeley, led to the scepticism of David Hume.

One of the conclusions of Hume's empiricism was the denial of the existence of any "substance" underlying the attributes which our senses perceive. Alexander agreed in part with Hume when he acknowledged that "the mind can acquire no knowledge of any substance but [by] its properties or qualities and its various relations to other things." But Alexander would not let go of belief in underlying "substance" that lay beyond all perception, and appealed to "intuition" to retain the concept. "It is absurd," he wrote, "to suppose a quality to exist without a subject. . . . It is an intuitive truth that every property must have a subject" (that is, must inhere in an underlying substance).[10] Immanuel Kant, of course, dealt quite differently with underlying substance—"the thing in itself," as he called it—and all along the line responded to Hume in a very different way from that of Thomas Reid and the Scottish philosophy. But Alexander had little use or appreciation for Kent's profound grappling with the question which Hume had raised. Thus in 1827 Alexander wrote to Hodge, who was at the time studying in Germany, reporting that he himself was currently reading Kant who was new to him and who, he confessed, "confounds and astonishes" him.[11] Alexander's rejection of Kant was to commit the Old Princeton Theology to enmity with some of the major theological forces of the next one hundred years.

In rejecting Kant's answer to Hume, Alexander chose to follow Thomas Reid and the Scottish philosophy which had been introduced into America by John Witherspoon, president of the College of New Jersey, and first conveyed to Alexander by his early teacher William Graham. By the time of Alexander's maturity and for a considerable time thereafter, this philosophy was in vogue among Americans of widely differing theological views.[12] Locke and his heirs, like many philosophers before them, saw human knowledge as consisting of awareness of the images of the external would transmitted to the brain by the senses. But Alexander, following Reid, adopted a philosophy of "realism"—that is, that we actually perceive the real world itself, not merely mental images of it.[13] This realism, its adherents felt, cut the root of Berkeley's alleged "solipsism" and of Hume's scepticism.

"Fundamental principle," or "self-evident," or "intuitive" truth, as it was often called, was an idea in the Scottish philosophy which greatly appealed to Alexander. When used loosely, without the safeguards that the fathers of the Scottish philosophy sought to place upon it, the concept could easily be made to endorse many a dogmatism. The basic point was that philosophy cannot float in midair, but must be built on some unproved assumptions.

Alexander was concerned to point out a difference between these "intuitive" truths and the "innate ideas" which Locke, asserting that the human mind started as a "blank tablet," had rejected. Of course,

Alexander conceded, no one is born with ready-formed ideas (assuming that this was indeed what Locke was refuting), but, Alexander asserted "God has so constituted our minds that we cannot avoid believing in certain truths as soon as they are presented to the mind."[14]

These primary truths ["intuitive" truths] are not in the mind until they are apprehended by the reason or understanding. The knowledge of them supposes the mind to have arrived at some degree of maturity, so as to be capable of understanding what is meant by the terms of the proposition by which they are expressed.[15]

Alexander has here admitted an essential subjective and historical—and therefore potentially variable—element in the individual's achieving awareness of foundational "intuitive truths." He shared the unhistorical assumption, widespread in the eighteenth century among deists and their opponents, that human "reason" was the same everywhere, at all times, and under all sociological conditions.

Alexander even admitted that "to distinguish between first [intuitive] truths and opinions founded on prejudice is not always easy." "But," he added, "these errors are never universal, extending to all nations and countries, and often the falsity of these opinions can be detected by reasoning."[16] The ability here attributed to reason to evaluate alleged "intuitive" principles is significant, but of more interest at the moment is Alexander's appeal to "universal" consensus as a corroboration and even a test of "intuitive" principles. The seventeenth and eighteenth centuries—after the era of great geographical discoveries—developed a concern to see the European cultural heritage in its relation to other cultures. Deism did this in its attempt to define a universal religion based on reason. The Scottish philosophy sought endorsement for some of its concepts in the universal opinion of mankind. Archibald Alexander—and later, to a much greater degree, Charles Hodge—went beyond the original Scottish philosophers in exploiting this convenient endorsement of their opinions by supposed "universal consent." To be used with validity, this argument would require an historical and sociological sophistication on the part of the researcher which eighteenth- and early nineteenth-century America certainly had not attained, because words and ideas that on their face appear the same often have radically different meaning in varying sociological contexts. But used superficially, the argument from universal consensus seemed to prove that people of widely different backgrounds and by very different routes had by "intuition" reached identical views of truth. Thus Alexander introduced two variables—"intuition" and supposedly "universal" consent—into his search for absolute truth.

At times Alexander frankly conceded subjective variations in conceptions of intuitive truth. "A definite number of intuitive truths cannot . . . be laid down," he wrote, because "some truths may appear self-evident to men of superior intellect, which are not immediately perceived to be true by common minds."[17] In fact, he admitted, "to distinguish between first [intuitive] truth[s] & those deduced by reasoning is not always easy or important."[18] His view of the perception of truth—whether attained by reasoning or accepted as "self-evident" by intuition—appeared at times almost as a mystical immediate awareness, as when he wrote: "Between truth and intellect the relation is such, that whenever any true proposition is distinctly apprehended, it is seen to be true; and, therefore, that the evidence of truth is in itself . . . . Intuitive truth needs no evidence, because they [sic] are at once before the mind and therefore seen at once to be true."[19]

This problem of the relation between reason and intuition in the identification of metaphysical truth closely paralleled a central religious problem in Alexander's life and in the Old Princeton Theology, namely, the relation between reason and mystical experience as the foundation of Christian certitude. It is striking that Alexander was willing to build his metaphysics on the almost mystical conception of intuition, and yet was so unwilling to express proportionate theological confidence in "the witness of the Holy Spirit" in any other than a purely rational sense, even though his own religious life had originated in an experience that quite transcended reason. One could almost say that at times Alexander's theology proved to be more rationalistic than his intuitionistic philosophy.

The inquiry as to how truth is known (epistemology) leads quite directly to the exploration of how the mind itself operates (psychology). This was the sequence within Western civilization, and Archibald Alexander was a rapt student of both subjects, partly because of the implications of both for the better understanding and analysis of religious experience. For general education, he ranked "mental philosophy" (psychology) just below the traditional staples of mathematics and the classical languages,[20] and felt that it should form "a necessary part of every complete theological course."[21]

Not only did he regard the study of psychology to be an excellent mental discipline, but he also thought that it provided a foundation for ethics because "the first principles of morals must necessarily be derived from the mind itself"—a quite "modern" statement, not entirely lacking in naturalistic implications. Psychology, he thought, "is highly useful to inquire into the nature of conscience, into the nature of liberty, & of moral agency." "It is necessary," Alexander continued, "to be acquainted with the philosophy of the mind to give a clear & consistent account of faith, hope & all other pious affections, all which have their seat in the mind."[22] It is interesting to see how much of the Christian's inmost religious experience Alexander was eager to throw open to rational scientific investigation (though of course assuming the already mentioned limitations on creative hypothesis which he would place on all natural science.)[23] Alexander also urged that the study of psychology could contribute to effective preaching, "for by this science a preacher of the gospel may learn how to adapt the truth to the minds of his hearers to produce a determinate effect."[24] Thus secular learning was to be made the valued handmaid of piety, Christian ethics, and popular preaching.

Alexander followed Berkeley, Hume, and others in the idea that the human mind is unceasingly active. He criticized John Locke's rejection of this view, charging that Locke had erred by "confounding consciousness with memory."[25] "The mind is active as soon as it exists," Alexander wrote, and added, "To conceive of a mind destitute of all mental exercise would be as hard to think of a body without extension."[26] He insisted that even in sleep the mind does not cease to be conscious. "I can conceive as easily," he said, "that the stone wh[ich] I cast into the sea exists without solidity or extension as that the soul in sleep exists without activity." As psychologists had not yet developed the concept of subconscious mental life, Alexander necessarily connected mental activity with consciousness, and ascribed to lapse of memory the large gaps which exist in our awareness of the past stream of our mental life. Thus, argued Alexander, the sleep walker or sleep talker is very obviously engaging in mental activity; yet on awaking he has often forgotten the whole thing.[27] At times Alexander seemed to be skirting near the idea of subconscious mental activity, but concluded that to have a sensation and not to know it seems to be an absurdity.[28]

Alexander, apparently identifying the "soul" with the mind, went so far as to say that "we can form no conception of the existence of a soul without thought, for it is by this property alone that we know anything of it."[29] But he refused to take the next step with Hume to deny the existence of an underlying "soul" substance and thus reduce mental life entirely to the stream of consciousness itself.[30] Rather, assured of the existence of a soul substance, Alexander argued its immortality from the unbroken stream of consciousness: "The mind is always active and therefore tho its mode of acting may be changed by the death of the body, yet its activity is not thereby destroyed."[31] In rejecting Hume's elimination of a "soul" substance and Hume's reduction of all to the stream of ideas, Alexander also rejected psychological "associationism" as developed by David Hartley and more fully later by James Mill. For associationism, the "mind" is passive and ideas associate mechanically after the pattern of Newton's physics. But for Alexander, mind itself, as the underlying "substance," remains always actively in charge.

Alexander's inner religious life was one of the motivations for his interest in psychology, and to the interpretation of this inner life he sought to relate some of his psychology and much of his theology. In spite of the importance to him of religious experience, he never succeeded in describing a relation between "reason" and "feeling" that did full justice to the experience—not an easy task.

Alexander agreed in rejecting the old "faculty" psychology,[32] but then practically reinstated it by the emphasis which he gave to the intellect, feeling, and will as separate faculties. If one separates these three, the view of the relation between them is important both for theology and for religious experience. Alexander inclined at times to place the "affections" above the will,[33] at other times to identify affections and will.[34] More particularly, the affections were for him the seat of both duty and pleasure. Thus he said in a sermon, "Man is not the mere creature of intellect. . . . He is susceptible of affections of a very exalted kind. And moral duty, in all cases, involves the exercise of the affections."[35]

This might seem to prepare the way for relating ethics to religious experience. But he did not do this, because, in the last analysis, intellect and affections are separate, and intellect controls. In a lecture he declared: "Every man's feelings & volitions are in accordance with the prevailing practical views of the understanding."[36] In his youthful sermons he had at times reflected the fine blending of "affections" and intellect seen in Jonathan Edwards's "Treatise on the Religious Affections," but in more mature life he seems to have kept intellectual functions quite separate from the "affections," a pattern more obviously suited to mathematics and to natural science than to religion or to relations between persons divine or human. And the twentieth century had challenged the possibility of completely "objective" knowledge even in natural science. Alexander's dualism of mind and heart tended to separate both theology and ethics from religious experience and to make it very difficult if not impossible for him to give full theological expression to the experience that was so central to his own Christian life. This dichotomy affected his heirs in the Old Princeton Theology even more seriously.

Those who, like Charles G. Finney, were more in the tradition of Edwards's blending of "affections" and intellect were able to apply religious experience and even revivalism directly to social action, sometimes, however, to the extent of "moralizing" theology itself. But those, like Alexander, who were in the psychological tradition of keeping "affections" separate from, and subordinate to, intellect were less able to give religious experience, as such, a central place in their theology or to relate Christian experience creatively to social action. This separation between affections and intellect would in twentieth-century America contribute to a dangerous dichotomy between "private religion" and "public religion" to the serious impoverishment of both.

When, for example, Alexander said that Christian experience was formed by the impact of God's truth (the Bible) on the human mind, exactly what did he mean by "mind"? Did the "mind" in this context include feelings (the "affections"), or was it purely rational, after the pattern of mathematics and of Newtonian physics? He appears ambivalent at this crucial point, and his heirs inclined increasingly to emphasize the latter, rationalistic, concept of mind. There were times when Alexander treated the "affections" and "understanding" as closely interrelated in Christian faith, as when he declared that the reason why an "unregenerate" person's religious knowledge is inadequate is because

it does not present truth in its true colours to the heart. It is called speculative knowledge . . . but it does not penetrate the excellence and the beauty of any one spiritual object; and it may be averred, that the affections of the heart do always correspond with the real views of the understanding. . . . Indeed, we hardly know how to distinguish between the clear perception of the beauty of an object, and the love of that object.[37]

In this statement one almost hears echoes of Edwards. But even here, instead of Edwards's blending of understanding and affections, with the affections coloring the nature of understanding itself, Alexander seems to see the understanding as a distinct function supplying the base for the religious delight of the "affections" which then follow. Thus the way is left open, in other contexts, to use the "understanding" quite separately to develop a rationalistic type of orthodoxy.

Changing his terminology somewhat, Alexander again brought understanding and affections into close relation when he told his students that in regeneration "the soul is . . . rendered capable of spiritual perception & feeling. To give a new heart, and to enlighten the understanding are therefore one & the same thing." The "regenerated" person, Alexander continued, "is firmly persuaded, not only of the truth, but of the excellence & beauty of divine objects." In this same lecture, however, he distinguished sufficiently between the feelings and the understanding to assert that "every man's feelings & volitions are in accordance with the prevailing practical views of the understanding." This understanding really remains separate and dominant, capable of being firmly committed to "orthodox" ways that identified with the rationalism of Alexander's seventeenth- and eighteenth-century roots.

Not unrelated to the question of the relation between the understanding and the affections, there was in Alexander's view of Christian experience a large superrational, almost mystical, conception that has at times been conspicuous in the mainstream of historic Christianity. "The unregenerate man," he said, "may think about God, may reason correctly . . . & express his opinions in correct words, but he knows not God, he has not a single idea of the right kind. . . . [But] the most illiterate believer has ideas of God, of an entirely different kind and far more perfect."[38] A truly psychological description of this phenomenon which he attributed to the direct action of God eluded him, and perhaps cannot be fully encapsulated in any human definition.

Meanwhile Alexander, reflecting his dualism, continued to speak and write about piety and learning as two quite separate experiences which must be brought together, instead of seeking to integrate them under some such single rubric as the knowledge of God. This dualism between piety and learning was prominent also in the plan of the Seminary which Alexander had had a part in drafting. He warned his students that "no accession to our stock of critical, & speculative knowledge can compensate for the diminution of our love to God." The danger, he explained, "mainly arises from a light & irreverent handling of sacred matters—from rashness in extending our researches too far." This last reference reflected his opinion, previously noted, that true knowledge is confined to experienced, "empirical" evidence, and does not extend to "mere" speculation. He also warned against "the pride of reason which is reluctant to acquiesce readily in the revelations of God" and against a "party spirit" which at the time was increasing amid the controversy over "Hopkinsianism."[39]

American Calvinism, ever since the early eighteenth century, had been under increasing pressure to give greater freedom to the human will. Alexander made indirect use of the stream of consciousness to reinforce the idea that human beings can change the direction of their thoughts and thus of their motives. "There is a perpetual flow of ideas & emotions in the mind," he wrote, "so that an exact equilibrium cannot remain." "We certainly have the power to a certain extent . . . to change the motives which influence the will. . . . The extent of this power is to change the train of our thoughts." But at the moment of decision, Alexander, like Jonathan Edwards, said that the will is inevitably determined by the prevailing desire, which the will cannot alter.[40]

An important aspect of the problem of human freedom was the question as to what was the divine role and what was the human role in "conversion" and the Christian life. Could the new revivalism, for example, be interpreted to accord with seventeenth-century scholastic tightening of early Calvinism without becoming smothered in the process?

In a day that was increasingly stressing human ability and initiative, Alexander emphasized the initiative of God in winning human beings. He rejected the implication "that a dead sinner can beget new life in himself." "In some places," he added, obviously with the revivalist Charles G. Finney in mind, "anxious inquirers are told that if they will hold on praying and using the means, that God is bound to save them; as though a dead, condemned sinner could so pray as to bring God under obligation to him."[41]

It is by means of the truth contained in the Bible, Alexander repeatedly taught, that God evokes a saving response in a human being. Alexander's love of dualisms was reflected in his sharp contrast between objective truth (in this case, revelation) and subjective truth (in this case, Christian experience). "There are," he wrote, "two kinds of religious knowledge . . . intimately connected as cause and effect. . . . These are the knowledge of the truth as it is revealed in the Holy Scriptures, and the impression which that truth makes on the human mind when rightly apprehended." He then likened this truth of God to a seal and the believing human being to the wax that receives the divine impression, an illustration which he used frequently through the years. Thus "it is evident that a knowledge of the truth is essential to piety." But even "where a true impression is made, it may be rendered very defective, for want of a complete knowledge of the whole system of revealed truth." This last statement contains a number of interesting implications. (1) The Bible contains a "system" of truth. (2) We have a moral obligation to receive and understand this system in its entirety. (3) Lack of knowledge of any part of the system will result in a corresponding defect in our religious experience, a view which implied strong warning against interdenominational unities. (4) Taken on its face, there is almost an implication that God's truth, like the seal on the wax, operates automatically. But this last inference would press a simile too far.

Eyeing critically the revivalistic extravagances of his day, Alexander warned: "There is nothing more necessary than to distinguish carefully between true and false experiences in religion. . . . And in making this discrimination, there is no other test but the infallible word of God." American denominational pluralism was a particular embarrassment in this quest for absolute certainty: "We find, that those denominations of Christians which receive the system of evangelical truth, only in part, have a defective experience."[42] All of this made orthodoxy in every detail crucially important both for true religious experience and for complete moral life, and obviously operated against compromise in the interest of church unity.

Because Alexander saw the human stream of consciousness as a continuum and not as a series of isolated moments, he sought antecedents of the individual's religious conversion. Although he denied "that special grace differs from common grace only in degree," he stressed the importance of previous religious instruction and suggested that there is "a gradual preparation, by common grace, for regeneration, which may be going on from childhood to mature age." Here, with this strong emphasis on rationality, he invoked supernaturalism only sparingly. The theological propositions of the catechism, memorized in childhood without being understood, can, he said, be valuable preparation for conversion and then are recalled with new understanding. Directly opposite to the more optimistic doctrine taught half a decade later by Horace Bushnell, Alexander declared that "the education of children should proceed on the principle that they [children] are in an unregenerate state until evidences of piety clearly appear."[43] Perhaps it was his emphasis on the rational foundations of Christianity that caused him to be unusually sceptical about manifestations of piety in early childhood. "I cannot remember," he wrote pessimistically to a friend, "one solitary instance of decided piety in childhood [under twelve years of age], where the child lived to adult age to prove the genuineness of the change." All others apparently had fallen from the faith. But he could mingle quite modern ideas with old, as when he emphasized training specialists to devote their lives to the Christian instruction of the young, because "our common preaching does the children no manner of good." In fact, he added, "I am doubtful whether the common custom of taking them and confining them during the [church] service is not injurious." It was his observation that "the talent of preaching to children is of all other preaching talents the most rare." He himself, however, delighted to do this kind of preaching.[44]

Alexander was very critical of revivalists like Finney who, he felt, overlooked the importance of instruction and nurture in concentrating their efforts to bring about the moment of conversion, as when he wrote: "The attempt at immediate [converting] effect, and the expectation of it, is one of the errors of the present times." But the criticism was really more psychological and pedagogical than theological. Both Alexander and those whom he here criticized were offering to God natural means—Finney and his followers concentrating on the most arresting and persuasive presentation of the gospel at the moment of appeal; Alexander focusing on more prolonged pedagogy. Much of the difference lay in the concept of human personality: Did the will have complete freedom every new moment, or was it ordinarily bound by its own "nature" and its own past experiences and choices? Perhaps each position contained part of the truth, if not stated in a form that excluded the other.

Alexander, like Edwards, had an element of existentialism in his conception of conversion. No descriptions from outside can transmit the experience of conversion. It can be understood only by involvement from within. At this point, reflecting again his ambivalence, Alexander went quite beyond his basic rationalism. Thus he wrote:

In regard to conversion, what a different thing does it turn out to be in experience, from what it was conceived to be beforehand. Whilst the anxious saint was expecting something miraculous, or entirely out of the way, he experiences a new train of thought, new and pleasing views of truth, with corresponding emotions.

The event is experienced in nature's own areas of the mind and heart, and only "afterwards" does the convert realize by faith that "the peace which he then enjoyed was the peace of reconciliation through our Lord Jesus Christ."[45] In all of this, he said, we cannot empirically identify the Holy Spirit as a separate person operating on our person. Speaking of the working of the Holy Spirit, he wrote: "We cannot be conscious of the agency of another spirit on ours, because our consciousness extends only to our own thoughts [has he here slipped into the epistemology of Locke and Berkeley which he had rejected?], and often when new feelings arise in our minds we are unable to trace them to their proper cause."[46] But for Alexander the witness of the Bible, received by faith, identifies the divine origin of this experience.[47] Thus for him the Bible guarantees the spiritual experience, rather than the reverse.

Emphasis on redemption and salvation involved the question of "assurance." Like Edwards, Alexander saw differences in the religious experiences of Christians, though he did not offer as diverse examples as had Edwards.[48] Some think they can date their conversion precisely; others mistake a later illumination for their rebirth which occurred earlier without their awareness. Throughout this discussion, Alexander presupposed that there is a precise moment in time when God "regenerates" a Christian, a moment of which many are entirely unaware when it happens. Though God's act occupies but a single instant, an extended process of preparation moving imperceptibly into awareness is sometimes experienced on the human side.[49] Here again, for Alexander, the natural and supernatural merge, as in some medieval scholastics.

More modern and optimistic than seventeenth-century Puritans, Alexander solved the problem of assurance more easily than they. "One who cordially embraces Xt. [Christ] may be assured of his election."[50] But he also offered some additional analytic self-tests, some of them involving piety—such as delight in Bible reading, prayer, meditation on God, and self-examination.[51] Elsewhere he mentioned "love of God" and "love to brethren," including concern for their physical needs, but gave little separate emphasis to the "witness of the Holy Spirit," to which Reformed theology traditionally gave first place among the evidences of regeneration. Reflecting the "objective" way by which he himself had attained a degree of assurance after fluctuating anxieties, he counseled a young relative: "You must learn to derive consolation from direct acts of faith in the Redeemer, rather than from exploring your own heart for marks of conversion."[52] Undoubtedly out of a desire to protect the doctrine of "the perseverance of the saints" against the seeming fact of lapsed believers, he emphasized that some appearances of conversion may after all be only operations of God's common grace.[53]

Alexander from his early years was interested in searching out personal examples of Christian piety. As a youth he had eagerly sought opportunities for conversation with surviving converts of the Great Awakening. Perhaps partly as a result of these early contacts he interpreted that movement much more favorably than did Charles Hodge, though criticizing some of its extravagances.[54] After the turn of the century, Alexander made much less use of Jonathan Edwards's theology than he had in his earliest years, but even in old age he declared that "few men even attained, as we think, higher degrees of holiness than Edwards."[55]

In his early years Alexander had discovered Thomas Halyburton (1674-1712), a Scottish Presbyterian contemporary of the high church Anglican William Law. Halyburton, like Law, sought to combat the coldness of deism with warm Christian piety, but unlike Law he had, in addition, written a rational treatise against deism. Halyburton's father had been ejected from his living at the Restoration of Charles II, and persecution had followed the family even after the father's death. In the closing years of his short life, Halyburton was Professor of Divinity at St. Andrews University. A mid-twentieth-century Scottish writer, influenced by reemphasis on interpersonal relations in his own day, found enduring values in Halyburton's emphasis on heart knowledge in religion and in the avoidance of a proof-text method in his extensive use of Scripture. By his life and writing, Halyburton influenced both John Wesley and George Whitefield.[56]

Early in life, as we have seen, Alexander had become interested in such Puritan devotional writers as John Flavel, though his own piety after it matured was less analytic, less introspective, less agonizing, milder, and more prevailingly cheerful than that of the Puritans. But both they and he combined emphasis on theology with emphasis on personal piety. What Alexander especially liked about the Scot Halyburton was that in him "there was a tincture of enthusiasm. "Indeed," he added, revealing his own ideal of feeling born of understanding (like the wax imprinted by the seal), "holy affections thus produced by the contemplation of truth is [sic] the very opposite of enthusiasm."[57] He admired Halyburton's ability to apply the Bible "to the various conditions and exigencies of believers" as well as his "extraordinary insight into . . . the complicated foldings of the human heart," a skill which Alexander cultivated diligently throughout his adult life.[58] A special Princeton reprint of Halyburton's Memoirs contained a "Recommendation" by Professors Samuel Miller and Charles Hodge and a nine-page "Preface" by Dr. Alexander, almost a semiofficial endorsement of Halyburton as an ideal of piety for the Seminary's faculty and students.

Alexander's piety was deep and genuine, but not arrogant or aggressive. He tended to be reticent about his most intimate affairs including his religious life. Rarely did he speak to strangers about religion, though among intimates he often spoke freely on the subject when in the mood.[59] His observation and psychological insights warned him that "indiscriminate disclosure of these secret things of the heart" in public often fosters "spiritual pride." He found the sameness and lack of spiritual conflict in routine "testimonies" at public meetings to be suspicious, and the pressure to say what was expected an unconscious temptation to hypocrisy which is "a fearful evil."[60] Because of his own deep religious experience, his psychological insights, and his transparent sincerity, Alexander was in demand as a spiritual adviser, a role which he accepted with modesty and reluctance. In his later years these individual requests for spiritual guidance by letters and in person became almost burdensome, but his services in this intimate area were one of the chief sources of his great influence. He found a dearth of helpful literature in this area.[61]

Like very many in his day, he attached special importance to the words and experiences of the dying and quoted special evidences of their unshaken faith, reflecting an other-worldly orientation which for him had priority over concerns for contemporary social evils. Religion was very much a part of his family life, where he with his wife and children would often engage in singing psalms. He would sometimes hum religious tunes, appropriate to the mood of the moment, while at his desk.[62] While Christ's divinity and redemption were for him the necessary access to God, his piety did not, like that of Bernard of Clairvaux, dwell on the details of the earthly life of Jesus, though his son, James Waddell Alexander, was the translator of Bernard's famous hymn, "O Sacred Head Now Wounded."

Recent scholarship has reemphasized and developed further William Warren Sweet's concept of the Second Awakening as a force that contributed powerfully to give organization and stability to an American society that was in rapid flux during the late eighteenth and early nineteenth centuries.[63] But Alexander was not responsive to these forces. The implications of his orthodox rationalism, though not explicitly developed in that direction by him, pointed toward freezing society in its old patterns. This would have been an impossible task, the dynamism of the times being what it was, which helps to explain why his church and the Congregationalists and the Episcopalians were losing the majority position which they had shared with the Baptists, even though the "New Measures" of some Congregationalists and New School Presbyterians were making some concessions to the forces of orderly social change.

# 13
# PROOF AND PRACTICE OF CHRISTIANITY

Apologetics and ethics ("moral philosophy") were Dr. Alexander's first and last writings, respectively, to be published. That is interesting, because both sought to start not from "revelation" or Christian experience, but from the rationality thought to be common to humanity. Both proceeded from there to lay foundations, respectively, for Christian faith and for a life consonant with Christian principles.

It has perhaps a symbolic significance that Dr. Alexander's first book was on apologetics, because in a sense the whole of the Old Princeton Theology was geared to the task of making their system of Christian truth appealing to the human mind.

"When about the year 1823 . . . a little knot of young skeptics began to make themselves busy in the College on New Jersey," Alexander was invited to preach in the College Chapel. One thinks of the somewhat similar situation of President Dwight at Yale a quarter of a century earlier. When Alexander was asked to make the sermon more widely available, he enlarged it into a book which appeared in 1825 under the title, *A Brief Outline of the Evidences of the Christian Religion*.[1] It went through various editions and was translated into a number of foreign languages.[2] A revised edition of 1836 contained much discussion of what books properly belong in the Bible (the "canon"). Its altered title significantly reflected the fact that argument for the Bible as the objective and absolute religious authority was the cornerstone of Alexander's apologetic.[3] We shall, however, postpone consideration of biblical portions of this revision until dealing with Alexander's biblical studies themselves.

Apologetics, even among those who valued it highly, always had a kind of ambivalent status. Thus President Francis Landey Patton wrote: "Apologetics is a subject that the encyclopaedists have difficulty with; some treating it as belonging to the Prolegomena of Theology and others as part of Systematic Theology."[4] By treating apologetics in the curriculum under "Studies Preliminary to Theology," Alexander obviously was placing it outside of systematic theology proper. But the whole discipline has fallen into desuetude, since most of its "proofs" of faith, even when they have been retained in a later day, depend on prior faith for their support.

From the outset, Alexander sought to give to reason a decisive role.

Truth and reason are so intimately connected, that they can never, with propriety, be separated. . . . No doctrine can be a proper object of our faith which it is not more reasonable to receive, than to reject. If a book claiming to be a divine revelation, is found to contain doctrines which can in no way be reconciled to right reason, it is a sure evidence that those claims have no solid foundation, and ought to be rejected.

Is there, then, no mystery in religion, nothing that transcends sensory experience and ordinary reasoning processes? Alexander hastened to reject any such conclusion. Referring to God, he wrote, "Every thing which relates to this Infinite Being, must be to us, in some respect, incomprehensible. . . . and all the plans and works of God are very far above and beyond the conception of such minds as ours." Thus he would emphatically distinguish between transcending reason and contradicting reason, but did not make clear what the distinction is. He acknowledged profound mystery which reason cannot fathom, while at the same time asserting that reason must be the test of its acceptability. Part of his problem was that he was treating a certain kind of reason (of which mathematics was the underlying model) as operable in every sphere of human experience. This was in sharp contrast to Immanuel Kant's positing of various kinds of "reason" adaptable, respectively, to the understanding of different kinds of reality.

While Alexander insisted that revelation is initiated by God, its "ultimate appeal is to reason." "There is no just cause for apprehending," he wrote reassuringly, "that we shall be misled by the proper exercise of reason, on any subject, which may be proposed for our consideration." But he acknowledged that there is the danger of "making an improper use of this faculty" (of reason), and cited such causes of irrationality as superstition, prejudice, passion, and biased interpretation of Scripture.[5] How was reason to be deterred from such aberrations, and how was the individual to know whether or not he was thus erring? Clearly, the task of laying the foundations for absolute norms in a rapidly changing and increasingly pluralistic American society was not an easy one.

In the course of its slightly more than a century of history, the Old Princeton Theology was deeply involved in a number of controversies—among them the struggle against deism; against the idealistic philosophy; against the historical reconstruction of Scripture; and against the ecumenical superseding of denominational distinctions. But the first of these—the counterattack against deism—placed a permanent stamp on that Princeton Theology both through the Seminary's original plan and through the influence of Alexander himself.

The fact that both Virginia and Philadelphia during Alexander's formative years had been principal American strongholds of deism left a lasting imprint on his mind. In an undated lecture he told his students, "Deism has at length descended to the common people, among whom its effects are very dreadful. . . . They [contemporary deists] are as much opposed to Natural as to Revealed religion."[6] The threat of deism, he warned, in another undated lecture perhaps written during the Jacksonian era, is all the greater "when so many of those who wield the destinies of our empire . . . use their civil power to promote their deistical or atheistical projects. And these are the very men who have raised the *war whoop* against the unoff[end]ing Sunday School & Bible Societies, &c." Clearly, Alexander's Federalists-Whig political and social predilections showed through. Deism, he declared, was a far greater peril than "Papal domination" itself.[7] He delivered a thirty-two page lecture on some of the principal deists, mostly English,[8] and an eight-page lecture on "French Infidelity,"[9] and supplied his students with a bibliography of more than a dozen deistical and nearly sixty antideistical writings.[10] As late as 1836 Alexander was still vigorously fighting deism,[11] but five years later he was ready to imply that deism was less "rampant" than it had been.[12]

The shallowness and inadequacy of deism as a religion had become evident to most Americans sooner than Alexander realized. Deism had virtually nothing to say to the depths or heights of human experience. But deism was only the tip of the Enlightenment iceberg. The Enlightenment was built into the political and economic structure of the new American nation, and even though Alexander's own scholasticism was inoculated with aspects of Enlightenment thinking, this could not give permanent immunity against the impact of the Enlightenment's critical rationalism. America began in the late nineteenth century to feel the real force of critical reason which the Enlightment had developed; and to experience its full results only in the last half of the twentieth century. It would be then that the real crisis would become more universally evident.

Alexander required his students to study the apologetic writings of the Anglican Latitudinarians Samuel Clarke (1675–1729) and William Paley (1743–1805),[13] and he himself often followed Bishop Joseph Butler's famous *Analogy* in seeking to show that the arguments used by deists against "revealed religion" applied also against their own "natural religion." As previously noted, this strategy of seeking to destroy the deist's "middle ground" was a dangerous one. While intended to persuade the deist to orthodoxy, it might, with equal logic, drive him to atheism.

Alexander's apologetics followed closely the main lines of the eighteenth-century antideistical writers, building on the "external evidences" of miracle and fulfilled prophecy to prove that the Bible contains divine revelation and on the "internal evidence" of the high spiritual and moral caliber of the biblical writings. In seeking to refute David Hume's rejection of miracles on the ground that they violated natural law, Alexander abandoned for the moment the Newtonian mechanistic conception of the universe which he otherwise quietly accepted, and argued that "natural law" is simply the way God operates and the fact that we have never seen him operate in any other way does not prove that he has not done so. But Alexander ignored another argument Hume offered against the evidential value of miracles; namely that even if one witnessed an actual miracle, this event would not of itself prove that it was God who had produced the miracle. Scripture itself corroborates this argument, where one reads that many who witnessed the biblical miracles did not view them as produced by God and therefore were not persuaded by them.

Fulfilled prophecy was the second pillar of the apologetes' "external evidences." "The Bible contains predictions of events," declared Alexander, "which no human sagacity could have foreseen, and which have been exactly and remarkably accomplished."[14] He then proceeded to set forth fulfilled prophecies originally made by "Moses," "Isaiah," "Daniel," and others. The historical reconstruction of Scripture would later show that some of these apparent predictions were written after the events described, while hermeneutical analysis would question traditional interpretations of many others. It is significant that Alexander would have nothing to do with attempts in his own day by premillennialists and others, who were using hermeneutical methods similar to his own, to apply as yet unfulfilled prophecies to contemporary and future events.

"Internal evidence"—based on the quality and value of the Bible's content—was of course the most enduring weapon in the apologete's arsenal. Alexander had never ceased to prize Soame Jenyns whose internal evidences of Christianity had contributed importantly to his own conversion as a youth. Jenyns, Alexander wrote in 1825, "exhibits the internal [evidences], in a light so strong, that his argument assumes the appearance of demonstration." Alexander himself considered the internal evidences of Christianity more effective than the external, and even included among these "internal evidences" the proof of God's existence and wisdom from the excellence of his material creation. But more particularly, it is from the Bible of the Israelites, he said, that all of the world's knowledge of the one true God stems, directly or indirectly. And he attributed this to divine revelation. "If the knowledge of the true God as received by the Jews was the discovery of reason, why was it that other nations, advanced far beyond them, in learning and mental culture, never arrived at the knowledge of this important truth?"

Alexander, like many before him and since, emphasized that the Bible gives "no profound metaphysical disquisitions; no discussion of philo-sophical principles . . . and no systematic arrangement of the subjects treated." Rather, "the method of speaking of God, in the Sacred Scrip-tures, is at once most simple, and sublime." "The glory of the Scriptures," he added, "is the revelation which they contain of the moral attributes of God"—especially his "holiness" and his "goodness," that is, his benevolence. Another "internal evidence" in the Scriptures which Alexander stressed was their realistic but hopeful picture of mankind, with the basic sequence of sin, redemption, and the life beyond. The high caliber of the New Testament's moral teachings proved for him their divine origin. He implied a broad international and even universal interpretation of human obligations when he answered the criticism that such civic virtues as patriotism, friendship, and bravery are not taught in the New Testament by saying that, so far as these "are moral virtues," they are included in the gospel precept "to love our fellow men"; but when they "interfere with the general obligation of loving all men, they are no longer virtues, but vices."[15]

On the centuries-old question of the extent of the Christian's obligation to obey civil government, Alexander's position was basically that of John Calvin, slightly updated to fit American democracy, except that Alexander—more conservative at this point than Calvin or even than Luther—said nothing about cases where the Christian for conscience' sake should disobey civil government and accept the penalty. "As long as a government has authority, so long we are bound to obey," wrote Alexander. "Christianity is so constituted as not to interfere with any civil institution." Slaveholders and all in positions of influence would find this comforting, as well as many other Americans who were appre-hensive of the dynamism and flux of the times. But, like Calvin, Alexander did recognize a right of change by orderly process—for Calvin, it was by the authority of the "Estates of the Realm"; for Alexander, in democratic America, change was by the right of "the majority of the nation" "of new modeling their government, or changing their rulers." Thus Alexander did see lawful possibility of political change but, as with Calvin, it was to be by the interaction of existing con-stitutional parts of government on each other, and not by individual revolt or by the overthrow of the constitution itself. This basic political stability Alexander found to be taught or at least to be implied in the New Testament, and he induced this as part of the evidence of the divine origin of Scripture. Alexander, of course, found in the character of Jesus the grand climax of the moral evidence of the divine origin of biblical teaching, noting particularly the balance and interrelation of the diverse excellencies portrayed in the life of Jesus.[16]

As indicated, almost the entire thrust of Alexander's apologetic was directed to proving by miracle, fulfilled prophecy, and internal evidence that the teaching contained in Scripture is of divine origin and therefore true. If one would insist on a rational apologetic, one might wish that it would seek to show that the gospel is suited to human needs, rather than concentrating almost exclusively on the effort to establish the Bible as an "objective" and absolute authority whose teaching is automatically binding at every point. Of course, as Alexander progressively set forth his interpretation of this authoritative Scripture, he did seek to show that, in accordance with God's gracious plan, the revealed truth did precisely fit the human situation.

While the lessons of history always tend to be ambivalent, Alexander, before closing his apologetic, drew some arguments from the larger human experience intended to show the beneficent impact which the gospel has had on the course of human affairs. Stimulated by the contemporary struggle of the Greeks for independence from Turkey (1821–1829), he launched into a comparison of the social influence of Christianity with that of "Mohammedanism," to the great disadvantage of the latter, amid which he stated his social claims for Christianity more broadly: "The Christian religion has been a rich blessing to every country which has embraced it. . . . What nations are truly civilized? Where does learning flourish? . . . Where are the poor and afflicted most relieved? . . . Where is the female sex treated with due respect? . . . Where do men enjoy most rational happiness?" The climatic answer was—not unexpectedly—that "every one" of these advantages "would be found in Christendom."[17]

A little later Alexander offered a similar historical argument in somewhat altered form. "We have seen in our own time, the wonderful effects of the Gospel in civilizing some of the most barbarous people. . . . Look at Greenland—at Africa— . . . and nearer home, at the Cherokees [this was written shortly before their brutal transplantation] . . . and see what the Gospel can effect." While history and sociology must pronounce these uncritical generalizations oversimplified, a case could be made that they contain important elements of truth.

Alexander also argued the divine origin of Christianity from its ability to comfort the needy and distressed.

The cottages of the poor are often blessed with the consolations of that Gospel, which . . . produces contentment, resignation, mutual kindness, and the longing after immortality. . . . The Gospel can render tolerable, even the yoke of slavery, and the chains of the oppressor. How often is the pious slave, through the blessed influence of the word of God, a thousand times happier than his lordly master! He cares not for his short deprivation of liberty; he knows and feels that he is "Christ's freeman."[18]

A post-Marxian and post-Niebuhrian era cries out for the biblical notes of divine judgment and human revolt in the face of such wrongs, but the social complacency of these quotations accurately reflected the dominant—though not quite universal—mood of prospering white America at that time. And there were evidences that some found this book helpful. Alexander's son told an intimate friend: "My father has received innumerable letters from persons converted as well as convinced by his 'Evidences,' "[19] and the president of Centre College informed Alexander that "your work on the 'Evidences' has been blessed to a man here . . . in converting him from infidelity."[20]

As we leave apologetics and turn to his ethics, we find that, in accordance with prevailing practice in eighteenth- and early nineteenth-century America, Alexander treated ethics under the category of "moral philosophy." Influenced strongly by the Enlightenment, the moral philosophers, like their close kin the eighteenth-century Christian apologists, assumed the rational unity of God's creation. Thus it was thought possible by reasoning—especially by psychological investigation of human nature—to discover and establish ultimate principles of right conduct both for individuals and for society. It was no accident that the conclusions of these nonbiblical and almost nontheological studies closely approximated, and were thought to confirm for all rational people, the ideals already professed by the nominally Christian society. A course in moral philosophy, taught to the senior class by the college president, was the climax of the typical college curriculum, offering a cosmic synthesis and the application of this to practical living. John Witherspoon set an influential, if not profoundly original, example for American moral philosophy in this period, and most such courses were based on the presuppositions of the Scottish philosophy.[21]

Alexander's lectures on moral philosophy antedated by many decades their posthumous publication by his son in 1852.[22] By that time, moral philosophy's too easy attempt to synthesize the methods and conclusions of critical science with inherited orthodoxy were already passing out of vogue.[23]

Alexander, in a method typical of the moral philosophy of his day, sought to build on ground shared by both Christian believers and non-believers. "We have at present [in this study] nothing to do," he declared, "with any principles or questions but such as can be learned from reason and experience."[24] Of course this kind of rationalistic method assigned basic importance to natural law which Alexander found "rooted in the holiness of God's nature." He took sharp exception to Thomas Hobbes, who grounded all moral authority in civil government. The extent of Alexander's effort to find in the "Law of Nature" the essence of biblical "Moral Law" is evident in his declaration that in substance there is no difference [between these two]. . . . Both prescribe the same duties to God & man. . . . The moral law [as revealed in the Bible] delivers clearly, distinctly & fully, wh[at] are by the Law of Nat[ure] taught obscurely & imperfectly."[25] The deists sought common ground with science, and with the larger non-Christian world of which Western civilization had become aware, by reducing revelation to reason; Alexander, in the area of moral law, almost elevated reason to the level of revelation. What Alexander was really seeking to do was not to bypass the Bible, but to impose on all people a moral obligation which would approximate biblical norms. And, injecting an apologetic note, he added that this moral obligation points directly to a divine Lawgiver, a kind of circular argument.[26] Thus, unlike some of his orthodox contemporaries, he did not argue that atheists are of necessity immoral; but rather that, because they have an inescapable moral sense, logically they should believe in the divine Lawgiver. Like Kant, he was using a moral argument for the existence of God, but he was arguing from very different presuppositions and by a very different method.

A major issue at the time was whether the moral quality of an ethical decision should be judged by its "intention," that is, by its motive or whether it should be judged by its "ends," that is, by the result which it achieved. *The Moral and Political Philosophy* (1786) by William Paley, an Anglican divine, was widely used as a textbook in America. Paley had the gift of clarity, albeit at the price of oversimplification. But a more immediate criticism by many Americans, including Alexander, was that Paley judged the correctness of moral decisions by "ends" rather than by intentions. For Paley, happiness was the goal which ethical decisions should seek, which marked him as a utilitarian before Jeremy Bentham whose goal was "the greatest happiness of the greatest number." Most American moral philosophers, including Alexander, preferred an ethic of intentions, and supplemented Paley with their own lectures, some later substituting their own published volumes for Paley's, as for example the widely used text by President Francis Wayland of Brown University. Alexander heartily approved of Wayland's method and emphasis on "intention," criticizing only the evident "haste" in which he wrote, by which Alexander seemed to intimate a slighting of psychological foundations of ethics which were particularly important to Alexander.[27]

Though always treating Edwards with respect, Alexander considered the central emphasis by Edwards and his followers on benevolence to be dangerously utilitarian in its thrust.[28] What particularly worried Alexander in utilitarianism was the ethical relativism that he found in it, which was an especially serious shortcoming to one who, like Alexander, was seeking "absolute" norms and ultimate certainty. Alexander also faulted utilitarianism for mistaking expediency for virtue.[29] Though thus vigorously opposing an ethics of ends, and of happiness as the ultimate end, Alexander acknowledged that the "desire for well-being is essentially wrought into our constitution" and that "if my pursuit of happiness interferes with the rights and interests of no others, it is innocent."[30] Alexander, in his eagerness to refute Samuel Hopkins's criterion of "willingness to be damned for the glory of God," appears for the moment almost as a hedonist himself.

If emphasis on "ends" by some late eighteenth- and early nineteenth-century ethicists pointed toward social concern and perhaps toward a degree of relativism, emphasis on "intention"—especially as developed by Alexander—tended to introvert ethics. Alexander's ethical thinking was even more psychological and also more introspective than that of most of his contemporaries.[31] In discussing moral norms, Alexander thus touched on problems related to religious experience, but had little to say about obligations to social involvement.

Alexander repeatedly said that intention or motive determines the moral quality of an action and even extended this somewhat dangerously to add that a good disposition which does not have occasion to act is also virtuous.[32] But before one can intend to do what is right, one must decide what is the right. Thus he felt required to establish objective standards of right based on reason.

Alexander disagreed sharply with John Locke's opinion "that there are no clear principles of morality in which all men are agreed."[33] For many, Locke's view appeared to be fully confirmed by the diversity which Western man had discovered overseas, as well as by the increasing cultural pluralism at home. But Alexander and many contemporary moral philosophers, seeking a universal foundation for morals, taught that without appeal to the authority of the Bible and without any previous conception of moral law or of a divine Lawgiver, the individual's conscience could be a sound moral guide. In fact, Alexander claimed, "the dictates of conscience are the law of nature, written on the hearts of all men."[34] Here, once again, the intuitionism of Scottish philosophy came to the rescue. "There are first principles or intuitive truths in morals, as certainly and as universally believed, as any mathematical axioms."[35] Here, as frequently elsewhere, Alexander used universal consent to confirm intuition: "Let an act of manifest injustice be performed before their eyes, and among a thousand spectators there will be but one opinion." Dr. Alexander's son and editor notes "the great earnestness with which . . . the author maintains the intuitive perceptions of conscience as independent of every doctrine of theology, even the greatest." Intuitive conscience perceives not universal moral laws, but what is right in individual cases; then reason inductively infers universal moral laws from these individual instances.[36] While this certainly is not twentieth-century situation ethics, it does appear to offer, potentially, a degree of flexibility. Alexander does not start with a universal moral law, but with individual instances where conscience, interpreted by reason, must make a moral decision in the light of the particular case.

In Alexander there is a complex relation between conscience (which he sometimes calls "the moral faculty"), intuition, and reason. Conscience acquires its information, both intuitively and empirically, then transmits this information to the reason which evaluates what it receives and decides upon suitable action. In this process, intuition and conscience, working together, function almost as a sixth sense. This process operates to make clear what is right in individual cases. By definition, Alexander claims, the very conception of "right" carries with it the moral obligation to perform what intuition and observation, interpreted by reason, have defined as the right. Conscience, thus interpreted by reason, is the best light that we have at any given moment and we have the moral obligation to obey it. But if, because of faulty interpretation by reason, our consciences lead us into error, we are nonetheless guilty of sin, because we are morally accountable for the evil of our nature which corrupted reason.[37] At this point, unannounced presuppositions, based on the author's Old Calvinism, have invaded what was to have been a purely rational argument.

Alexander offers an organizing concept when he says: "Reason or understanding is the genus; the judgments of conscience are the species. Reason has relation to all intelligible subjects; the moral faculty [conscience] is conversant about moral qualities alone." For Alexander, "reason or understanding" is supreme in all aspects of human personality—it is the executive committee or clearinghouse for all normal and proper human functions. But in the last analysis, Alexander, in spite of all his effort to be "rational," has introduced at the very center of conscience the element of "intuition" which he cannot define in rational terms. It is the same problem which appeared in his discussions of epistemology, psychology, and piety—a paradox which he failed to acknowledge as such, while assuming that he had treated these subjects with uninterrupted rationality.

The analogy of Alexander's concept of "conscience" to both piety and aesthetics comes out clearly when he says:

Conscience, or the moral sense, is not a simple but a compound faculty, including both an intellectual act or judgment and a peculiar feeling or emotion. . . . It will serve perhaps to illustrate this subject, if we bring into view another faculty between which and the moral sense there is a remarkable analogy. I refer to what is commonly called Taste, or that faculty by which men are in some degree capable of perceiving and relishing the beauties of nature and art. In this there is a judgment respecting that quality denominated Beauty, but there is also a vivid emotion of a peculiar kind accompanying this judgment.[38]

There is here a clear echo of Lord Shaftesbury who gave new impetus to aesthetic theory and who treated aesthetics and ethics in tandem. Influenced by the Cambridge Platonists, Shaftesbury emphasized presence of an emotional and intuitive element in aesthetic and ethical values and greatly influenced both Francis Hutcheson and Jonathan

Edwards.[39] It was characteristic of Alexander's inner dichotomy that he was responsive to such Platonic tendencies to mystical awareness and to wholeness, but was unable to synthesize these with the dominating dualism of his Scottish realism. Thus in the last analysis, he rejected any independent or fully assimilated insights of "taste" by bringing these completely under the domination of reason: "Instead, therefore, of making our moral feelings mere instinctive emotions, as is done by Hutcheson and Shaftesbury, we make them depend on the clear dictates of the understanding; for, as we have often explained, the judgments of conscience are no other than the understanding judging on moral subjects."

In discussing ethics, Alexander could not of course escape the problem of human freedom. He rejected any suggestion that an individual's moral decisions are merely the product of his environment, appealing for support to his old standbys, intuition and universal consensus.[40] In view of the slight regard he had for the relation between ideas and their social context, the problem of environmental determinism did not loom large for him.

American Calvinists in the early nineteenth century were deeply involved in debates about the nature of the human will and its freedom. Alexander was concerned to root moral responsibility more deeply than in ungrounded and fluctuating acts of volition of the passing moment. Such unpredictable and uncaused acts of willing seemed to dissolve the concept of the individual's underlying continuous "character," and might even be viewed as weakening social stability, though Alexander, who seldom referred to social implications, did not mention the latter possibility. Thus in discussing the will or volition, Alexander viewed it as a function of something continuous and stable—an underlying substance, the person's nature or "latent dispositions" which were the real seat of the person's moral character. Here, again, for confirmation he looked to "the common sense of mankind." Sometimes he related these "underlying dispositions" to the "affections," as when he said, "The proper seat of moral qualities is not in the will, considered as distinct from the affections, but in the affections themselves. . . . The internal affections or desires are properly the springs of our actions, and our wills are the executive power by which they are carried into effect."[41]

Alexander distinguished between "volitional," as restricted to an act of willing, and "voluntary" as including any spontaneous feeling or desire. It was in this kind of spontaneity that Alexander found moral quality. Thus, for him, as already noted, there can be virtue or sin apart from any acts of the will.[42] Because the mind is continually active, it is possible to sin even during sleep. On the other hand, Alexander thought that some states of mind are not voluntary, in this sense of being spontaneous. Here he almost seems to lapse into the associationist psychology which he had rejected. Such involuntary states of mind are without moral character.[43] While the will cannot will to change itself, the will can, to a degree, get control of its stray thoughts and thus can influence the future choices of the will itself.[44]

True freedom, Alexander insisted, does not require a self-determining power in the will. It requires only that a person have "the power to will and act in accordance with his own inclination. . . . Men feel accountable, not only for their volitions and actions, but for the views and feelings which precede volition." To suppose, he continued, that a person has "a power to act independently of all reasons and motives, would be to confer on him a power for the exercise of which he could never be accountable." True freedom, he declared, is not incompatible with "necessity," for God himself is bound by the necessity of his nature to do good and to avoid doing evil.[45] On this issue of the freedom of the will, Alexander stood solidly on "Old Calvinism."

Dr. Alexander's moral philosophy, by a rational study of human nature, particularly of conscience, sought to set forth the principles on which right conduct should be based. The appeal to "conscience" can stimulate radicalism, but when based on a static view of human nature and of society, it tends to support the status quo.[46] Under such circumstances, conscience readily becomes a negative "response" to an outside "stimulus," rather than a creative force. Nor did Alexander, in his general thinking, give large room to the postmillennial ideas which were stimulating many of his contemporaries to innovative movements. But Alexander's moral philosophy, in its suggestive wrestling with some of the deepest contemporary aspects of the subject, was in its day a distinguished representative of its genre. James McCosh, later president of the College of New Jersey, but at that time professor in Queen's College, Belfast, Ireland, called Alexander's *Outlines of Moral Science* "one of the very best which we have on the subject of man's Moral Nature," and recommended the book to his own students.[47]

In his moral philosophy, Alexander did not apply his basic principles in detail to specific social issues, but other writings of his indicate that he endorsed, with his customary spirit of moderation, many of the social concerns of the day. He did not, however, support the antislavery movement, but favored instead the more neutral African colonization effort. He continued to support "Sabbath" observance—more by encouraging voluntary participation than by legislative enactment—and to oppose the theater.[48] Like his contemporaries, Alexander assumed that social needs were to be met by caring for individuals rather than by attempting to reform social structures, as many Christians sought to do in the more interdependent era of rapid industrialization after the Civil War.

In his inaugural address in 1812, Alexander, reflecting the growing optimism of that era, gloried that under their [the Scriptures'] benign influence, war has become less sanguinary and ferocious [this following the French Revolution, while the Napoleonic Wars were still in progress, and six months after America's entrance into the War of 1812]; justice has been more equally distributed; the poor have been more generally instructed and their wants supplied; asylums have been provided for the unfortunate and distressed; the female character has been appreciated and exalted to its proper standard in society; the matrimonial bond has been held more sacred; and polygamy, the bane of domestic happiness, discountenanced.[49]

More specifically, on occasion, Alexander attacked economic sins. "A voracious spirit of avarice," he warned in an undated sermon, "has pervaded the mass of the people. Gain has been their God. . . . A swindling sort of speculation has greatly banished honest and fair dealing. . . . Failures to an enormous amount far above what the person ever possessed of his own have drawn thousands into ruin."[50] In similar vein, in another undated sermon. Alexander denounced covetousness as "an excessive love of riches," and then proceeded to list some typically Protestant virtues which are not to be regarded as covetousness—"industry in our lawful callings"; thrifty living that avoids undue "pride and fashion"; enforcing one's "just rights" of property. On the other hand, he saw real evidence of covetousness "if riches . . . be our chief object of affection"; or if we "use unlawful means to obtain" riches. Here he faced the moral problem of the acquisition of wealth, but seemingly was inclined to limit acquisition only by what existing law forbids. "It is," he continued, "an evidence of covetousness when we do not relieve the necessities of the poor and promote the general welfare as far as we can."[51] If these economic views did not go beyond the prevailing social ideals of his day, neither did they fall short of those standards, and there is abundant evidence that the seeking of wealth was never for Alexander himself an "ultimate concern."

Alexander's attitude toward the rapidly expanding temperance movement of his day was characteristically moderate. Dr. Hodge has aptly summarized it: "Dr. Archibald Alexander, as a general rule, never drank wine; but when the use of wine came to be pronounced sinful, he would sometimes, in company, take a glass for conscience sake."[52] In the moral crusades of his day, Alexander, like Hodge after him, opposed denouncing as sin what was not explicitly defined as such in the Bible. Thus a very wide area of conduct was permanently left open to rational ethical deliberations, free from specific divine injunctions.

# 14
# A PROTESTANT SCHOLASTICISM

Classes in colleges and theological schools in Alexander's early days were commonly referred to as "recitations"—an ominous term. In some institutions they were exactly that. But Alexander was too spontaneous a person to be satisfied with mechanical routine. He did use a textbook in theology—the *Institutes* of the Swiss Reformed Scholastic Francis Turretin (1623–1687), written in Latin, from which the students "recited" on assigned portions.[1] Alexander had a flare for extemporaneity, and supplemented both the text and the students' summary of it with original and stimulating comments. In addition, students were assigned topics for papers which were discussed by him and by their peers. He also developed over the years lectures of his own which updated and modified the seventeenth-century textbook. In his courses he often supplied syllabi, lists of questions, and names of authors of differing viewpoints, which many of the more interested students followed up. Before long a "Theological Society" was created, which had parallels in other institutions, and where theological discussion could be pursued more informally under the stimulus of the professor.[2]

We have said that Alexander's thinking was not highly systematized. A corollary was that he escaped being stereotyped or boringly predictable. His manuscripts show that rather than reading verbatim the same lectures year after year, he commonly lectured from outlines which varied both in structure and content even when dealing with the same subject. A comparison of extant student notes on his course in "Didactic Theology" for the successive years 1842–1843 and 1843–1844 indicates that in the interval—even though at that time over seventy years of age—he had made numerous changes in both the sequence and the identity of the major subdivisions of the course.[3]

Thus, in seeking to trace the development of Alexander's thought after his coming to Princeton, the historian finds an abundance of quite separate manuscripts of varying length, but a paucity of dated material. There are, however, revealing student notes on Alexander's course in

"Systematic Theology" (later designated "Didactic Theology") from November 1814 to June 1815, Alexander's third year of teaching. These notes are mostly confined to what Alexander later defined as "introductory" to theology proper and to which these early years he devoted more lecturing than to theology proper—undoubtedly because of his extensive use of Turretin's textbook in the latter area. These lectures of 1814–1815 touch on the history of systematic theology as a study; the nature of truth and how it is known; the existence of God and the immortality of the soul; the necessity of revelation; the "internal evidences" that God is revealed in the Bible; and a lengthy discussion of the canon of the Old and New Testaments.[4]

An undated manuscript of Alexander entitled "Introductory Lecture" outlines the forthcoming course under thirty-eight headings, indicating by its fuller development a considerably later date than that of the student's notes of 1814–1815.[5] Five topics, he told his students, will discuss the importance, difficulty, and prerequisites of Didactic Theology; three will deal with the problem of knowledge; seven with natural and revealed religion; four with the inspiration, canon, and interpretation of Scripture (hermeneutics). The last half of this introductory series then announced what would be the arrangement of the theological substance of the course. The material will be set forth systematically in logical order which Alexander acknowledged was that "pursued by the schoolmen, & . . . by most systematic writers among Protestants," rather than in the biblical order of the "covenants" as exemplified by the seventeenth-century Dutch theologian, Johann Cocceius. Thus he was deliberately selecting the more abstract and rational approach rather than the more personal and biblical and historical method of Cocceius. The plan chosen started with God and his attributes, then came the Trinity, the divine decrees, creation and providence, man's original state and fall, the nature of sin and freedom of the will, the covenant of grace, Christ the Mediator and the application of his New Covenant, justification, regeneration, and sanctification, good works and perseverance, the Sacraments, and then "the last things" (eschatology)—"death, judgment, resurrection, heaven, and hell."[6]

It is very noticeable that there is here no heading devoted to the church, an omission which has often been commented on in the *Systematic Theology* of Alexander's successor, Charles Hodge. This omission is the more striking in view of the fact that in Alexander's day the American churches were developing new home and foreign missionary activities, were confronting rapidly increasing religious pluralism, and the functions of ministers were becoming more diversified. This pluralism was contributing to intense denominational competition, especially on the frontier. Meanwhile the nonecclesiastical voluntary societies were organizing pragmatic cooperation of Christian individuals across denominational lines. All of this implied real problems of self-identification for the American churches. At the same time, the American nation, with its mounting sectionalism and expanding pluralism, was itself experiencing an acute problem of self-identification. But there was a notable differ- ence in the way nation and church treated their respective problems of self-identification. On the national stage there was continual and agoniz- ing debate concerning the true meaning of the Constitution of the United States and the nature of the union of the states; while among the churches, deep exploration concerning the nature of the church itself was confined almost entirely to high churchmen and to those who had been influenced by the new wave of idealistic philosophy.[7] In most American denominations, including the Presbyterian, the needed thorough theological reexamination of the nature of the church itself and of its ministry was postponed until stimulated by the international ecumenical movement of the twentieth century.

In giving a brief introductory history of systematic theology, Dr. Alexander told his students, "Theology is not taught systematically in the s[acred] s[criptures] of the O[ld] & N[ew] T[estament]."[8] One is startled to read this historical approach, for elsewhere Alexander seemed to regard the system of theology to which he adhered as actually taught in Scripture and as being almost as absolute in its derived correctness as he felt the Scripture itself to be. "Nor," continued Alexander, "have the doctrines of S[acred] s[cripture] been reduced into system by any of the Fathers unless we shd. choose to call the creeds by the name of a system." It should be noted in passing that the Apostles' Creed of the late fourth century, with its brief treatment of Father, Son, Holy Spirit, Church, and Last Things served as a structural model—with of course extensive amplification—for many systematic theologies of Reformed and other churchmen. Alexander's historical summary then declared that "Systematic Theology took its rise in the sixth century" following which he named, among others, Isidore of Seville and especially Peter Lombard in the Western Church, and before him, John of Damascus in the Eastern Church.

Alexander found a "dark period of the church wh[ich] intervened between the origin of Scholastic Theology & the Reformation. . . . True learning & Theology were in a lamentable state during the whole period. . . . At the Reformation, Theology was purged from the filth & errors of the Schoolmen."[9] This way of viewing the late Middle Ages— which the twentieth century regards as the climax of centuries of cul- tural development and a chief ancestor of the Protestant Reformation and of modern Western civilization—was widespread in America in Alexander's day and helps to explain the fear and hostility felt at that time toward the rapid immigration of Roman Catholics into the United States.

Somewhat anomalously, immediately following this disparaging reference to the medieval schoolmen, Alexander frankly acknowledged that their "method of treating it [theology] systematically, was not laid aside," and cited the *Common Places* (1521) of the Lutheran Philip Melanchthon as "the commencement of Systematic Theology among the Protestants." Among the Reformed he mentioned Zwingli, Bullinger, Calvin, Beza, and others. In America, though he named Samuel Willard of the late seventeenth century, he called Samuel Hopkins's *System of Doctrines* "the only professed system of Theology written to America to date," but added, somewhat disparagingly, that "it does not treat of a great number of questions commonly handled in Systems of Theology." He also acknowledged that "Dr. [Timothy] Dwight's sermons contain a system of Theology, written with elegance & good sense."[10]

In commenting on specific aspects of Alexander's "Didactic Theology," it should be noted that no extant manuscript sets forth his theology in continuous form. Instead, there are separate brief topical manuscripts which have been collected by the Seminary librarians and packaged under various umbrella titles such as "Lectures on Didactic Theology." The present writer has arranged the treatment of these separate topics and some others from Alexander's pen in an order that corresponds in general with the student outlines of 1843–1845 previously mentioned, and which roughly parallels various Reformed sequences of treatment. Though Alexander's extant presentation of systematic theology exists only in fragments, it can be fitted together with a degree of self-consistency which suggests that his underlying thought patterns were much more systematic and fully developed than his rather fragmentary and sometimes extemporaneous presentation might imply.

Dr. Alexander seems to have confined his Apologetics (he did not use that term) to "evidences" of the divine authority of the Bible and left "natural theology" (that is, philosophical arguments for the reality—"existence" was his word—of God) to theology proper.

It reflects some degree of breadth in Alexander's thinking that he recommended as "very good" books on the existence and perfections of God the *Natural Theology* (1794) of William Paley, whom he elsewhere denounced as a Utilitarian; and the widely used *Demonstration of the Being and Attributes of God* by Samuel Clarke, who had been formally accused of heretical views in the Church of England Convocation. Students were even requested "to read & digest with care" Paley's book.[11]

Alexander laid basic emphasis on "natural religion." "Take away," he wrote, "all belief of a First Cause—obliterate from the minds of men all ideas of the perfections of God, and the establishment of revelation becomes impossible." "Imagine," he continued, "a whole people atheistic. Missionaries going to them would first have to prove to them the existence of God."[12] Here, in true scholastic fashion, "reason" leads up to the threshold of faith, and appears as an indispensable precondition of faith. The nonrational "intuition" which Alexander so stressed in his epistemology here finds no parallel in any action by the Holy Spirit's illumination in making the Christian conception of God come alive directly to the formerly unbelieving hearer. Seemingly a person must previously be intellectually convinced by an entirely separate process of the "existence" of such a God. "In receiving a revelation," Alexander said, "it must be assessed as true that there is a God who makes the revelation. . . . Therefore this truth cannot originally be established by revelation."[13] One almost gets the impression that an atheist must be brought by rational argument to deism then to theism as a necessary preparation for becoming a Christian believer. Yet, once again, Alexander appears to be ambivalent on the relation between head and heart—the rational and the affective—as when he said, "Atheism has been properly denominated a disease of the heart, rather than of the head. . . .Atheism seems to be incapable of a cure from mere reasoning."[14] This statement seems to depend on a direct illumination by the Holy Spirit which bypasses rational argument—unless the "atheist" is assumed to be quite beyond God's reach, which certainly was not Alexander's opinion.

Alexander suggested three possible sources of natural theology—that is, of the idea of God: it is innate; it is handed down by tradition through the diverging races and peoples of the world from an original revelation; or it is discovered by reason. He found practical truth in all three views. Consistently with his announced epistemology, he found the idea of God innate not in the sense that it is already formed at birth, but in the limited sense that all human beings have the capacity to recognize the reality of the idea when it is properly presented.

Alexander saw in revelation a second source of the idea of God which, although corrupted, he found scattered among all peoples. There were in him, as in Reformed scholasticism in general, a precarious combination of a high Calvinistic conception of universal human sinfulness with an extravagant optimism about the competence of human reason. The first of these led him to conclude that "the knowledge of God has been preserved in the world by tradition. . . . It has been transmitted like language from father to son" from the original revelation by God—presumably God's self-revelation to the first humans, as recorded in the Genesis narrative.[15]

Inevitably Alexander found in reason a third source of belief in God. This gave him the opportunity of reviewing some of the classical philosophical arguments for God's existence. Descartes's ontological argument—in which Descartes was preceded by Augustine and Anselm—that the idea of a perfect being proves that such a being exists, because existence is necessary to perfection—seemed too *a priori* for Alexander's strong empirical emphasis on experience. Alexander considered this "attempt to prove the being of God with[ou]t any reference to the existence of the external world" as reflecting "the evil consequences of doubting or denying the truth of the inform[atio]n of the senses." Apparently it savored too much of philosophical idealism for Alexander's philosophical realism. But he did accept Dr. Samuel Clarke's somewhat similar argument for the infinity of God based on the analogy of infinite time and infinite space.[16]

Without referring to Kant, Alexander often used a moral argument for the existence of God, as when he asserted that "the existence of God may be fairly inferred from the operations of the moral faculty." He was careful to repudiate the narrowness of some contemporaries who were arguing that atheism inevitably produced immorality, when he added: "But the belief of a divine existence is not necessary to all exercise of conscience."[17] This recognition that "atheists" retained a moral nature was necessary to give universal validity to the moral argument for God's existence.

The cosmological argument for God's existence—seemingly strengthened by Newton's mathematically based synthesis—argued that so marvelous a machine as the universe must be the product of a divine intelligence. This argument of course confronted a challenge from Hume's critique of causality which Alexander dismissed as "denying the existence of power or efficiency, and reducing the whole to mere precedence & sequence in events, excluding all idea of any agency of a cause on the effect." Here, as usual in answering Hume, Alexander drew on Scottish realism which he oversimplified to yield an easy refutation: "That every effect must have a cause is one of the clearest & most evident of the class of intuitive truths."[18] Alexander felt that the only plausible objection to the cosmological argument was the view of the "Modern or French Philosophy," related to the French Revolution, "that the intelligence necessary to produce these effects, does not exist in one independent Being, but resides in all nature, in various degrees & kinds according to the different species of being which exist." This he rejected outright as "a deification of the Universe itself" in which "there is no freedom and choice" and "no being to be worshiped."[19] The Old Princeton Theology, with its sharp dualism between God and man and between observing subject and observed object, was always specially hostile to anything that savored of pantheism.

Alexander's zeal for "Natural Religion" implied that the reasoning processes used in science are competent also for at least partial understanding of religious truth; that knowledge of persons whether human or divine is the same kind of knowledge as the knowledge of physical science. "Is it so indeed," he wrote, "that the reason of man has dived into the depths of philosophical & mathematical science, unaided by any revelation; and yet the same minds if they had been impartially directed to the inquiry, could never have hit upon a single conclusive argument to prove the existence of a Supreme Being?"

Moving beyond natural theology, Alexander turned to God's "attributes." It would be hard to imagine a subject farther removed from religious experience than the philosophic discussion of this. But Alexander often vitalized his scholasticism by adding an emphasis on God's direct relation to human affairs. Thus he sounded almost like a twentieth-century exponent of "salvation history" when he told his students that "the s[acred] s[criptures], avoid all abstruse disquisitions & make God known to us principally in the relations which he bears to his creatures, as Creator, Preserver, Benefactor, Witness, Saviour, Judge &c." But, on the other hand, he did not avoid more speculative treatment of the divine attributes. Discussing God's infinity, he pronounced this a negative idea, derived from the fact that no matter how far we extend the concept of space or of time we can always imagine it to be capable of extension still further.[20] Thus he declared that the concept of infinity transcends human experience.

Alexander treated the doctrine of the Trinity following his discussion of God's attributes. It is of course no surprise to find him affirming the historic Christian doctrine, but it is somewhat of a surprise to see him saying that "it is a strong presumptive evidence that this doctrine is taught in the Bible, that it has been the doctrine of the Christian church in all ages."[21] The authority here conceded to Christian consensus contrasts with his emphatic denial that the authority of the Church was involved in deciding what books belong in the Bible. His doctrine of the Person of Christ was also strictly orthodox, in which he discussed in some detail Christ's bodily resurrection.[22]

In treating the topic "Creation," Alexander noted that some people used the term to refer to God's molding preexisting matter. But he rejected the idea of an eternally existing chaos antedating creation as "most inconceivable," and insisted that "creation" meant creating out of nothing—"a stupendous and incomprehensible work! but not impossible to omnipotence."

Alexander's pervasive dualism between mind and matter is reflected in his readiness to consider the possibility "that the matter of the earth might have been created millions of years" before the creation of man. Here, of course, he was addressing the problems being raised at that time by geology. Sir Charles Lyell's three volumes on *Principles of Geology* (1830–1833) had precursors in ancient Greece, in the Renaissance, and since the seventeenth century, but Lyell laid the solid foundation of modern geological science in his first volume by announcing his "attempt to explain the former changes of the earth's surface by reference to causes now in operation." Thus the vast age of the universe was being widely discussed decades before Darwin.

Alexander was fully aware of the discovery of fossils "of numerous animals both of the land and water entirely different from any species now found upon earth." He acknowledged that in the "coal strata, we find enormous reeds, bamboos, fern, unknown in the climate where these beds are deposited." Speaking of calcarious strata, he noted that "as we rise to the superior calcarious strata, the shells approach in form nearer to living animals" and that "t[he] same sort of shells . . . are found every where round the globe, in strata of the same kind." But instead of heeding the scientific hypotheses being offered to explain these remarkable facts, he noted that some were construing the "six days" of Genesis as "periods of great and unequal length," and he lightly dismissed the matter with the comment that this stretching of time "seems inconsistent with the simplicity of the Mosaic narrative" and that there was "no purpose to be served by making the world older than Moses has made it." "Mosaic history," he said quite truly, "is written in popular language & not intended to teach men Natural Philosophy." He might have added quite logically, "and therefore it cannot be used to refute the findings of science." But this was far from his intent.

Alexander's considerable interest in the exciting discoveries of science was not in order to join the scientists in seeking to explain inductively these data, but to borrow their findings to buttress his own theology. Thus near the end of his lecture on Creation he told his students: "Instead of curious, but useless inquiries into the primordial elements of the universe, it would be much more profitable to contemplate the wonderful wisdom of God, in the several parts of creation." "Take," he continued, "a single example from the atmosphere; wh[ich] consists of 79 parts of azote [nitrogen] 21 parts of oxygen with a small proportion of carbonic acid gas." From this he drew the teleological argument that this combination was exactly suited to human needs.[23]

Alexander's treatment of providence followed logically his discussion of Creation for, as he said, "it w[ould] be absurd to suppose that God w[ould] create t[he] world without having any end in view." Our theologian's logic proceeds inexorably: "And if he had an end in bringing t[he] world into existence he will of course so direct and govern his creatures as t[hat] the end designed shall be attained." Having gone this far, logic takes another step. "The doctrine of a general providence extending to the events of a great magnitude . . . cannot be maintained while a particular providence extending to all creatures & to all events is denied." This doctrine of providence, as Alexander clearly recognized, encountered two problems—the so-called laws of nature, and human freedom. Concerning the first, he answered rather casually that "the power by wh[ich] all material causes act is the power of God" and "there is . . . nothing to hinder the occasional departure from these laws, when any exigense [sic] of the divine government renders it expedient. These deviations are called miracles."[24]

Starting with God's absolute sovereignty, Alexander's thought moved from creation to providence to double predestination. "Besides the decree of election," he said, "there is also an eternal decree of reprobation. . . . God reprobates no one but such as he foresees will be & continue in a state of sin & unbelief."[25] Alexander has here softened somewhat the Westminster Confession which declares that God has "not decreed any thing because he foresaw it as future, or as that which would come to pass on certain conditions."[26] Alexander continued: "They [the Calvinists, including himself] say that God c[ould] have saved all men if it had so pleased him—But for wise reasons & having regard to his div[ine] attributes he otherwise determined." He then went on to say—not altogether convincingly in the light of what had preceded—that "God loves all his creatures & does them good in many ways."[27] Writing late in life, he referred to predestination as "this awful and mysterious doctrine."[28]

Double predestination was taught by Augustine and further developed by many medieval Augustinians. John Calvin, the Westminster Confession of Faith, and others gave classic expression to the doctrine.[29] Calvin acknowledged that "the decree [of reprobation] is dreadful indeed, I confess" ("Decretum quidem horribile, fateor"), and warned against indulging in idle curiosity about predestination.[30] The problem of the relation between the divine and human wills, between God's sovereignty and human freedom, must always remain a baffling one for Christians interested in such unanswerable speculations. The underlying intent of the "Calvinistic" position was a noble one in both its religious insight and its moral seriousness—to give to God the glory for human redemption while at the same time ascribing to human beings full moral responsibility for their conduct. Probably this profound insight is best expressed in paradox or in poetry.

This Calvinistic emphasis on God's sovereignty had begun to raise serious questions about human freedom and responsibility among New England Calvinists early in the eighteenth century under the impact of the Enlightenment. By Alexander's day the discussion had intensified and included Presbyterians. "The greatest difficulty," Alexander acknowledged, "lies in conceiving how the actions of free agents are directed & governed by providence, consistently with their freedom, & the accountableness [sic] of the creature. . . . It is sufficient for us to know that he can do it, and does perform it."[31] In considering the relation of God's will to human will, two extremes should be avoided, he said—"the one wh[ich] ascribes such a liberty to man as makes him independent of his Creator . . . The other, that wh[ich] makes man's dependence so great, that God is considered as working all things in all."[32] He criticized the view of Nathanael Emmons who, with others, was being accused of emphasizing God's sovereignty in such a way as to make God the actual author of human sin. At the opposite pole he insisted that "liberty as it consists in spontaneity is essential to a moral agent"; and thus construing liberty as spontaneity, he could say reassuringly: "We possess liberty. . . . it is the intuitive perception of every mind."[33]

In an article in 1831 on the "inability of Sinners," Alexander sought to answer the criticism made by many revivalists and others that Calvinistic preaching that human beings were " 'dead in trespasses and sins,' and utterly unable to put forth one act of spiritual life" called hearers into the complacent conclusion that they were "excusable" and need make no effort "until it should please a sovereign God to work." The problem was similar to the question of the possibility and role of human "preparation" for conversion in early New England.[34] Alexander's answer was similar to that of the Puritans: "The true system is, to exhort sinners to be found in the use of God's appointed means; that is, to be diligent in attendance on the word, and at the throne of grace. . . . While they are reading, or hearing, or meditating, or praying, God may, by his Holy Spirit, work faith in their hearts." This was silent as to the way, if any, in which the human decision was causally related to the divine. He argued that the opposite doctrine that people "can repent, at any moment, by a proper use of their own powers," was much more likely to produce over confidence, postponement of action, and a failure to make an affirmative Christian decision than was his own Calvinistic emphasis on God's ultimate sovereignty.[35]

Amid the debates about Calvinism in Alexander's day, the relation between God's sovereignty and human responsibility was not the only topic being reexamined. The related questions of the origin of sin and its transmission—that is, the doctrines of "original sin" and "imputation"—were also in hot contention.[36] Surely no one could accuse the Calvinism of that era of dodging the hard, recondite questions! The speculative problem was a real one. If God the Creator is good and all-powerful, how did sin originate? And what connection, if any, is there between the origin of sin in the human race and the present manifestations of sin? Of course the nature of the problem later became drastically altered in the wake of biological evolution.

The traditional view was that because of "Adam's" sin both he and all his descendents became both guilty before God and corrupted in nature, with the result that inevitably thereafter they repeatedly yielded to sin. Jonathan Edwards asserted that Adam's descendants were really in him biologically and spiritually and that therefore they actually participated in his sin, thus incurring personal guilt. The more widely held view was that God had appointed Adam to be "federal" (that is, covenantal) representative of the human race. Adam, because initially innocent and not influenced by a corrupt ancestry, provided his posterity with their best chance of using the gift of freedom sinlessly and thereby confirming this freedom in righteousness. But this idea of an "appointed" representative was increasingly foreign to Americans, who had fought the Revolutionary War partly against being "represented" in Parliament by persons whom they had not themselves elected. Other forces also in the contemporary culture operated against this view. For example, even if interpreted symbolically, the organic concept of human solidarity in sin—or of solidarity in anything else for that matter—was quite alien to an age and a land in which nominalism and individualism were dominant. But in the twentieth century, as industrialization and interdependence began to make organic conceptions of society once again more intelligible and applicable, Reinhold Niebuhr and some others found symbolic, though not literalistic, conceptions of "original sin"—in drastically altered form, to be sure—helpful in describing the human predicament.

Alexander's orthodox rationalism often ran into a dead end when it became evident that his ultimate guide was really not speculative logic, but simple faith. "Now if we were at liberty," he admitted to his students with admirable frankness, "to make our own reason the standard of what it is proper & right for the Governor of the universe to do in dealing with his own creatures we would be apt to come to the conclusion that such a principle [as "original sin"] should not be admitted into the righteous government of God." But, he added, "are we competent judges" of this? "Is not the course proper to be pursued by us, to learn from divine revelation what the principles are, on which God governs the world?"[37] Thus his ardent rationalism, in the last analysis, habitually surrendered to traditional doctrine which was supposedly derived from biblical authority. And it might be added that he seemed to have been happier and really more convincing in his metaphysical and psychological speculations where he had a freer hand than he was in his theological speculations where his conscience forced him to steer for conclusions that were predetermined by authority. Deeper for him than his elaborate argument defending the authority and inspiration of Scripture was his faith in the reality of God as he had found him in Christ.

In somewhat the same vein, this man who found free-soaring speculation so delightful where matters of faith and of the Bible did not appear to be involved, was irritated by the speculations of theologians which diverged from his own inherited speculations. Thus, after reading sermons on the problem of sin by Professor Eleazar T. Fitch of Yale Divinity School, and anticipating another publication on the same subject by Fitch's more famous colleague, Nathaniel W. Taylor, Alexander in 1827 wrote to Charles Hodge, who was then studying in Germany: "I am sick of these controversies." "O that men would learn to be contented with the plain doctrines of the Bible, & give up their refinements in theology!"[38] Clearly Alexander was torn between the deep and simple faith on which his inner life was built and the intellectual speculations to which he believed that faith committed him.

In treating the problem of original sin, Alexander affirmed the "federal" view. "Adam," said Alexander,

was constituted the federal head and legal representative of all his posterity . . . his sin is to be considered not merely the sin of an individual but of a public person, in fact the sin of our whole race. . . . Therefore the penalty incurred falls on his posterity just as it fell on him. . . . This has been termed the imputation of Adam's sin to his posterity.

Alexander hastened to explain what he meant by the "imputation" of Adam's sin. In imputation, he said,

God does not view us as having been personally active in eating the forbidden fruit, but as having sinned in & by our representative. . . . The word impute in both the orig[inal] languages [of the Bible] is a commercial word, having relation to accounts. To impute anything to any one is to set down that item to his account, either in his favor or against him."[39]

Similarly, in 1830 he wrote: "Although personal acts cannot be transferred, the consequences or legal penalties of those acts may be transferred."[40] An illustration which he used to support this view clearly indicated the conception of organic rather than individualistic moral responsibility on which the doctrine was based. "Husband and wife being one in the law," he said, "the acts of the latter are treated as if performed by the former."[41] Thus this doctrine of imputation regarded moral account-ability for acts as detachable from the person who performed the acts (analogously to monetary debts), and also as ascribable to another than the performer. This detachment of "guilt" and the liability to penalty for guilty actions contains an obvious threat to both individual and social ethics. This danger became especially great when the conception of im-putation was given unprecedented emphasis by Alexander and Hodge in the face of attack by New England Trinitarians who were revising many traditional Calvinistic tenets to strengthen their own position against their Unitarian neighbors.[42]

It will be recalled that Alexander, in his discussion of psychology, found all acts of will rooted in the individual's underlying nature or char-acter. Thus, individual sinful acts are the product of a corrupted nature, and this corrupted nature is guilty, he thought, even before it expresses itself in specific actions. "To admit a sinful state, wh[ich] is the true source & cause of all evil actions, and still to hold that there is nothing culpable in this state, appears to me very unreasonable; for the true & proper cause of moral evil must be itself a moral evil. . . . We ought to feel guilty on account of this latent depravity."[43]

While this doctrine of imputation was a part of the inherited Calvin-ism, Alexander—stimulated by the attacks currently being made on it—blew it up to extravagant importance. "If the doctrine of imputation be given up, the whole doctrine of original sin must be abandoned. And if this doctrine be relinquished, then the whole doctrine of redemption must fall."[44]

Moses Stuart of Andover Theological Seminary replied to Alexander the same year with the questions, "Have men no sins of their own, from

which they need to be redeemed?" "I ask also, whether the first principles of moral consciousness do not decide, that sin, in its proper sense, is
the result of what we have done ourselves; not of what others have done
for us, without our knowledge and consent? I ask, in what part of the
bible we are called upon to repent of Adam's sin?"[45] Alexander in class
argued against Stuart's view of original sin to the satisfaction of a student
who reported that "he did it most admirably. . . . We have 2 of Prof.
S[tuart's] disciples (one of whom has frequently turned instructor to our
Professors). . . . They endeavored to divert our attention by wondering
at our blind minds, that should be perverted by such sophistry."[46] Not
surprisingly, students, too, were hotly debating on both sides the
challenges being made to the Calvinistic heritage.

Not only Andover but Yale, particularly under the leadership of
Nathaniel W. Taylor, disagreed with Alexander's view of original sin and
imputation. Taylor emphasized that the human will was morally free
and not precondemned to sin by any inheritance from Adam, but he
offered no explanation as to how it happens that all human beings do sin,
as Taylor himself acknowledged. Alexander opposed this view at length
in a lecture,[47] and Alexander and Hodge, in turn, were criticized in the
Yale organ, the *Quarterly Christian Spectator,* for declaring human beings
liable to punishment for the sin of Adam without showing that Adam's
heirs had any personal responsibility for their ancestor's sin.[48] Needless
to say, Alexander also denied the possibility of human beings living sinlessly in the present life.[49] Under the cultural pressures of the time,
American Calvinism was in process of disruption.

How did children, dying in infancy, fare under this doctrine of original
sin? Alexander cited Augustine as teaching that the baptism of infants
attests that they are born guilty of sin, a view which Alexander shared.[50]
Are these unconverted infants, then, to be damned for sins they themselves had never committed? Alexander, like most Calvinists, would not
affirm such a possibility. "Regeneration" (which was defined as God's
invisible and often unfelt gift of new birth to an individual, based on
Christ's redeeming work and bestowed in accordance with God's foreor-
dained election) was considered quite separate from that person's "conversion" (which Alexander viewed as a conscious act of personal faith in
Christ). Thus God's act of regeneration might long precede the human
experience of faith and conversion, or, in exceptional cases such as of
those dying in infancy, might never be followed by conscious faith at all.

Thus even strict Calvinism left room for speculation about extensive
divine clemency, an opening of which Alexander and others cautiously
made use. On this basis of "regeneration," without the exercise of faith
following it, Alexander could write to an inquirer: "As the Holy Scriptures have not informed us that any of the human family departing in
infancy will be lost, we are permitted to hope that all such will be
saved."[51] To his sister, grieving over the death of a daughter who had

given no clear evidence of personal Christian faith, he wrote: "We know not how far the promise of God to believing parents, in behalf of their offspring, extends, when they are taken away in tender youth. . . . Many who never profess religion exhibit more of the Christian temper than some who are professors."[52] Alexander was a zealous supporter of foreign missions, but he speculated that God might

in an extraordinary way unknown to us save some individuals who never were blessed with an external revelation; but if this is the fact wh[ich] we neither affirm nor deny, these persons were not saved by the Religion of Nature much less by conforming themselves conscientiously to their Heathen superstitions . . . . If it hath pleased God to save any individuals of the Heathen world, He hath done it by uniting them to Christ, in some way to us unknown, as in the case of infants.[53]

The door was open a crack; others would open it much more widely.

Alexander's doctrine of the atonement was the counterpart of his doctrine of original sin. His doctrine of original sin taught that Adam's sin was imputed to all his descendants; while his doctrine of the atonement taught that the sins of all the redeemed were imputed to Christ who then bore the punishment for them. In an article in the *Christian Advocate* in 1824—one of his earliest publications—Alexander attacked the "governmental" view of the atonement.[54] Hugo Grotius (1583–1645), a Dutch international jurist and theologian, reflected early influences of Enlightenment emphasis on God's benevolence when he turned from the orthodox Calvinistic doctrine that the atonement was grounded in God's justice to the idea that it was based not on God's vindicatory justice, but on God's need as ruler of the universe to make an example of the consequences of sin, in order to deter his creatures from wrongdoing, an objective for which Christ willingly offered himself. The idea was adapted by Jonathan Edwards, Jr., and soon became popular in New England.

Alexander's chief ground of attack against this governmental view of the atonement was that, in his opinion, it left the justice of God, which he considered essential to the divine nature, doubly violated. Because, said Alexander, this theory does not regard human sin as imputed to Christ, God is viewed as pardoning sinners without any vicarious punishment for their sins; and he is further viewed as allowing Christ, who had no sin of his own and to whom no sins of others were imputed, to be punished as a common criminal. And, furthermore, Alexander charged, Christ's death, according to the governmental theory, does not warn sinners that their own sins will be punished, as it claims to do; but merely indicates that somebody suffered, who in no way was involved in their wrongdoing, which is no deterrent at all.[55]

In stating positively his own view of substitutionary atonement,

Alexander, unlike many advocates of the theory, said that Christ literally suffered "punishment" for the sins of others. Quoting Scripture, he declared, "We cannot understand how it can be said that Christ was "made sin,' 'bore our sins,' 'died for our sins,' 'was made a curse for us,' &c unless he suffered the punishment due to sin." He clearly implied that Christ's death was a necessary fulfillment of the justice inherent in God's inviolable law: "If the death and sufferings of Christ have no relation to law and justice, we cannot conceive how they can answer any valuable purpose." And, again, he rejected all other theories of the atonement because they imply "that the law of God can be dispensed with."[56] He warned that a denial of the substitutionary atonement pointed toward universalism: "If a penalty is not to be considered of the nature of a prediction of the consequence of transgression, it is the same as if there were no penalty; & the inevitable consequence is, that we have no assurance whatever, that any of God's threatenings against sin will ever be executed either in this world or the next."[57]

Somewhat paradoxically, in the very lecture in which Alexander insisted on Christ's atonement as a full legal equivalent of the punishment which God's law requires of sinners, he seemed to relax his legalistic precision. Christ's atoning sufferings, he said, did not need to be "identical w[ith] t[hose] wh[ich] w[oul]d have been endured by t[he] sinner."[58] Elsewhere he conceded that the substitutionary atonement "indeed is a relaxation of the rigid demands of the Law, for the Law knows nothing of substitution. The sentence of the Law is, The soul t[hat] sinneth it shall die."[59] Though he had argued at some length to rationalize substitutionary atonement, he finally had to admit that, like all divine mysteries, it transcended human reason. "If it sh[oul]d be alleged," he conceded, "that in no circumstances, can it be reconcilable with justice, that an innocent person sh[oul]d bear the punishment of the guilty, I answer that human reason is incompetent to decide this question."[60]

Alexander was an orthodox Trinitarian, and we have noted some of his teachings about God the Father as Creator and Sovereign and concerning Christ as Redeemer. As to the Holy Spirit, Alexander asserted that he is a divine "Person distinct from the Father & the Son," and "endowed with intelligence & will, which supposes consciousness."[61]

In his inaugural address at the opening of the Seminary in 1812, Alexander gave a fleeting glimpse of what was really central in Christianity for him, when he said to the three students of the entering class and to the assembled audience:

When the serious mind falls into doubt respecting divine truths, the remedy is not always reasoning and argument, but divine illumination. . . . At such times a

lively impression made by the [Holy] Spirit of truth, banishes all doubt and hesitation. . . . This may appear to some to savour of enthusiasm. Be it so. It is, however, an enthusiasm essential to the very nature of our holy religion, without
which it would be a mere dry system of speculation, of ethics and ceremonies.[62]

Alexander on occasion said similar things in some of his sermons. But
he never fully integrated his heritage of pietism with his more formal
orthodox rationalism. The doctrine of the Holy Spirit might conceivably
have suggested such an opportunity; but he did not undertake the task.
Instead, contrary to his procedure in many theological areas, in an
undated lecture on the Holy Spirit, he told his students that he would
avoid "metaphysical disquisition on a subject so far above the comprehension of human reason," since "such speculations shed no light on this
mysterious subject. . . . All we know are the various effects produced
[by] the divine agency." He listed, without amplification, the conventional doctrine concerning the Spirit's operations, which included the
"work of making application of the purchased redemption . . . of preparing the elect of God" and of restoring "the image of God, lost by the
fall," all of which faith "is the effect of the illumination of the Spirit."[63]
One might wish that with his interest in speculation in many other areas
he had attempted to elaborate more fully, on the basis of Scripture and
Christian history, the action of God on the inner life of Christian
believers. This he did not do in his doctrine of the Holy Spirit. The
inherited Reformed and Presbyterian doctrine of the "Word" and the
"Spirit" lends itself to highly dynamic treatment, in which the concepts
of Word, Spirit, and their interrelationship can each be variously
interpreted. But it remained for others to explore more fully these
possibilities.

When the Protestant Reformers declared that human beings are
accepted by God's grace which is received by faith alone they were
emphatic that by faith in this context they meant not merely intellectual
"assent" to propositions about God, but meant "trust" in God himself
and in his mercy.

As previously noted, Alexander's painful emotional fluctuations at the
time of his youthful conversion had driven him to seek stability by giving
central place to the role of the intellect in Christianity, an emphasis
which in some respects blended quite readily with the rational spirit of
the Enlightenment. It is not surprising, therefore, that in his discussion
of faith and of the relation in the act of faith between intellectual assent
and personal trust, Alexander tended toward the same kind of ambivalence between intellect and affections that appears elsewhere in his
thinking. Thus, in treating the New Testament word for faith ("pistis"),
he said that to believe "is to be persuaded of any truth upon any evidence whatever."[64] Clearly, this avoided distinctions between different

kinds of faith and tended to subsume all faith under the category of intellectual assent.

On another occasion, Alexander used an illustration of trust which
seemed to suggest that trust was something quite different from mere
belief in a proposition, when he spoke of an imprisoned debtor trusting
the promise of wealthy friend to pay the debt for him. But then
Alexander promptly reduced this trust to assent by the interpretation
which he added: "Trust . . .is nothing else than a firm persuasion of the
truth of a promise."[65] When discussing "assent" and "trust" in still
another connection, Alexander again defined trust as a form of intellectual assent. "Trust or confidence . . . at first view," he said,

seems to be a different act from assent, as it contains the element of reliance, not
included in this. But when we attend accurately to the exercises of our minds;
when we trust or confide in anyone, it differs from other acts of firm belief, only
in this, that the object is a promise of some good. . . . This act of trust or
confidence is not distinct from the act of believing, but one and the same.

Thus trust in a person has once again been treated merely as assent to a
proposition of a particular kind.

When, however, he applied psychology's rejection of the "faculty psychology," his treatment of Christian trust became less narrowly intellectual. Alexander was quite aware that the views just summarized exposed
him to criticism.

The principal objection which I foresee to all that has been said is, that by this
theory we make faith to be a mere assent of the understanding, whereas the
s[acred] s[criptures] continually speak of believing with the heart. . . . The
answer is, that the s[acred] s[criptures] do not make this distinction between the
understanding & will, & therefore we need not do it. . . . Heart in S[acred] S[crip-
tures] almost always means the whole soul. In sound philosophy [in psychology]
there is no foundation for so wide a distinction as is made between the understanding & will. . . . The account of faith given, does not exclude the will, & is not
a simple assent of the understanding."[66]

Here he comes much closer to the traditional Protestant view of "trust"
as a commitment of the whole self in faith. But then he felt it necessary
to add that it is the intellect that defines the object of trust.[67]

Alexander distinguished sharply between acts of "faith" where the
objects of faith are emotionally neutral such as that "2 & 2 make four"
(if indeed that is "faith") and objects of faith where "there is a persuasion of the excellence, importance, or pleasantness of the truth"; that is,
between a supposedly objective understanding and an understanding
that includes emotional involvement. He used as an illustration persons

reared in Christianity who "afterwards have received that faith which is the gift of God. Altho they are bro't to the knowledge of no truth not known before, they now know these things after a very different manner. . . . It is, as to the effect produced, much as if they had never heard of them before."[68] This new kind of knowledge he declared to be the result of the testimony of the Holy Spirit.[69] Here, clearly, religious knowledge for him did go beyond mere rational knowledge. But he did not distinguish relations between persons—including relations to the Divine Person—from relations to nonpersonal things and to abstract truths as specifically as some twentieth-century philosophy has demanded. It would, however, be anachronistic to fault him for that particular shortcoming.

On the doctrine of Last Things (eschatology) Alexander was modestly brief. To imply that the core of his theology was "Believe in Jesus and go to heaven" would be the grossest caricature. While concerned with "saving souls" in accordance with the evangelical presuppositions of the times, he was much more a Calvinist than a revivalist. As reflected in his emphasis on divine sovereignty and in other ways, his highest avowed objective was not individual bliss throughout eternity but "the glory of God." Translated into philosophical language, this was a supreme concern about Ultimate Reality, which he conceived of as personal and also as fixed, certain, and inherently unchangeable. This offered stability and confidence to many in an era of rapid mobility and change. Though a man of gentle and benevolent sentiments, he had the honesty to avow the logic of his convictions. God himself, Alexander declared, was bound by eternal principles of justice. Thus, he said, God punishes sin not for the good of the sufferer, or for the good of all people, or because God delights in human misery, but because "God must ever act towards his creatures according to the perfection of his own nature."[70] Alexander neither dwelt on this thought nor delighted in it.

In early nineteenth-century America, most orthodox Christians believed in an ultimate physical return of Christ to the earth. Most of those who were interested in such matters, following the earlier lead of Jonathan Edwards, Samuel Hopkins, and others, believed that this return would be "post-millennial," that is, it would be preceded by a "millennium" of special blessing and multiplied evidence of God's working. This expectation was an important stimulus for many Christians to missionary outreach and social reform. But Alexander's emphasis was more on day-to-day routine faithfulness and devotion than on special events or incentives, and his appeals to millennial expectations were notably sparse. He was vigorously opposed to the crassly supernatural "premillennial" view that Christ would return to earth before the millennium and set up a millennial rule in person, "which has been zealously revived in our day by the prophetic men of Great Britain," presumably a reference to the Darbyites.[71] Referring to William Miller's specific prediction of Christ's return in 1843, he commended indulgently, "If it did not damp the spirit of missions, it would do little harm."[72]

Alexander emphasized the "immortality of the soul" on nonbiblical as well as on biblical grounds, arguing from supposed universal consensus that even "the fierce & wandering savages of N. America & the degraded & brutish inhabitants of Guinea do both believe in an existence after death." He invoked his Cartesian dualism between mind and matter to assert that "there is nothing wh[ich] takes place in the death of the body with wh[ich] we are acquainted that can affect the existence of an active & immaterial substance" such as the soul.[73]

"Polemic Theology," which concentrated on refuting "erroneous" religious beliefs, was set forth in the Seminary's Plan as a separate discipline from Didactic (Systematic) Theology, and Alexander so treated it from his early days at Princeton. But his surviving manuscripts on Polemic Theology are less copious than those on Didactic Theology, so that one must depend on student notes for much of the contents of the Polemic Theology course. His manuscripts include translations of portions of the Latin of the *Institutes of Comprehensive Polemic Theology* (1743–1747) of Johann Friedrich Stapfer,[74] a Swiss Reformed orthodox rationalist, of whom he made extensive use and to whom he acknowledged credit, a further reminder of the pervasive influence on Alexander of Reformed scholasticism.

A student who two years later became pastor of the Old South Church in Boston, writing to a friend in 1819, described the procedure used by Alexander in Polemic Theology where "he reads to us his Lecture & besides gives out to different members of the class the different hypotheses & objections of the adversaries & they are to bring in in writing a concise summary of the arguments by which they are refuted."[75]

Student notes as well as Alexander's biographer, who was himself a former student, indicate that Alexander used an historical method in dealing with Christian controversies in his Polemic Theology, which we are told constituted a kind of *"Dogmengeschichte."*[76] It is significant that in his Didactic Theology, where he was setting forth "correct" doctrine, he did not use an historical method which would have illustrated how orthodox positions had developed out of dialogue with conflicting views. The Old Princeton Theology, with some later exceptions, was reluctant to treat systematic theology in such an historical way, presumably lest it might imply a relativism that would undermine the absolutistic character that was attributed to "true" theology. But to present "error" as a product of relativistic forces was of course quite appropriate, because error appeared to be mired in historical relativism; whereas truth did not.

Alexander as a former pastor never lost sight of practical objectives. He wished to arm his students against ancient heresies in whatever guise they might reappear, as well as to equip them against more contemporary error. He was very much aware of the religious turbulence of his own day. Though favoring American religious liberty, he warned that it made possible "some of the most monstrous heresies."[77] He distinguished between "infidels" as those "who deny Revelation" and "heretics" as those who only deny fundamentals of doctrines," but added that "heretics, however blameless & amiable cannot be treated as Christians," and "cannot be admitted into the Church." This was quite in accord with the revulsion that Alexander had experienced against theological inclusivism in his visit to New England in 1801, and remained a central, though seldom advertised, characteristic of the Old Princeton Theology until the reorganization of the Seminary in the early twentieth century, though with minority exceptions toward the end of that period.

In urging this strict exclusivism, however, Alexander was careful to confine it to the "fundamental articles" of religion. That of course raised the problem of what are these "fundamental articles." In one lecture he mentioned among other "fundamental" truths the "guilt & depravity of human nature, on which [the] whole mediatorial system depends"; the "Divinity & humanity of Xt."; the "obligation of moral law"; and the "necessity of [the] operat[ion] of [the] Spirit in regeneration." But along with his strict orthodoxy, Alexander was by temperament a reasonable and moderate person who did not appear happy with the problem of defining specifically what was and what was not "fundamental" to the faith. He was torn between asserting the entire "system" of the Bible's teaching, on the one hand, and on the other the claims of Christian charity, though he was unwilling to sacrifice to charity what he was convinced was truth.[78]

It was more in accord with Alexander's intellectuality to suggest broad principles for recognizing the "fundamental articles" of Christianity, rather than to name specific doctrines. On one occasion, he offered two kinds of tests of these articles. "The first [is] Theoretical—The second Practical. All doctrines essential to the integrity & existence of the Xn. system is [sic] fundamental." Alexander's strong pietistic and practical bent found expression in his second test: ' Every truth necessary to real piety is fundamental." This letter was long a conscious or unconscious test of fundamental Christian truth in American revivalistic circles. Alexander then proceeded, with strongly sectarian implications, to distinguish between things essential to the visible church and things essential to salvation,

If all the truths of God are held, and all his appointed ordinances administered, there is a visible church, altho few of its members shd. be true believers. But if a number of believers neglect to profess publicly their belief, and to attend on the ordinances of God, there is no visible church, tho' the persons thus believing . . . are in a state of salvation.[79]

This used the Calvinistic doctrine of the visible church and the invisible church to go far beyond Calvin[80] in making individual faith quite independent of the institutional church, reflecting the individualism of the era, and of the American environment in particular. This way of stating the cleavage seemed to relate Alexander's more rationalistic side to the visible church and to the older ecclesiasticism; and to relate his more pietistic side to the invisible church and to the newer individualism.

Lecturing six years after the damaging Old-School–New-School Presbyterian disruption of 1837, Alexander discussed the nature of Christian unity, while leaning heavily on the invisible church-visible church dichotomy. "Unity of [the] Church," he said, "does not consist in union of visible Societies, but [in] union by invisible bonds. . . . So long as [they are] on [the] same foundation, [the] same Bible, [they are] members of the same church." Speaking of the diversity of denominations, he commented: "When they differ in doctrine & practice, [there] must be error on one side; and those in error are guilty of some degree of schism; but so long as neither excludes [the] other, [they] are not guilty of schism in the highest sense. But where one refuses communion with others, [they are] guilty of schism." This statement clearly differed from the more institutional conceptions of Christian unity held by such churchly bodies as the Roman Catholics, Episcopalians, and Lutherans, who attached far more significance to what Old Calvinists called the "visible" church.

Admission to the church was properly on profession on faith—faith in the objective reality of God's redeeming action and in his promises, but not faith about one's own supposedly redeemed condition, as the Protestant Reformers were incorrectly accused of teaching and as some contemporary revivalists seemed to imply, a conception under which Alexander had suffered acutely during his own conversion experience. Since this kind of objective, substantive faith was required for membership in the Presbyterian Church, Alexander toyed with the question whether members of other denominations which did not require examination of faith for membership should be excluded from communion in Presbyterian churches.[81]

Alexander's "Rules for Controversy" attest his desire to be moderate and fair, even while remaining strictly orthodox. "Consider," he urged his students, "whether [the] danger & importance of error justifies public controversy"; "be satisfied of the purity of our motives"; "avoid whatever is apt to create prejudice in opponents or auditors"; "attribute to an antagonist no opinion [he] does not own, though [it be a] necessary consequence"; strive "for truth not victory. If [you are] convinced of error confess it''; ''know when to put a stop to controversy. [It is a] great evil in keeping it up, after [the] controversy [is] exhausted.''[82] Alexander's own life reveals that, in spite of strong convictions, he kept his involvement in active controversy to a minimum, stating, when he felt it necessary, his own views with uncompromising clarity and thereafter remaining silent.

In an undated manuscript, Dr. Alexander listed ''errors'' which would be dealt with in his Polemics course—a heterogeneous collection which included ''Atheism, Pantheism, Indifferentism, Deism, Paganism, Judaism, Mohammedanism [sic], Humanitarianism, Socinianism . . . Popery . . . Arminianism, Fanaticism, Cambellism.''[83] One student recorded a few additional objects of critical study: Brahminism, Religion of Thibet . . . Anabaptists, Mysticism.''[84]

The distinguished Lutheran leader and early advocate of church union, Samuel S. Schmucker, was a student at Princeton Seminary from 1818 to 1820. On the first page of his notes on Alexander's Polemic Theology course he quoted Alexander as saying: ''A perfect union of opinion cannot be expected. . . . Therefore all who hold the fundamental doctrines *ought to be united into one church.*''[85] This sentiment was certainly not characteristic of Alexander if the reference was to the ''visible'' church, but the ideal of church union evidently impressed Schmucker (the underlining is his) while still a student at Princeton Seminary. Regarding atheism, Schmucker explicitly attributed to Alexander a strange rationalistic procedure inferred previously in the present writing in another context: ''The proper method is to make first a deist of the atheist & then a christian of the deist.'' Alexander's rationalism was continually forced to confess its ultimate limits. Thus he argued that infinity could not be rationally comprehended. ''We have no idea of duration without succession. . . . The application of numbers to space & duration gives us our best idea of infinity. Yet the absurdity of an infinite succession of dependent beings may be demonstrated.''[86]

The direct contribution of Alexander's orthodoxy to social stability was not absent from his mind. ''Their [the atheists'] system,'' he said, ''is not consistent with the existence of society. They say they admit the law of nature &c—but take away God & no one will care whether he violates this law or not.'' Thus reason without religious faith, he felt, could not support either morality or social order. To clinch the argument, he cited the French Revolution: ''France has tried the atheistic system; all the bonds of society were severed—all its relations destroyed.'' Schmucker was stimulated to comment on atheism in a parenthesis: ''The question . . . is which was eternal, mind or matter—There is more reasonableness in believing that mind created matter than matter, mind.''

When it came to treating deism, which had long been a decisive factor in determining his own theological strategy, Alexander still thought in 1820 that ''there are many deists in America, ten times more than is supposed.'' He attacked the Englishman Matthew Tindal (1653–1733) as "the ablest advocate of Deism" and for the criticism of deism drew heavily, among others, on such standbys as Bishop Butler, John Leland, and William Paley. He highly recommended the technique used against Thomas Paine and much later against Robert Ingersoll of preaching "a course of sermons on the . . . pretended inconsistencies of S[acred] S[cripture]—such as the destruction of the Canaanite nations."[87]

In discussing "Mohammedanism," Alexander charged that "Mohammed was a cruel, sensual man & a robber." He thought that Islam "had its origin in enthusiasm," a psychological condition which Alexander consistently considered highly perilous, whether found in American revivalism or elsewhere. He related Mohammed's enthusiasm to "epileptic fits."[88]

Roman Catholicism, Alexander warned his students, as early as 1820, was "becoming more important" as an issue. He summarized its "errors" under three headings—those which relate to the "popish hierarchy," to "faith," and to "ceremonies." He charged that Roman Catholics "still maintain the doctrine of persecution for conscience sake," and recommended as "the best English author against them" the English seventeenth-century Latitudinarian William Chillingworth,[89] whose dictum is still remembered: "The Bible only is the religion of Protestants." More than twenty years later, after extensive Roman Catholic immigration had stimulated anti-Catholicism in America to a high pitch, Alexander devoted ten lectures to Roman Catholicism.[90] Though hostile, his tone was not inflammatory. He considered "points of controversy very numerous indeed," but noted the difficulty of debate because of disagreement as to ultimate authority, Catholics appealing not only to the books which Protestants accepted as their Bible, but also to the Apocrypha and to oral tradition and to the Catholic principle of interpretation by church authority.

Judaism also came in for treatment. By 1843 American had experienced some increase in its Jewish population, though the great influx of Jewish immigration was to come later. Alexander's tone was basically objective, noting that there had been controversy between Christians and Jews from the early days of Christianity over such matters as the interpretation of prophecy and the coming of the Messiah. Among other subjects, he mentioned the Talmud as a great repository of Jewish law and summarized the theology of the famous medieval Jewish philosopher, Moses Maimonides.[91]

Alexander's lectures also touched on Eastern Orthodoxy, commenting that the "Oriental Ch[urches] have the leaven of mysticism among them."[92]  Opposition to "mysticism" was more characteristic of Alexander's younger colleague, Dr. Charles Hodge, Alexander himself—sometimes inconsistently with his own admixture of rationalism—giving large place to inner religious experience.

But Alexander was always careful to set bounds to subjective religious experience. Thus in his Polemic Theology course he devoted three lectures to "Enthusiasm" and "Fanaticism" during February 1844, which fell in the period between the first and second failures of William Miller's prediction of Christ's physical return to earth. Like Philip Schaff in this same decade, Alexander noted two extremes to be avoided—enthusiasm (Schaff called it "sectarianism") and rationalism—and then Alexander concentrated his warnings on the first. He charged enthusiasts with a "low estimate of God's word"; a "disposition to entertain all sorts of impulses"; "overweening pride & conceit"; "pretension to extraordinary gifts—tongues"; "expect[ation] of extraord[inary] events as [the] coming of Xt. or [the] millennium"; "new worship—new rules of conduct contrary to the Bible."[93]

Toward fellow "evangelical" denominations, Alexander's attitude was more friendly. He distinguished the Arminianism of the Methodists from that of the Dutch Remonstrants as "much sounder," though he took exception to their teaching of "sinless perfection" and their view that "God has not been able to carry into effect that system . . . which he intended." Lecturing in 1844, he declared that "within a few years past the Methodists have become favourers of learning, & now have more colleges than any other sect." His treatment of the Lutherans dealt particularly with Lutheran controversies in Germany and the rise of biblical studies there, following which he discussed the Baptists, devoting three lectures to the controversy over infant baptism.[94]

We turn now to Biblical Studies, which came first in the seminary curriculum, but the approach to which was predetermined by the philosophy and theology which we have been considering. Alexander taught biblical studies for a few years, until he could hand them over to a third professor, as contemplated in the Seminary's original plan. In the meanwhile, Alexander had established the approach which the Seminary, with increasing depth and elaboration, would take toward this basic subject for more than a century.

# 15
# BIBLICAL STUDIES

In the summer of 1812 Archibald Alexander faced an almost unprecedented task. While the teaching of the Bible and of theology to prospective ministers, in one way or another, was centuries old, the creation of a curriculum specifically for the new American type of theological seminary was in its infancy. Although Alexander had been a member of the General Assembly's committee chaired by Dr. Green that had drafted a "plan" for the proposed seminary, this was merely a suggestive skeleton. How should the available three years be fleshed out with specific courses? What should be the content of such courses? What books were available? What methods of instruction should be employed?[1]

Though called to be professor of theology, Alexander decided to devote the students' entire first year to the Bible. As he wrote to Samuel S. Schmucker, who was applying for admission in 1818, the first year was given to "the study of the original tongues of scripture, Jewish antiquities, Biblical History, Sacred Chronolgy, etc."[2]

As he expressed it a decade and a half later, Alexander had great hopes for the scientific study of the "authenticity, canonical authority and correct interpretation of the sacred books," that is, textual criticism, canon, and hermeneutics. He expected such studies to become widely popular and thought that, in proportion as the Bible is truly understood, "the mere doctrines of men will disappear; and the dogmas of the schools and the alliance with philosophy being renounced, there will be among sincere inquiries after truth, an increasing tendency to unity of sentiment."[3] This type of empirical study, analysis, and organization of "objective" facts, seemingly free from the type of metaphysical "speculation" which he thought he deprecated, was particularly congenial to Alexander, although both its spirit and its conclusions were, as we have seen, uncritically predetermined by the metaphysics which he actually loved.

Diverse groups in America were turning to the Bible with renewed interest and high expectations in the early nineteenth century. Some, like the Christian Church "primitivist" movements, were rejecting man-made creeds and hoping to find Christian unity in the Bible alone; some, like Archibald Alexander and such solid biblical students as Moses Stuart of Andover, hoped that direct, intense study of the Bible would lead to a greater degree of unity among the denominations. Others, like the early Unitarians at Harvard, hoped to see their anti-Trinitarian views confirmed by the critical study of the New Testament.[4] But actually biblical study—critical or otherwise—did not reduce ecclesiastical divisions, not only because of differences within Scripture, but also because very different theological presuppositions were brought to the study; and even when a degree of consensus developed on some critical questions, ecclesiastical structures continued to be self perpetuating.

Alexander, in the statement quoted, almost seemed to be anticipating later biblical theology, but actually his biblical positions were determined both by dogma and also, to a greater degree than he acknowledged, by the very "alliance with philosophy" which he was deprecating. He even dared to hope that critical study of the Bible would stimulate the laborer and the merchant to turn in those decades of rapid economic expansion from personal ambition and avarice to give their strength and resources to spreading the gospel at home and abroad.[5] This was a truly millennial vision, more directly served by popular evangelicalism than by critical biblical studies.

Biblical studies in America were in a rudimentary state when Alexander began his work in Princeton. No American had yet gone to Germany for biblical or theological work, and it would be three quarters of a century before there would be real seminars in the United States. William F. Albright has said that in 1810, when Moses Stuart joined the Andover Seminary faculty, "there was probably no native-born American who knew enough Hebrew to teach it properly."[6]

Moses Stuart, like Alexander called directly from the pastorate to a seminary chair without special preparation, when he came knew no German, was deficient in Hebrew, and lacked knowledge of the cognate Semitic languages. It was by diligent self-teaching that he became second to none in America in his acquaintance with contemporary critical biblical scholarship in Germany. In 1813 he published A Hebrew Grammar Without the Points, type for part of which he set with his own hands. He superseded this with still another Hebrew grammar of his own eight years later,[7] a work which did not escape scholarly criticism.[8] When faced with the blockade of imports caused by the War of 1812, Stuart was in a hurry to see the printing in America of Hebrew Bibles.[9]

During his first three years at Andover Seminary, Stuart's lectures paid little attention to critical methods, but his purchase in 1812 of a copy of J. G. Eichhorn's Einleitung in das alte Testament awakened his interest in German biblical criticism. Starting the next year, Stuart's lectures at

Andover dealt critically with the Old Testament canon, the genuineness of Old Testament books, prophecy, and the recognition of separate Elohist and Yahwist sources in Genesis, though he still held that Moses was the compiler of the work. The Old Testament canon, he thought, was assembled in the time of Ezra. The publication of his *A Critical History and Defence of the Old Testament Canon* in 1845 showed that his views had changed but little since his early lectures, though he was now ready, for example, to acknowledge the possibility of a plural authorship of Isaiah.[10] Stuart applied his philological attainments to his commentaries, where he aspired to a strict grammatico-historical method of exegesis, as he wrote to a friend: "The double sense is a desperate throw in Hermeneutics. . . . If the Bible be a revelation to men, in the language of men, then it is to be interpreted agreeably to the laws of human language."[11]

In spite of the theological orthodoxy that dominated Stuart's critical studies, some of his best friends were alarmed at the fearlessness with which he studied the more radical critics. In 1825 a special investigating committee appointed by the trustees of Andover Seminary reported that "the unrestrained cultivation of German studies has evidently tended to chill the ardor of piety," and urged that students be encouraged to study the Bible with "reverence, meekness, simplicity, and implicit submission."[12] Samuel Miller of Princeton Seminary, commenting apprehensively to a Boston friend on the spread of Unitarianism, wrote as early as 1822: "It grieves me to be obliged to say that I fear the influence of Andover, in this respect, will, in the end, be on the wrong side. . . . The constant recommendation of German criticks [sic] . . . must lead (however far from the present views of the excellent man referred to) to a mischeivous [sic] result. May the Lord avert it!"[13] But Alexander's opinion was more favorable after partly reading Stuart's first volume on Hebrew, which dealt with critical questions. "It is a learned accurate, & able work," Alexander commented to a friend. "Perhaps he pursues some objections too minutely and laboriously, but he always seems to maintain the right side of the question."[14]

Harvard College fostered a critical study of the Bible which was much less closely related to traditional orthodoxy than that at Andover Seminary. Joseph Stevens Buckminster, a Harvard graduate and from 1804 eloquent young pastor of the influential Brattle Street Church of Boston, reflected in his sermons critical views of the canon, inspiration, and text of the Scriptures, influenced by J.D. Michaelis, J. J. Griesbach, and other European scholars. He used the various differences in the text of the Bible as an argument against verbal inspiration, and attacked any view of inspiration that regarded the Bible as a textbook of doctrines. He emphasized the historical context of the biblical writings, declaring some of their teachings applicable only to the age in which they were written.

In 1811 he was appointed to the new Dexter Lectureship on Biblical Criticism at Harvard, but died the next year. His influence, however, through his sermons and through the library which he had collected, survived his brief career.[15]

Andrews Norton (1786–1853) became Dexter Lecturer at Harvard in 1813 and Dexter Professor six years later. He urged greater attention to the individuality of the various biblical writers and the influence of time and place on the meaning of words. Though basically Unitarian in his view of Christ, he proposed that the biblical writings be tested by "the intellectual and moral character of our Saviour and his apostles" and accepted or rejected accordingly. Bypassing the much discussed questions of historicity, authorship, and what books properly belong in the Bible (canon), he sought by a correct understanding of the various biblical writers' individual characteristics and historical setting to discover "the great truths of religion" and then to judge particular biblical passages by these. But he was often incompletely critical, allowing theological presuppositions to determine historical facts. Following John Locke, Norton attached special credence to the Gospels and resisted some of the recent critical work being done on the Gospels by German scholars such as Eichhorn and Griesbach. Norton focused on the New Testament and paid relatively little attention to Old Testament critical studies which were currently developing in Germany. The New Testament books themselves, Norton felt, did not constitute revelation, but revelation was to be found in a few central truths which the New Testament contained.[16]

Meanwhile other American Unitarians were contributing to the critical approach to Scripture. William E. Channing in 1819 urged an historical understanding of the Bible, in which reason would separate what was temporary from what was of permanent value and even "the laws of nature" would have some normative significance. The apostolic writings should be the criterion for evaluating all other Scripture. Other Unitarian scholars after the period covered in the present study carried critical biblical studies beyond the point reached by Norton, but by the time of the Civil War their creative interest in the subject had largely declined. Further American developments in the field awaited the closing decades of the century, and then were no longer primarily led by Unitarians. The Unitarian pioneers in the field had hoped to establish their theological position on the basis of a more critical study of Scripture, but their later coreligionists shifted from a biblical to a theological and philosophical base, with resulting decline of interest in critical biblical questions.[17]

What were Archibald Alexander's qualifications in biblical scholarship when he came from the pastorate to teach at Princeton Seminary in 1812? He had the traditional grounding in the Latin and Greek classics which enabled him to read readily the Latin writings of seventeenth- and eighteenth-century scholars on biblical and theological subjects, a pursuit which he maintained zealously to the end of his life.[18] His knowledge of Greek made the daily reading of the Greek New Testament a delight. When still in Virginia, he had acquired a Hebrew Old Testament and a copy of the Septuagint translation of the Old Testament into Greek.

Later, apparently while in Philadelphia, he acquired "the splendid . . . Michaelis edition of Halle" of the Hebrew Old Testament.[19] It was during his Philadelphia pastorate that Alexander made "his first successful attempts" to master Hebrew, studying there under "a learned Jew."[20] At least two years before coming to Princeton, he had acquired a Syriac New Testament,[21] and before long made enough progress in this "cognate" language to teach it to a student; but he was less successful with Arabic. His most serious deficiency as a teacher of biblical studies lay in an apparent lack of facility in—or at least a relative indifference to—the German language. His son and biographer concedes his lack of interest in "the modern languages."[22] In Alexander's extant manuscript lectures and in his notes on his reading, as well as in student notes on his lectures, references to works in German are almost nonexistent, although older and very solid biblical works by Germans and others in Latin are cited profusely, as are some writings in French and such English works on the subject as were available.

It is evident that Alexander possessed extensive knowledge about scholarly discussions of the canon and text extending across many centuries, but with limited insights into and with even less sympathy for the newer critical questions and methods that were currently supplementing and reconstructing the older materials. It was perhaps, then, with some sense of relief that in 1828 he transformed to his young protégé Charles Hodge, fresh from nearly two years of study in Germany, the responsibility for instruction in biblical work.[23] But by that time the theological presuppositions and something of the methodology underlying the Seminary's approach to biblical studies had become fixed for a full century. Alexander's successors in biblical teaching built with up-to-date learning and many new insights, but with much the same basic pattern, on the foundation which he had laid.

Alexander had the habit of making notes on his scholarly reading.[24] The lengthiest of his extant summaries of writings of biblical scholars are two pamphlets of manuscript notes on a writing in Latin by the German scholar Johannes Franciscus Buddeus (1667–1729).[25] Buddeus, a man of very wide scholarly interests, after an education in classical and oriental languages, taught philosophy at Wittenberg, history at Jena, classics at Coburg, moral philosophy at Halle, and finally theology upon returning to Jena. While his theology reflected something of the transitional period in which he lived, as a textual critic he clung unyieldingly to the received text of Scripture. As Alexander notes, Buddeus battled by name against such proto-"higher critics" as Thomas Hobbes, Benedict Spinoza, and Richard Simon, defending against them and against others the Mosaic authorship of the Pentateuch. Buddeus suggested that denying that books of the Old Testament were written by the persons whose names they bear undermines the doctrine of biblical inspiration. Alexander noted that Buddeus held to the historicity of Job whom he placed in the patriarchal period, and that he attributed some of the Psalms to David and other Psalms to both earlier and later authors, with Ezra finally compiling the whole. Buddeus considered Proverbs, Ecclesiastes, and the Song of Solomon as genuine writings of Solomon, and rejected the idea that Ezra wrote the historical books of the Old Testament. While Alexander's biblical lectures do not by any means slavishly reproduce his notes on Buddeus, the general attitude of his own lectures toward biblical problems is very similar to that of Buddeus, and many, though far from all, of the biblical scholars whom he cites are also mentioned by Buddeus.

But Alexander made extensive use of other biblical scholars also. For example, he set great store by Humphrey Prideaux's *The Old and New Testament Connected in the History of the Jews and Neighboring Nations*, commonly known as Prideaux's *Connection*, an early classic that sought to use what was known in the first part of the eighteenth century about ancient Oriental history to illuminate the history of Israel from the days of King Ahaz to the time of the New Testament, including also an attempted chronology of the Hebrew prophets.[26] Alexander thought enough of Prideaux's work to publish its contents later in abbreviated and popular form for the layman, with full credit to Prideaux, using the Book of Acts, the ancient Jewish historian Flavius Josephus, and the eighteenth-century Englishman Nathaniel Lardner, to extend the story beyond the terminal point of Prideaux.[27] Alexander also used for his seminary teaching Samuel Shuckford's *Connection* of 1727.[28] Clearly Alexander sought to place the history of Israel in its larger context of world history. Thus he told an applicant for admission in 1818 that both Prideaux and Shuckford were required textbooks for first-year students along with a Hebrew Bible and lexicon, a Greek Testament and lexicon, and—perhaps as a concession to the weakness of the flesh—an English Bible and concordance.[29]

This explains why, as early as 1813, the General Assembly—which in those early days had close control of the Seminary—authorized the Seminary's board of directors to purchase forty copies of the Hebrew Bible "without points" and forty "with points."[30] For critical study of the Old Testament text, Alexander made extensive use of the work of Benjamin Kennicott (1718–1783) who had laboriously collected and compared more than 600 manuscripts. This enterprise, utilizing many researchers, elicited widespread support and was up to that time unprecedented in magnitude, but was sharply criticized by some German and other contemporaries as being insufficiently critical in its methodology and for other shortcomings. Alexander was aware of these criticisms, but esteemed the work for its ground-breaking contribution.[31] He also made extensive use of Bishop Robert Lowth's study of Hebrew poetry (1753), and of Johann David Michaelis's (1717-1791) studies in language and in Old Testament versions, though repudiating Machaelis's effort to avoid distinctively Christian assumptions in interpreting the Old Testament.

Alexander, whose conscious sincerity is above question, set a norm for scholarship which the entire Old Princeton Theology avowedly embraced, namely, readiness to consider and to test honestly any claim to truth or challenge to one's own position from whatever source it might come. He repeatedly urged this courageous attitude both in his lectures to students and in his published writings. Thus he boldly wrote in 1826: "That faith which is weakened by discussion is mere prejudice, not true faith. They who receive the most important articles of their religion, upon trust, from human authority, are continually liable to be thrown into doubt; and the only method of obviating this evil, is to dig deep and lay our foundation upon a rock."[32]

An article of 1833 attributed to Alexander and appearing seven years after he had encouraged Charles Hodge to study in Germany, declared quite characteristically:

If the church consents to close her eyes upon the increasing facilities for biblical investigation which are possessed in Germany, and to turn away from the controversies which are there waged, she will find herself in a field of battle without armour, or, if armed, with the mail and greaves and heavy weapons of a former age, wholly unsuited to the emergency, and the new modes of attack.[33]

This brave claim to openness is reminiscent of the spirit of William Graham, the teacher who had so greatly inspired Alexander in his youth. But it will be recalled that Alexander had noted at that time that Graham took it ill if a student did venture to disagree with him.

There was a certain ambivalence here which prevailed throughout the long history of the Old Princeton Theology. How did Alexander reconcile his own bold advocacy of openness with his determined and undeviating adherence to strict orthodoxy? Certainly part of the answer is that he was so convinced of the ultimate truth of his tenets that he was certain that no adequate evidence could ever be adduced that would overthrow them. But an important part of the answer undoubtedly lay in the fact that he was, from the beginning, more determined than he realized to prove, come what might, the correctness of his convictions. Such an *a priori* commitment was less than fully "open" in the "scientific" noncommitted sense of the form that he seemed to be endorsing. Thus in his writing of 1826 we find him inveighing against the spirit of contemporary biblical criticism: "There is something reprehensible, not to say impious, in that bold spirit of modern criticism, which has led many eminent Biblical scholars in Germany, first to attack the authority of particular books of Scripture, and next to call in question the inspiration of the whole volume."[34] Similarly, in his article of 1833, he rejected the view that Genesis incorporated earlier diverse records even if actually edited by a single author, and he lamented that among some German scholars "the noble predictions of Isaiah, have been torn asunder and mutilated, until they seem scattered leaves of the Sibyl." By the same token, high praise was accorded to Ernst Wilhelm Hengstenberg and to Friedrich August G. Tholuck for their defense of biblical positions which were more acceptable to him.[35]

Alexander, assured of the correctness of his own view of Scripture, felt that "erroneous" views were the result of a wrong methodology: "We are sorry to see, even in some who have approached the nearest to the truth, a sort of tacit admission, that the principles of criticism which the rationalists hold, are sound." Rather, reflecting the influence of Scottish "common-sense" philosophy, Alexander favored an approach which he called "the English ground of faith and common sense instead of the German ground of scepticism and nonsense." But like the proverbial optimist, he thought he saw signs of coming improvement.[36] While Alexander here retained old thought forms and offered no adequate critical methodology to replace the professedly "objective" methodology which at times he seemed uncritically to accept, he was unconsciously facing in the direction of modern awareness that complete detachment and disinterestedness are impossible in questions involving human values and human existence. This whole problem of the psychological relation between existing convictions or biases and "objectivity" or "openmindedness" remains a central one of twentieth-century hermeneutics and for the problem of the relation between faith and knowledge.

If one subsumes biblical scholarship of both Testaments under the three categories of Biblical Introduction, Biblical History, and Biblical Theology, Alexander's courses concentrated on the first category, Biblical Introduction. Biblical Theology had not yet fully emerged as a distinct approach and furthermore was quite foreign to the non-historical dominantly dogmatic approach that characterized Alexander and the Old Princeton Theology. Theology, rather, was treated extensively in the Seminary under the categories of "Didactic Theology" and "Polemic Theology." Biblical History was committed to Dr. Samuel Miller, presumably as part of his professorship of Ecclesiastical History and Church Government. In his teaching of Biblical Introduction—"Biblical Criticism" as he called it—Alexander concentrated almost entirely on what books properly belong in the Bible (canon) and especially on textual or lower criticism, treating literary and historical criticism (the so-called higher criticism) only very indirectly and incidentally, and then in a vigorously negative way.[37]

The attempt to reconstruct Alexander's biblical lectures for the years 1812–1828, during which he had responsibility for instruction in this field, involves a critical problem. He did not publish these lectures, nor did he leave manuscripts explicitly identified as such lectures. More important than his notes on Buddeus, already discussed, as indicating the content of Alexander's lectures on Old Testament textual criticism, are his detailed notes on Georg Lorenz Bauer's Latin work, *Critica Sacra* of 1795. Bauer was teacher of Oriental studies in the University of Altdorf in Germany. Alexander frankly acknowledged that his lectures on this subject were "principally derived" from Bauer's book, and Hodge's student notes attest that Alexander explicitly acknowledged this fact to his class.[38] Corroborating Alexander's frank avowal, the student notes of both Crowe and Hodge show that most—though not all—of Alexander's extant lecture material on Old Testament textual criticism is to be found in Bauer. This is interesting because, though Bauer's views on the Old Testament text were quite conventional, works which he published in German in 1799 and 1802[39] indicate that he belonged to the emerging school of mythological interpretation of Scripture whose work he summarized and to which he offered compact general principles for interpreting Scripture. Charging Bauer with "rationalism," colleagues at the University of Altdorf refused to admit him to membership on the theological faculty there.[40]

Was Alexander—whose interest in the German language was not extensive, as has been noted—unaware of these later writings of Bauer; or was he unconcerned with such "errors" so long as Bauer's textual views were acceptable? The latter alternative cannot be entirely ruled out, as Alexander ranged rather widely in the chronological, denominational, and even theological backgrounds of those whose ideas he used on the text of the Old Testament. Occasionally, in marginal notes in his manuscript, Alexander took exception to Bauer's textual views, but such disagreements were usually on technical rather than on theological matters. Thus, based on Alexander's notes on Bauer, and on Crowe's and Hodge's student notes, it is possible to reconstruct the basic lines of Alexander's lectures on Old Testament textual criticism.

The larger part of Alexander's lectures on the text of the Old Testament was devoted to the period after the beginning of the era of Masoretes, who flourished from the late fifth or early sixth century A.D. to the tenth century. They were so called because of their work on the textual criticism of the Old Testament, which was known as the Masorah. There emerged among the Masoretes three diverging schools—the Babylonian, the Palestinian, and the Tiberian—with the last-named becoming dominant. Within the school of Tiberias, two rival texts appeared, that of ben Naphtali and that of ben Asher, with the latter achieving recognition as the prevailingly received text. Early translations of the Old Testament are also of value for their independent witness to the text, but of course these translations inevitably involve questions as to the translator's methods and accuracy and also as to the transmission of the text of the versions themselves.[41] After the invention of printing, Jacob ben Chayyim (sometimes written as Hayyim) published a text (Venice, 1524–1525) based on many manuscripts which resulted in contaminating the ben Asher text with elements from the ben Naphtali text. The third edition of Gerhard Kittel's *Biblia Hebraia* in 1936, however, was based on a purer ben Asher text, which owed much to the critical work of Paul E. Kahle.[42]

In treating this material, Alexander briefly mentioned the importance of the Masoretes, naming both ben Naphtali and ben Asher. He then proceeded to discuss at considerably greater length the history of the text after the days of the Masoretes. He rejected the older view that a perfect Old Testament text had been preserved through the centuries, and also repudiated the opinion that the Hebrew vowel points belonged to the original text and were divinely inspired. He praised highly the work of Louis Cappel of Saumur, who asserted the later origin of the vowel points against Johann Buxtorf and against the hyperorthodox Helvetic Consensus Formula of 1675.[43] This is the more interesting, because in the Old-School–New-School Presbyterian controversy, the New School, which Alexander stoutly opposed, asserted theological positions concerning human moral ability which somewhat resembled views taught by the school of Saumur.

In mentioning the importance of the ancient translations as aids to recovering the best possible Hebrew text, Alexander gave special praise to Brian Walton's six-volume polyglot Bible (1654–1657) which contained nine texts including the Samaritan Pentateuch, the Greek Septuagint, the Syriac Peshitta, an Ethiopic version of the Psalms and Song of Solomon, and the Latin Vulgate, as well as the New Testament in Greek and in a number of translations. Alexander praised the acumen of Walton's accompanying critical "Apparatus" which speculated on the origin of human language and discussed critically the shape of Hebrew letters, principal editions of the Hebrew Bible and of versions, as well as variant readings of the Masoretes. Alexander told his students that "in this work the learned author has taught the true principles of Sacred Criticism." Though hostile to Richard Simon's questioning of the Mosaic authorship of the Pentateuch, Alexander, closely following Bauer,[44] said that Simon "greatly distinguished himself" as a textual critic by his discussion of causes of corruptions in the biblical text and by his treatment of versions and of various editions of the Hebrew Bible.[45] It was quite characteristic of Alexander's basic fairness of mind to be able to recognize and to endorse acceptable elements in the thinking of those with whom he was otherwise in basic disagreement, as he was with both Cappel and Simon, though not for the same reasons.

Alexander emphasized the work of the Moravian bishop, Daniel E. Jablonski (1660–1741), who in the preface to his edition of the Old Testament pointed out the importance of correcting the printed text by careful critical comparison with the best extant manuscripts. Jablonski described and evaluated some of these manuscripts, noting that many of their readings diverged considerably from the existing text. In particular he pointed out that some of the Keri, or marginal readings of the Masoretes, belonged more properly in the text itself. He also showed that some of the ancient manuscripts had been altered to accommodate them to the text of the Masoretes. Alexander regretted that, in spite of these insights, Jablonski published a traditional rather than a critically revised text, because of the conservative pressures still prevailing in Germany on such matters, Alexander himself being quite open-minded on purely textual questions.[46] The previously mentioned partial edition of the Hebrew Bible published at Halle in 1720 by Johann Heinrich Michaelis profited from Jablonski's work, as did Benjamin Kennicott's collating of more than 600 manuscripts for his two-volume Hebrew Old Testament.[47]

Again reflecting his willingness to learn from scholars whose views he could not fully endorse on other matters, Alexander, closely following Bauer,[48] told his students: "Before all John [Johann] David Michaelis [1717–1791] deserves to be mentioned, who greatly distinguished himself in every department of Sacred Philosophy, & in promoting the true interpretation of the S[acred] S[criptures] in general." He possessed the necessary learning and also "discernment & profound sagacity which are so requisite in a Biblical critic, thus greatly stimulating and extending interest in Biblical criticism in his native Germany." Even so, the brief extant records of Alexander's lectures scarcely do detailed justice to the wide range of Michaelis's scholarship as author of a periodical, of introductions to both New and Old Testaments, and as philologist, lexicographer, biblical commentator, and theologian. From his own strictly orthodox viewpoint, Alexander, evaluating Michaelis as a biblical commentator, conceded that "although he often errs from the truth, he renders others attentive to it and frequently furnishes the occasion of discovering it."[49]

It will be recalled that it was Johann Gottfried Eichhorn's *Introduction to the Old Testament* (3 volumes, 1780–1783) which awakened Moses Stuart to the crucial important of current German biblical scholarship and to the use of critical methods. Alexander, following his informant,

G. L. Bauer,[50] emphasized Eichhorn's contribution to the history of the text of the Old Testament, his careful description of manuscripts, his analysis of the sources of textual errors, and his instruction concerning critical methods by which erroneous texts might be corrected. "In our opinion," said Alexander, "he [Eichhorn] deserves to be ranked among those Heb. Critics & Philologists who hold the very first place." But Alexander added a comment of his own on the opposite page of his lecture sheets which did not get into the extant notes of his two students: "We shd. be on our guard in listening to these high commendations bestowed on Michaelis & Eichhorn lest we should be led to imitate them in the badness of their opinions. As Critics they do indeed stand unrivalled but either of them & especially the last would be a very unsafe guide in Theology." It was Alexander's clear separation of textual criticism from theology which made it possible for him to use the textual work of those with whose theology he disagreed sharply. Alexander's independent note also added a word of appreciation for Herbert Marsh, at that time Lady Margaret Professor of Divinity at Cambridge, for translating J. D. Michaelis's *Introduction to the New Testament* as well as "for the influence which he has had in turning the attention of his countrymen to this subject [to biblical criticism]."[51]

After bringing down to his own day his overview of the history of Old Testament texual criticism based on Bauer, Alexander undertook a summary evaluation of the status of the Hebrew text. For this he used, among others, the *Philologia Sacra* (Jena, 1623–1636), of Salomon Glass, an orthodox Lutheran noted in his own day for his piety and his Old Testament scholarship. In the course of these lectures, Alexander argued in some detail for the basic purity of the existing Masoretic text of the Old Testament. Quite ignoring the somewhat loose way in which the New Testament often cites the Old Testament, Alexander argued that the Old Testament text could not have been corrupted before Christ's time because Christ and his apostles endorsed the Old Testament text by their quotations of it; and it could not have been corrupted after Christ's time because the citations of Christ and his apostles still remained in the later Old Testament text. This argument of course implied that by Christ's time, the Old Testament as a whole was a single universally recognized body of authoritative writings, a closed canon,[52] whereas the Jewish canon was probably not finally fixed until near the end of the first century A.D. But Alexander did allow for copyists' errors, noting that the original writers of Scripture might have used amanuenses and that, thus, copyists' errors might even have crept into the original Old Testament writings.[53] This was a somewhat broader view than that of his successors who later were to insist on the "inerrancy" of the original autographs of Scripture.[54]

For Alexander's lectures on the ancient translations of the Old Testament, one must depend on the student notes of Charles Hodge. Like scholars before and since his time, Alexander recognized the wide discrepancy between the text of many of these versions and the accepted Hebrew text of the Masoretes, and he prevailingly preferred the Masoretic text. He devoted special attention to the famous Septuagint Greek translation, noting with appropriate scepticism the tradition that it was translated by seventy-two Jewish elders sent from Jerusalem at the request of Ptolemy about 285 B.C. Alexander added the correction that parts of it were translated much later. He noted also that the Jews later repudiated this translation in favor of the quite different Masoretic text, from which they then made new Greek translations. Alexander also observed that it was the Septuagint text of the Old Testament which was used by the early church Fathers down to the time of the scholarly Jerome in the fourth century.[55]

As early as the eighth century B.C., Aramaic was appearing in the Near East, becoming more widespread by the time of the Persian period. Oral translations at the public reading of the Hebrew Scriptures thus became necessary and, later still, written translations of the Pentateuch and other portions of the Old Testament into Aramac were made.[56] Bypassing these earlier oral translations, Alexander mentioned the written Targums, treating them as "paraphrases" of the Old Testament in "Chaldaic," and dating them later than modern scholars do. Alexander also mentioned the famous translation of the Old Testament into Syriac, the Peshitta, declaring it, according to his student Hodge, to be "ancient and highly esteemed," but recognizing that its actual date of origin was "a matter of dispute." He considered it "a very excellent version" which often illuminates "an obscure passage."

Alexander's lectures also discussed the interesting Samaritan Pentateuch. "Written in the Hebrew language but in the Samaritan letters, supposed by many to have been the ancient Hebrew," this text, Alexander reminded his students, has been transmitted to us "by a perfectly distinct channel." He noted the wide difference of opinion among scholars as to the accuracy of its text, and—quite characteristically where difference of theological doctrine was not involved—tended toward a median view of its textual value. Alexander also treated the Latin versions, noting that the earliest of these were made not from the original Hebrew, but from the widely used Greek Septuagint, Jerome later pioneering in going back to the Hebrew for his monumental Vulgate translation. Hodge's student notes also summarize Alexander's lectures on the Jewish Talmuds, which contain oral traditions and comments by the teachers of the Jewish law. One was completed in Palestine in the fourth century A.D., and the larger and more significant Talmud a century or more later in Babylonia.[57]

Logically, perhaps, the question of what books properly belong in the

Old Testament (that is, the question of "canon") precedes the study of the way the text of these books was preserved. But historically great care in the preservation of the text of the sacred writings was exercised long before there was official agreement as to precisely what writings possessed this special religious authority.

A turning point in Alexander's religious life as a youth had been, as we have seen, the discovery of Soame Jenyns's subjective evidences for the truth of Christianity, and Alexander had subsequently had a transforming—though not clearly datable—inner experience of conversion. But in his biblical lectures at Princeton Seminary, Alexander was reaching after a clear "objective" foundation for Christian faith, which he sought in a text of Scripture that correctly preserved in all essentials the words of the original authors and in an authoritative list of what writings constituted sacred Scripture. But interestingly, Alexander's own notes on Buddeus emphasize a subjective factor also, as when Alexander translates Buddeus verbatim: "This is certain that those books which by the Jewish church were received as divinely inspired demonstrate themselves to be such in internal [Buddeus wrote "by their own"—"suis"] characteristics."[58]

Alexander's early Princeton lectures on the Old Testament—so far as these are attested by his notes on G. L. Bauer and by the student notes of Crowe and Hodge—concentrated almost entirely on textual questions. Of these three sources, only Hodge's notes preserve any references to canon in Alexander's lectures, and even these are relatively brief. But the heart of Alexander's "objective" emphasis on canon is already here in these early lectures. According to Hodge's notes, Alexander asserted that Moses wrote the Pentateuch and that Moses' original manuscript was preserved in the Ark of the Covenant and rediscovered during the reign of Josiah. As to other Old Testament books, "as long as there was a succession of prophets in the land, every spurious work could be instantly detected." It is unimportant, we are told, whether a collection of the sacred writings was made before the exile. It is probable that the original writings were destroyed, Alexander thought, before the return of the Jews from exile, and that Ezra restored the writings from extant copies. "The corrections and additions made by this eminent scribe are as authentic as if made by the original writer[s]; for he was an inspired man commissioned to perform this very work." Alexander, according to Hodge, accepted the idea that Ezra might have been aided by a "Great Synagogue" of 120—not all of whom lived at the same time—which included Zechariah, Haggai, and Malachi. This Great Synagogue, Alexander thought, might have completed Ezra's work after his death, perhaps by the end of the fourth century B.C.[59]

Thus Dr. Alexander saw the Old Testament canon definitely agreed upon centuries before the Christian era. How do we know that we possess all the books of that canon? For one thing, "they were guarded with sedulous care.'' Then, too, Christ and his apostles endorsed as authoritative the Scriptures of their day. Thus, according to Alexander, all that remains is to discover what writings were contained in Christ's Scriptures. Modern scholarship recognizes that it is difficult to make such an identification with precision. The problem is further complicated by the fact that the New Testament quotes some writings not contained in what is now accepted as the Old Testament ''canon.''[60] Alexander cited catalogues of Old Testament books left by such ancient Christian churchmen as Melito, Athanasius, Cyril, Jerome, and Augustine, but actually these lists do not agree with each other exactly, Jerome including in his list so-called apocryphal books found in the Septuagint translation and not in the accepted Jewish lists. Similarly the versions, which Alexander cites in confirmation of the canon, do not agree entirely on the books to be included. Alexander divides the extant Jewish religious books into three categories—canonical, apocryphal, and spurious. One test proposed of the ''spurious'' books is that they are never quoted as Scripture in the New Testament, apparently overlooking the fact that Jude cites the book of ''Enoch.''

In 1826 Dr. Alexander published a work on *The Canon of the Old and New Testaments Ascertained.* This elaborated what was very embryonically touched on in his early lectures. The Old Testament canon was formed by Ezra assisted by others and completed at about the end of the fourth century B.C.. ''It seems probable,'' Alexander wrote, that the canon at that time was viewed as being divided into the three categories of Law, Prophets, and Sacred Writings or Hagiographa.[61] From the fact that Christ and the apostles cited Scripture as authoritative, Alexander drew the somewhat dubious conclusion that ''we have, therefore, an important point established with the utmost certainty, that the volume of Scripture which existed in the time of Christ and his apostles, was uncorrupted, and was esteemed by them an inspired and infallible rule.'' But how do we know from these individual citations that Christ and the apostles had the same authoritative collection of books as now constitutes the Protestants' Old Testament canon? Here again he invoked the list of Old Testament books given by Josephus (A.D. 37?-95?) and early church Fathers as containing the identical books accepted by Protestants as authoritative.[62] This was the view which Alexander has expressed in his inaugural address in 1812.[63] If the canon is defined as those books which constitute our present Old Testament, it was a circular argument to affirm sweepingly that ''no canonical book of the Old Testament has been lost.'' Citation by New Testament authors of writings now lost should not be construed, Alexander argued, to imply that such lost writings had ever been canonical, although Alexander had previously argued from New Testament citations of Old Testament books to prove the canonicity of the books thus cited.[64]

In treating the Old Testament canon, Alexander sought to avoid the opposite extremes of a canon determined by fiat of church authority on the one hand, and a canon subjectively determined by "internal evidence" of the religious caliber of the material on the other. He readily acknowledged that "the internal evidence of the Scriptures is exceedingly strong . . . but that every sincere Christian should be able, in all cases, by this internal light, to distinguish between Canonical books and such as are not, is surely no very safe or reasonable opinion. . . The tendency of this doctrine is to enthusiasm."[65] The result of Alexander's median position, which was widely held among Protestants, was to make the authority of Scripture dependent upon historical assumptions which were vulnerable to the historical scholarship which was already developing in Germany and whose impact would be felt widely and acutely in America later in the nineteenth century.

When Dr. Alexander turned to lecture on the text of the New Testament, he conceded, as he had done in the case of the Old Testament, "that it is even possible that some of the autographs, if we had them, might not be altogether free from such errors as arise from the slip of the pen, as the Apostles and ["had"] amanuensis [-es] who were not inspired."[66] Thus here, as in treating the Old Testament, Alexander avoided asserting the literal "inerrancy" of the original autographs of the New Testament. Trifling as it might seem to a later day, this was a concession that logically weakened his desire for an absolute base for theology, a concession which his successors, A. A. Hodge and B. B. Warfield, in the process of tightening up the theology, declined to make. Alexander suggested that an interlinear correction by the author himself of such a pen slip would be impossible to distinguish from an emendation by a later scribe. He then sought deftly to turn this concession to advantage by arguing that "the loss of the autographs therefore need not be considered of so much importance as we know that they were copied with the utmost care."[67] For the later Old Princeton position, the argument at this point tended to be reversed. The loss of the unknown original autographs made it possible to blame existing discrepancies on supposed errors in transmission of the text.

While acknowledging that none of the original manuscripts of the New Testament has survived, Alexander noted that there are a few New Testament manuscripts dating from the fourth to the sixth century, such as the Codex Alexandrinus, the Codex Bezae, and the Codex Vaticanus.[68] He estimated that, taking all extant manuscripts into view, there are perhaps as many as 60,000 variant readings, but hastened to reassure his students that "generally they [these variations] do not affect the sense in any degree. . . . But in a few instances, important texts are found in some MSS. whilst they are omitted in others; but the doctrine taught in these passages, is repeated[ly] taught in other parts of S[acred]

S[cripture]."[69] Alexander saw in this excellent preservation of the biblical text both "the care of Providence" and "the veneration & esteem in
which the s[acred] vol[ume] has always been held." While God could
have prevented the entrance of any error whatever in the transmission of
the text, this "wd. have required a perpetual & unnecessary miracle."[70]
He noted that when the critical comparison of New Testament manuscripts began, and the public became aware of the great number of variant readings, this "excited much alarm in the friends of revelation. . . .
But when it was found that these thousands and tens of thousands of var.
readings were so far from presenting us with a new bible, that not one
important truth is weakened or obscured by the whole of them, the
alarm of the pious and the triumph of the infidel were of short
duration."[71]

After noting very briefly some of the causes of textual variations,
Alexander summarized rules for critically recovering the original text.
While attaching more weight to the number of attesting manuscripts
than modern scholarship would do, he fully recognized the important
fact that "any major number of MSS. evidently copied from one, adds
nothing to the weight of the testimony." "Other things being equal," he
said, "the more ancient the MS. the more weight it has." But he also was
clearly aware that "a modern MS. may be copied from a more ancient
and might thus have more value than a MS. older than itself." He also
called attention to a fact that greatly complicates tracing lines of textual
descent, namely that "eclectic MSS." are copied from more than one
MS. and thus cannot give consistent testimony to a single textual tradition. In spite of his dominating desire to build theology on an "objective"
biblical foundation, Alexander recognized important subjective factors
in the transmission of manuscripts. Thus "a MS. written with care shd.
be preferred to one carelessly written, other things being equal." A manuscript where the transcriber obtruded his own criticisms is worthless.
When a variant reading "might have proceeded from an oversight in the
transcriber it may be neglected." Similarly, "in comparing var[iant]
read[ings] it is important to inquire wh. wd. be most likely to occur from
a mistake of the transcriber." "A passage not necessary to the construc-
tion wh. is found in some MSS. & not in others equally good is suspicious." "Words wh. seem to be superfluous if they be found in no
anc[ient] version may be reckoned suspicious." "Readings wh. convey
no meaning whatever shd. be ascribed to the carelessness of tran-
scribers, yet the obscurity of a single word is not suff[icien]t reason for
rejecting a passage."[72]

While reflecting acquaintance with both the "family" descent of manuscripts and with geographical divergence between Alexandrine, Syrian,
Western, and Byzantine types of text, Alexander was less inclined than
some later scholars have been to trace resemblances between contrasting

types in the effort to postulate a common early reading from which both were derived. It is quite accord with Alexander's desire for an "objective" authority that, although he was ready to correct textual errors due to incidental mistakes of scribes, he did not suggest "conjectual emendations" of unclear passages as a whole.

Alexander's lectures described some of the most important ancient translations of the New Testament, noting the special value of literal translations as a witness to the Greek text on which they were based. He considered the Latin versions before Jerome's day "wretchedly imperfect" and warned that they "shd. never be used in [textual] criticism." Realizing that versions, too, suffered from copyists' errors in transmission, he felt that therefore "we must be careful in taking var[iant] read[ings] from them lest we adopt a mod[er]n corruption instead of an anc[ient] version of a text." "Many Translations were made from other versions, these of course are of no use in Bib. criticism." He devoted considerable space to the famous Syriac Peshitta translation printed in Vienna in 1555, which he considered "very ancient," and probably made at Edessa. He also mentioned the translation into Coptic, the common language of ancient Egypt, and into Sahidic, as spoken in upper Egypt.[73] He referred also to the Ethiopic, Armenian, and Persic versions, and then gave more detailed attention to Jerome's revised Latin translation—the famous Vulgate—giving him less credit than his due for translation from critically revised texts of the original languages. Dr. Alexander's lectures also named some of the most important printed editions of the New Testament starting with the sixteenth century.[74]

Alexander's well-informed, analytic interest in scholarly methods for critical recovery of the best New Testament text is impressive. The Old Princeton Theology from Dr. Alexander to Dr. Benjamin B. Warfield, with its very high and tight view of the Bible, was characteristically devoted to careful and able textual criticism. His successors used much more contemporary scholarship than he had done, and were not working as he had been under the necessity of creating a curriculum almost instantaneously in several diverse fields at the same time. But Alexander continually held up scholarly ideals, which his successors were able to implement more fully along the lines which he laid down.

In approaching the question as to what books properly belong in the New Testament (that is, the question of the New Testament canon), Dr. Alexander, like everyone else, came with certain presuppositions and objectives already in mind. He believed that it was both necessary and divinely made possible to have an absolute religious standard in a day of uncertainty and rapid change; and he believed that this standard was to be found in the Bible. This goal and these presuppositions he inherited from Francis Turretin and other Protestant scholastics as well as earlier writers who had preceded them. If the Bible was to perform such a function, it was of course crucially important to be able to list its contents precisely.

Nineteenth- and twentieth-century scholarship has shown that the New Testament canon developed by an historical process. At first, Christians had only the Jewish Scriptures (the Christian "Old Testament") as their canon, which they applied to Christ prophetically and allegorically. Meanwhile oral traditions concerning Jesus were circulated and treasured in various Christian congregations out of which emerged in final form the four canonical Gospels, as well as other peripheral writings not accepted by the early churches as authoritative. Meanwhile Paul's letters to particular churches were copied and circulated. How much of this material was to be accepted by Christians as normative? Varying theological values and religious needs of the early Christian communities entered into the selective process, as well as more strictly historical criteria. It is of great significance that church leaders of the early and middle second century were citing parts of the epistles and parts of what became the four canonical Gospels, sometimes by name. By the end of the second century there was extensive agreement among the widely scattered churches as to which books were authoritative sources, with only a few books still in dispute. By the time of Origen of Alexandria, a widely traveled scholar who died in the middle of the third century, the designation of books properly belonging in the New Testament was almost completely agreed upon.

The Protestant Reformation witnessed a basic controversy between Roman Catholics and Protestants concerning the ultimate source of religious authority. Roman Catholics asserted that the Scriptures had been authenticated by the authority of the church, an assertion of ecclesiastical authority which Protestants were unwilling to accept. John Calvin and the Gallican Confession, which he had had a large part in drafting, the similar Belgic Confession, and the later and quite differently constructed Westminster Confession taught that the witness of the Holy Spirit attested the authenticity of the books of Scripture as well as their true meaning. This divine inner attestation worked well when it involved attesting the deep spiritual value of the Old and New Testaments viewed as a whole, or perhaps even as a means of discounting the religious and moral value of the Apocrypha. But it was far too subjective a criterion to deal with the rational biblical criticism which was developing in the eighteenth and nineteenth century. One could hardly invoke the witness of the Spirit to decide between the relative authority of two biblical documents or between portions of a single verse. If an absolute biblical authority was to be maintained at all in this new situation, the criterion of authenticity seemed to some to depend upon either the authority of the church or the historical determination of apostolic authorship or at least of apostolic endorsement.

"The internal evidence of the Scriptures is exceedingly strong," Alexander acknowledged, but added,

Suppose, that a thousand books of various kinds, including the Canonical, were placed before any sincere Christian, would he be able, without mistake, to select from this mass, the twenty seven books of which the New Testament is composed if he had nothing to guide him but the internal evidence. . . . The tendency of this doctrine is to enthusiasm, and the consequence of acting upon it, would be to unsettle, rather than establish the Canon of Holy Scripture.[75]

Rather than base the New Testament on either the ecclesiastical authority of the church or the inner witness of the Holy Spirit, Alexander followed the principle of basing it on history: "We must have recourse to authentic history," he wrote, "and endeavour to ascertain, what books were received as genuine, by the primitive church and early Fathers." He quoted with approval the historical maxim of the French Roman Catholic prelate Pierre Daniel Huet (1630–1721): "That every [New Testament] book is genuine, which was esteemed genuine, by those who lived nearest to the time in which it was written, and by the ages following, in a continued series."[76] To invoke in this way the historical testimony of individual churchmen was very different from basing the canon on the corporate authority of the church.

Actually, however, Alexander went dangerously beyond this broad historical test of canonicity to the much more specific and elusive criterion of the actual authorship of each New Testament book. "The question to be decided," he wrote, "is a matter of fact. It is an inquiry respecting the real authors of the books of the New Testament; whether they were written by the persons whose names they bear; or by others under their names."[77] This view appeared to offer several advantages. It was construed as connecting the writer of every New Testament book with statements of Jesus such as that found in John 16:13 concerning the Holy Spirit: "He will guide you into all the truth." Inspiration—closely related to Jewish conceptions of the Old Testament—was construed as going beyond the revelation of great divine truths to deliverance from error even in the most minute statements. This supreme emphasis on the identity of the New Testament authors left no need or opportunity for ancient Christians—or for modern Christians either, for that matter—to evaluate the theological or moral quality of the books to be accepted as canon. The issue was thought to be purely objective and absolute.

In thus making the authority of the New Testament dependent on the authorship of the New Testament books rather than on the witness of the church—actually a difficult separation to carry through—Alexander made the Old Princeton Theology, which followed him in this matter, extremely vulnerable to the higher criticism which was already emerging in his own day. Charles Hodge's student notes on Alexander's biblical lectures indicate that as early as 1817–1818 Alexander was teaching the above view. A modern writer would comment that whether or not the Gospels were written or even edited by those whose names they bear, there is strong evidence that they embody the attitude and views of very early Christian communities concerning Jesus and the meaning of his life.

Interestingly, Alexander suggested to his students a number of purely rational critical tests of canonicity which conceivably could have been used—in the spirit of the "higher criticism" itself—to challenge supposedly historical evidence, but Alexander did not so apply them. Thus, according to Hodge, Alexander told his students, "That book which contains contradictions is spurious." So, too, is "anything inconsistent with authentic facts"; or "any thing of a ludicrous, trifling silly kind"; or "facts of a date more recent than the time in which the person lived to whom the book is ascribed"; or "when the style is entirely different from the style of the author whose name it bears"; or "when the idiom and dialect are different"; "if it contains nothing but what is copied from other books"; or "when a spirit is exhibited totally different from the known temper of the author."[78] Here, as we have often already seen in Alexander, were critical principles, reflecting the rationalistic spirit of his age, which would, if consistently applied, have created extremely serious problems for his own ideal of "objective," absolute certainty.

Alexander lectured not only on philosophical, theological, and biblical subjects, but also on the application of faith and knowledge to the concrete problems and duties of the pastor's work.

# 16
# PUTTING THEOLOGY TO WORK

"Pastoral Theology" in the early decades of the American seminary movement was the name often given to everything then offered that theological education would later subsume under the broader title of "Practical Theology." It was usually postponed to senior year, and was offered, not by a specialist in the subject, but by one or more specialists from other fields. At Harvard Divinity School it was taught by the professor of theology and included the composition and delivery of sermons, church polity, and "the practical problems of the minister."[1] Yale Divinity School devoted most of senior year to Practical Theology, having two professors in the field by 1839, both of whom had other duties also. In addition to sermon preparation and rhetoric, there was instruction in expository preaching, public worship, religious revivals, church polity, the history of missions, and pastoral theology properly so called. The effort was also made to show the student the practical bearing of his earlier theological studies and how the gist of this might best be presented to his future parishioners. But as with some other early theological schools, students were not permitted the practical experience of preaching in churches until almost the end of their senior year.[2] This postponement of the opportunity for real preaching was the practice at Princeton Seminary also, according to Melancthon W. Jacobus of the class of 1838, and later a professor at Western Theological Seminary, who made the same complaint.[3]

Thus the professors virtually became a substitute for the students' professional contact with the churches. It is not surprising therefore that contact, when it suddenly came, sometimes proved to be a real shock. Lyman Beecher, with his keen eye for the practical, was aware of this very danger. When considering a call to the presidency of Lane Seminary, he warned against having theological students worship on Sundays by themselves in a seminary chapel "to be edified by classical accuracy at the expense of feeling and untrammeled eloquence . . . a kind of preaching having no more relation to that for which they should be preparing than a sham fight with friends bears to a real battle."[4] And Charles G. Finney, never reluctant to point out faults in conventional churches or ministers, summarized a lifetime's criticism of theological education, with the charge that though ministers were now "vastly more learned" in theological subjects, "they do not know how to use it."[5] It was no easy task which the new theological schools, and more immediately their practical departments, faced.

At Princeton Seminary the "Pastoral Theology" course had the customary broad range with the obvious intent of whetting the student's appetite for his coming ministerial duties and of supplying practical suggestions for their successful performance. Dr. Alexander gave the course, except for a two-year interval, and Dr. Hodge indicated the tone and spirit of it by his recollection many years later that Dr. Alexander's lectures in pastoral theology were "devotional exercises which we attended as we would attend church."[6]

Knowledge of the content of Dr. Alexander's course is in part dependent on the notes of two students of successive years in the last decade of his teaching. As with other courses which he gave repeatedly, the basic pattern and objective remained the same, but his continuing freshness even here in his later life was reflected in numerous changes of content and arrangement within the lapse of this one year. He discussed the nature of the pastoral office, its "excellency and dignity," the minister's "call" and qualifications, his responsibilities to home and foreign missions, pastoral visitation and religious instruction, with major concern for the minister's studying and preaching, and—as might be expected in that era—gave much less attention to public worship and the sacraments, which were confined to a single lecture.[7]

Dr. Alexander's theological and biblical courses were filled with bibliographical suggestions, and he reemphasized in his Pastoral Theology the importance of the minister's continued study. But he introduced an additional idea here, growing out of his own youthful experience of preaching on the frontier. The itinerant minister's library, he said, is sometimes confined to the Bible alone, but this affords him the valuable opportunity of learning to think systematically and profoundly without books. But, we warned, the minister "must take care not to get into the habit of preaching without thought or preparation." It will be recalled that he himself had read very solid books as a young minister even under difficult circumstances.

Alexander retained to the end a vivid awareness of frontier life and of the importance of "domestic missions." "Many pioneers," he said, "[are] so restless [that they] will not bear laws human or divine & [keep] constantly moving further. Missionaries thus must be supported [by mission funds] though [the local] people [are] able to support them." Under these circumstances, the Presbyterian ideal of an educated minister, settled full-time in a congregation, was a physical handicap in competition with more mobile ministries. Alexander did not say this, although he did note that "our missionary boards confine support to existing weak churches, but recently have sent some itinerants . . . but [it is] difficult to find good men. Young men [are] inexperienced—others can't go."[8] Apparently the more experienced were, in a sense, intellectually priced out of the market. Presbyterianism was geared to a stable Old World situation, and was not sufficiently flexible to adapt rapidly to the new conditions. The frontier was not only highly dynamic. Its population was also heterogeneous and was not sorted into ready-made denominational groupings such as would have suited Presbyterians with their precise definitions of theology and church government. Presbyterians, Alexander told his class, "should have gone in bodies . . . capable of supporting ministers and schools." It might be added that Roman Catholics, who had a stronger sense of the church than Presbyterians had, often did have sufficient numbers and discipline to do this kind of group colonizing.

"What increases the difficulty," Alexander lamented, "[is that] teachers of error all go to [the] the new settlements, and found churches before our ministers." Alexander did not mention that the uprootedness of the new settlers and their contact with others of diverse backgrounds would greatly reduce their desire for theological and ecclesiastical particularities such as characterized Old School Presbyterianism of that day. In keeping with his pacific character, Alexander advised his students not to contend with competing movements, but rather simply to "preach [the] pure gospel."

But in this lecture, only half a decade after the Old-School–New-School rupture of 1837, in which nondenominational voluntary societies had been an issue, he did say that it was "very important that [the] church judicatories shd. take this matter [of home missions] as much as possible out of [the] hands of [the] voluntary associations." Confronting the home mission problem, Alexander offered a piece of advice which in altered forms the church often considered and which would have strengthened both the ministry and the church in Alexander's day: "Every young man I think, unless, [the] course of Providence [is] very marked, should spend a few yrs. in itinerant preaching."[9] Alexander's own early missionary ministry had given him an acquaintance with aspects of the life of the church and of the nation which he could have acquired in no other way, as well as rendering valuable service.

Itinerancy was temporarily necessary for the frontier, but long-settled pastorates remained the ideal for Alexander. He lamented the current shortening of pastorates as "lowering the character [that is, professional standing and influence] of the minister." Instead of interpreting the phenomenon sociologically in such terms as the mobility and increasing lay influence of the times, Alexander sought the corrective in a more "sincere & tender affection for the flock" on the part of the pastor.[10]

Much of the teaching of preaching—homiletics—in Alexander's day was called "Sacred Rhetoric," although rhetoric is a discipline which through the centuries has had a somewhat ambivalent reputation. Plato frowned on rhetoric as giving influence to the speaker rather than to truth, but Aristotle saw it as the means of making truth effective. In medieval education, rhetoric, along with grammar and logic, became part of the basic "trivium." Changes in philosophy affected conceptions of rhetoric and the *Lectures on Rhetoric and Belles Lettres* (London, 1783) of the Scotsman Hugh Blair quietly influenced American preaching and literature in the direction of the Scottish Realistic philosophy. Blair was among the texts used at Harvard Divinity School when Ralph Waldo Emerson was a student there, and the attempt has been made to trace the influence of Blair's thought on Emerson's early style.[11] Blair's *Rhetoric* was also used at Princeton Seminary; but in spite of its welcome underlying Scottish philosophy, it was undoubtedly overshadowed as a homiletic influence by Alexander's own less formal pulpit vitality.

"Elocution" was another discipline which could remove obstacles to natural self-expression or, on the other hand, could create artificial barriers to communication. Thus a biased critic commented on the preaching of a young minister: "Should a man adopt those terms in a drawing room . . . he would be esteemed an idiot, or a buffoon."[12] With Alexander's strong emphasis on naturalness in reality in preaching, there was little danger that his students would be led into faults of this kind.

Alexander exalted preaching. "In a large city," he told a young minister, "preparation for the pulpit is the main thing, and except in case of illness, comparatively little good is accomplished by running from house to house."[13] One recalls Alexander's own exasperation over the time consumed by his early pastoral visitations in Virginia. He and the other professors had the responsibility of criticizing student practice preaching,[14] and in his Pastoral Theology course, he devoted four of his lectures to preaching. In his own preaching he was occasionally criticized for excessive simplicity, but he was in great demand as a preacher and was very effective. He condemned the grandiloquent oratory that characterized much of the preaching and political life of his day. Preaching, he said, "should not be [in the] style of books or [of the] Senate."[15] "The pulpit," he told his students,

is no place for historical, philosophical, or political discussions. . . . Sometimes [a preacher becomes] so enveloped in criticism or metaphysics, [that] plain people cannot understand [him]. [The minister] should be [a] critic & metaphysician, but carry only [the] result to [the] pulpit. . . . Preaching [the] Gospel [is] not to gratify a refine[d] taste . . . [but the preacher should] avoid disgusting men of taste. [It is] a grievous fault to speak nonsense in [the] name of [the] Lord. . . . The main object . . . [is] to make preaching useful to [the] souls of men.[16]

"Avoid generalities," said Alexander, "they convey no instruction. Do not preach [on subjects] that [you] don't understand." He suggested concentrating on the "greatest truths," because people are "generally lamentably deficient as to even these." In fact, the preacher should "go over [the] whole system of theology and natural religion and evidences." He then listed as appropriate for the core of preaching doctrines that were central in his own Didactic Theology course. He did not neglect ethics, which should be taught by pointing out the "injury to society" of wrongdoing and not by "denunciation." "Party politics [is] not admissible. But . . . [discussion of] duties or rulers [is appropriate]." "Constant preaching of moral duties alone tend[s] to harden people. The minister should also preach on "Xtian [Christian] experience, afflictions & temptations" and "should know how to deal with awakened souls." He should set forth the "doctrine of election . . . as a ground of joy."[17]

Alexander offered some pointed caveats. "Want of variety will weary anybody," he said. "Have enough subjects, and preserve the peculiar dress given to each text." He warned against a "cold" or "formal-pompous manner," "ranting, noisy preaching," an "angry" or a "timid method." "There are no discourses," said this successful preacher, "heard with so little attention as sermons. . . . [It is] not easy to propose truth . . . clearly, level to [the] meanest capacity; yet [to] preserve dignity of style . . . such as the bulk of people can understand."[18]

Alexander's own preaching embodied the ideals he taught. His extant manuscript sermons are not the place to weigh the full measure of his mind's range and depth. He deliberately avoided too many abstract ideas and cultivated a "plain style" but without the aesthetic pithiness of the best seventeenth-century Puritan preachers. Sometimes sermon-tasters came away disappointed. His preaching was biblical in language and thought, though he seldom expounded long passages. A college student in a religious revival during the last year of Alexander's life commented that his preaching "was addressed almost exclusively to the conscience," and his reading of the Scriptures was interspersed with shrewd comments . . . as barbed arrows into the heart."[19]

One evening a week, "the two lower classes assembled for public speaking, Dr. Alexander presiding and criticizing the performances."[20] Some doubt emerges as to the thoroughness of this exercise from the fact that Dr. Alexander dismissed one student preacher with a single sentence: "A very fine specimen of public speaking: call the next." But the student, who later had a distinguished career, commented appreciatively: "He encouraged me by making only one remark, and that a compliment, which was said to be unusual with him."[21]

The task of criticizing the weekly preaching of the senior class fell to Dr. Samuel Miller. Leroy J. Halsey, later well known as professor at McCormick Seminary, commented that "as a critic, he was acute, skillful, and faithful to the last degree in detecting everything like an error or a blemish; and yet his keenest criticisms were given with all the gentle kindness of a father."[22] A pseudonymous letter to Miller reflected a rather stereotyped conception of biblical interpretation as well as of preaching in its suggestion that Miller receive students' sermon texts in advance in order that he might show the class how the text "should have been" analyzed and presented.[23] One would expect Miller to be a helpful sermon critic. His own sermons were meaty, clear, and well ordered rather than sparkling or sensational.[24] His mind was analytical and critical, as his numerous controversies reveal, while his attitude toward students was unfailingly kindly and helpful. Preaching at an installation service, Miller urged "expounding large passages of the sacred text." This would facilitate presenting "sound doctrine in its proper connection and order." It was particularly important that truth be presented "in a manner adapted to impress the heart as well as the head"—an emphasis which was central for Alexander also.[25]

In 1826 the Seminary's board of directors proposed to the General Assembly an amendment to the Seminary's plan requiring the writing and preaching of sermons by all students, and six years later the board refused the Seminary's certificate of graduation to a student who had not submitted the required written sermons.[26] This added up to a lot of paper work for both students and faculty, as Hodge told his brother: "Every year each student of the graduating class is required to present two discourses to each professor. I have therefore annually some sixty or seventy to look over. One handed in by Mr. Shields [just called to the pastorate of the church of which Hodge's brother was a member] is the only one I ever read through."[27] This confession did less than justice to Hodge's lifelong industry, but suggested limits to the value of this particular exercise.

In Alexander's day there was a notable difference between the preaching of Southern Presbyterians and New Englanders, with Northern Presbyterians fluctuating somewhere in between. Southern preaching tended to be more grandiloquent, emotional, and delivered without notes, whereas New England sermons were more commonly read and were much less emotional. Thus Alexander's son, preaching for a time in Virginia, reported that "there is no toleration here for reading sermons; so that my extempore powers are called constantly into requisition."[28] A somewhat critical Southern writer suggested that in New England the

Edwardsean philosophical influence had "produced a dry analytical method, which is greatly at war with high-toned fervid eloquence. Feeling, instead of being exemplified, is analyzed."[29] As loyal a New Englander as the ebullient Lyman Beecher warned his friend, Professor Leonard Woods at Andover Seminary,

I have been troubled at the complaints which have been made at the want of animation of the Andover students, and of the impression beginning to be made in favor of Princeton. . . . I believe there is a false taste prevailing about eloquence at the South, and threatening to make irruption into New England. . . . Your preachers must wake up. . . . They must get their mouths open, and their lungs in vehement action.[30]

Clearly, Alexander's "Southern" eloquence was having impact in his classroom and beyond. When the Old School General Assembly adopted a resolution against reading sermons in the pulpit, a practice which it found to be "on the increase," Dr. Hodge's always uninhibited annual review of the Assembly flatly contradicted the Assembly with the declaration, "We hail the increase of this method [of reading sermons] as proof of the intellectual progress of our church, and as one of the best omens of its true prosperity," and he proceeded to brand any extempore preaching which involved more or less preparation as "the laziest of all methods." Four months later, Dr. Alexander privately warned Hodge that to create the impression that "preaching without reading is discouraged in our Seminary" would cost the Seminary a loss of students, "as at least four fifths of the churches south of the Delaware are prejudiced against reading sermons." Along with this admonition, Alexander enclosed for publication in Hodge's journal an article from a Southern alumnus on the opposite side. But it was never published. In spite of his reverence for his mentor, Hodge was by now his own boss. Samuel Miller habitually wrote his sermons and in earlier life memorized them, but later commonly read them, but with such skill as to be scarcely noticeable. But practises differed. Alexander's son, distinguished pastor of the Fifth Avenue Presbyterian Church in New York City, commented adversely on the increase of read sermons during the first half of nineteenth-century America. Read sermons were also being discussed among Scottish Presbyterians at this time.[31] Old School Presbyterians were very strict as to what doctrines were to be proclaimed, but left wide freedom as to the method by which they were to be preached.

Although, as already observed, Alexander so exalted preaching as seemingly to disparage pastoral visitation, he did reserve a place for "pastoral theology" properly so called. Though he had read extensively in the psychology and "mental philosophy" of his and earlier days, the more scientific development of the pastoral art lay still in the future. For him pastoral visitation was still a combination of piety, authority, compassion, and common sense, each of which he possessed in generous measure.

"The first object of a pastor," he said, "should be to get a correct knowledge of his flock."[32] To do this one would suppose that he would need to do more listening than the lecture suggests. "Once in a year if practicable, the pastor shd. visit every family in his parish." These visits were not to be mere social occasions, but "shd. be devoted entirely to religious instruction & devotional exercises." As in the earliest days of the Reformed faith, the spiritual function of the lay elder was stressed, for "it is of advantage to be accompanied with the elder of the district."

The function of the minister was changing during this period and the prestige of his office was declining; so Alexander was emphatic in his exhortation: "In these visits a pastor should act with freedom & authority. . . . Timidity must be laid aside." The minister, in Alexander's view, was still a special personage, somewhat aloof, and not just a good fellow. "The effect of much familiar intercourse is not good. A good degree of reserve in ministers . . . increases their authority." Pastors should be more faithful in giving private admonition. "No part of ministerial duty [is] so much neglected. . . . The certainty of meeting with reproof from a pastor wd. act as a powerful restraint." People, Alexander said, should be encouraged to come to their pastor with cases of conscience and with their sorrows.[33]

Alexander, like Jonathan Edwards in describing phenomena of the Great Awakening, was particularly concerned with inner religious experience. Alexander stressed the difference between religious fear and true repentance. "Sinners in the near prospect of death," he noted, "are often awfully alarmed, and yet they have no clear & distinct views of their own sinfulness. . . . These persons, when the prospect of death passes away are found as careless as ever." Without mentioning Edwards, he substantiated Edwards's findings when he reported that "the deepest conviction is often accompanied with very little terror."[34] These observations, like much of Alexander's other writing, place feelings and thought in interesting confrontation.

Heroic measures were proposed for the sick. If such are "stupid [that is, in a stupor] he [the minister] should endeavor to awaken him. . . . If you find them hardened—Beware of giving them any comfort [concerning their future state]." But "if he appear pious—Exhort him to gratitude, to humility, and announce the absolution of his sins in the name of Christ."[35]

Alexander, as a member of the General Assembly of 1837, voted to abrogate the Plan of Union with the Congregationalists of which he, a third of a century earlier, had been a bearer, but he was never a man who delighted in controversy. He exhorted prospective pastors that "religious controversies should be excluded from the church." He warned against the minister's "attempting to moderate in disputes lest he give reason of a suspicion of partiality." Rather, he advised invoking the help of the lay elders. "Call the parties before the session, not for trial, but for advice & counsel. Hear both sides in full . . let the Session make up a deliberate opinion . . . recommending the course to be pursued in order to reconciliation."[36] Alexander emphasized the pastor's dignity and authority, but he also was ready to share some of this with the elected lay representatives of the congregation.

During the late eighteenth and early nineteenth centuries, deadly epidemics swept many American communities. Ministers reacted differently, some seeking safety, others remaining at their fever-stricken posts. Alexander suggested that "nearly the same rules should guide the pastor & the physician in attending on, or withdrawing from pestilential diseases." In a day that understood less about contagion, he suggested that "there are few cases in which it is proper to shut up the temples of God."[37]

During the early years of Princeton Seminary, piety was greatly stressed there and at such other leading theological institutions as Andover Seminary and Yale Divinity School. Thus, Professor Leonard Woods of Andover, describing the regular Wednesday evening "Conferences" for students, declared: "We poured out the feelings of our hearts . . . on the character and work of the Saviour and the Holy Spirit, and on the great interests of time and eternity." Professor Moses Stuart, the biblical scholar, also delighted in these meetings.[38] Francis Wayland, a student at Andover in 1816–1817 and later a prominent Baptist leader and president of Brown University, reminisced that "the value of these conferences was inestimable. I think they did more to keep alive the spirit of piety than any other service of the week.[39] Professor George P. Fisher, writing of the early days of the Yale Divinity School, noted that zeal for theological discussion did not "chill the spirit of piety." "The instructors . . . were familiar with revivals of religion; and their pupils in many cases caught their spirit."[40]

Princeton Seminary also emphasized spiritual nurture. During its first quarter century its students came "in great numbers from the very midst of revival scenes," some of them "valorous youth who were wiser than their teachers, and eager to beard a professor, and make converts among their fellows," "a zeal . . . . which sometimes demanded the cautious hand of repression and guidance."[41] Some zealous students felt that still greater fervor was needed. Thus Benjamin B. Wisner, a year out of the seminary and already pastor of Boston's historic Old South Congregational Church, while expressing deep affection for the Seminary, confided to Hodge that he thought that its piety fell below that of Andover.[42] Similarly, Albert Barnes, later famous as a New School Presbyterian leader, arriving at Princeton Seminary with too high expectations, was disappointed to find that "a spirit prevailed here very much allied to the spirit of the college," but reported that currently he found an improvement with the "spirit of missions . . . gaining ground."[43]

Of course much is in the eye of the beholder. A very different interpretation of piety at Princeton Seminary in these early years was offered by John W. Nevin, who later became one of the leading American theologians of his day.[44] Nevin was a student at Princeton Seminary from 1823 to 1826 and instructor there for two years afterwards during Charles Hodge's absence in Europe. He had been reared in a religious life-style somewhat in the tradition of eighteenth-century antirevivalistic Old Side Presbyterianism at its best. Emphasis was on the objective side of religion, with four days devoted to the solemnities of the Lord's Supper. Later, as a student at Union College in Schenectady, Nevin found himself suddenly immersed in agonizing introspection amidst a religious revival rooted in a New England Puritanism which contrasted sharply with his own more objective religious heritage.

Entering Princeton Seminary after a year's intermission, Nevin evaluated its religious life in terms of subjective-objective polarization. As a boy in his home church, he had thought that Princeton Seminary students "had a certain air of conscious sanctimony about them, which . . . gave the notion of a *Young Presbyterianism,* which was in a fair way to turn into old-fogeyism soon all their [of congregations like Nevin's] existing religious life." At the Seminary, Nevin found the teaching of Drs. Alexander and Samuel Miller predominantly on the side of the older nonrevivalistic Presbyterianism of the seventeenth century, and yet, he added, "our teaching was not steadily and consistently in one direction." A particular case in point was Dr. Alexander's Sunday afternoon "conferences," which were characterized by "searching and awakening casuistry" and from which, said Nevin, some students went away "in a state bordering on despair." The students themselves, he thought, were not being won over to the scholastic theology. Rather, "the tide of actual living . . . around us lay all now another way; and all of us, whether we would have it so or not, fell inwardly and experimentally, more or less, under captivity to its power."[45] At the time Nevin wrote these reminiscences, his perspective had been formed not only by the objective Presbyterianism of his boyhood, but also by his later catholic and sacramentarian "Mercersburg Theology." Alexander did not thus view revivalism and Scholastic Calvinism as being in complete disjunction, but for a lifetime sought, with mixed success, to synthesize elements from both.

In the autumn of 1812, some two months after the founding of the Seminary, Alexander started Sunday evening services in his own home, which were soon moved to a college building and were forced later by overflowing attendance to move to the larger college refectory. The services were later discontinued in favor of the Sunday evening services of the village church. Those who heard Dr. Alexander's sermons often were moved to seek his spiritual counsel privately. Alexander's colleague, Dr. Samuel Miller, often led these services also.[46] In 1815 a notable revival occurred in the college, in which President Ashbel Green took deep personal interest and in which both Alexander and Miller actively cooperated, addressing groups and counseling individuals.[47] A number of converts presently became students in the Seminary, and influences of the revival radiated in many directions and extended over many years. Meanwhile the Seminary community worshiped along with the college in the College Hall on Sunday mornings, until the Seminary in 1826 withdrew for its own worship in the "Oratory" of the Seminary building.[48]

Highly as Alexander regarded preaching, he saw clearly that it was not in every situation the most effective means of instruction, and emphasized something not entirely unlike the twentieth century's broadly conceived ideal of religious education. "Preaching," he said, "[is] inadequate for [the] instruction of [the] very young, or [the] wholly uninstructed. [In preaching] truths are not held up long enough. [The] import of words [is] not known." He suggested a discussion method: "Try by inquiring what idea[s] they attach to words—law, grace, satisfaction, &c." He did not approve of the rite of "confirmation," "but at 14 or 15 . . . [there] should be a class for preparation for [the] Lord's table." His noting of the "diff[iculty]" of refusing admission of this class of persons not baptized" had parallels in the widespread late twentieth-century discussions among the denominations as to the conditions under which children should be admitted to the Lord's Supper. Both cases involved the democratic issue as to whether or not inheritance (that is, infant baptism based on God's "covenant" with the child's parents) should convey special religious privileges. In teaching the Bible to children, he said that the "historical comes first. On these [historical] facts, the important doctrines should be grafted."[49] This pedagogical common sense unconsciously accorded well with twentieth-century salvation-history and emphasis on story.

Perhaps recalling his own youthful wrestling with doubt and his discovery of Christian "evidences," Alexander suggested that it would be "well to deliver a course of lectures to young people on evidences." He also warned that "they should be well instructed against infidelity," presumably referring to deism, as late as 1842. He also urged that pastors lecture on biblical history "as connected with other authentic history," and promote "study of [the] customs of [the] East, Geography, [and] antiquities." In addition, "every clergyman should give (better in lecture or Bible Class) [a] sketch of Ch[urch] H[istory]." He proposed adult Bible classes which "might, if they could not at [any] other time, meet an hour before worship."[50] Clearly, Alexander was implying that nearly everything a student learned in seminary was useful for passing on to his parishioners—after, of course, thorough digestion and appropriate popularization. This was to be done either from the pulpit or by extra-pulpit lectures—almost an anticipation of late twentieth-century ideals of the "continuing education" of lay adults in the solid study of biblical, historical, and theological aspects of Christianity.

Undoubtedly with a certain kind of contemporary revivalism in mind, Alexander warned that "a great many efforts to promote religion in our day . . . are not founded on the principle that divine truth is t[he] great instrument of reforming & saving men." But he saw an opposite failing when "some seem contented to have the head full of sound opinions while t[he] heart remains unaffected & the life unreformed."[51]

In a "Pastoral Letter" immediately following the Old-School–New-School disruption, the Old School General Assembly warned that the current expanding Christian literature was no substitute for instruction in the venerable Westminster Shorter Catechism.[52] A dozen years later, the Assembly announced that interest in the catechism was increasing with instruction in it being given "to the young in almost the entire number of our congregations." The same Assembly ordered that an "illuminated" edition be published "with interesting and instructive illustrations."[53]

But Alexander needed no urging to emphasize catechising. He commended to his students the early Calvinistic practice of dividing a congregation into districts, with an elder assisting the pastor in this work in each district.[54] Whether catechising children or slaves, questions and answers should be simple, with frequent repetition. Questions should start with "historical" and factual material, moving on later to meanings and applications. Patience was crucial. "Every thing shd. be so managed as to produce pleasure & alacrity . . . and every thing avoided wh[ich] tends to mortify or discourage." The same method was recommended for catechising slaves.[55] The catechist should seek to ensure understanding by asking the same questions in simpler form and demanding simpler answers. The districts should be catechised quarterly and the whole congregation once a year.[56]

Religious instruction of slaves had been a concern of Alexander during his own youthful ministry, and to this subject he devoted a lecture in his Pastoral Theology course. It should be noted that this lecture was delivered a decade after the heightening of the slavery controversy by the founding of the American Antislavery Society and the radical abolition activity of William Lloyd Garrison, Theodore Dwight Weld, and others, but before the further exacerbation of the issue by the Mexican War and the problem of organizing the territories acquired by that war.

In his lecture Alexander saw in the bringing of slaves from Africa to

America a divine providential purpose, although for him as a Calvinist this did not of itself justify human involvement in either the slave trade or slaveholding. The descendants of Noah's three sons would now all have their successive blessing. Shem (the Hebrews) had been favored first, then Japheth (white Gentiles) had "for 2,000 years . . .ascendancy," but now Ham (black Africa) was about to be elevated "from barbarism to civilization." As early as his pseudonymous writing in the *Virginia Religious Magazine*, Alexander—like others in the slaveholding states—had intimated moral qualms about slavery as an institution, and he appeared to be on the moral defensive in this lecture also, noting quite rightly that there was "no reason for [the] North to glory" since slaves had been brought in "Northern ships." He recognized, too, that slavery was actually uneconomic, a fact hidden by its continued expansion into virgin land. "It is evident," he said, "[that] slaves [are] a wasteful possession . . . [and] bankruptcy would result, but for [the] great extent of new country."[57]

For him God's mysterious and ultimately gracious purpose was to be seen in the fact that "in [the] U.S. [slaves are] brought within sound of [the] Gospel, & many [are] called. And now [it] seems as if God intended to civilize & Christianize Africa." Taking the gospel to the slaves is the "duty of ministers. [It is] one of the most interesting and inviting field[s] of missionary labour in [the] world." He acknowledged that the Baptists and Methodists "have paid most attention" to this work, but felt that these denominations "place religion too much in [the] feelings," without suggesting that this accounted for their greater numerical success. By implication he seemed to look upon blacks as inherently different from whites when he said that it is "hardly worth while to teach [slave] adults to read. . . . With them emphatically truth comes by hearing." Therefore one should "first teach [the] historical facts of the Bible." This should be followed by instruction concerning the "Attributes of God, in plainest language," the "Ten Commandments," and their "Lost condition." But "with this preach [the] Gospel—[the] love of God—encouraging prayer—[and giving a] call to repentance." The slaves' "duties" should be taught—"to obey [their] masters" and (pace Karl Marx!) that "outward condition in this world [is] of little importance" and "afflictions are useful." He suggested that a simplified catechism should be used, since the church's official Westminster Shorter Catechism was "too abstruse."

In spite of some inward misgivings that Alexander seems to have felt, he—like countless citizens North and South—was the captive of the institution. He warned his predominantly Northern students that the missionary to slaves

must have [the] confidence of [the] masters. [There can be] no meddling directly or indirectly. [The] best means of abolishing slavery [is] to preach the

gospel. . . . [The] apostles . . . did not form abolition Soc[ieties]. . . . [It] may be
the duty of some men to try to bring about abolition [sic], but not of ministers as
such; especially in the S[outhern] States. . . . [Some] free people [are] in worse
condition than slaves.[58]

Colonization of freed slaves in Africa was a longstanding interest of
Alexander. He had encouraged the founding of the American Colonization Society and wrote a history of it,[59] and he told his students that the
"only plan of disposing of free slaves [is] to send [them] to Africa. [It is]
well," he said, "to patronize [this enterprise] as far as [circumstances]
permit." But by 1843, even colonization, which earlier had been looked
upon by many as a potential compromise between slaveholding and abolition, was now regarded in many quarters as too radical. So Alexander
warned his students: "If [a minister] wishes to benefit slavery [it is] best
not to be too strong [an] advocate of [the] Colonizat[ion] Soc[iety]. . . .
Slavery will never be abolished by denunciation. Northern men," said
this distinguished Virginian, "have notions far from correct as to
slavery."[60]

One lecture on public worship was included in Alexander's course on
Pastoral Theology. Ways of worship, whether casual or highly liturgical,
consciously or unconsciously reflect the worshiper's concepts concerning human nature, social relations, and ultimate reality in addition to the
more explicit theological affirmations which Christian worship
expresses. Thus early Reformed worship—as exemplified, for example,
in Calvin's liturgy at Geneva—assumed the radical immateriality of God
and centered everything in words—the word of God in particular—to be
apprehended by hearing, the most abstract of the physical senses. This
seemingly "simple" service, which had a liturgy, was anything but primitive, for it presupposed a highly sophisticated worshiper who could
bring understanding to the service and find deep meaning without the
help of symbols. Early Puritans, battling the symbolism of Anglicanism,
exaggerated this ideal of meaningful simplicity, and on the American
frontier amid intense activism and competition, worship often degener-
ated into mere slovenliness which was increased by highly emotional revivalism. If revivalistic conversion tended to discipline and guide social
change, more formal worship had the tendency to restrict social change
and to preserve the status quo.

Presbyterians in 1788, while reorganizing on a more national basis,
adopted a new Directory for the Worship of God, to replace the Westminster Directory of 1644. This directory omitted the prayer topics of the
Westminster document and also the model prayers proposed by its own
drafting committee while at the same time it offered "no underlying
theory of worship." The directory rebuked the prevailing casualness and
lack of reverence during public prayer, and urged careful preparation by

the minister for this part of worship. Perhaps the problem was not unrelated to the fact that the "pastoral prayer" among late eighteenth-century Presbyterians was twelve to twenty minutes in length. The original draft suggested a sermon length of thirty to forty-five minutes, and longer if only one Sunday service was held. But this stipulation was deleted by the adopting Synod.[61] In spite of this deletion, the heroic pulpit marathons of the early Puritan era were abandoned, except in the case of revivals and camp meetings. As late as 1852 a Princeton Seminary alumnus who served in distinguished pulpits and seminary chairs in both the North and South could still tell a correspondent, "When I preach I do not like to be limited to 45 minutes, though I seldom exceed that time."[62]

During the nineteenth century, discussions continued among Presbyterians concerning the singing of hymns in addition to the biblical Psalms and also concerning the use of organs and choirs. By mid-nineteenth century, sitting had largely replaced standing as the prevailing posture in public prayer, in spite of Dr. Miller's consistent resistance.[63] American Presbyterian creative interest in the improvement of Presbyterian public worship was greatly stimulated by publication of historic Reformed Church liturgies by Charles W. Baird in 1855, a work which was given added influence by Dr. Charles Hodge's commendation in the *Princeton Review*.[64]

A lecture on public worship was included in Alexander's course in Pastoral Theology. He saw much of the form of Christian worship inherited from the Jewish synagogue, including the reading of Scripture (to which Christians early added the reading of portions of what later became the New Testament plus exposition); prayer, "whether extempore or not is disputed"; and benediction. To Jewish worship was of course added the preaching of the Christian gospel and "praise to [the] Trinity & especially [to] Xt." and "doxologies . . . [in the] very early age of [the] church." Alexander, presumably with sectarians and the more extreme forms of revivalism of his own day in mind, emphasized that "everything [is] to be done decently & in order," calling attention to the fact that "Paul reprehends disorders as to [the] use of gifts." Because the first Christians were "in great danger, [they] met at night, and in [the] cemeteries of martyrs that [they] might encourage [one another] to meet death firmly." There was the rule—"no vestige of which [is] in S[acred] S[cripture]" —that "none must be present but members during prayer, or at communion."[65]

Declaring standing to have been the prevailing posture during public prayer in the early church, Alexander noted the variety of postures in his own day. Many American Presbyterians of an earlier time had the custom of standing, but now many were sitting during prayer and rising for singing. He thought "some instruction should be given as to behaviour in the house of God" because the "practice of standing about [the] doors and conversing [is] unfriendly to religion, [although it is] not possible to prevent it entirely in the country." He stressed the importance of the pastor's public prayers. "Some have no gift of prayer—who preach very well. [They] should prepare for prayer. . . . Some . . . ramble in prayer. . . . [Some] have not unction. [I] know no part of a pastor's duty more diff[icult] to attain perfect[ion] in than prayer."

To the question whether a convert from Roman Catholicism should be rebaptized, Alexander in his lecture replied, "I think not." This was an advanced position to take in 1843 at the height of anti-Catholic feeling in the nation, even though he added that "each [is] to form [his] own opinion."[66] Two years later the General Assembly decided "by a nearly unanimous vote, that baptism so administered [by the Roman Catholic Church] is not valid."[67] In the next issue of the *Biblical Repertory* Charles Hodge refuted the General Assembly in language far more positive than Alexander had used. The Assembly later straddled the issue, leaving the decision to each local church session.[68] Almost like the early Protestants who viewed marriage as a civil ceremony, Alexander considered the performance of a marriage ceremony as "not strictly [a] pastoral duty. [I] don't know [that the] Apostles had anything to do with it; but as it falls to [his] lot [the minister] must prepare [for it]. [He] must acquaint himself with the laws," which differ in the various states.[69]

# EPILOGUE

Archibald Alexander's life is, to a degree, the struggle for stability for himself, and in behalf of others, in the face of religious, social, and intellectual change. His grandfather was a successful pioneer in the Valley of Virginia, a late and quite different expansion of the Old Dominion. Thus family traditions extended back to the earliest frontier of the region, and Alexander himself had boyhood recollections of Revolutionary War days. He had seen evidence of the widespread social and cultural dislocations that followed the war in the disorderliness of students both when he attended Liberty Hall and when he was president of Hampden-Sydney College.

In a sense, the dual phenomena of Enlightenment and Pietism set the stage for the deepest experiences of Alexander's inner life and of his outward labors. These two great forces of the era, antithetical in so many ways, yet had strange parallels. Both had a tendency to weaken the authority of the group and to strengthen the authority of the individual, the Enlightenment by its appeal to the critical reason of the individual, and Pietism by its emphasis on the individual's experience of conversion and of divinely illuminated conscience. Was there some similarity, after all, between "reason" and inner "illumination"?

The Reformed faith, particularly as seen in seventeenth-century English Puritanism, contributed to the early stages of both of these movements. From its inception the Reformed faith had emphasized the authority of the written "word of God," which must be interpreted by grammatico-historical exegesis. Inevitably this task involved the careful use of rational processes, a function which the controversies and rationalistic forces of the seventeenth century greatly heightened. But latent Pietistic tendencies were also present from the beginning in the Reformed emphasis on the inner witness of the Holy Spirit as an indispensable guide to the true understanding of the Bible's meaning and in giving "assurance of salvation."

At the age of sixteen, Alexander, who, like his parents, had led a

respectable but not ardently religious life, found himself suddenly confronted head on by these two major forces of the era, the Enlightenment
and Pietism. This occurred while he was tutor in the home of General
Posey, on the edge of Virginia's Tidewater. At Posey's table were
exponents of Enlightenment "scepticism" and also an ardently
evangelical senior lady who persuaded him to accompany her to the
emotional meetings of the rapidly increasing "Separate" Baptists. In the
midst of these enthusiastic and quite unconventional gatherings, he preserved enough of his characteristic judicious detachment to recall, many
years later, some of the odd sights he witnessed there. But the impact of
these meetings, together with private conversations along similar lines,
stimulated within him agonizing fluctuations between spiritual ecstasy
and utter despair. Meanwhile Alexander maintained his extensive reading, including writings of such Puritan divines as Flavel, Owen, and
Baxter. But his anguish continued for a time after he left the Posey
household and while he attended other revival meetings. Alexander
found more stable inner peace only when he turned his dependence
away from fluctuating subjective feelings to objective dependence on
God himself. But this "objective" dependence on God as presented by
evangelical Christians presupposed the basic trustworthiness of the Biblical record, with the result that he became a lifelong student of the
Bible.

Alexander's theological study under William Graham, coming soon
after his revivalistic conversion, was formative for his intellectual life.
Graham had studied Francis Turretin's seventeenth-century Reformed
scholasticism and was a graduate of the College of New Jersey, where he
had come under the influence of President John Witherspoon's Scottish
Philosophy of Realism. But Graham had also been much influenced by
Jonathan Edwards, as a student's extant notes on Graham's lecturing
make clear. This Edwardsean influence on young Alexander was at first
quite strong, as manuscripts of his early Virginia sermons attest, in
which, like Edwards's *Treatise Concerning Religious Affections*, Alexander
showed a tendency to fuse the affections and intellectual activity. Such a
fusion of affections (that is, feelings) and intellect not only transcended
the old "faculty" psychology, but might have broken down the dualism
between "piety and learning" proclaimed by John Witherspoon and
made a cornerstone of Princeton Seminary's basic "plan." The tendency
of the Enlightenment, and even before that of the Renaissance, was to
compartmentalize Christianity as one of numerous special interests in a
compartmentalized "secular" world. This flatly contradicted Christianity's claim that its God ruled and was concerned with the whole
world, a claim to which the medieval church attempted to give some
semblance of reality.

Whatever may have been the ultimate intentions of Jonathan

Edwards's uncompleted writings, some have suggested that the form of his philosophic idealism—in spite of his theological orthodoxy—contained seeds of a possible synthesis between Christian faith and culture. Be that as it may, the sharp dualism which Alexander posited on the base of his philosophic realism pointed directly to a separation between "Christ and culture," between Christianity and cultural forms that diverged basically from the clearly bounded system of religious thought which he inherited. Whether or not it would be possible to create any kind of viable synthesis between historic Christianity and a new emerging world culture would be a central and keenly debated problem in late twentieth-century America.

Alexander was concerned not only with inner spirituality and with wide-ranging scholarship. From the time of his "conversion," he maintained a lifelong interest in the church itself, first as youthful itinerant preacher, then as pastor, college president, and active participant in the work of the church judicatories. The Synod of Virginia had extensive frontier contacts and, because of this, experienced a greater than average need for more ministers. Amid this crisis, Alexander was one of the earliest Presbyterian leaders who were seeking some new method and structure which would not only increase the quantity of ministers, but would at the same time improve their intellectual quality. He had little understanding of, or sympathy with, the democratic leveling forces in the newer settlements and among the less privileged in the older areas, which created resentment of professionals and of the increased specialized training being planned for them. While still in Virginia Alexander took a leading part in planning for a theological school which would be under the synod, an objective which the synod achieved after his departure for Philadelphia. Alexander was also a leader in the synod in establishing one of the nation's early theological journals to which he contributed pseudonymous articles gently satirizing slavery and sharply critizing the anticlerical sectarianism which was conspicuous in part of the revivalism of the times. It is interesting to recall that as some of these "sects" became more settled and secure, many of them also aspired toward greater training and professionalism for their ministers.

Alexander's moving to a pastorate in Philadelphia, the largest city on the continent, introduced him to a quite different lifestyle and to a very different ecclesiastical situation. Here in Philadelphia he became involved in the burgeoning voluntary society movement and participated in founding the Philadelphia Bible Society and in organizing an "Evangelical Society" whose concern was the poor and which had an important part in founding the first black Presbyterian church in the nation. Alexander's sermon as retiring moderator of the General Assembly in 1808 gave wide publicity to the idea of a Presbyterian theological seminary, an objective which Dr. Samuel Miller by private correspondence had already been pursuing for several years. As the proposal gained momentum, Alexander was elected to the Assembly's committee to draft the "plan" of the Seminary, which became its constitution. He also played a prominent role as a representative of the General Assembly in very delicate and important negotiations with the College of New Jersey which resulted in the agreement, in substance, that the Seminary would not function as a college, and that the College would not function as a divinity school.

Alexander was elected by the General Assembly to the Seminary's first professorship, with the title of "Professor of Didactic and Polemic Theology," and Dr. Samuel Miller, pastor of the First Presbyterian Church of New York City, was elected the next year as "Professor of Ecclesiastical History and Church Government." To Alexander fell the task of devising a curriculum that would implement the Seminary's "Plan," a task for which his solid studies and his varied ministerial experience had for that era given him good preparation.

Alexander's deeply rooted religious experience gave him special interest in epistemology and psychology, and he emphasized the value of these as a help in analyzing Christian experience, as an introduction to the study of theology, and as preparation for preaching and pastoral counseling. In his apologetics he sought to meet nonbelievers on their own ground and to demonstrate that Christian faith was tenable for a rational person. Faith, he said, though it transcends reason, may not contradict reason. His ethics, following the fashion of the day, was rational and philosophical, rather than biblical or theological. His theology, which had its seventeenth-century core in the theology of Francis Turretin and of the Westminster Confession, was seen through the perspective of the eighteenth-century epistemology of the Scottish Philosophy of Realism. But Alexander's realism was tinctured at times with Jonathan Edwards's philosophic idealism, in which the "affections" were blended with the intellect, thus suggesting to Alexander a fleeting possibility that the sharp dualism between Pietism and the Enlightenment, religious experience and reason, piety and learning, might be synthesized. But Alexander, apparently, never systematically or seriously concentrated on this objective. During his lifetime, a quite different expression of philosophic idealism, entering America from Germany, offered organic conceptions and many kinds of basic syntheses, but Alexander's philosophic realism and the theological system which stood on it fully immunized him against philosophic idealism, except for a few scattered—and for him not fully integrated—ideas of Jonathan Edwards.

Alexander's dependence on and love for the Bible led to his interest in textual criticism and exegesis, but he avoided extended study of historical and literary criticism, pursuit of which was not widespread among American scholars during his lifetime. Biblical theology and the history of doctrine, which also came later to America, would likewise have challenged the somewhat complacent method of his "didactic theology" and of his "polemic theology," which, supposedly, were drawn inductively from Bible passages, but were not facing the challenge of relativism that would come from a critical dealing with the origin, viewpoint, and historical development of the biblical documents and their contents. The theme of religious stability became a hallmark of the Old Princeton Theology which Alexander fathered and which had particular appeal to an emerging elite whose college education had not included critical methodology, and whose own achieved status was threatened by the social mobility of others.

Pastoral theology, which in Alexander's day included all the material then offered that would later be sussumed under "Practical Theology," at that time lacked the specialization and scientific development that these disciplines would later receive. But within those serious limitations, many students found helpful Alexander's contagious zeal, his practical suggestions drawn from extensive reading and broad ministerial experience, and the importance which he attached to their anticipated labors.

In the earliest days of the American seminary movement, there remained some resemblances to the earlier "apprentice" system of ministerial education under one minister who continued in the meantime his active pastorate. Seminary faculties and libraries for a time remained very small, and the teachers were former pastors without postgraduate training who usually continued to preach in various pulpits, though now without pastoral ties. But the new seminary movement had basic differences from its informal predecessor. Faculty members increasingly became learned specialists in particular fields; libraries grew significantly; larger bodies of students came from wider geographical areas, all of which created an academic community which approached the prospective duties of the ministry in a more analytic and knowledgeable way. Although supervised and instructed "field education" was not introduced until much later, many students, whether under financial pressure or from eagerness to sample anticipated service, gained practical experience preaching in neighboring churches. In spite of some "sectarian" and other criticism, the American seminary movement made rapid progress, and Princeton Seminary, as an early and successful pioneer in the movement, continued among those in its forefront.

# NOTES

Manuscript packages marked by an asterisk contain numerous brief manuscripts of Dr. Alexander. Citations in the present volume give the initials of the package followed by the title of the manuscript contained in that package. Bracketing of the page number in the citation indicates that the MS itself it not paginated.

*Abbreviations Used in the Notes*

| | |
|---|---|
| *BRPR* | *Biblical Repertory and Princeton Review* under its various names: vols. I–V (1825–1829) *Biblical Repertory;* N.S. vols. II–VIII (1830–1836) *Biblical Repertory and Theological Review;* vols. IX–XLIII (1837–1871) *Biblical Repertory and Princeton Review.* Continued later under other titles. |
| *DAB* | *Dictionary of American Biography,* Allen Johnson and Dumas Malone, eds.. 22 vols.. New York, 1928–1944. |
| *DNB* | *Dictionary of National Biography.* Leslie Stephen and Sidney Lee, eds.. 63 vols.. New York, 1885–1900. |
| G.A. *Minutes* | *Minutes of the General Assembly of the Presbyterian Church in the U.S.A..,* designated by the year. |
| HP | Hodge Family Papers. Firestone Library, Princeton University. |
| HSP | Historical Society of Pennsylvania, Philadelphia. |
| *IL | "Introductory Lectures, 1814–1839," by Archibald Alexander. Package of MSS in Princeton Theological Seminary (PTS). |
| *LAA* | *The Life of Archibald Alexander, D.D.,* by James W. Alexander. New York, 1854. |
| *LCH* | *The Life of Charles Hodge, D.D., LL.D.,* by A. A. Hodge. New York, 1880 |
| *LDT | "Lectures on Didactic Theology," by Archibald Alexander. Package of MSS in PTS. |
| *LMMS | "Lectures on Mental and Moral Science," by Archibald Alexander. Package of MSS in PTS. |
| *LPstlT | "Lectures on Pastoral Theology," by Archibald Alexander. Package of MSS in PTS. |
| *LPT | "Lectures on Polemic Theology," by Archibald Alexander. Package of MSS in PTS. |

| | |
|---|---|
| *LSM* | *The Life of Samuel Miller, D.D., LLD.,* by Samuel Miller. 2 vols.. Philadelphia, 1869. |
| MP | Samuel Miller Papers. Firestone Library, Princeton University. |
| PHS | Presbyterian Historical Society, Philadelphia. |
| PTS | Speer Library, Princeton Theological Seminary. |
| PU | Firestone Library, Princeton University. |

*Preface*

1. While Donald G. Matthews, *Religion in the Old South* (Chicago, 1977) gives an admirable fresh portrayal of what has been traditionally regarded as "Southern" religion, E. Brooks Holifield, *The Gentlemen Theologians: American Theology in Southern Culture, 1795–1860* (Durham, N.C., 1978) has shown that an intellectually solid theology—much of it closely akin to the Old Princeton Theology—was influential in the South in "towns" and among the more sophisticated. Theodore Dwight Bozeman, *Protestants in an Age of Science: The Baconian Ideal and Antebellum American Religious Thought* (Chapel Hill, N.C., 1977) has made it clear that Old School Presbyterians showed considerable interest in the immediate empirical aspects of pre-Darwinian science.

2. Fred J. Hood, *Reformed America: The Middle and Southern States, 1783–1837* (University, Alabama: University of Alabama Press, 1980) has discussed in detail the contents and social implications of the philosophy and theology of Presidents John Witherspoon and Samuel Stanhope Smith.

*1: Roots in Virginia*

1. Richard B. Davis, *Intellectual Life in Jefferson's Virginia, 1790–1830* (Chapel Hill, N.C., 1964). For Presbyterianism in the antebellum South, Ernest Trice Thompson, *Presbyterians in the South, 1607–1861* (Richmond, Va., c.1963) contains helpful material.

2. Carl Bridenbaugh, *Myths and Realities: Societies of the Colonial South* (Baton Rouge, La., 1952), pp. 1-53; Robert E. Brown and B. Katherine Brown, *Virginia 1705–1786: Democracy or Aristocracy?* (E. Lansing, Mich., 1964) pp. 32ff., 253-265.

3. *LAA,* pp. 8, 25.

4. Ibid., p. 15.

5. Archibald Alexander, "Rejoice with Trembling" (1794), in "Sermons MSS," Package 1, PTS, p. 23.

6. Freeman H. Hart, *The Valley of Virginia in the American Revolution, 1763–1789* (Chapel Hill, N.C., 1942); Bridenbaugh, op. cit., pp. 119-196.

7. Archibald Alexander, *Biographical Sketches of the Founder, and Principal Alumni of the Log College* (Princeton, N.J., 1845), p. 355; *LAA,* pp. 1-2.

8. "Ersbell's" grandfather had migrated from Scotland to Northern Ireland in 1652. *Alexander Family Genealogical Chart,* in Virginia State Library, Archives Division, Richmond.

9. "Deed Book 1, 1745–49," Augusta County, pp. 463-465, in County Courthouse, Staunton, Virginia. (At that time, Rockbridge County had not yet been divided from Augusta County.)

10. Archibald Alexander, "Memoir of the Rev. Wm. Graham First President of Washington College Va." (MS, [1842], PTS), p. 199.

11. "Deed Book A, 1778–1788, Rockbridge County," pp. 105, 122, 277, 278, 307, 616, 686, 687, in Rockbridge County Courthouse, Lexington, Virginia.

12. J. A. Alexander to H. Alexander, June 9, 1855, in Henry C. Alexander, *The Life of Joseph Addison Alexander, D.D.* . . . , (2 vols. (New York, 1870), II, p. 757.

13. "Minutes of the Presbytery of Lexington," vol. I (1786–1792), pp. 8, 66, for September 27, 1786, and October 27, 1790; "Minutes of the Synod of Virginia," vol. I (1788–1798), p. 16 for October 24, 1789. Both are MSS in Library of Union Theological Seminary in Virginia. Alexander was elected, but did not attend, *LAA*, pp. 1-9, 36.

14. *LAA*, p. 8; A. Alexander to S. I. Prime, February 25, 1850, MS in HSP. The Rockbridge Historical Society in 1958 erected a marker in the present hamlet of Cornwall at the junction of Irish Creek and South River at the site of the log house where Alexander was born.

15. The chronology here in *LAA* is obscure. We are told that Archibald Alexander was born on April 17, 1772 (p. 8); that he went to school "when not more than five years old" (p. 12); and that "before the year was out" at this school "the war had commenced" (p. 13). The Revolution began in April 1775, which would make Alexander three years old when he started to school. Similar lack of critical editing is evident (p. 8) where Alexander is quoted as saying "I was the third of nine children" and then proceeds immediately to name nine brothers and sisters in addition to himself. A valuable part of this biography is Alexander's interpretive reminiscences of his intellectual and religious development, some of which were made at the age of sixty-seven, some ten years later (pp. 8, 72).

16. *LAA*, pp. 9, 12-15.

17. Samuel E. Morison, *The Founding of Harvard College* (Cambridge, 1935), pp. 53-78, 126-139; see also Perry Miller, *The New England Mind: The Seventeenth Century* (New York, 1954); Howard Miller, *The Revolutionary College: American Presbyterian Higher Education, 1707–1837* (New York, 1976); Douglas Sloan, *The Scottish Enlightenment and the American College Ideal* (New York, 1971).

18. John S. Brubacher and Willis Rudy, *Higher Education in Transition: An American History: 1636–1956* (New York, 1958), pp. 16-17; Mary L. Gambrell, *Ministerial Training in Eighteenth-Century New England* (New York, 1937), pp. 82-83.

19. "Minutes of Hanover Presbytery," II (1769–1785) and III (1786–1795); "Minutes of Lexington Presbytery," I (1786–1792), MSS in Library of Union Theological Seminary in Virginia.

20. "Minutes of Hanover Presbytery," II (1769–1785), pp. 68, 74, 90, 92, 121, 158-159; "Minutes of Lexington Presbytery," I (1786–1792), pp. 4-6, 12-13.

21. "Minutes of Hanover Presbytery," II (1769–1785), pp. 71-72, 100, 121; IV (1796–1804), p. 89.

22. "Minutes of Hanover Presbytery," II (1769–1785), pp. 81-109, 115, 148; III (1786–1795), p. 43.

23. "Minutes of Lexington Presbytery," I (1786–1792), pp. 14, 30, 152.

24. Texts of Jefferson's three bills are reproduced in *The Papers of Thomas Jefferson*, edited by Julian P. Boyd et al., II (Princeton, 1950), pp. 526-545; see also Philip A. Bruce, *History of the University of Virginia, 1819–1919*, I (New York, 1920), pp. 67-83; Henry B. Adams, "The College of William and Mary," *Circulars of Information of the Bureau of Education*, no. 1 (Washington, 1887), pp. 37-58.

25. Alfred N. Whitehead, *The Aims of Education and Other Essays* (New York, 1929), pp. 2-6, 139-144.

26. A. Alexander, "Memoir of the Rev. Wm. Graham First President of Washington College Virginia," (MS [1842] in PTS), p. 41.

27. Ibid., p. 94; Donald R. Come, "The Influence of Princeton on Higher Education in the South Before 1825," *William and Mary Quarterly*, 3rd Series, II (1945), pp. 366-378; "Minutes of Hanover Presbytery," II (1769–1785), pp. 2-42, *passim*.

28. "Minutes of Hanover Presbytery," II (1769–1785), pp. 55-56, 63, 67, 76-79; Hugh E. Grigsby, "The Founders of Washington College," in Washington and Lee University, *Historical Papers*, no. 2 (Baltimore, 1890), pp. 9-13.

29. Archibald Alexander, "Memoir of the Rev. Wm. Graham," pp. 78-93; text of the charter is given in Edgar W. Knight, ed., *A Documentary History of Education in the South*, IV, pp. 5-7. The name of the institution was changed from Liberty Hall to Washington Academy in 1798, to Washington College in 1813, and to Washington and Lee University in 1871.

30. A. Alexander, "Memoir of the Rev. Wm. Graham," p. 93; *LAA*, p. 23.

31. William Graham, "Lectures on Human Nature Aula Libutatis [Libertatis]: Delivered by Wm. Graham; Notes Taken by Joseph Glass, 1796." MS in Library of Washington and Lee University (microfilm in PTS).

32. Henry Ruffner, "Early History of Washington College," in Washington and Lee University, *Historical Papers*, no. 1 (Baltimore, 1890), pp. 46, 91-92; see also ibid., no. 4, p. 96.

33. John Witherspoon, "Address to the Inhabitants of Jamaica, and other West-Indian Islands, in behalf of the College of New Jersey" (1772), in *The Works of the Rev. John Witherspoon, D.D., L.L.D.*, vol. IV (Philadelphia, 1802), pp. 185-186, 193-194.

34. *LAA*, pp. 22-24.

*2: What Is Conversion?*

1. See, for example, William B. Sprague, *Lectures on Revivals of Religion* (Albany, N.Y., 1832), which includes letters by Old School leaders with qualified endorsements of revivalism. For a suggestive treatment of Alexander's conception of religious experience, see Gordon E. Jackson, "Archibald Alexander's *Thoughts on Religious Experience*, a Critical Revisiting," *Journal of Presbyterian History*, vol. 51 (1973), pp. 141-153.

2. *LAA*, p. 72.

3. Ibid., pp. 8, 72.

4. Katherine Brown, *Virginia 1705–1786: Democracy or Aristocracy?* (E. Lansing, Mich., 1964), p. 250; Richard B. Davis, *Intellectual Life in Jefferson's Virginia, 1790–1830* (Chapel Hill, N.C., 1964), p. 11; Archibald Alexander, "Memoir of the Rev. Wm Graham First President of Washington College Virginia" (MS [1842], in PTS), pp. 41, 146-153, 233-236; *LAA*, p. 42.

5. Wesley M. Gewehr, *The Great Awakening in Virginia, 1740–1790* (Durham, N.C., 1930), pp. 168-177.

6. *LAA*, pp. 36-37, 32-33. Among the "few pious" was his uncle by marriage, John Lyle, whose devout life greatly impressed Alexander. Lyle had been converted through reading *The Rise and Progress of Religion in the Soul* (1745) by Philip Doddridge, the English Dissenter who was an important influence on American evangelicals. See Alexander, "Memoir of the Rev. Wm. Graham," pp. 245-247.

7. *LAA*, pp. 24-31.

8. Here again the chronology of *LAA* is confusing and self-contradictory. We are told that he went to Posey's in 1789 (chapter heading, p. 32), which is twice corroborated by the statement that he went at the age of seventeen (pp. 24, 34). He was born on April 17, 1772 (p. 8). But elsewhere the sojourn at Posey's is dated as "this year 1788–1789" (p. 46); Alexander says that his regeneration took place while "I resided at General Posey's, in the year 1788" (p. 72); and it is said that he returned home in the year 1789 (p. 48). By August 1789, we know from other sources that Alexander was accompanying William Graham on a trip to Prince Edward County, which is the latest terminal date possible for his stay at Posey's. Even if Alexander had only a short "year" at Posey's, he must have arrived there at least as early as the late summer or early autumn of 1788, perhaps staying there until July 1789.

9. *LAA*, pp. 36, 41.

10. Ibid., p. 38.

11. Ibid., p. 34.

12. Ibid., p. 41.

13. Ibid., pp. 38-39.

14. Wesley M. Gewehr, *The Great Awakening in Virginia, 1740–1790*, pp. 106-137; A. Alexander, "Memoir of the Rev. Wm. Graham," pp. 247-248; "Minutes of Virginia Synod," I (1788–1797), pp. 59-60; "Minutes of Hanover Presbytery," IV (1796–1804), pp. 50-52, 53-56, 70-71 (MSS, Union Theological Seminary in Virginia).

15. Robert B. Semple, *A History of the Rise and Progress of the Baptists in Virginia* (Richmond, 1810), pp. 141, 155.

16. *LAA*, pp. 39-41.

17. Ibid., pp. 35-36.

18. Louis B. Wright, "Pious Reading in Colonial Virginia," *Journal of Southern History*, VI (1940), pp. 383-392.

19. *LAA*, pp. 35-36, 42; C. H. Firth, "Paul de Rapin," in *DNB*, II (New York, 1896), pp. 297-300.

20. *LAA*, pp. 42-43.

21. Soame Jenyns, "A View of the Internal Evidence of the Christian Religion" (1776), in *The Works of Soame Jenyns*, 2 vols. (Dublin, 1790–1791), II, pp. 217-301; A. H. Bullen, "Soame Jenyns," *DNB*, XXIX, pp. 332-333.

22. *LAA*, pp. 44-47.

23. He perhaps means *Submission to the Righteousness of God*, by Benjamin Jenks, an Anglican clergyman who argues vigorously for justification by faith.

24. Presumably this was *Expository Notes, with Practical Observations on the New Testament* (1724), by William Burkitt (1650–1703), an evangelical Anglican.

25. *LAA*, p. 76.

26. Ibid., pp. 49-50.

27. Ibid., p. 41.

28. Ibid., pp. 43-44.

29. Ibid., pp. 44-45.

30. Ibid., pp. 45-47.

31. Charles G. Sellers, Jr., "John Blair Smith," *Journal of the Presbyterian Historical Society*, XXXIV (1956), pp. 201-225; Wesley M. Gewehr, *The Great Awakening in Virginia, 1740–1790*, pp. 177-185; William H. Foote, *Sketches of Virginia, Historical and Biographical* (Philadelphia, 1850), pp. 408-438.

32. *LAA*, p. 56.
33. Ibid., p. 61.
34. Ibid., p. 62.
35. Ibid., p. 62-72.

*3: Educational Background*

1. Moore had married Alexander's cousin, Sarah Reid. There was perhaps ten-sion between Moore and Graham, for Moore had favored ratification of the United States Constitution by Virginia, whereas Graham had vigorously opposed it. Moore was an alumnus and trustee of Liberty Hall, and a United States sena-tor, 1804-1808. *DAB*, XIII, pp. 113-114.

2. *LAA*, pp. 76-83.

3. The basic source on the life of Graham—particularly his preministerial years—is "A Memoir of the Late Rev. William Graham, A.M.," *Evangelical and Literary Magazine and Missionary Chronicle IV* (1821), pp. 75-79, 150-152, 253-263, 397-412. (Hereafter cited as [E. Graham], "A Memoir.") Alexander states (in his "Memoir of the Rev. Wm. Graham First President of Washington College Vir-ginia," MS [1842] in PTS, p. 48) that Edward Graham, William Graham's brother, was the author of this anonymous article. The article's elaborate praise of their mother corroborates this authorship, and the fact that Edward Graham married Alexander's older sister Margaret (*LAA*, p. 8) further substantiates it. Edward Graham seems to have had access to his brother's manuscripts (p. 398). The article is a brief factual chronicle and must be supplemented for both facts and interpretations by various much later writings by Alexander.

4. [E. Graham], "A Memoir," pp. 75-79, 150-152; *Records of the Presbyterian Church in the United States of America* (Philadelphia, 1841), pp. 180-183; William H. Foote, *Sketches of Virginia Historical and Biographical* (Philadelphia, 1850), pp. 133-138.

5. [E. Graham], "A Memoir," pp. 253-258; A. Alexander, "Memoir of the Rev. Wm. Graham, pp. 61-69, 84-86.

6. A. Alexander, *Address Delivered before the Alumni Association of Washington College Virginia . . . 1843* (Lexington, 1843) (hereafter cited as Alexander, *Address, Washington College, 1843*), pp. 27-28; A. Alexander, "Memoir of the Rev. Wm. Graham," p. 215; *LAA*, p. 90; "Minutes of the Synod of Virginia" (MS in Union Seminary in Virginia), I (1788-1797), p. 5; [E. Graham], "A Memoir," pp. 254, 256, 398, 403-408.

7. "Minutes of the Synod of Virginia," I (1788-1797), pp. 74-84; "Minutes of Lexington Presbytery" (MSS in Union Seminary in Virginia), I (1786-1792), pp. 119, 127, 132; II (1793-1794), pp. 12, 190; Henry Ruffner, "Early History of Washington College," part I (1844) in Washington and Lee University, *Historical Papers*, no. 1 (Baltimore, 1890), pp. 44-49.

8. [E. Graham], "A Memoir," pp. 397-399; Alexander, *Address, Washington College, 1843*, pp. 26-27; *LAA*, pp. 105-109.

9. *LAA*, pp. 84, 123.

10. Thomas Reid, *Essays on the Intellectual Powers of Man* (Edinburgh, 1785), pp. 569-575.

11. Thomas Reid, "Essays on the Active Powers of the Human Mind" (1788), in

*Works*, III (New York, 1822), p. 202; *Essays on the Intellectual Powers of Man*, pp. 373, 43, 522.

12. Thomas Reid, *An Inquiry Into The Human Mind or the Principles of Common Sense*, 2nd ed. (Edinburgh, 1765), pp. 4-10, 88, 90; *Essays on the Intellectual Powers of Man*, pp. 41-42, 62-63, 133, 581.

13. Thomas Reid, "Essays on the Active Powers of the Human Mind," pp. 155-167, 243-245.

14. Ibid., pp. 5, 63, 174-176, 136-139, 119-124.

15. Thomas Reid, *Essays on the Intellectual Powers of Man*, pp. 608-611; Reid, "Essays on the Active Powers of the Human Mind," pp. 302-317.

16. Reid, "Essays on the Active Powers of the Human Mind," pp. 97-108, 145-151, 171, 271.

17. I. Woodbridge Riley, *American Philosophy: The Early Schools* (New York, 1907), p. 480.

18. John Witherspoon, *Lectures on Moral Philosophy*, edited by V. L. Collins (Princeton, 1912), pp. 37-43, 1, 2.

19. Ibid., pp. 14, 15, 38, 39.

20. Ibid., pp. 4, 10, 17, 24-31, 52, 64-65, 140-141.

21. See Robert W. Landis, "Imputation, Part I," *Danville Quarterly Review*, I (1861), p. 425; Lyman H. Atwater, "Witherspoon's Theology," *Biblical Repertory and Princeton Review*, XXXV (1863), pp. 596-610.

22. William Graham, "Lectures on Human Nature, Aula Libutatis [Libertatis]: Delivered by Wm. Graham; Notes Taken by Joseph Glass, 1796" (p. 117) says: "Copied by Harry Waddell Pratt: M.A. in A.D. in 1896. W. & L. University" (MS in Library of Washington and Lee University, Lexington, Virginia; microfilm in PTS).

23. Ibid., pp. 15, 65, 5.

24. Ibid., pp. 5-13, 103, 115.

25. Ibid., pp. 9, 17, 3.

26. John Witherspoon, *Moral Philosophy*, p. 10.

27. Graham, "Lectures on Human Nature," pp. 57-59, 53, 21, 33, 37, 41.

28. [William Graham], *An Essay on Government* (Philadelphia, 1786), pp. 20, 25.

29. Graham, "Lectures on Human Nature," p. 53.

30. Ibid., pp. 63-67, 71-77.

31. A. Alexander, *Address, Washington College, 1843*, p. 27.

32. Graham, "Lectures on Human Nature," p. 43.

33. Ibid., p. 67.

34. Ibid., pp. 91, 93, 105, 125-127.

35. Ibid., pp. 21, 25, 81-83.

36. Archibald Alexander, *Address, Washington College, 1843*, p. 27.

37. Graham, "Lectures on Human Nature," pp. 83, 85.

38. A. Alexander, "Memoir of Graham," pp. 221-223; also *LAA*, pp. 107-108.

39. W. Graham, "Lectures on Human Nature," p. 123.

40. Ibid., pp. 79, 63, 83.

41. William Graham, *The Scriptural Doctrine of Water Baptism* (Richmond, 1799), p. 6.

42. Ibid., pp. 1-41; Alexander, "Memoir of Graham," pp. 224-225.

43. Alexander, "Memoir of Graham," pp. 159-160, 176-180. Incidentally,

Alexander offers additional testimony (p. 224) that Graham was the author of this anonymous pamphlet, *An Essay on Government*.

44. [William Graham], *An Essay on Government*, pp. 4-6, 11, 20-21.

45. Ibid., pp. 7-9, 15; Graham, "Lectures on Human Nature," p. 141.

46. Alexander, "Memoir of Graham," p. 180; Graham, "Lectures on Human Nature," pp. 161-167; Graham, *The Scriptural Doctrine of Water Baptism*, p. 34.

47. Henry Ruffner, "Early History of Washington College," part I (1844), in Washington and Lee University, *Historical Papers*, no. 1 (Baltimore, 1890), p. 60.

48. *LAA*, pp. 78, 111 ff.

*4: Applied Theology*

1. "Minutes of Lexington Presbytery" (MS in Union Theological Seminary in Virginia) vol. I (1786–1792), April 28, 1790, p. 59; October 27, 1790, p. 67; See also *LAA*, pp. 84-85, which erroneously gives the date as October 20.

2. "Minutes of Lexington Presbytery," vol. I (1786–1792), pp. 67, 78-82; *LAA*, pp. 110-111.

3. *LAA*, pp. 90-104.

4. "Minutes of Lexington Presbytery," vol. I (1786–1792), pp. 67, 78-82, 90, 102-103, 112-116; *LAA*, pp. 110-112.

5. *LAA*, p. 110.

6. This sermon MS in PTS is dated October 18, 1790, and to it is added in Alexander's hand, "The first sermon I ever wrote."

7. A. Alexander, Sermon on John 6:45, March 1791, "his second sermon" (MS, PTS).

8. "Minutes of Lexington Presbytery," April 28, 1791, vol. I (1786–1792), p. 78; *LAA*, p. 110.

9. A. Alexander, "A Treatise in Which the Difference between a Living and a Dead Faith is Explained. A Homily Read before the presbytery of Lexington, April 1791" (MS PTS), pp. 2-11.

10. Ibid., pp. 13-20.

11. A. Alexander, "A Sermon on the Gospel Ministry. A Trial Sermon . . . before the Revd. Presbytery of Lexington, September 20, 1791" (MS, PTS), pp. 8-13.

12. "Journal" (MS, PTS), for April 17, 1792; see also *LAA*, p. 75.

13. This explicit statement of his contemporary "Journal," in the entry for April 17, 1792, must supersede the contrary statement of his recollections half a century later, in *LAA*, pp. 85-86. The date March 1791, given in *LAA*, p. 122, as the completion of preaching for a "whole winter" should, in the light of *LAA*, p. 123, undoubtedly be March 1792.

14. *DAB*, XIII, pp. 166-167.

15. Ibid., XVIII, pp. 161-162.

16. *LAA*, pp. 112-125.

17. "Minutes of Lexington Presbytery," I (1786–1792), p. 129; *LAA*, p. 125.

18. *LAA*, pp. 125-167.

19. Ibid., pp. 119, 122.

20. A. Alexander, "A Book Containing the Year, the Month, the Day, the County, the House & the Text on which I Have Preached" (MS, PTS).

21. A. Alexander, "Memoir of the Rev. Wm. Graham First President of Washington College Virginia," (MS [1842] PTS), p. 258.

22. *LAA*, p. 116.

23. Ibid., pp. 124, 172.

24. Ibid., pp. 114-115, 142-143, 178.

25. A. Alexander, "To Be Carnally Minded Is Death, but to Be Spiritually Minded Is Life and Peace" (Sermons MS, Package no. 1, PTS), pp. 7-16.

26. Ibid., pp. 23, 29, 33.

27. Ibid., p. 16.

28. "Minutes of Lexington Presbytery," April 25 and 26, 1792, April 27, October 8 and 9, 1793, vol. I (1786–1792), pp. 123-125, vol. II (1793–1794), pp. 19, 40, 42-43; "Minutes of Hanover Presbytery," Nov. 9, 1793, May 2, June 7, and Oct. 22, 1794, vol. III (1786–1795), pp. 116, 188-189, 197-200 (MSS in Union Theological Seminary in Virginia); *LAA*, p. 167; *LAA*, pp. 169 and 175 give two different dates for Alexander's ordination, both erroneous.

29. "Minutes of Hanover Presbytery," April 14, 1797, April 20 and November 16, 1798, April 8 and November 28, 1801, April 15, 1802, vol. IV (1796–1804), pp. 19, 33, 66, 86; "Minutes of Hanover Presbytery," MS copy, vol. IV (1796–1804), pp. 207-208 (all in Union Theological Seminary in Virginia); the original MS calls from Briery Church (February 7, 1801) and from Cumberland Church (November 28, 1801) are in PTS. This second Briery call was at £70 per year and the Cumberland call at $200 per year, each for "one half of your ministerial labours"; but starting in 1796 Alexander was also president of Hampden-Sydney College.

30. *LAA*, pp. 156, 168.

31. Ibid., pp. 169-171.

32. Richard B. Davis, *Intellectual Life in Jefferson's Virginia, 1790–1830* (Chapel Hill, N.C., 1964), pp. 411-416; William H. Foote, *Sketches of Virginia, Historical and Biographical*, 2nd Series (Philadelphia, 1855), pp. 446-447.

33. "The Session Book of Briery Church," vol. I (MS in custody of Mr. Matthew Lyle, Keysville, Virginia), "Early History" preceding official minutes; also official minutes for March 20, 1819, p. 30; also James W. Douglas, *A Manual for the Members of the Briery Presbyterian Church, Virginia* (Richmond, 1828), p. 3.

34. "Minutes of Hanover Presbytery," April 16, 1802, vol. IV (1796–1804) (MS in Union Theological Seminary in Virginia); W. H. Foote, *Sketches of Virginia* (Philadelphia, 1850), p. 285; E. V. Gaines, *Cub Creek Church and Congregation, 1738–1838* (Richmond, 1931), p. 51.

35. "Minutes of Hanover Presbytery," vol. II (1769–1785), pp. 114; vol. III (1786–1795), pp. 169, 223; M. W. Jernegan, "Slavery and Conversion in the American Colonies," *American Historical Review*, XXI (1916), pp. 504-527.

36. "The Session Book of Briery Church," vol. 1, pp. 20-25.

37. *LAA*, 169, 176-177, 183-193.

38. Ibid., pp. 177, 201.

39. A. Alexander, "If Any Man Love Not the Lord Jesus Christ; Let Him Be Anathema Maranatha" (MS Sermon "A.D. 1794" in PTS), pp. 3, 7-11, 17-18.

40. A. Alexander, "Almost Christians" (MS Sermon, "A.D. 1794," PTS), pp. 8-16.

41. Ibid., pp. 13-19.

42. Ibid., pp. 22-24.

43. Ibid., p. 25.

44. Ibid., pp. 25-26.

45. Ibid., pp. 26-27.

46. A. Alexander, "Rejoice with Trembling" (MS Sermon, "A.D. 1794," PTS), pp. 13-31.

47. Ibid.

48. *LAA*, p. 177.

49. A. Alexander, Sermon on 2 Cor. 4:13, "We Also Believe and Therefore Speak" (MS, PTS), p. 5. This undated sermon is stitch-bound in a 1795 newspaper, and may tentatively be dated 1795, the year following publication of Paine's *Age of Reason*, which it seeks to refute.

50. Ibid., p. 14.

51. Ibid., pp. 19-20.

52. Ibid., pp. 25, 30-31.

53. Ibid., pp. 15-19.

54. A. Alexander, "But As He Who Hath Called You Is Holy So Be Ye Holy in All Manner of Conversation" (MS Sermon, "A.D. 1795," PTS), pp. 1-3.

55. Ibid., p. 5.

56. Ibid., pp. 6-7.

57. Ibid., pp. 9-12.

## 5: The Leader Matures

1. Richard B. Davis, *Intellectual Life in Jefferson's Virginia, 1790–1830* (Chapel Hill, N.C., 1964), pp. 30, 122; Herbert Clarence Bradshaw, *History of Hampden-Sydney College*, vol. I, *From the Beginnings to the Year 1856* (Privately printed, 1976).

2. *LAA*, p. 195.

3. "Records of Hampden-Sidney College," (MS in Hampden-Sydney College Library) (Hereafter cited as "Records of H.S. College") vol. I, pp. 180-181, 192, 209, 235, 250, 254, 257; A.J. Morrison, *The College of Hampden-Sidney: Calendar of Board Minutes, 1776–1876* (Richmond, 1912), p. 23 (hereafter cited as *H.S. Calendar*); William H. Foote, *Sketches of Virginia: Historical and Biographical*, vol. I (Philadelphia, 1850), p. 408.

4. A. J. Morrison, *H.S. Calendar*, pp. 12-14, 29-30, 33, 35; "Minutes of Hanover Presbytery" (MS in Library of Union Theological Seminary in Virginia), vol. II (1769–1785); Nov. 8, 1775, p. 70; "Records of H.S. College," pp. 216, 222, 250.

5. A. J. Morrison, *H. S. Calendar*, pp. 53, 66; "Records of H. S. College," Sept. 23, 1799, p. 198; also pp. 304, 306, 324.

6. *LAA*, pp. 195, 200, 273, 276-277; William Maxwell, *A Memoir of the Rev. John H. Rice, D.D.* (Philadelphia, 1835), p. 18.

7. Archibald Alexander to Charles Hodge, n.p., n.d., HP.

8. Drury Lacy to William Williamson, Ararat, Va., July 17, 1801, photostatic copy of MS, in library of Union Theological Seminary in Virginia.

9. *LAA*, p. 47; *DNB*, XXI, p. 355.

10. Drury Lacy to William Williamson, July 17, 1801, as cited; Abraham Booth, *Paedobaptism Examined on the Principles, Concessions and Reasonings of the Most Learned Paedobaptists*, 2nd ed., 2 vols. (London, 1787); *DNB*, V, pp. 373-374.

11. Drury Lacy to William Williamson, July 17, 1801; George Campbell, *The Four Gospels, Translated from the Greek, with Preliminary Dissertations and Notes Critical and Explanatory* (first published 1789), 4 vols. (Boston, 1811), vol. I, Dissertation VI, "Hagios and Hosios," pp. 333-370; *DNB*, VIII, pp. 357-358.

12. John Claude, *An Essay on the Composition of a Sermon*, translated with notes by Robert Robinson, 2 vols. (Cambridge, 1779); *DNB*, XLIX, pp. 40-43.

13. Drury Lacy to William Williamson, July 17, 1801, as cited.

14. *LAA*, p. 204-223.

15. Henry Hammond, *The Baptizing of Infants Reviewed and Defended from the Exceptions of Mr. Tombs . . .* (London, 1655); John Lightfoot, *The Whole Works of the Rev. John Lightfoot, D.D.*, 13 vols. (London, 1822-25), VI, pp. 399-414; William Wall, *A Conference between Two Men that Had Doubts about Infant Baptism*, 2nd ed. (London, 1708), pp. 16-49; *DNB*, XXIV, pp. 242-246; XXXIII, pp. 229-231; LIX, p. 97.

16. William Graham, *The Scriptural Doctrine of Water Baptism* (Richmond, 1799).

17. Richard B. Davis, *Intellectual Life in Jefferson's Virginia*, p. 121; William H. Foote, *Sketches of Virginia, Historical and Biographical*, I, p. 502; Donald R. Come, "The Influence of Princeton on Higher Education in the South before 1825," *William and Mary Quarterly*, 3rd series, II (1945), p. 378; *LAA*, pp. 201, 243, 254; statement by Alexander in William Maxwell, *A Memoir of the Rev. John H. Rice, D.D.* (Philadelphia, 1835), p. 32; Archibald Alexander, letter to the editor, Jan. 25, 1802, in *Connecticut Evangelical Magazine*, II (1801-02), p. 354.

18. P. B. Price, "The Life of the Rev. John Holt Rice, D.D.," Mimeographed (Richmond, 1963), p. 34; Cyrus Kingsbury to Archibald Alexander, Lexington, Va., June 21, 1816, MS in Dreer Collection, HSP; see also R. B. Davis, *Intellectual Life in Jefferson's Virginia*, p. 58.

19. William Maxwell, *A Memoir of the Rev. John H. Rice, D.D.*, p. 28; these were Clarke's Boyle Lectures of 1704–1705, popularly referred to as above, but actually entitled *The Being and Attributes of God* and *The Evidences of Natural and Revealed Religion*.

20. Samuel Clarke, *A Demonstration of the Being and Attributes of God*, 6th ed., (London, 1725), "Preface" and p. 7.

21. Ibid., pp. 8-11.

22. Ibid., p. 50.

23. Ibid., p. 23.

24. Ibid., p. 15.

25. Ibid., p. 44.

26. Ibid., pp. 47-48, 54-56, 62.

27. Ibid., pp. 54, 106-107.

28. Samuel Clarke, *The Leibniz-Clarke Correspondence . . . .*, edited by H. G. Alexander (New York, 1956); for a modern comment on Clarke, see John J. Dahm, "Science and Apologetics in the Early Boyle Lectures," *Church History*, vol. 39 (1970), pp. 172-186.

29. William Maxwell, *A Memoir of the Rev. John H. Rice, D.D.*, pp. 17-18, 26-28.

30. "Records of H.S. College," vol. I, pp. 210-211; *LAA*, pp. 225-226.

31. *LAA*, pp. 226, 233.

32. G. A. *Minutes*, pp. 222-223.

33. Ibid., pp. 229, 233.

34. Ibid., p. 218.

35. Ibid., p. 231.

36. Ibid., pp. 212, 220, 221, 224-225.

37. *LAA*, pp. 233–237.

38. For New England Arminianism, see Conrad Wright, *The Beginnings of Unitarianism in New England* (Boston, 1955).

39. *LAA*, pp. 237-240.

40. Ibid., pp. 243-244.

41. Ibid., pp. 244-249; A. Alexander, LDT, "Providence" (MS, n.d., PTS), p. 12.

42. *LAA*, pp. 245, 238, 240.

43. Ibid., pp. 252-253, 256. In New Hampshire Noah Worcester reported that ministers were almost equally divided among Calvinists, Hopkinsians, and Arminians—Noah Worcester to Samuel Miller, Feb. 4, 1803, MP.

44. *The Life of Ashbel Green*, edited by J.H. Jones (New York, 1849), pp. 217, 221, 222, 225; *LAA*, p. 245.

45. *The Life of Ashbel Green*, pp. 218, 223.

46. *LAA*, pp. 251-253.

47. Ibid., p. 238.

48. Ibid., pp. 240, 242, 255, 263, 270.

49. Ibid., pp. 238, 239, 243, 249.

50. Ibid., pp. 262, 264-271.

51. See ibid., pp. 268-269; Charles Hodge, "Memoir of Dr. Alexander," *BRPR*, XXVII (1855), p. 138; Archibald Alexander to Jedidiah Morse, Dec. 2, 1801, in Simon Gratz MSS, HSP.

52. *LAA*, pp. 223-224.

53. A. J. Morison, *H.S. Calendar* (as cited), p. 54 note 2.

54. William Wirt, *The Letters of the British Spy* (New York, 1832), letter VII, pp. 195-205; *LAA*, pp. 226-228, 272-273, 664-667; *Forty Years' Familiar Letters of James W. Alexander, D.D.*, edited by John Hall, 2 vols. (New York, 1860), II, p. 113; W.H. Foote, *Sketches of Virginia*, I, pp. 349-388; A. Alexander in William B. Sprague, *Annuals of the American Pulpit*, 9 vols. (New York, 1857–1869), III, p. 242.


*6: A Shortage of Ministers*

1. Drury Lacy to William Williamson, July 24, 1799, MS in Union Theological Seminary in Virginia; "Minutes of Hanover Presbytery," IV (1796–1804), May 2, 1800, April 11, 1801, pp. 59, 74; *Connecticut Evangelical Magazine*, II (1801–1802), pp. 354-360; Drury Lacy to Ashbel Green, Oct. 6, 1804, in Simon Gratz MSS, HSP; "Address from Presbytery of Hanover," n.d. in *Virginia Religious Magazine*, III (May and June, 1807), p. 153; *LAA*, pp. 275, 294.

2. The statistics of the Synod of Virginia are based on the respective years in the "Minutes of the Synod of Virginia" (MS in Union Theological Seminary,

Richmond, vol. II (1798-1806); the General Assembly statistics are based on the G.A. *Minutes* at the end for each of the ten years.

3. "Minutes of Hanover Presbytery," II (1769-1785), pp. 37, 51, 57 (MS in Union Theological Seminary, Richmond).

4. Ibid., III (1786-1795), p. 204; IV (1796-1804), pp. 16, 27.

5. Ibid., vol. V, pp. 196-202.

6. Trustees' Minutes, in "Records of Hampden-Sydney College" (MS in Hampden-Sydney Library), p. 256.

7. "Minutes of Hanover Presbytery," V, pp. 196-202.

8. G. A. Baxter, in *Virginia Religious Magazine*, II (July, 1806), p. 231.

9. "Address from Presbytery of Hanover," p. 160.

10. "Minutes of the Synod of Virginia," (MS in Union Theological Seminary in Virginia), II (1798-1806), Oct. 17, 1803, p. 129.

11. Henry S. Stroupe, *The Religious Press in the South Atlantic States, 1802–1865* (Durham, N.C., 1956), pp. 4-5.

12. Frank L. Mott, *A History of American Magazines, 1741–1850* (Cambridge, Mass., 1939), p. 133.

13. *Virginia Religious Magazine*, I (October 1804), pp. iii-iv.

14. "Minutes of the Synod of Virginia," II, Oct. 12 and 14, 1805, pp. 150-151, 157-159.

15. *Virginia Religious Magazine*, II (January 1806), pp. iii-iv.

16. "Minutes of the Synod of Virginia," II, Oct. 20, 1806, pp. 177, 183.

17. *Virginia Religious Magazine*, I (September 1805), pp. 270-277.

18. Ibid., II (1806), pp. 199, 49; and I, pp. 370-374; II, pp. 48-53, 92-100, 193-201, 262-269, 346-352. These articles are signed pseudonymously "Philander," who is identified as Speece by Speece's close friend, John H. Rice, in William Maxwell, *A Memoir of the Rev. John H. Rice, D.D.* (Philadelphia, 1835), p. 39.

19. The pseudonyms of Alexander and of Rice himself are also identified in W. Maxwell, op. cit., pp. 38-40.

20. *Virginia Religious Magazine*, III (May and June 1807), pp. 161-170.

21. This portion of presbytery's pastoral letter to its congregations is printed immediately before the Jervas episode, ibid., p. 159.

22. Ibid., II (September 1806), pp. 291-296.

23. Ibid., III (May and June 1807), pp. 172-174.

24. Ibid., pp. 175-176.

25. Ibid., pp. 177-179.

26. Ibid., p. 180.

27. Ibid., pp. 199-202.

28. Ibid., pp. 203-205; see also Speece's individual views on theological curriculum in a sermon bearing his name, ibid., pp. 317-321.

29. Ibid., pp. 207-208.

30. "Records of Hampden-Sidney College" (MS in Hampden-Sydney College library), vol. I, pp. 186-187, 198, 231-255, *passim*; Alfred J. Morrison, *The College of Hampden-Sidney: Calendar of Board Minutes, 1776–1876* (Richmond, 1912), pp. 62-63; *LAA*, pp. 275, 282.

31. *LAA*, p. 200.

32. Ibid., pp. 275-276.

*7: A Philadelphia Orientation*

1. John F. Watson, *Annals of Philadelphia and Pennsylvania in Olden Time . . .*, 2 vols. (Philadelphia, c.1850), I, pp. 175-185.

2. *Letters of Benjamin Rush*, edited by L. H. Butterfield, 2 vols. (Princeton, 1951), I, p. 295.

3. Jonathan Powell, "Presbyterian Loyalists: A 'Chain of Interest' in Philadelphia," *Journal of Presbyterian History*, vol. 57 (Summer 1979), pp. 135-160.

4. Benjamin Wickes to Philip Milledoler, Sept. 22, 1812, MS in Milledoler Papers, New York Historical Society.

5. Hughes Oliphant Gibbons, *A History of Old Pine Street* (Philadelphia, 1905), p. 144. The figures here given show the membership increase to have been over 50 percent, not the stated 40 percent.

6. Third Presbyterian Church, Philadelphia, "Minutes of Session" (1809–1828), pp. 22, 23, 26, MS in Third Church; *LAA*, p. 288.

7. G. A. *Minutes*, 1812, p. 512.

8. *LAA*, p. 280.

9. Ibid., pp. 287-288.

10. Ibid., p. 283; also p. 285.

11. Ibid., pp. 284-285.

12. Thomas J. Janeway, *Memoir of the Rev. Jacob J. Janeway, D.D.* (Philadelphia, 1861), p. 130.

13. See Henry F. May, *The Enlightenment in America* (New York, 1976), pp. 197-204, 221-226, 243.

14. Carl and Jessica Bridenbaugh, *Rebels and Gentlemen* (New York, 1965), pp. ix, 363-371.

15. E. M. Geffen, *Philadelphia Unitarianism, 1796–1861* (Philadelphia, 1961), pp. 17-28, 34, 90.

16. *A View of the Principal Deistical Writers that Have Appeared in England in the Last and Present Centuries*, 2 vols. (London, 1754–1756).

17. Joseph H. Jones, ed., *The Life of Ashbel Green* (New York, 1849), pp. 124-126.

18. Ibid., p. 270; James D. Richardson, *A Compilation of the Messages and Papers of the Presidents, 1789–1902*, 10 vols. (Washington, 1896–1899), I, p. 285.

19. Archibald Alexander, *A Sermon Delivered at the Opening of the General Assembly of the Presbyterian Church in the United States, May 1808* (Philadelphia, 1808), pp. 7-8.

20. Ibid., p. 8.

21. Ibid., pp. 8-10.

22. Philip Schaff, *The Principle of Protestantism* (Chambersburg, Pa.,1845). Schaff, newly arrived in America, warned against the rationalism and the "sectarian-ism" which he found there. More perceptively than Alexander, Schaff noted the individualism and subjectivism of both and their common lack of roots and historical consciousness.

23. Alexander, *Sermon at General Assembly, 1808*, pp. 11-12.

24. Ibid., pp. 14-20.

25. Ibid., pp. 26-28.

26. A. Alexander, "Rom[ans] VI.2: How Shall We That Are Dead to Sin Live Any Longer Therein? 1808" ("Sermons MSS," Package 1, PTS), pp. 10-13.

27. Ibid., pp. 13, 15.

28. Ibid., pp. 15-17.

29. Ibid., pp. 19-24.

30. A. Alexander, "Repent Ye For the Kingdom of Heaven is at Hand . . ." (In "Sermons MSS," Package 1, PTS), pp. 9-11.

31. Ibid., p. 12.

32. Ibid., p. 13.

33. Ibid., pp. 15-16.

34. "Minutes of Philadelphia Presbytery (1782–1806)," in PHS, Oct. 22, 1783, pp. 22-24.

35. Ibid., pp. 141-144.

36. For example, ibid., pp. 120-157 *passim*.

37. Ibid., pp. 424-428; Archibald Alexander's letter of July 7, 1840, in *Journal of the Presbyterian Historical Society*, V (1909), pp. 151-152; see also *LAA*, p. 297.

38. On the Evangelical Society, see Alexander's letter of July 7, 1840, cited immediately above, pp. 150-153; and *LAA*, pp. 298-304.

39. W. E. B. DuBois, *The Philadelphia Negro: A Social Study* (Philadelphia, 1899), pp. 1-23, 199-201.

40. Benjamin Rush, *The Autobiography of Benjamin Rush, His "Travels through Life" Together With His Commonplace Book for 1789–1813*, edited by George W. Corner (Princeton, 1948), p. 202.

41. "Evangelical Society of Philadelphia, Appeal for Funds," MS in PHS.

42. William T. Catto, *A Semi-Centenary Discourse. Delivered in the First African Presbyterian Church, Philadelphia . . ., May, 1857: With a History of the Church . . . .* (Philadelphia, 1857), p. 50. The author was a later pastor of this church.

43. Ibid.

44. Ibid., pp. 51-52.

45. "Charter of the First African Church of Philadelphia, December 11, 1809," in PHS; "Evangelical Society of Philadelphia, Appeal for Funds," MS in PHS; William T. Catto, op. cit., p. 54; see also Andrew E. Murray, *Presbyterians and the Negro—A History* (Philadelphia, 1966), pp. 30-35.

46. Benjamin Rush, *The Autobiography of Benjamin Rush . . .*, p. 275; Thomas I. Janeway, *Memoir of the Rev. Jacob J. Janeway, D.D.* (Philadelphia, 1861), p. 149, in recalling the four drafters, named Ashbel Green instead of Alexander.

47. E. R. Beadle, *The Old and the New, 1743–1876. The Second Presbyterian Church of Philadelphia: Its Beginning and Increase* (n.p., 1876), p. 26.

48. *The First Report of the Bible Society Established at Philadelphia . . . May 1, 1809* (Philadelphia, 1809), pp. 3-6; *Second Report . . .* (Philadelphia, 1810), pp. 4-5; "The Third Report . . ." in *The Christian's Magazine*, IV (1811), p. 402.

49. *The First Report*, pp. 7-8.

50. Ibid., p. 10.

51. *LAA*, p. 306.

52. Ibid., p. 305.

53. Ibid., pp. 302-304.

54. [Matthew Carey], *Essays on the Public Charities of Philadelphia* (pamphlet, n.p., 1828), p. 30.

55. "Plan of the Female Charity School, Philada.," MS in Philip Milledoler Papers, New York Historical Society.

56. J. Thomas Scharf and Thompson Westcott, *History of Philadelphia,*

*1609–1884*, 3 vols. (Philadelphia, 1884), I, pp. 537-538; Jacob J. Janeway, *The Blessedness of the Charitable. A Sermon Preached at the Request of the Female Hospitable Society of Philadelphia . . . December 22, 1811* (Philadelphia, 1812), pp. 22, 24.

57. "Minutes of the Synod of Philadelphia (1788–1816)," MS in PHS, pp. 345-349.

58. For a study of the significance of the "Sabbath" in an earlier American context, see Winton U. Solberg, *Redeem the Time: The Puritan Sabbath in Early America* (Cambridge, Mass., 1977).

59. "Minutes of the Synod of Philadelphia (1788–1816)," pp. 349, 356, 374, 375, 411, 425-426.

60. Second Presbyterian Church, "Session Records (1798–1817)," II [not paginated], MS in PHS.

61. John F. Watson, *Annals of Philadelphia and Pennsylvania the Olden Time*, I, pp. 471-474.

62. *LAA*, pp. 306-312.

63. Second Presbyterian Church, "Session Records (1798–1817)," II, MS in PHS.

64. *LAA*, pp. 296, 353-357.

65. Ibid., pp. 289-290.

66. Ibid., pp. 286-287.

67. Ibid., p. 355.

68. Ibid., p. 295; also p. 277.

69. Ibid., p. 285.

70. Ibid., p. 374.

71. Third Presbyterian Church of Philadelphia, "Minutes of the Session (1809–1828)," MS in PHS, 1813, *passim*.

72. *LAA*, p. 329.

73. Ibid., p. 295.

## 8: A Private Letter

1. A MS copy (by Miller's son and biographer) of this letter is in PTS, in which the son conjectures that the letter was addressed to Ashbel Green, a conjecture which is fully corroborated by internal evidence. Excerpts of the letter are given in *LSM*, I, pp. 191-192. Green, reminiscing in old age, did not mention this communication and gave credit for originating the specific proposal of a seminary to Archibald Alexander's 1808 sermon as retiring moderator of the General Assembly (*The Life of Ashbel Green*, p. 332), as did also *LAA*, p. 314. But more correctly, Alexander himself, speaking of the Seminary, said of Miller: "He and Dr. Green may more properly be considered its founders than any other persons" (*LAA*, p. 581). Miller's biographer is a notably honest and factually correct chronicler, and his attestation of the authencity of this letter and therefore of Miller's priority must be accepted as final. Miller himself, in a latter to Green in 1808, mentioned having sent the 1805 letter (*LSM*, I, p. 242). Even if the 1805 letter was not delivered, it attests Miller's pioneering thought at that date.

2. John McVickar, *The Professional Years of John Henry Hobart, D.D.* (New York, 1836), pp. 129-145; Samuel Miller, *A Continuation of Letters Concerning the Constitution and Order of the Christian Ministry* (New York, 1809), pp. 13-35.

3. G. A. *Minutes*, 1810, pp. 455, 458; see also [Samuel Miller], *A Brief History of the Theological Seminary of the Presbyterian Church at Princeton . . .* (Princeton, 1838), p. 4; *Life of Ashbel Green*, p. 332; *LSM*, I, pp. 230, 233, 237-238; John Rodgers to Jedidiah Morse, Jan. 31, 1807, in Simon Gratz MSS, HSP. For suggestive views of denominationalism, see Russell E. Richey, ed., *Denominationalism* (Nashville, 1977).

4. G. A. *Minutes*, 1803, p. 274.

5. An admirable analysis of the cultural factor in the Cumberland division is provided by Haskell M. Miller, "Institutional Behavior of the Cumberland Presbyterian Church, an American Protestant Religious Denomination" (Ph.D. dissertation, New York University, 1940); for a critical historical evaluation, see Ben M. Barrus, "Factors Involved in the Origin of the Cumberland Presbyterian Church," *Journal of Presbyterian History*, 45 (1967), pp. 273-289; 46 (1968), pp. 58-73.

6. See Jerald C. Brauer, "Conversion: From Puritanism to Revivalism," *Journal of Religion*, 58 (1978), pp. 227-243.

7. John Witherspoon, *Address to the Inhabitants of Jamaica, and Other West-India Islands in Behalf of the College of New-Jersey* (Philadelphia, 1772).

8. S. S. Smith to Benjamin Rush, Nov. 10, 1794, in Rush Papers, Library Company of Philadelphia, HSP; an informing discussion of President Smith's administration is in Douglas Sloan, *The Scottish Enlightenment and the American College Ideal* (New York, 1971), pp. 146-184.

9. *Memoirs of the Life of Eliza S. M. Quincy* (Boston, 1861), p. 68.

10. Thomas J. Wertenbaker, *Princeton, 1746–1896* (Princeton, 1946), p. 123.

11. Trustees Minutes, II, pp. 33, 41, 50 (MS in PU.)

12. Michael Kraus, "Charles Nisbet and Samuel Stanhope Smith—Two Eighteenth-Century Educators," *Princeton University Library Chronicle*, VI (November 1944), p. 22.

13. Samuel S. Smith, *An Essay on the Causes of the Variety of Complexion and Figure in the Human Species* (original ed. 1787), edited by Winthrop D. Jordan (Cambridge, Mass., 1965), p. xx; see also M. L. Bradbury, "Samuel Stanhope Smith: Princeton's Accommodation to Reason," *Journal of Presbyterian History*, 48 (1970), pp. 189–202. Fred J. Hood, "Presbyterianism and the New American Nation, 1783–1826, a Case Study of Religion and National Life" (Ph.D. dissertation, Princeton University, 1968) discusses President Smith's philosophical and theological views.

14. William Hill to Ashbel Green, Jan. 20 and May 12, 1804; Ashbel Green to John M. Bradford, July 1, 1804, MSS in PU; S. S. Smith, *The Lectures . . . on the Subjects of Moral and Political Philosophy*, 2 vols. (Trenton, N.J., 1812), II, p. 120.

15. Trustees Minutes, II (1797–1823), pp. 60, 68, 97-98; V. L. Collins, *Princeton* (New York, 1914), pp. 109, 115.

16. S. S. Smith to Jedidiah Morse, March 10, 1802, MS in S. S. Smith Collection, PU.

17. Trustees Minutes, II, pp. 62, 64.

18. Ibid., I, p. 71; II, p. 37.

19. Ibid., II, pp. 111-112.

20. John Rodgers to Ashbel Green, Oct. 27, 1803, in Simon Gratz MSS, "Presbyterian Moderators," HSP; S. S. Smith to Ashbel Green [1803], in S. S. Smith Collection, PU.

21. Trustees Minutes, II, pp. 117-118, 125; John Rodgers to Ashbel Green, Nov. 28 and Dec. 3 1803; Feb. 15, 1804, MSS in HSP; S. S. Smith to Ashbel Green, Dec. 5, 1803, in S. S. Smith Collection, PU.

22. Trustees Minutes, II, pp. 147, 163.

23. Ibid., pp. 126, 128-129; G.A. *Minutes*, 1806, p. 363.

24. G.A. *Minutes*, 1806, pp. 362-363.

25. *Life of Ashbel Green*, pp. 145-146.

26. Ashbel Green to John M. Bradford, July 1, 1804, MS in PU.

27. Samuel Miller, *A Brief Retrospect of the Eighteenth Century*, 2 vols. (New York, 1803), II, p. 500; S. Miller to Eliphalet Nott, Dec. 26, 1803, in MP.

28. *LSM*, I, pp. 191-195.

29. Ibid., p. 192.

30. Trustees Minutes, II, pp. 87, 93.

31. G.A. *Minutes*, 1805, pp. 341-344.

32. Ibid., 1806, pp. 356, 366-367; see also *LSM*, I, p. 203.

33. G.A. *Minutes*, 1806, p. 363.

34. Trustees Minutes, II (1797–1823), p. 216; Dr. John Rodgers, in resigning from the trustees, had strongly pressed for Miller's election: John Rodgers to Ashbel Green, Sept. 9, 1807, in Simon Gratz MSS, HSP.

35. *LSM*, I, pp. 240-242.

36. Ibid., pp. 243-244. For example, Green's own distinguished parishioner, Ebenezer Hazard, a little later voiced opposition to seminaries: Ebenezer Hazard to Jedidiah Morse, June 30, 1816, in PHS.

*9: The College and the Seminary*

1. Archibald Alexander, *A Sermon Delivered at the Opening of the General Assembly of the Presbyterian Church in the United States, May 1808* (Philadelphia, 1808), pp. 24-25.

2. *Letters of Benjamin Rush*, edited by L. H. Butterfield, 2 vols. (Princeton, 1951), II, p. 946; see also II, p. 294.

3. "Minutes of the Presbytery of Philadelphia" (1806–1826), April 20, 1809 (MS in PHS); *The Life of Ashbel Green*, edited by J. H. Jones (New York, 1849), pp. 332-333; A. Green to Edward D. Griffin, July 28, 1808, in PU.

4. G.A. *Minutes*, 1809, pp. 417, 430-431.

5. *LSM*, I, pp. 280-281; S. Miller to A. Green, January 23, 1810, MS copy in PTS.

6. *Panoplist*, III (1807–1808), p. 314.

7. [Samuel Miller], *A Brief History of the Theological Seminary of the Presbyterian Church, at Princeton, New Jersey* (Princeton, 1838), p. 6n.

8. G.A. *Minutes*, 1810, pp. 437, 439, 453-455.

9. Ibid., p. 454.

10. A statement by Miller attests Green's authorship (*Life of Ashbel Green*, p. 529). But Green's extravagant assertion that other committee members contributed only "one idea" to the document (ibid., p. 334) is rendered highly dubious by the fact that two strong members of the committee, Miller and Alexander, had both had more zeal and experience in promoting the idea of a seminary than had Green, and by the fact that Alexander's son and biographer declared that, though the document "was framed by Dr. Green, Dr. Alexander's views were largely

contributed" (*LAA*, pp. 363). The same was undoubtedly true of Miller, some of whose previously proclaimed ideas appear in the plan.

11. *Report of a Committee of the General Assembly of the Presbyterian Church, Exhibiting the Plan of the Theological Seminary to be Submitted to the Next Assembly* (New York, 1810). Miller, who had been dubious about including collegiate education in the proposed plan for a seminary, was now enthusiastic for it. *LSM*, p. 287.

12. Dr. Green's signature as committee chairman is dated September 26, 1810. See also Andrew Flinn to Ashbel Green, Charleston, S.C., Jan. 28, 1811, in Simon Gratz MSS, HSP.

13. *LSM*, I, pp. 287, 307-308.

14. Ibid., I, pp. 243-244.

15. Trustees Minutes, II (1797–1823), pp. 184, 187.

16. Ibid., p. 355.

17. Ibid., p. 305.

18. Manuscript AM4234, in PU.

19. G.A. *Minutes*, 1811, pp. 466, 470-472. Text of the plan as adopted in 1811, but including also the two postponed articles, is in *Extracts from the Minutes of the General Assembly of the Presbyterian Church in the United States of America A.D. 1811* (Philadelphia, 1811), pp. 327-346.

20. Trustees minutes, II (1797–1823), pp. 305, 314-315; identical texts of the agreement are found in Trustees Minutes, II, pp. 377-380, and G.A. *Minutes*, 1812, pp. 499-501.

21. Gardiner Spring, in *Brick Church Memorial . . .* (New York, 1861), pp. 11-14.

22. Gardiner Spring, *Personal Reminiscences of the Life and Times of Gardiner Spring*, 2 vols. (New York, 1866), II, pp. 102-103; Philip Milledoler, "Memoirs, or an Outline of the Life of Philip Milledoler of New York," pp. 49-50 (MS in New York Historical Society); "Minutes of the Presbytery of New York" (1810–1813), pp. 40-43 (MH in PHS).

23. G. Spring, *Personal Reminiscences*, I, pp. 131-137; Philip Milledoler, "Memo of February 19 and 25, 1812, Meeting with Gardiner Spring," in Milledoler Papers, New York Historical Society; "Minutes of the Presbytery of New York" (1810–1813), pp. 89-96, and Ezra Stiles Ely's caricature of Hopkinsianism, *A Contrast Between Calvinism and Hopkinsianism* reflect the tensions created among New York Presbyterians by the "Hopkinsian" issue at this time.

24. Philip Milledoler, "Events Which Occurred at Philada. during the Session of the Gen'l Assy., in May 1812"; *idem*; "Memoirs, or an Outline of the life of Philip Milledoler of New York," pp. 59-60, 84-94; Milledoler to James Stuart, September 19, 1812, all MSS in Milledoler Papers, New York Historical Society.

25. William B. Sprague, ed., *Annals of the American Pulpit*, 9 vols. (New York, 1857–1869), III, pp. 374-375.

26. G.A. *Minutes*, 1812, pp. 496-501.

27. Ibid., 1813, p. 533; Trustees Minutes, II (1797–1823), p. 368.

28. Ibid., 1812, pp. 503, 509, 512; Directors Minutes, June 30, 1812, pp. 4, 19 (MS in PTS).

29. Their names are given in G.A. *Minutes*, 1812, p. 509 and in *Biographical Catalogue of the Princeton Theological Seminary, 1815–1932* (Princeton, 1933), pp. viii-ix (hereafter cited as *Biographical Catalogue PTS*).

30. Samuel Miller to (probably) Lieutenant Governor William Phillips of Boston, 1811, copy in PTS.

31. Trustee Minutes, II (1797–1823), pp. 337-341, 345-346; *The Life of Ashbel Green*, pp. 338-340.

32. S. S. Smith to Joseph C. Breckinridge, March 13, 1817, in Breckinridge Family Papers, Library of Congress.

33. John F. Hageman, *History of Princeton and Its Institutions,* 2 vols. (Philadelphia, 1879), I, pp. 19-24, 35, 121-123.

34. *LSM,* I, p. 281; S. Miller to A. Green, January 23, 1810, MS copy in PTS.

35. *LSM,* I, p. 341.

36. Philip Lindsly to "Dear Sir," April 26, 1823, in Lindsly Miscellaneous Papers, PU.

37. Trustees Minutes, II (1797–1823), p. 370, May 5, 1813.

38. G.A. *Minutes,* 1812, pp. 504, 511, 512; *LAA,* pp. 327-329.

39. Trustees Minutes, II (1797–1823), p. 297.

40. G.A. *Minutes,* 1813, pp. 536-537; *Life of Ashbel Green,* p. 348.

*10: Ministers as Professionals*

1. John Calvin, *Institutes of the Christian Religion,* 2 vols. (Philadelphia, 1960), IV:III:1-3;IV:VIII:2; see also "The Westminster Confession," XXV:3 in *The Constitution of the United Presbyterian Church in the U.S.A.,* part I, *Book of Confessions* (Philadelphia, c.1967), section 6.127.

2. Calvin's *Institutes,* IV:I:22, IV.XI–IV.XII; *Heidelberg Catechism,* Questions 83-85, in *Constitution,* as cited, Sections 4.083–4.085.

3. James L. Ainslie, *The Doctrines of Ministerial Orders in the Reformed Churches of the 16th and 17th Centuries* (Edinburgh, 1940).

4. Wilhelm Pauck, in *The Ministry in Historical Perspectives,* edited by H. Richard Niebuhr and Daniel D. Williams (New York, 1956), pp. 147, 143; see also Sidney E. Mead, in ibid., pp. 207-249; David S. Schuller, Merton P. Strommen, and Milo L. Brekke, eds., *Ministry in America . . .* (San Francisco, 1980); David D. Hall, *The Faithful Shepherd: A History of the New England Ministry in the Seventeenth Century* (Chapel Hill, N.C., 1972); J. William T. Youngs, Jr., *God's Messengers: Religious Leadership in Colonial New England, 1700–1750* (Baltimore, 1976); Donald M. Scott, *From Office to Profession: The New England Ministry, 1750–1850* (Philadelphia, 1978).

5. Samuel Finley, *The Successful Minister of Christ, Distinguished in Glory . . .* (Philadelphia, 1764), pp. 8, 13; Finley, *Faithful Ministers the Fathers of the Church . . .* (Philadelphia, 1752), pp. 4, 17.

6. Samuel Davies, *The Duties, Difficulties and Reward of the Faithful Minister . . .* (Glasgow, 1754), pp. 44-45.

7. Samuel S. Smith, *A Discourse on the 22d of February, 1797 . . .* (Philadelphia, n.d.), p. 33.

8. Samuel Davies, *The Duties, Difficulties, and Reward of the Faithful Minister . . . ,* pp. 58, 59.

9. Samuel Finley, *The Approved Minister of God . . ., 1749* (Philadelphia, n.d.), pp. 5-6.

10. Ibid., p. 15.

11. Caleb Smith, *Diligence in the Work of God* . . . (New York, 1758), p. 26.

12. Samuel Finley, *The Successful Minister of Christ* . . . , p. 19.

13. Edward D. Griffin, *A Sermon Preached July 22, 1807* . . . (New York, 1807), pp. 33-34.

14. Samuel Davies, *The Duties, Difficulties and Reward of the Faithful Minister*, p. 49.

15. Samuel Finley, *Faithful Ministers*, p. 14.

16. S. S. Smith, *A Discourse Delivered on the 22d of February, 1797*, p. 30.

17. *Annual Reports of the American Bible Society* (New York, 1838), I, p. 10; *First Annual Report of the American Tract Society* (New York, 1826), p. 7; *Tenth Annual Report of the American Sunday-school Union . . . 1834* (Philadelphia, 1834), p. 2.

18. *BRPR*, N.S., III (1831), p. 567.

19. Philip Lindsly, *A Learned and Honest Clergy Essential . . ., 1818* (Trenton, N.J., 1821), pp. 16-18.

20. G.A. *Minutes*, 1811, p. 465; Archibald Alexander, "Sermon on Acts 20: 26, 27." Farewell sermon to his Third Church parishioners in Philadelphia in 1812. MS, PTS.

21. *Panoplist and Missionary Magazine United*, IV, N.S. (1811–1812), pp. 271-274.

22. Eleazer Lord, in *Literary and Theological Review*, II (1835), p. 10.

23. Daniel H. Calhoun, *Professional Lives in America: Structure and Aspiration, 1750–1850* (Cambridge, Mass., 1965), pp. 107-117, 133, 167.

24. John H. Rice, *The Importance of the Gospel Ministry* . . . (Richmond, 1817), p. 4.

25. Timothy Dwight, *A Sermon Preached at the Opening of the Theological Seminary in Andover* . . . , *1808* (Boston, 1808), pp. 16, 8, 9, 23-27.

26. Jacob Van Vechten, *Memoirs of John M. Mason* . . . (New York, 1956), pp. 360-361, 364.

27. John H. Rice, *The Importance of the Gospel Ministry*, p. 8.

28. Abraham Flexner, *Medical Education in the United States and Canada* . . . (New York, 1910), p. 14.

29. Ibid., p. 46.

30. Richard H. Shryock, *The Development of Modern Medicine: An Interpretation of the Social and Scientific Factors Involved* (New York, 1936), p. 262.

31. Alfred Z. Reed, *Present-day Law Schools in the United States and Canada* (New York, 1928), pp. 6-7.

32. Abraham Flexner, *Medical Education in the United States and Canada*, p. 6.

33. See Benjamin Rush, *The Autobiography of Benjamin Rush* . . . , edited by G. W. Corner (Princeton, 1948), p. 38.

34. Esther L. Brown, *Physicians and Medical Care* (New York, 1937), pp. 12-14.

35. Josef Redlich, *The Common Law and the Case Method in American University Law Schools* . . . (New York, 1914).

36. Talcott Parsons, *Essays in Sociological Theory*, rev. ed. (Glencoe, Ill., 1954), pp. 378-385.

37. John S. Brubacher and Willis Rudy, *Higher Education in Transition; an American History: 1636–1956* (New York, 1958), pp. 6-12.

38. Richard Hofstadter and Wilson Smith, eds., *American Higher Education: A Documentary History*, 2 vols. (Chicago, 1961), I, pp. 153-156.

39. Samuel B. Morison, *The Founding of Harvard College* (Cambridge, 1935); Morison, *Harvard College in the Seventeenth Century*, 2 vols. (Cambridge, 1936), pp. 267-275; see also Mary L. Gambrell, *Ministerial Training in Eighteenth-Century New England* (New York, 1937).

40. M. L. Gambrell, *Ministerial Training in Eighteenth-Century New England*, pp. 101, 130-139.

41. See Philip Lindsly, *A Plea for the Theological Seminary at Princeton, N.J.* (Trenton, 1821), pp. 11-18.


*11: What Should a Minister Study?*

1. Friedrich Schleiermacher, *Kurze Darstellung des theologischen Studiums* (Berlin, 1811; revised 1830); Eng. transl. by Terrence N. Tice, *Brief Outline on the Study of Theology* (Richmond, 1966).

2. Daniel T. Jenkins, in Jenkins, ed., *The Scope of Theology* (Cleveland, 1965), pp. x-xi.

3. *The Constitution and Associate Statutes of the Theological Seminary in Andover* (Andover, 1817), pp. 12, 5.

4. Leonard Woods, *History of the Andover Theological Seminary* (Boston, 1885), pp. 186-197.

5. The text of the Plan of 1811 is in *Extracts from the Minutes of the General Assembly of the Presbyterian Church in the United States of America A.D. 1811* (Philadelphia, 1811), pp. 327-346. See especially Article IV "Of Study and Attainments," section 1; G.A. *Minutes*, 1810, p. 454.

6. Plan, op. cit., article III, section 1.

7. Directors Minutes, May 25, 1813, p. 38.

8. Ibid., May 16 and Sept. 26, 1815, pp. 119, 155.

9. Conrad Wright in George H. Williams, ed., *The Harvard Divinity School: Its Place in Harvard University and in American Culture* (Boston, 1954), p. 27.

10. See Jerry Wayne Brown, *The Rise of Biblical Criticism in America 1800–1870: The New England Scholars* (Middletown, Conn., 1969).

11. Daniel W. Howe, *The Unitarian Conscience: Harvard Moral Philosophy, 1805-1861* (Cambridge, Mass., 1970).

12. Conrad Wright in *The Harvard Divinity School*, p. 59.

13. Ibid., pp. 27-28.

14. This summary is based on the detailed statistics supplied in ibid., pp. 58, note 7.

15. John T. Wayland, "The Theological Department in Yale College, 1822–1858" (Ph.D. dissertation, Yale University, 1933), pp. 176-181, 189, 225; Roland H. Bainton, *Yale and the Ministry . . .* (New York, 1957), pp. 79-95.


*12: Psychology and Religious Experience*

1. Archibald Alexander, "Nature and Evidence of Truth October 1812." MS in PTS.

2. Joseph Addison Alexander to Charles Hodge, May 3, 1856, in HP as cited by Earl William Kennedy, "An Historical Analysis of Charles Hodge's Doctrine of Sin and Particular Grace" (Th.D. dissertation, PTS, 1968), p. 230.

3. *LAA*, p. 367.

4. LDT, "Lectures Introductory to the Study of Theology," [p. 16].

5. LPT, "The Best Method of Reconciling," [p. 7].

6. See Theodore Dwight Bozeman, *Protestants in an Age of Science: The Baconian Ideal and Antebellum American Religious Thought* (Chapel Hill, N.C., 1977).

7. LDT, "General Principles."

8. LMMS, "Lecture. The Principles of Human Knowledge," [pp. 10-11]; LMMS, "Origin of Our Knowledge," [pp. 1-6].

9. LDT, "Introductory Lecture"; and LDT, "Necessity of Revelation," p. 6.

10. LMMS, "Origin of Our Knowledge," [p. 3].

11. A. Alexander to Charles Hodge, January 29 and July 27, 1827, HP.

12. For the Scottish background and extensive American influence of this philosophy, see Sydney E. Ahlstrom, "The Scottish Philosophy and American Theology," *Church History*, XXIV (1955), pp. 257-272.

13. LMMS, "Part of Lecture on Sensation," pp. 3-5.

14. LMMS, "Nature & Evidence of Truth," pp. 14-15.

15. LMMS, "Truth, 1846," p. 5.

16. LMMS, "Nature & Evidence of Truth," pp. 16-17.

17. LMMS, "Truth, 1846," p. 9.

18. LMMS, "Nature & Evidence of Truth," p. 17.

19. LMMS, "Principles of Truth and Knowledge," p. 9.

20. LPstlT, "Qualifications for the Ministry. Lecture III," [p. 12].

21. *LAA*, p. 366.

22. LMMS, "Usefulness & Importance of Mental Philosophy," [pp. 1, 3, 4].

23. See T. D. Bozeman, op. cit.

24. LMMS, "Usefulness & Importance of Mental Philosophy," [p. 4].

25. LMMS, "Truth, 1846," pp. 19-20.

26. LMMS, "Principles of Truth and Knowledge," p. 7; see also LDT, "Providence," p. 21; LMMS, "Pneumatology," [p. 1].

27. LDT, "The Immortality of the Soul," [pp. 8, 6].

28. LMMS, "Pneumatology," [p. 2].

29. LMMS, "Truth, 1846," p. 21.

30. LDT, "Faith," p. 22.

31. LDT, "The Immorality of the Soul," [p. 8].

32. LMMS, "Pneumatology," [p. 1].

33. Archibald Alexander, "Chalmers' Mental and Moral Philosophy," *BRPR*, XX (1848), p. 531.

34. LDT, "Lecture on Faith," p. 5; LDT, "Holy Spirit: The Holy Spirit a Divine Person," p. 2.

35. "Sermon on Ecclesiastes XII:1" in Archibald Alexander, "Sermons" MS Package No. 1, PTS; see also LDT, "Lecture on Faith," p. 5.

36. LDT, "Faith," p. 20; also LMMS, "Lecture on the Active Powers of Man," [p. 2].

37. A. Alexander, "An Inquiry into that Inability under Which the Sinner Labours," *BRPR*, N.S. III (1831), p. 366.

38. LDT, "Faith," pp. 16, 18, 20.

39. LD, "Can Anything Be Done to Raise the Standard of Piety in this Seminary?" [p. 22].

40. LMMS, "Lecture on the Active Powers of Man," pp. 19, 21.

41. Archibald Alexander, *Thoughts on Religious Experience* (Philadelphia, 1841), pp. 45, 46.

42. Ibid., pp. 5-9; see also *Memoirs of the Rev. Thomas Halyburton* (Princeton, 1833), "Preface" by A. Alexander, pp. v-x; *LAA*, p. 694.

43. Alexander, *Thoughts on Religious Experience*, pp. 15, 13, 26.

44. *LAA*, pp. 529, 533-535.

45. *Thoughts on Religious Experience*, pp. 16, 146.

46. Ibid., p. 75; LDT, "Faith," p. 22; LDT, "Holy Spirit: The Holy Spirit a Divine Person," [p. 14].

47. *Thoughts on Religious Experience*, p. 75.

48. Ibid., p. 39.

49. A. Alexander, "A Practical View of Regeneration," *BRPR*, VIII (1836), p. 495.

50. LPT, "The Best Method of Reconciliation," [p. 27]; similarly, LDT, "Faith," p. 5; *Thoughts on Religious Experience*, p. 25.

51. *Thoughts on Religious Experience*, p. 27.

52. *LAA*, p. 545.

53. *Thoughts on Religious Experience*, p. 15.

54. A. Alexander, *Biographical Sketches of the Founder and Principal Alumni of the Log College* (Princeton, 1845).

55. *Thoughts on Religious Experience*, p. 43.

56. E. P. Dickie, "Thomas Halyburton," *Scottish Journal of Theology*, V (1952), pp. 1-13.

57. *Thoughts on Religious Experience*, p. 132.

58. A. Alexander, "Preface" in *Memoirs of the Rev. Thomas Halyburton*, pp. xi, xiii.

59. *LAA*, pp. 682, 694; *LCH*, p. 17.

60. *Thoughts on Religious Experience*, pp. 45, 46.

61. *LAA*, pp. 378, 393-394; *Thoughts on Religious Experience*, p. 61.

62. *LAA*, p. 406; Thomas Smyth, *Autobiographical Notes, Letters, and Reflections* (Charleston, S.C., 1914), p. 539.

63. For example, Donald G. Mathews, "The Second Great Awakening as an Organizing Process, 1780–1830," in John M. Mulder and John F. Wilson, eds., *Religion in American History: Interpretive Essays* (Englewood Cliffs, N.J., 1978), p. 199; Henry F. May, *The Enlightenment in America* (New York, 1976), pp. 324, 325.

*13: Proof and Practice of Christianity*

1. The second edition here used (Princeton, 1825) was published in the same year as the first. Hereafter cited as *Evidences*, 2d ed. (1825).

2. *LAA*, p. 429.

3. *Evidences of the Authenticity, Inspiration, and Canonical Authority of the Holy Scriptures*. Philadelphia, c.1836. Hereafter cited as *Evidences* (1836).

4. *Biblical and Theological Studies by the Members of the Faculty of Princeton Theological Seminary* (New York, 1912), pp. 6-7.

5. *Evidences*, 2d ed. (1825), pp. 10-19.

6. LPT, "Hist[ory] of Pol[emic] Theology," [p. 1].

7. LDT, "Necessity of Revelation," p. 51.

8. LPT, "Deistical Writers."

9. LPT, "French Infidelity."

10. LPT, "Deistical Objections."

11. *Evidences* (1836), p. 242 and *passim*.

12. A. Alexander, *Thoughts on Religious Experience* (Philadelphia, 1841), p. 232.

13. LDT, "External Evidences of Revelation," [p. 17].

14. *Evidences*, 2d ed. (1825), pp. 59-62, 127ff.

15. Ibid., pp. 190-220.

16. Ibid., pp. 222-233.

17. Ibid., p. 178.

18. Ibid., pp. 234, 238.

19. J. W. Alexander to John Hall, July [no day] 1840, in J. W. Alexander, *Forty Years' Familiar Letters*, edited by John Hall, 2 vols. (New York, 1860), I, p. 310.

20. John C. Young to A. Alexander, Danville, Jan. 8 [no year], in Simon Gratz MSS, "Presbyterian Moderators," Case 8, Box 39, HSP.

21. Fred Hood, "Presbyterianism and the New American Nation, 1783–1826, a Case Study of Religion and National Life" (Ph.D. dissertation, Princeton University, 1968) contains a discussion of the moral philosophy of John Witherspoon and Samuel Stanhope Smith.

22. Archibald Alexander, *Outlines of Moral Science* (New York, 1852). Hereafter cited as Alexander, *Moral Science*.

23. D. H. Meyer, *The Instructed Conscience: The Shaping of the American National Ethic* (Philadelphia, 1972) treats the American moral philosophers suggestively; see also Daniel W. Howe, *The Unitarian Conscience: Harvard Moral Philosophy, 1805–1861* (Cambridge, 1970).

24. Alexander, *Moral Science*, p. 148.

25. LMMS, "Of the Law of God," [pp. 2, 3, 7].

26. Alexander, *Moral Science*, p. 86.

27. A. Alexander, "Wayland's Moral Science," *BRPR*, VII (1835), pp. 377-400; see also William G. McLoughlin, *The American Evangelicals, 1800–1900: An Anthology* (New York, 1968), p. 101.

28. LDT, "Lectures on the Atonement of Christ, No. 1," p. 5.

29. Ibid., p. 6; Alexander, "Wayland's Moral Science," pp. 377, 382, 388, 389.

30. LMMS, "Benevolence O[ld] & N[ew] School Theo[logical] Disquisitions," [p. 3.].

31. See LMMS, "Phil[osophy] of Mind," [p. 1], where he criticizes the *Edinburgh Review* for insufficient interest in psychology.

32. Alexander, *Moral Science*, pp. 94, 138-140, 204-206.

33. Alexander, "Wayland's Moral Science," p. 390.

34. LMMS, "The Law of God," [pp. 5, 7].

35. Alexander, "Wayland's Moral Science," p. 377.

36. Alexander, *Moral Science*, pp. 36, 13, 73-77.

37. Ibid., pp. 41, 65-71, 187-190.

38. Ibid., pp. 43, 44-45.

39. See Stanley Grean, *Shaftesbury's Philosophy of Religion and Ethics: A Study in Enthusiasm* (Athens, Ohio, 1927); Ernst Cassirer, *The Platonic Renaissance in England* (1953).

40. Alexander, *Moral Science*, pp. 194, 97-100.

41. Ibid., pp. 82, 202.

42. On this point he differed from the Scottish churchman Thomas Chalmers, whom he greatly admired. A. Alexander, "Chalmers's Mental and Moral Philosophy," *BRPR*, XX (1848), p. 534.

43. A. Alexander, *Thoughts on Religious Experience*, pp. 178, 179.

44. LMMS, "Lecture on the Active Powers of Man," pp. 19, 21.

45. Alexander, *Moral Science*, pp. 111, 120, 127, 102-103.

46. John Macquarrie, *3 Issues in Ethics* (New York, 1970), p. 42.

47. James McCosh to the Rev. W. Blackwood, Belfast, June 23, 1854. Typed copy in PU.

48. A. Alexander to Charles Hodge, May 31, 1828 in HP; G.A. *Minutes*, 1839, p. 178; LDT, "Necessity of Revelation," p. 45.

49. A. Alexander, *The Sermon Delivered at the Inauguration of the Rev. Archibald Alexander* . . . (New York, 1812), p. 72.

50. Undated sermon on Proverbs 14:34 in "Archibald Alexander, Sermons MSS, Package 1," in PTS.

51. Ibid.

52. Charles Hodge, "Retrospect of the History of the Princeton Review," *BRPR Index Volume* (Philadelphia, 1871), p. 19.

*14: A Protestant Scholasticism*

1. Francis Turretin, *Institutio Theologiae Elencticae* . . . , 3 vols. in 2, Genevae, 1679-1685; also New York, 1847. English translation by George M. Giger, MS in PTS; also microfilm of this translation in PTS.

2. *LAA*, pp. 368-369.

3. A. Alexander, "Notes on the Lectures of—, by an unnamed student: Didactic Theology 1842-3," MS package in PTS; Allen Henry Brown, "Lectures on Didactic Theology by Dr. Alexander, 1843-1844," bound MS in PTS.

4. John Finley Crowe, "Systematic Theology from the Lectures of Dr. Alexander," in Crowe, "Notes on Lectures at Princeton Theological Seminary, 1814-1815," MS in PTS.

5. A. Alexander, LDT, "Introductory Lecture," n.d., not paginated.

6. Ibid.

7. See H. Shelton Smith, Robert T. Handy, and Lefferts A. Loetscher, *American Christianity: An Historical Interpretation with Representative Documents*, 2 vols. (New York, 1960, 1963), II, pp. 66-118.

8. LDT, "Valuable History of Systems," [p. 25].

9. Ibid., [pp. 25-27].

10. Ibid., [pp. 27-34].

11. LDT, "Lecture on the Existence of God," [p. ii]; LDT, "On the being of a God," [p. 24].

12. LDT, "Scriptural Theology," [pp. 1, 7].

13. LDT, "Nat[ural] Rel[igion], [p. 7].

14. LPT, "History of Atheism," [p. 18].

15. LDT, "Lecture on the Existence of God," [p. 2].

16. LMMS, "Truth, 1846," p. 17; LDT, "Lecture on the Existence of God," [pp. 10-12]. Much of the twentieth-century philosophy rejected philosophical argu-

ments for God's existence because these arguments assumed the underlying rationality of the universe, a presupposition which this philosophy rejected. Langdon Gilkey, *Naming the Whirlwind: The Renewal of God-Language* (Indianapolis, 1969), pp. 210-228.

17. LMMS, "The Law," p. 1.

18. LMMS, no title; first sentence reads: "The existence of all self-evident truths . . . ." [p. 33].

19. LDT, "On the Being of a God," [p. 15].

20. LDT, "Theological Lectures: The Attributes of God," [p. 4]; LDT, "Lecture on the Existence of God," [p. 21].

21. LDT, "Trinity," p. 1.

22. LDT, "Mediatorial Character of J[esus] C[hrist]," p. 19; LDT, "Exaltation of Christ," pp. 1-4; LDT, "Scripture Doctrine of the Trinity by Dr. Clarke," [pp. 1-8].

23. LDT, "Creation," [pp. 21-28].

24. LDT, "Providence," pp. 1, 3, 6.

25. LPT, "The Best Method of Reconciling," [p. 27].

26. *The Westminster Confession of Faith*, chapter III:2.

27. LPT, "The Best Method of Reconciling," [pp. 27, 29].

28. A. Alexander, *Biographical Sketches of the Founder and Principal Alumni of the Log College* (Princeton, 1845), p. 288.

29. John Calvin, *Institutes of the Christian Religion*, III: XXI: 5 and 7 and III:XXI-XXIV *passim; The Westminster Confession of Faith*, chapter III.

30. *Institutes*: III:XXIII:7; III:XXI:1.

31. LDT, "Providence," p. 5.

32. LPT, "The Best Method of Preaching," [p. 10].

33. LDT, "Providence," pp. 11-22; LDT, "Primeval State," [p. 4]; LMMS, "Theories of the Will," [p. 4].

34. A. Alexander, "Inability of Sinners," *BRPR*, III, N.S. (1831), pp. 360-361; see Norman Pettit, *The Heart Prepared: Grace and Conversion in Puritan Spiritual Life* (New Haven, Conn., 1966).

35. Alexander, "Inability of Sinners," pp. 381, 382.

36. See H. Shelton Smith, *Changing Conceptions of Original Sin: A Study in American Theology Since 1750* (New York, 1955).

37. LMMS, "Original Sin," [p. 1].

38. A. Alexander to Charles Hodge, October 30, 1827, in File D, PTS.

39. LMMS, "Original Sin," [pp. 1-3].

40. A. Alexander, "The Early History of Pelagianism," *BRPR*, II, N.S. (1830), p. 90.

41. LMMS, "Original Sin," [p. 4]; also LMMS, "Imputation of the First Sin," p. 5. Alexander also mentioned Adam's "real" headship of the race as taught by Jonathan Edwards, as well as this federal headship. See LMMS, "Original Sin," [p. 20].

42. Charles Hodge's view of imputation is treated with factual detail in Earl William Kennedy, "An Historical Analysis of Charles Hodge's Doctrines of Sin and Particular Grace" (Ph.D. dissertation, PTS, 1968).

43. LMMS, "The Fall," p. 9.

44. A. Alexander, "The Early History of Pelagianism," p. 93.

45. Moses Stuart, "Inquiries Respecting the Doctrine of Imputation," *Quarterly Christian Spectator*, II (1830), pp. 339, 341-342.

46. Andrew B. Cross to Robert J. Breckinridge, March 26, 1833, in Breckinridge Family Papers, Library of Congress.

47. LPT, "New Haven Theory of Original Sin," [pp. 1ff].

48. "The Biblical Repertory on the Doctrine of Imputation," *Quarterly Christian Spectator*, III (1831), pp. 497-512.

49. LPT, "President Mahan on Perfection."

50. Alexander, "The Early History of Pelagianism," pp. 99-100.

51. *LAA*, p. 585.

52. Ibid., p. 455.

53. LDT, "Valuable History of Systems," [pp. 17-19].

54. The article is extensively excerpted in *LAA*, pp. 430-447.

55. Ibid., pp. 434-447.

56. LDT, "Vicarious Atonement," pp. 36, 33, 57.

57. LDT, "Lectures on the Atonement of Christ, No. 1," p. 20.

58. LDT, "Vicarious Atonement," p. 22a.

59. LDT, "Lectures on the Atonement of Christ, No. 1," p. 13.

60. LDT, "Mediatorial Character of J[esus] C[hrist]," p. 5.

61. LDT, "Holy Spirit: The Holy Spirit a Divine Person," pp. 2-3.

62. Archibald Alexander, *The Sermon Delivered at the Inauguration of the Rev. Archibald Alexander, D.D. . . .* (New York, 1812), p. 92.

63. LDT, "Holy Spirit: The Holy Spirit a Divine Person," pp. 3, 13-14.

64. LDT, "Faith," pp. 9-10.

65. LDT, "Lecture on Faith," p. 13.

66. LDT, "Faith," pp. 25, 26, 31-32.

67. LDT, "Lecture on Faith," pp. 21-25.

68. Ibid., pp. 4, 5, 10.

69. LDT, "Faith," p. 14.

70. LDT, "Lectures on the Atonement of Christ, No. 1," p. 3.

71. A. Alexander, *The Pastoral Office, A Sermon at Philadelphia . . . before the . . . Alumni . . .* (Philadelphia, 1834), p. 23.

72. *LAA*, p. 550; see also *BRPR*, XIX (1847), p. 576.

73. LDT, "The Immortality of the Soul," [pp. 1, 3].

74. In LPT.

75. B. B. Wisner to Charles Hodge, Jan. 27, 1819, in HP; see also *LAA*, p. 372.

76. LPT; *LAA*, p. 371.

77. Unnamed student, "Polemic Theology. Notes of Dr. Alexander's lectures to First Class, 1843–44," MS in PTS (hereafter cited as "Student's Polemic Theology Notes, 1843–44").

78. Ibid., pp. 16-17, 12-14.

79. LMMS, "Fundamental Articles," [pp. 1, 3]; also LPT, "Lecture 2d, Object of Polemic Theology," [pp. 7-8].

80. See John Calvin, *Institutes of the Christian Religion*, IV:I:4.

81. "Student's Polemic Theology Notes, 1843–44," pp. 25-28.

82. Ibid., pp. 8-11.

83. LPT, "Lecture 2d Object of Polemic Theology," [p. 30].

84. Allen Henry Brown, "Lectures on Didactic and Polemic Theology by Dr. Alexander, 1843," PTS [not paginated].

85. Samuel S. Schmucker, "MS Notes on A. Alexander's lectures on Polemics at Princeton Theological Seminary 1820" in Gettysburg Theological Seminary Library, Gettysburg, Pa. (not paginated).

86. Ibid.

87. Ibid.

88. Ibid.

89. Ibid.

90. "Unnamed Student's Polemic Theology Notes, 1843–44," pp. 138-164.

91. Ibid., pp. 89-109.

92. Ibid., pp. 164-168.

93. Ibid., pp. 168-177.

94. Ibid., pp. 168-177, 185-188, 190-193.

*15: Biblical Studies*

1. *LAA*, pp. 362-364.

2. Ibid., p. 364; A. Alexander to S.S. Schmucker, July 26, 1818, in Gettysburg Theological Seminary Library, Gettysburg, Pa.

3. A. Alexander, *The Canon of the Old and New Testaments Ascertained; or, The Bible Complete Without the Apocrypha & Unwritten Traditions* (Princeton, 1826), pp. 15-16.

4. Jerry Wayne Brown, *The Rise of Biblical Criticism in America, 1800–1870: The New England Scholars* (Middletown, Conn., 1969), pp. 18, 75, 99.

5. Alexander, *The Canon*, pp. 16-17.

6. William F. Albright, "Moses Stuart," in *DAB*, XVIII (New York, 1936), p. 174.

7. John H. Giltner, "Moses Stuart: 1780–1852" (Ph.D. dissertation, Yale University, 1956), pp. 151, 152, 160, 161, 400.

8. J. Addison Alexander to George Bush, Sept. 30, 1834, in Simon Gratz MSS, HSP.

9. M. Stuart to J.M. Matthews, Nov. 25, 1812, in "Prominent Clergy" box, New York Public Library.

10. Giltner, op. cit., pp. 190-203, 443-450.

11. M. Stuart to Charles Hodge, June 27, 1826, in HP.

12. J.W. Brown, *The Rise of Biblical Criticism in America*, pp. 49, 97.

13. Samuel Miller to Benjamin B. Wisner, April 15, 1822, in MP.

14. A. Alexander to Charles Hodge, Nov. 29, 1827, in HP.

15. J.W. Brown, *The Rise of Biblical Criticism in America*, pp. 10-26.

16. Ibid., pp. 31-32, 72-82, 92-93.

17. Ibid., pp. 62-63, 180-182.

18. *LAA*, pp. 386-387.

19. Ibid., p. 356. Presumably this was the critical partial edition of the O.T. by Johann Heinrich Michaelis, 1720, an important edition in its day, but which has been declared too hastily done to be thoroughly dependable.

20. Ibid.

21. John H. Rice to A. Alexander, July 15, 1810, in William Maxwell, *A Memoir of the Rev. John H. Rice, D.D.* (Philadelphia, 1835), p. 52.

22. *LAA*, pp. 387, 679.

23. Ibid., p. 365.

24. Ibid., p. 387f.

25. These MSS, entitled "Budd" and "Buddeus," are in a package marked "Biblical Criticism Notes by Archibald Alexander . . ." in PTS. Alexander does not name the writing of Buddeus, but comparison with the original text identifies his notes as based on Buddeus's *Isagoge* (1727), pp. 1442-1458 of the "Posterior Section" Chapter 8, which deals with "Exegetical Theology." His notes often give verbatim quotations in English translation of the original Latin.

26. Two volumes, London, 1716–1718, re-edited as late as 1876. Prideaux had some indebtedness to Archbishop Ussher's still earlier *Annals of the World to the Beginning of the Emperor Vespasian's Reign*, 1659.

27. A. Alexander, *Annals of the Jewish Nation During the Period of the Second Temple* (New York, 1832), p. v.

28. Samuel Shuckford. *The Sacred and Profane History of the World Connected from the Creation of the World to the Dissolution of the Assyrian Empire at the Death of Sardanapalus, and to the Declension of the Kingdoms of Judah and Israel under the Reigns of Ahaz and Pekah*, 2 vols. (London, 1727; re-edited in London as late as 1858).

29. A. Alexander to Samuel S. Schmucker, July 26, 1818, MS in Gettysburg Theological Seminary Library.

30. G.A. *Minutes* (1813), p. 537.

31. Alexander was emphasizing Kennicott as early as 1815, as evidenced by the student notes of John F. Crowe, "Biblical Criticism . . . Jany. 26, 1815" in Crowe, "Notes on Lectures at Princeton Theological Seminary, 1814–1815," MS in PTS, not paginated, hereafter cited as J.F. Crowe, "Biblical Criticism," 1815.

32. A. Alexander, *The Canon of the Old and New Testaments Ascertained . . .* (Princeton, 1826), p. 13.

33. [A. Alexander], "Survey of Modern German Works on Interpretation," *BRPR*, V (1833), p. 9.

34. Alexander, *Canon* (1826), pp. 211-212.

35. "Survey of Modern German Works . . . ," pp. 12, 17.

36. Ibid., pp. 18-19.

37. J.F. Crowe, "Biblical Criticism," 1815; Charles Hodge, "Critica Sacra, or Biblical Criticism. Princeton Decem. 31st 1817," bound MS in PTS, containing Hodge's unpaginated but very carefully written student notes on Alexander's lectures on biblical criticism. (Cited hereafter as Hodge, "Critica Sacra, 1817."

38. Hodge, "Critica Sacra, 1817"; Bauer's work continues a work of Salomon Glass and is entitled *Salomonis Glassii Philologia Sacra . . . Continuata a Geo. Lud. Bauero . . . Tomus Secundus Sectio Prior, Critica Sacra*, Lipsiae [1795]. This Georg "Ludwig" Bauer is the same as Georg Lorenz Bauer; see *British Museum General Catalog of Printed Books*, vol. 12 (London, 1965), col. 981. Alexander's notes erroneously cite this author as "J. Bauer" as do also Hodge's student notes, but Alexander's close summary and frequent extensive verbatim translations of pages 7-32 of Bauer's book establish this identification of the work. Alexander's notes on Bauer are entitled "Biblical Criticism," Nos. I, II, IIIa, and IIIb, four MS pamphlets in a package entitled "Biblical Criticism Notes by Archibald Alexander" in PTS, not paginated.

39. *Entwurf einer Hermeneutik des Alten und Neuen Testaments* (Leipzig, 1799); and *Hebraischen Mythologie des Alten und Neuen Testamentes, mit Parallelen aus der*

*Mythologie anderer Völker vornehmlich der Griechen und Römer,* 2 Teile (Leipzig, 1802).

40. On G.L. Bauer, see Christian Hartlich and Walter Sachs, *Der Ursprung des Mythosbegriffes in der Modernen Bibelwissenschaft* (Tübingen, 1952), pp. 79-87; Klaus Leder, *Universität Altdorf: zur Theologie der Aufklärung in Franken, die theologische Fakultät in Altdorf 1750–1809* (Nürnberg, 1965), pp. 321-324; Ernst Wolf, "Georg Lorenz Bauer," *Die Religion in Geschichte und Gegenwart,* I (Tübingen, 1957), column 924.

41. Arthur Jeffery, "Text and Ancient Versions of the Old Testament," in *The Interpreter's Bible* (New York, 1952), I, pp. 46-62.

42. Robert Davidson and A.R.C. Leaney, *Biblical Criticism* (Harmondsworth, England, 1970), pp. 102-113. See also Paul E. Kahle, *The Cairo Geniza* (Oxford, 1959).

43. A. Alexander, "Biblical Criticism"; J.F. Crowe, "Biblical Criticism," 1815; C. Hodge, "Critica Sacra," 1817.

44. G.L. Bauer, op. cit., p. 11.

45. Alexander, Crowe, and Hodge, each as cited above.

46. Ibid.

47. Ibid.

48. G.L. Bauer, op. cit., p. 24.

49. Alexander and Crowe, as cited.

50. G.L. Bauer, op. cit., p. 25.

51. Alexander and Crowe, as cited. Crowe's student notes here at times reproduce verbatim Alexander's notes on Bauer.

52. Alexander, "Biblical Criticism" nos. III and IV and "Of the Antiquity & Corruption of the Hebrew Text"; also MS pamphlet in package, "Biblical Criticism Notes by Archibald Alexander" in PTS (not paginated); also student notes of Crowe and Hodge, as cited.

53. A marginal comment by Alexander, in his "Biblical Criticism," no. IV.

54. A.A. Hodge and B.B. Warfield, "Inspiration," *Presbyterian Review*, II (1881), pp. 225-260.

55. C. Hodge, "Critica Sacra, 1817."

56. Arthur Jeffery, "Text and Ancient Versions of the Old Testament," pp. 57-58.

57. C. Hodge, "Critica Sacra, 1817."

58. J.F. Buddeus, *Isagoge*, p. 1454b.

59. This follows Dr. Alexander's notes on J.F. Buddeus, *Isagoge*, p. 1453b.

60. Arthur Jeffery, "The Canon of the Old Testament," in *The Interpreter's Bible*, I (New York, 1952), pp. 34, 37.

61. A. Alexander, *The Canon* (1826), pp. 26, 29.

62. Ibid., pp. 31-32.

63. Alexander, *The Sermon Delivered at the Inauguration of the Rev. Archibald Alexander, D.D. . . . * (New York, 1812), pp. 62-63.

64. Alexander, *The Canon* (1826), pp. 95-103.

65. Ibid., pp. 133-134.

66. Alexander, "Biblical Criticism of the New Testament" no. 1, MS pamphlet in package, "Biblical Criticism Notes by Archibald Alexander," not paginated, PTS.

67. Ibid.

68. Ibid., no. 2.

69. C. Hodge, "Critica Sacra, 1817"; see also Archibald Alexander, *A Brief Outline of the Evidences of the Christian Religion,* 2nd ed. (1825), p. 88.

70. Alexander, "Biblical Criticism of the New Testament," no. 1.

71. Ibid.

72. Ibid.

73. Ibid.

74. Alexander, ibid., no. 2; also Hodge, "Critica Sacra, 1817."

75. Alexander, *Canon,* pp. 133-134.

76. Ibid., p. 132.

77. Ibid., p. 136.

78. Hodge, "Critica Sacra, 1817."

*16: Putting Theology to Work*

1. Conrad Wright, in George H. Williams, ed., *The Harvard Divinity School: Its Place in Harvard University and in American Culture* (Boston, 1954), pp. 54-56.

2. John T. Wayland, "The Theological Department in Yale College, 1822–1858" (Ph.D. dissertation, Yale University, 1933), pp. 211-219, 435.

3. *In Memoriam. Melanchthon W. Jacobus, D.D., LL.D.* (n.p., n.d.), p. 17.

4. *The Autobiography of Lyman Beecher,* edited by Barbara M. Cross, 2 vols. (Cambridge, Mass., 1961), II, p. 191.

5. *Memoirs of Rev. Charles G. Finney Written by Himself* (New York, c.1876), p. 88.

6. Charles Hodge, *Princeton Theological Seminary. A Discourse Delivered at the Re-opening of the Chapel, September 27, 1874* (Princeton, 1874), p. 20.

7. Allen Henry Brown, "[Lectures on] Pastoral Theology 1841 [-42]," [by Archibald Alexander], bound MS, PTS, not paginated; Archibald Alexander, "Notes on the Lectures of [by an unnamed student]: Pastoral Theology Lectures to 2d Class, 1842-3," MS package, PTS (hereafter cited as "Student's Pastoral Notes, 1842–43").

8. "Student's Pastoral Notes, 1842–43," pp. 49, 46–47.

9. Ibid., pp. 46-49.

10. LPstlT, "Reasons for Leaving a Pastoral Charge," [p. 4].

11. A.M. Baumgartner, " 'The Lyceum is My Pulpit': Homiletics in Emerson's Early Lectures," *American Literature,* vol. 34 (January, 1963), pp. 477-486.

12. Samuel Whelpley to Samuel Miller, May 25, 1813, MP.

13. *LAA,* p. 515.

14. Charles Hodge, "Memoir of Dr. Alexander," *BRPR,* XXVII (1855), p. 157.

15. "Student's Pastoral Notes, 1842–43," p. 124.

16. Ibid., p. 57.

17. Ibid., pp. 57-62.

18. Ibid., pp. 63, 66, 123-124.

19. Quoted in *Texas Presbyterian,* March 7, 1879.

20. Charles Hodge, "Memoir of Dr. Alexander," p. 157.

21. Samuel Irenaeus Prime, *Autobiography and Memorials,* edited by Wendell Prime (New York, 1888), p. 194.

22. *LSM*, II, pp. 409-410.

23. "Aliquis" to Samuel Miller, January 25, 1842, MP.

24. *LSM*, I, pp. 365-367.

25. Samuel Miller, *Holding Fast the Faithful Word: A Sermon . . . 1829; at the Installation of the Reverend William B. Sprague, D.D. . . .* (Albany, N.Y., 1829), pp. 36-37.

26. PTS "Minutes of the Board of Directors," May 23, 1826, p. 346; September 24, 1832, p. 181.

27. Charles Hodge to Hugh Hodge, July 8, 1850, HP.

28. John Hall, ed., *Forty Years' Familiar Letters of James W. Alexander*, 2 vols. (New York, 1860), I, p. 94.

29. "H.," "A Journey in New England," *Evangelical and Literary Magazine* (Richmond, 1823), p. 141.

30. *The Autobiography of Lyman Beecher*, I, p. 324.

31. *LSM*, I, pp. 365-366; G.A. *Minutes*, 1849, p. 271; Charles Hodge, "The General Assembly," *BRPR*, XXI (1849), p. 453; A. Alexander to C. Hodge, November 7, 1849, HP; James W. Alexander, "Sprague's Annals of the Presbyterian Pulpit," *BRPR*, XXX (1858), p. 410; William M. Scott, "English Diction," *BRPR*, XXII (1850), p. 90.

32. LPstlT, "Lec[ture] VIII. On the Pastoral Office," [p. 10].

33. Ibid., pp. 10, 12.

34. LPstlT, "Duty of the Pastor in Regard to the Awakened," [pp. 4-5].

35. Ibid., "Lec[ture] VIII. On the Pastoral Office," [pp. 13-15].

36. Ibid., "Duty of Pastors as Peacemakers," [pp. 2-5].

37. Ibid., [p. 15].

38. Leonard Woods, *History of the Andover Theological Seminary* (Boston, 1885), pp. 50, 153.

39. Francis Wayland, Jr., and H.L. Wayland, *A Memoir of the Life and Labors of Francis Wayland, D.D., LL.D.*, 2 vols. (New York, 1867), I, p. 63.

40. George P. Fisher in *Semi-centennial Anniversary of the Divinity School of Yale College* (New Haven, Conn., 1872), p. 19.

41. *LAA*, pp. 426, 480; see also A. Alexander, *Home Missionary and American Pastor's Journal*, I (1828–29), p. 6.

42. B.B. Wisner to Charles Hodge, Boston, November 12, 1821, HP.

43. Albert Barnes to John Dunlap, Princeton, February 6, 1822, PHS.

44. For Nevin's theology, see James Hastings Nichols, *Romanticism in American Theology: Nevin and Schaff at Mercersburg* (Chicago, 1961).

45. John W. Nevin, *My Own Life: The Earlier Years* (originally 1870; reprinted Lancaster, Pa., 1964), pp. 1-29.

46. *LAA*, pp. 376-377; *LSM*, II, p. 16.

47. *LAA*, pp. 392-393.

48. *LSM*, II, p. 17.

49. "Student's Pastoral Notes, 1842–43," pp. 69, 72.

50. Ibid., pp. 59, 62, 71.

51. LPT, "Method of Catechising," [p. 7].

52. G.A. *Minutes*, 1838, p. 50.

53. Ibid., 1850, pp. 476, 604.

54. "Student's Pastoral Notes, 1842–43," p. 71.

55. LPstlT, "Method of Catechising," [pp. 2-3].

56. Ibid., "Lec[ture] VIII. On the Pastoral Office," [p. 5].

57. "Student's Pastoral Notes, 1842–43," p. 74.

58. Ibid., p. 76.

59. *LAA*, p. 450; Archibald Alexander, *A History of Colonization on the Western Coast of Africa* (Philadelphia, 1846).

60. "Student's Pastoral Notes, 1842–43," pp. 74-77.

61. Julius Melton, *Presbyterian Worship in America: Changing Patterns Since 1787* (Richmond, 1967), pp. 17-27.

62. William S. Plumer to unnamed, December 1, 1852, Simon Gratz MS, "Presbyterian Moderators," Case 3, Box 38, HSP.

63. J. Melton, op. cit., pp. 35, 38.

64. Charles W. Baird, *Eutaxia, or the Presbyterian Liturgies, Historical Sketches, By a Minister of the Presbyterian Church* (New York, 1855); Charles Hodge, "Presbyterian Liturgies," *BRPR*, XXVII (1855), pp. 445-467.

65. "Student's Pastoral Notes, 1842–43," pp. 116-117.

66. Ibid., pp. 117-121.

67. G.A. *Minutes*, 1845, p. 34.

68. Ibid., 1875, p. 514.

69. "Student's Pastoral Notes, 1842–43," p. 121.

# BIBLIOGRAPHICAL ESSAY

James H. Smylie, Union Theological Seminary, Virginia

Archibald Alexander (1772–1851) was present at the creation of the American Republic and had a profound impact, not only on Princeton Theological Seminary and Presbyterians, but also on Protestantism in the United States. Therefore, it is important to consider him in the broadest context. In order to do this, American religious history in general and developments in the early national period of the nation's history must be kept in mind.

Sydney Ahlstrom provides the best general overview in *A Religious History of the American People* (New Haven: Yale University Press, 1972), while Alan Heimert in *Religion and the American Mind* (Cambridge, Mass.: Harvard University Press, 1966), Henry F. May in *The Enlightenment in America* (New York: Oxford University Press, 1976), Perry Miller in *The Life of the Mind in America, From the Revolution to the Civil War* (New York: Harcourt, Brace & World, Inc., 1965), and Rush Welter, *The Mind of America, 1820–1860* (New York: Columbia University Press, 1975) provide social, religious and cultural background, sometimes in a provocative manner. Richard B. Davis in *Intellectual Life in Jefferson's Virginia, 1790–1830* (Chapel Hill: University of North Carolina Press, 1964) gives an account of the local milieu that helped to shape Alexander's life and thought. Princetonians who were Alexander's associates and students left pioneering works about this period. They are still relevant. Samuel Miller broke fresh ground in intellectual history in *A Brief Retrospect of the Eighteenth Century . . . A Sketch of the Revolutions and Improvements in Science, Arts, and Literature During that Period* (New York: Lenox Hill, 1803), as did Princeton graduate Robert Baird in *Religion in the United States of America* (Glasgow: Blackie and Son, 1844). William Henry Foote, also of Princeton, gave us a mine of information and insight about Virginia, *Sketches of Virginia: Historical and Biographical* (First Series: Philadelphia: William Martien, 1850) (Second Series: Philadelphia: J. B. Lippincott & Co., 1855).

Unfortunately, a satisfactory history of American Presbyterianism spanning the life of Alexander has not yet been written. Although old, Robert Ellis Thompson's *A History of the Presbyterian Churches in the United States* (New York: The Christian Literature Co., 1895), is still useful. Leonard J. Trinterud has provided the best treatment of colonial Presbyterianism in *The Forming of an American Tradition, A Re-examination of Colonial Presbyterianism* (Philadelphia: The Westminster Press, 1949), while Fred J. Hood in *Reformed America: The*

*Middle and Southern States, 1783–1837* (University, Alabama: University of Alabama Press, 1980) covers the story of the early national period. Interpretation of this early history of Presbyterianism was a part of the theological conflict which was carried on during Alexander's lifetime as seen, for example, in Charles Hodge, an Old School Presbyterian, in *The Constitutional History of the Presbyterian Church in the United States of America* (2 volumes: Philadelphia: William S. Martien, 1839), New School advocate William Hill's *History of the Rise, Progress, Genius, and Character of American Presbyterianism. . .* (Washington: J. Gideon, 1839), as well as the later interpretation by Charles Augustus Briggs, *American Presbyterianism, Its Origins and Early History* (New York: Charles Scribner's Sons, 1885). George M. Marsden sorted out the theological dimensions of Presbyterianism in *The Evangelical Mind and the New School Presbyterian Experience, A Case Study of Thought and Theology in Nineteenth-Century America* (New Haven: Yale University Press, 1970). In a review of the interpretations of the Old School-New School division in an Appendix, Marsden stresses the important of doctrinal issues, rather than the conflict over slavery as the decisive factor in the controversy. This is still a controverted point.

Alexander's was an age of revivals, as well as one of the expansion of educational institutions. He was influenced by the currents of his time and helped to shape them. Alice F. Tyler interprets the fervor of these early years in *Freedom's Ferment: Phases of American Social History to 1860* (Minneapolis: University of Minnesota Press, 1944). William B. Sprague included a letter from his mentor Alexander in an Old School interpretation of what the Christian experience should be in *Lectures on Revivals of Religion* (Albany, N.Y.: Packard & Van Benthuysen, 1832). In more recent years William G. McLoughlin, Jr., has given us an interpretation of the whole tradition in *Modern Revivalism: Charles Grandison Finney to Billy Graham* (New York: The Ronald Press Company, 1959), and an analysis of the conflict between Princeton and Finney in his introduction to Charles Grandison Finney, *Lectures on Revivals of Religion* (Cambridge: Belknap Press of Harvard University Press, 1960).

Douglas Sloan explored the impact of the Scottish educational system on American institutions in *The Scottish Enlightenment and the American College Ideal* (New York: Teachers College Press, Columbia University, 1971), while Howard Miller traced the impact of the educational developments on American Presbyterianism in *The Revolutionary College, American Presbyterian Higher Education 1707–1837* (New York: New York University Press, 1976). Since clergy were expected to be the educators the older works by Donald G. Tewsbury, *The Founding of American Colleges and Universities before the Civil War, with Particular References to the Religious Influences Bearing on the College Movement* (New York: Columbia University Press, 1932), and George P. Schmidt, *The Old Time College President* (New York: Columbia University Press, 1935), and the more recent studies, for example, Lawrence A. Cremin, *American Education, the National Experience, 1783–1876* (New York: Harper & Row, 1981) form essential aspects of this history. The impact which the clergy as teachers had on society has been studied by Wilson Smith, *Professors and Public Ethics: Studies in Northern Moral Philosophers before the Civil War* (Ithaca: Cornell University Press, 1956), and Donald H. Meyer, *The Instructed Conscience: The Shaping of the American National Ethic* (Philadelphia: University of Pennsylvania Press, 1972). For an account of the establishment of

Princeton Seminary which focuses on its relationship to the college, see Mark A. Noll, "The Founding of Princeton Seminary," *Westminster Theological Journal,* XLII (Fall 1979), pp. 72-110.

Tensions arose in American Presbyterianism and Protestantism in general over the role of the minister as spiritual leader and educator. Elwyn Allen Smith analyzes some of the problems in *The Presbyterian Ministry in American Culture, A Study in Changing Concepts, 1700–1900* (Philadelphia: Westminster Press, 1957), as does Sidney E. Mead in "The Rise of the Evangelical Conception of the Ministry in America (1607–1850)," in H. Richard Niebuhr and Daniel D. Williams, eds., *The Ministry in Historical Perspective* (New York: Harper & Brothers, 1956), 207-249. W. Andrew Hoffecker in *Piety and the Princeton Theologians* (Phillipsburg, N.J.: Presbyterian & Reformed Publishing Company, 1981) shows how the leading professors at the Presbyterian institution attempted to hold together their spiritual and intellectual selves. Daniel H. Calhoun sets a larger context in which to consider the clergy in the age of Alexander in *Professional Lives in America: Structure and Aspiration, 1750–1850* (Cambridge: Harvard University Press, 1965). Changing perceptions of the clergy's role as a leader in worship, with Princeton's contribution to these changes, have been traced by Julius Melton, *Presbyterian Worship in America: Changing Patterns Since 1787* (Richmond: John Knox Press, 1967).

With regard to theological controversy, mention has already been made of general intellectual works, and to studies by Hodge, Hill, Briggs, and Marsden. Theodore Dwight Bozeman focuses attention on the influence of Francis Bacon on Presbyterians in *Protestants in an Age of Science, the Baconian Ideal and Antebellum American Religious Thought* (Chapel Hill, N.C.: The University of North Carolina, 1977), while Sydney E. Ahlstrom pointed out the impact of the Scottish School of Common Sense in "The Scottish Philosophy and American Theology," *Church History,* XXIV (September, 1955), pp. 257-72. Alexander and Princeton Theological Seminary disseminated a "doxological" approach to all learning based on Baconianism and the Scottish Enlightenment. These assumptions touched Presbyterian approaches to the Bible as Jerry Wayne Brown has shown in *The Rise of Biblical Criticism in America, 1800–1870: The New England Scholars* (Middletown, Conn.: Wesleyan University Press, 1969), and John C. Vander Stelt in *Philosophy and Scripture: A Study in Old Princeton and Westminster Theology* (Marlton, N.J.: Mack Publishing Company, 1978). H. Shelton Smith has shown the shifts in the interpretation of sin, so important to Calvinism, in *Changing Conception of Original Sin, A Study in American Theology since 1750* (New York: Charles Scribner's Sons, 1955). H. Shelton Smith, Robert T. Handy, and Lefferts A. Loetscher, eds., in "The Christocentric Liberal Tradition," *American Christianity, an Historical Interpretation with Representative Documents,* II (2 volumes: New York: Charles Scribner's Sons, 1963), pp. 255-308, show how emphasis upon Jesus modified American Calvinism, although they do not indicate how strong was such an emphasis on American Presbyterianism itself. Perry Miller has some interesting comments on how Unitarians turned to Princeton for help in dealing with Transcendentalism, despite disagreements over doctrine, in *The Transcendentalists: An Anthology* (Cambridge: Harvard University Press, 1950).

American Presbyterian concerns for the society, especially slavery, and for missions have been explored by a number of writers. Lois W. Banner in "Presbyterians and Voluntarism in the Early Republic," *Journal of Presbyterian History*, 50 (Fall, 1972), 187-205, demonstrates how vigorous was the activity of Princetonians in shaping American life in voluntary societies of their own, in the New York and Philadelphia areas. John R. Bodo analyzes the opinions of various Presbyterian clergy in *The Protestant Clergy and Public Issues, 1812–1848* (Princeton, N.J.: Princeton University Press, 1954), who in cooperation with Congregationalists and Dutch Reformed ministers, among others, attempted to extend their influence on American life. As indicated in this biography, Alexander, a Virginian transplanted in the North, was greatly concerned about the problem of slavery. A book which may have been decisive in shaping Presbyterian attitudes at Princeton was that of Samuel Stanhope Smith, *An Essay on the Causes of the Variety of Complexion and Figure in the Human Species*, (2d, 1810; reprint, Cambridge: The Belknap Press of Harvard University Press, 1965), in which he argued for the unity of the human race, but appeared to postpone emancipation of slaves until they were prepared to take their place in civil society with whites. Alexander's own volume, *A History of Colonization of the Western Coast of Africa* (Philadelphia: W. S. Martien, 1846), is still useful to indicate the reasons for his support of colonization. More recently, P. J. Staudenraus has investigated the movement in *The African Colonization Movement, 1816–1865* (New York: Columbia University Press, 1961). With regard to missions, Clifton Jackson Phillips has shown how Presbyterians and Congregationalists cooperated in early endeavors, in Protestant America and the Pagan World, *The First Half Century of the American Board of Commissioners for Foreign Missions, 1810–1860* (Cambridge: Harvard University Press, 1969), and points to how the former began to develop their own boards. A number of authors explore mission theory, covering the early part of the nineteenth century, in R. Pierce Beaver, ed., *American Missions in Bicentennial Perspective* (South Pasadena, Calif.: William Carey Library, 1977) including the ideas emanating from Princeton. John T. McNeill and James Hastings Nichols show Presbyterian concern for Christian cooperation in the early part of the nineteenth century in *Ecumenical Testimony, The Concern for Christian Unity within the Reformed and Presbyterian Churches* (Philadelphia: The Westminster Press, 1974).

Alexander and Princeton made an impact on, and interacted with a number of notable persons in nineteenth century American life. The following biographies represent examples which are worth surveying: William Maxwell, *A Memoir of the Rev. John H. Rice* (Philadelphia: J. Whetham; Richmond: R. J. Smith, 1835); Archibald Alexander Hodge, *The Life of Charles Hodge* (New York: Charles Scribner's Sons, 1880); Albert Barnes, *Life at Three Score and Ten* (New York: American Tract Society, 1871); Theodore Appel, *The Life and Work of John Williamson Nevin* (Philadelphia: Reformed Church Publication House, 1889), along with James Hastings Nichols, *Romanticism in American Theology, Nevin and Schaff at Mercersburg* (Chicago: The University of Chicago Press, 1961); P. Anstadt, *Life and Times of Rev. S. S. Schmucker* (York, Pa.: P. Anstadt and Sons, 1896); William Carus, ed., *Memorials of the Right Reverend Charles Petit McIlvaine* (New York: Thomas Whittaker, 1882). Hodge, Barnes, Nevin, Schmucker, and McIlvaine attended the seminary during Alexander's tenure there. Three volumes of biographical sketches of early graduates of The College of New Jersey contain much information on individuals who also played a role in the seminary:

*Princetonians 1748–1768,* ed. James McLachlan, *Princetonians 1769–1775* and *Princetonians 1776-1783,* ed. Richard A. Harrison (Princeton: Princeton University Press, 1976, 1980, 1981). While James McCosh came to New Jersey after Alexander's death, J. David Hoeveler, Jr., shows in *James McCosh and the Scottish Intellectual Tradition: From Glasgow to Princeton* (Princeton: Princeton University Press, 1981, 374 pp.) the continuity and the changes in the college and seminary with which Alexander was so closely associated.

Princeton's shadow was a long one. It continued to influence American Presbyterianism and Protestantism. This is demonstrated by Lefferts A. Loetscher in *The Broadening Church, A Study of Theological Issues in the Presbyterian Church since 1869* (Philadelphia: University of Pennsylvania Press, 1954); Ernest R. Sandeen, *The Roots of Fundamentalism, British and American Millenarianism, 1800–1930* (Chicago: The University of Chicago Press, 1970); George M. Marsden, *Fundamentalism and American Culture, The Shaping of Twentieth-Century Evangelicalism, 1870–1925* (Oxford University Press, 1980); and William R. Hutchinson, *The Modernist Impulse in American Protestantism* (Cambridge: Harvard University Press, 1976).

# INDEX

Mark A. Noll, Wheaton College, Illinois

Theological and philosophical topics are indexed both individually and under Alexander, Archibald. The following abbreviations are used in the index: AA = Archibald Alexander, PTS = Princeton Theologial Seminary.

PRESBYTERIAN HISTORICAL SOCIETY PUBLICATIONS

1. *The Presbyterian Enterprise* by M. W. Armstrong, L.A. Loetscher and C.A. Anderson (Westminster Press, 1956; Paperback reprinted for P.H.S., 1963 & 1976).

*2. *Presbyterian Ministry in American Culture* by E. A. Smith (Westminster Press, 1962)

3. *Journals of Charles Beatty, 1762–1769,* edited by Guy S. Klett *(Pennsylvania State University Press, 1962)*

*4. *Hoosier Zion, The Presbyterian in Early Indiana* by L. C. Rudolph (Yale University Press, 1963)

*5. *Presbyterianism in New York State* by Robert Hastings Nichols, edited and completed by James Hastings Nichols (Westminster Press, 1963)

6. *Scots Breed and Susquehanna* by Hubertis M. Cummings (University of Pittsburgh Press, 1964)

7. *Presbyterians and the Negro—A History* by Andrew E. Murray (Presbyterian Historical Society, 1966)

8. *A Bibliography of American Presbyterianism During the Colonial Period* by Leonard J. Trinterud (Presbyterian Historical Society, 1968)

9. *George Bourne and "The Book and Slavery Irreconcilable"* by John W. Christie and Dwight L. Dumond (Historical Society of Delaware and Presbyterian Historical Society, 1969)

10. *The Skyline Synod: Presbyterianism in Colorado and Utah* by Andrew E. Murray (Synod of Colorado/Utah, 1977)

11. *The Life and Writings of Francis Makemie,* edited by Boyd S. Schlenther (Presbyterian Historical Society, 1971)

12. *A Younger Church in Search of Maturity: Presbyterianism in Brazil from 1910 to 1959* by Paul Pierson (Trinity University Press, 1974)

13. *Presbyterians in the South,* Vols. II and III, by Ernest Trice Thompson (John Knox Press, 1973)

14. *Ecumenical Testimony* by John McNeill and James H. Nichols (Westminster Press, 1974)

15. *Iglesia Presbiteriana: A History of Presbyterians and Mexican Americans in the Southwest* by R. Douglas Brackenridge and Francisco O. Garcia-Treto (Trinity University Press, 1974)

16. *The Rise and Decline of Education for Black Presbyterians* by Inez M. Parker (Trinity University Press, 1977)

17. *Minutes of the Presbyterian Church in America, 1706–1788* edited by Guy S. Klett (Presbyterian Historical Society, 1977)

18. *Eugene Carson Black, Prophet With Portfolio* by R. Douglas Brackenridge (Seabury Press, 1978)

19. *Prisoners of Hope: A Search for Mission 1815–1822* by Marjorie Barnhart (Presbyterian Historical Society, 1980)

20. *From Colonalism to World Community: The Church's Pilgrimage* by John Coventry Smith (Geneva Press, 1982)

21. *Facing the Enlightenment and Pietism: Archibald Alexander and the Founding of Princeton Theological Seminary* by Lefferts A. Loetscher (Greenwood Press, 1983)

*Out of print.

## About the Author

LEFFERTS A. LOETSCHER served as a Professor of American Church History at Princeton Theological Seminary, from which he earlier received his Th.B. and Th.M. degrees. His extensive writings on Presbyterian history include *A Brief History of the Presbyterians* and *The Broadening Church: A Study of Theological Issues in the Presbyterian Church Since 1869.* He served as editor-in-chief of the *Twentieth Century Encyclopedia of Religious Knowledge* and as coeditor of *The Presbyterian Enterprise: Sources of American Presbyterian History* and *American Christianity: An Historical Interpretation with Representative Documents.*